BLACK-SCHOLES
AND BEYOND
OPTION PRICING MODELS

Neil A. Chriss

Boston, Massachusetts   Burr Ridge, Illinois
Dubuque, Iowa   Madison, Wisconsin   New York, New York
San Francisco, California   St. Louis, Missouri

McGraw-Hill

A Division of The **McGraw·Hill** *Companies*

Library of Congress Cataloging-in-Publication Data

Chriss, Neil.
    Black-Scholes and beyond : option pricing models / Neil Chriss.
      p.   cm.
    Includes bibliographical references and index.

    ISBN-13: 978-0-7863-1025-8

    ISBN-10: 0-7863-1025-1
    1. Options (Finance)—Prices—Mathematical models.   I. Title.
HG6024.A3C495   1997
332.64′5—dc20   96-17361

Printed in the United States of America

12 13 14 15 16 17 18 19 BKM BKM   0 9 8 7

⑥ CONTENTS

1 STOCKS, OPTIONS, AND FUTURES 11
  1.1 A preliminary definition of options, 11
  1.2 Stocks, 13
  1.3 Stock indexes and foreign currencies, 17
  1.4 Riskless zero-coupon bonds, 23
  1.5 Derivative securities, 24
  1.6 The value of an option, 26
  1.7 Security positions, 34
  1.8 Arbitrage and the basic properties of options, 38
  1.9 Put-call parity for European options, 40
  1.10 The economics of put-call parity, 43
  1.11 Early exercise of American options, 45
  1.12 Valuing Forward contracts, 48

2 FUNDAMENTAL MATHEMATICAL CONCEPTS 57
  2.1 The exponential, compound interest, and natural logarithms, 57
  2.2 Probability theory, 66
  2.3 The normal distribution, 78
  2.4 Cumulative normal distribution function, 85
  2.5 Four formulas for $N(x)$, 88
  2.6 Properties of the cumulative normal distribution function, 90

3 THE GEOMETRIC BROWNIAN MOTION MODEL OF PRICE MOVEMENTS 93
  3.1 Volatility and risk, 94
  3.2 The model, 96
  3.3 Calibrating the model, 103
  3.4 The distribution of stock prices, 109
  3.5 Brownian motion and call options, 112
  3.6 Geometric Brownian motion: fact or fiction?, 115

4 THE BLACK-SCHOLES FORMULA 119
  4.1 Self-financing, replicating hedging strategies, 120
  4.2 The expected rate of return on a stock, 127
  4.3 Hedging, 128
  4.4 Dynamic Hedging, 129
  4.5 The delta of an option, 132

4.6 The Black-Scholes hedging strategy, 140

4.7 How and why the Black-Scholes formula works, 145

4.8 Formulas for Δ_t and B_t, 152

4.9 Black-Scholes with dividends, 154

4.10 Hedge parameters, 162

5 MORE ON THE BLACK-SCHOLES FORMULA   185

5.1 Questions about Black-Scholes, 185

5.2 Risk-neutral valuation, 190

5.3 Delta hedging, 195

5.4 A common misconception about Black-Scholes, 197

5.5 The economic assumptions behind Black-Scholes, 200

5.6 Simulated Black-Scholes hedging, 204

6 BINOMIAL TREES   219

6.1 Continuous versus discrete time models, 221

6.2 Binomial trees, 221

6.3 Binomial trees and stock returns, 228

6.4 Binomial trees and volatility, 230

6.5 Building a standard binomial tree, 233

6.6 The most general standard trees, 239

6.7 The numbering system of the nodes, 241

6.8 Risk-neutral worlds and binomial trees, 241

6.9 Forward interest rates and binomial trees, 243

6.10 Binomial trees and dividends, 250

6.11 Arrow-Debreu prices, 260

6.12 The distribution of returns, 265

6.13 Arrow-Debreu prices and butterfly spreads, 271

7 BASIC OPTION PRICING WITH BINOMIAL TREES   273

7.1 One-step models, 274

7.2 Hedging the option, 278

7.3 Binomial pricing and risk-neutral probabilities, 282

7.4 Pricing European options on multiple-step trees, 284

7.5 Option valuation and Arrow-Debreu prices, 296

7.6 Stock price quantization and specification error, 299

7.7 Introduction to valuing exotic options on a binomial tree, 303

7.8 Hedge Parameters, 308

7.9 Pricing American options on a flexible tree, 315

7.10 The early exercise barrier, 323

8   THE VOLATILITY SMILE   327

    8.1   Implied volatility and the theory of option pricing, 327

    8.2   Computing implied volatility, 329

    8.3   The Newton-Raphson method, 336

    8.4   The Volatility Smile, 341

    8.5   The Volatility of Volatility—Stochastic Volatility, 343

9   IMPLIED VOLATILITY TREES   361

    9.1   Preliminaries—interpolation and extrapolation, 364

    9.2   Building implied trees—European options, 367

    9.3   Building implied trees with American input options, 373

    9.4   The false position method, 377

    9.5   Arrow-Debreu prices and bad probabilities, 379

    9.6   Implementing a system for building implied trees, 384

    9.7   Sample implied volatility computations, 390

    9.8   Hypothetical implied volatility tree: The S&P 500, 396

    9.9   The S&P 500 and the volatility smile, 400

    9.10   Bilinear interpolation of implied volatilities, 405

10   IMPLIED BINOMIAL TREES   411

    10.1   Inferring distributions directly from option prices, 413

    10.2   Building implied binomial trees, 417

    10.3   Sample implied binomial tree, 420

    10.4   Skewing a probability distribution, 423

    10.5   A complete example, 426

    10.6   Implied binomial versus implied volatility trees, 430

11   PRICING BARRIER OPTIONS IN THE PRESENCE OF THE SMILE   433

    11.1   What are barrier options?, 433

    11.2   In-out parity and barrier options, 436

    11.3   The price behavior of barrier options, 438

    11.4   Valuing barrier options on a binomial tree, 452

    11.5   Enhanced numerical methods, 464

    11.6   Final Words . . . What's it all good for?, 473

BIBLIOGRAPHY   477

AUTHOR INDEX   484

INDEX   486

⑥ FOREWORD

Neil Chriss has done a wonderful job explaining the core body of knowledge and most important extensions relating to option pricing. Starting with the Black-Scholes model and continuing with discussions of the binomial model, implied volatility, and implied binomial trees, Mr. Chriss makes the arcane quite understandable.

Since the benchmark Black-Scholes theory was introduced, it has been studied, restudied, and analyzed in real-time trading situations on the world's futures and options exchanges and over-the-counter markets. In fact, few theories have ever been put to such a rigorous empirical test. Even fewer have passed, let alone surpassed, the applicability and flexibility of the Black-Scholes Model. In fact, most of the modern options pricing is derived from ideas presented in the original Black-Scholes theory.

Even more to its credit, the model has served as the basis for numerous generalizations and extensions by academics and financial professionals. Indeed, the continued expansion of listed options and futures trading, plus the phenomenal growth of the over-the-counter options, exotics, and swaps markets, is intrinsically tied to this powerful model. But the theory is even more fundamental in that it can be applied to virtually any economic or financial activity where some aspect of contingency is inherent.

In *Black-Scholes and Beyond: Modern Options Pricing,* Neil Chriss, a very readable author, explains how one of the most important forces in capital market theory has been created. As a good teacher explains a complex theory, Mr. Chriss breaks down the theory into its component parts and delivers the mechanics of Black-Scholes with solid examples. Nothing is assumed. The necessary mathematics is patiently explained using formulas in the simplest form possible.

He starts by presenting a clear and detailed explanation of how and why the Black-Scholes formula works, without using any higher mathematics. The mathematics never goes beyond basic probability theory, and all necessary formulas are explained in the body of the book.

Organizationally, the first half of the book is devoted to the Black-Scholes formula. The actual model is then put into its analytical framework so readers of all levels will understand its critical components. Then, because the model has taken on a life of its own, been re-examined and extended by some of the financial industry's greatest minds, Mr. Chriss devotes roughly the last half of the book to changes that have occurred in option pricing theory since the introduction of the Black-Scholes model in 1973.

Mr. Chriss has culled perhaps the three most significant new theoretical developments—the binomial model (Cox, Ross, and Rubinstein, 1979), now an industry standard, the implied volatility trees model (Derman and Kani, 1994), and the implied binomial trees model (Rubinstein, 1994)—to pick up where the Black-Scholes model leaves off. All of these approaches carry on the spirit of Black-Scholes and are being used to help explain options pricing under less restrictive (i.e., more realistic) assumptions. With these three advances, our ability to understand and value options has been significantly improved.

The discussions of "volatility smiles," how to price options "in the presence of the smile," and the discussions on implied volatility and implied binomial trees are offered in a clear manner with numerous helpful examples. Other chapters in the second half of the book explain how the post-Black-Scholes option pricing models can be used to price instruments such as barrier options and other, more exotic, instruments.

Because of his teaching and research experience, Mr. Chriss provides new insights into complex concepts. It is very clear that he has spent the time needed to unravel, understand, and reflect on this critical component of modern capital market theory. It shows. Reading this book is time worth spending.

Ira Kawaller
Vice President–Director
New York Office
Chicago Mercantile Exchange

November 1995

INTRODUCTION

The development of modern option pricing began with the publication of the Black-Scholes option pricing formula in 1973.[1] This elegant and beautiful formula has forever changed the way both practitioners and theoreticians view the pricing of derivative securities.

This book has two purposes. The first half develops the Black-Scholes options pricing formula "from scratch." That is, we develop the necessary financial and mathematical background to understand what the formula means and how it is used *before* studying the formula itself. Moreover, we concentrate specifically on why the formula works and what the terms of the formula mean, rather than giving a rigorous account of its derivation.

Next, we move beyond Black-Scholes to discuss what I believe are the most important developments in modern options pricing since its introduction: the binomial model, the implied volatility trees model of option valuation, and the implied binomial trees model of option valuation. Lastly, as a demonstration of their power and flexibility, we explain how to apply these methods to value American and barrier options.

---

[1]In general, there is a distinction in economics between "price" and "value." Roughly speaking, the price of an option is the premium one pays for it, and the value is what it is worth. While this definition is perhaps a little circular, and is by no means rigorous, the point remains that throughout this book, we shall be concerned primarily with option valuation. That is, we shall be concerned with producing techniques for deducing the value of options. Despite this, there is a tendency to use the term "option pricing" when we mean "option valuation." In this book, we will maintain the value-price distinction, but we will refer to "option pricing" as the art and science of determining the value of an option.

1

The binomial model, developed by Cox, Ross, and Rubinstein, was introduced to provide a simplified derivation of the Black-Scholes formula and to extend its usefulness beyond the original narrow confines of European options. The method clarifies and elucidates why Black-Scholes works, and it also significantly extends the types of options one can easily price within a single framework. Indeed, the original Black-Scholes formula is only suitable for European call and put options on non-dividend-paying stocks.

Despite this, the Black-Scholes formula is vitally important. First, the basic ideas underlying it are very much the basis for all option pricing models. These methods will be a consistent theme throughout this book and can be summed up as follows: To value an option, one must form a self-financing hedging strategy that replicates the payoff of the option. Explaining what this means, and how it allows us to value options, is a central goal of this book.

Second, the Black-Scholes formula itself is very much here to stay, in part due to the notion of implied volatility. Volatility is a measure of the "riskiness" of a stock—the more volatile it is, the more risky it is. Technically, it measures the standard deviation of short-term returns on the stock. One ordinarily computes a stock's volatility by looking at historical price data and performing a series of statistical computations. The Black-Scholes formula gives a second method of computing volatility—it allows us to compute the volatility *implied* by the market price of an option.

An input to the Black-Scholes formula is the volatility of the underlying stock. All things being equal, the more volatile a stock is, the more valuable options on that stock are. Given an exchange-traded option, one can ask, What volatility makes the Black-Scholes value of an option agree with the market price of that option? This volatility is called the Black-Scholes implied volatility of the option, and it is frequently quoted as a substitute for price.

The Black-Scholes formula assumes that the volatility of a stock is the same at all times and will remain the same in the future, irrespective of the direction of price movements: If the stock's price rises, its volatility will remain the same; if the stock's price drops, its volatility will remain the same.

The Volatility Smile and Implied Theories

Despite this assumption, if we look at the Black-Scholes implied volatility of a variety of options on a single stock, a persistent pattern emerges. Rather than seeing a constant volatility, as assumed in the model, there is a pronounced pattern, called the *volatility smile*. The name "smile" derives from the fact that if we graph strike price versus implied volatilities of a set of options with the same expiration, we see a smile-shaped curve centered around the at-the-money option.[2]

The volatility smile is the origin of the third development in options valuation we will discuss: implied theories of option pricing. An implied theory takes as its starting point market prices of liquidly traded options, under the assumption that these options provide economically significant information about the nature of stock price movements, which can in turn be used to price illiquid options.

The two theories of this sort we will study are the implied volatility trees model of Derman and Kani (1994a and 1994b) (along with its extension for use with American options by the author of this book. See Chriss, 1996) and the implied binomial trees model of Rubinstein (1994 and 1995).[3] This model evaluates options "in the presence of the smile" (a phrase frequently heard around Wall Street). It takes the position that the volatility smile is the market's way of telling us how far the Black-Scholes formula deviates from a perfect option valuation formula, and it uses the smile to derive better option prices.

When implied theories first emerged, they made headlines. In the May 16, 1994, issue of *Pension and Investments,* Steve Hemmerick wrote an article called, "New Options Pricing Models Gain Ground: Investors Look Past Black-Scholes." Here is Mr. Hemmerick's description:

> Puzzling changes in the way some investors value options have prompted the development of new options pricing models that seek to improve on the popular Black-Scholes model . . . .
>
> Using what they call an implied tree, Goldman, Sachs & Co. researchers Emanuel Derman and Iraj Kani have developed what they call an extension of the Black-Scholes formula. Their extension, like Mr. Rubinstein's formula, attempts to deal with what is called 'the volatility smiles' . . . .

So, what were these "puzzling changes" in the way investors price options, and why did these models suddenly appear? To begin, the volatility smile has always existed. However, two things have changed since the 1987 stock market crash. First, the extent of the smile and its consequences for option pricing have increased dramatically. As Mr. Hemmerick puts it,

---

[2]Even the volatility smile is changing; some say it is now more of a sneer. See Whaley (1996).

[3]For a description of a similar model, developed independently, see "Pricing with a Smile," Dupire (1994), as well as Derman, Kani, Chriss (1996).

"Since the 1987 stock market crash, what was a gentle smile has become kind of a pronounced, if not insane, grin."

Second, investors are using "exotic" options more frequently now than ever before. Exotic options are options with nonstandard features, such as barrier prices, which, when breached, make the option contract null and void (we will discuss exotic options and, in particular, barrier options in Chapter 11). In general, these options are much more sensitive to the volatility smile than ordinary options.

Whereas one might reasonably be able to "correct" for the volatility smile when dealing with ordinary calls and puts, it becomes difficult, if not impossible, to do this for exotic options, especially when the smile is severe. Because of this, the Black-Scholes "no smile" assumption, which might have sufficed for ordinary calls and puts (especially before 1987), becomes inadequate for volatility-sensitive exotics.

Here is a more detailed discussion of the contents of this book.

Options Basics
In Chapter 1, we discuss the basic types of securities we will use throughout the book: stocks, indexes, options, zero-coupon bonds, and forward and futures contracts. In Chapter 2, we give a basic account of the mathematics necessary for understanding and using the Black-Scholes formula, focusing on probability distributions, especially the normal distribution. This chapter can be read from the outset, or if the reader prefers, it can be skipped and used strictly as a reference.

Both of the first two chapters are user-oriented. That is, we focus on what is necessary for this book, rather than giving an encyclopedic introduction to either financial instruments or probability theory. To make up for this brevity, there are references at the end of each chapter pointing the reader to more detailed expositions.

Once the mathematical and financial necessities are taken care of, we move on to the study of the stock price model that underlies Black-Scholes: the geometric Brownian motion model of stock movements.

We describe this model in detail using only the basic probability theory. Because the goal is to understand the Black-Scholes formula, the exposition is tailored specifically for that purpose. Two aspects are most important in this regard: the model for stock returns and the model for stock volatility (in particular, the constant volatility assumption itself is discussed). Because these are so crucial, we also discuss some of the more important critiques of the geometric Brownian motion model, including statistical evidence against the model.

What Is the Black-Scholes Formula?

The Black-Scholes formula computes the value of an option based on certain information: the strike price of the option, the price of the underlying, the risk-free rate of interest, the volatility of the stock, and the time until the option expires. If, in addition, the underlying pays dividends during the option's life, then the expected dividend payments play a role as well. While all of these parameters can be easily explained to someone with only a little knowledge of finance and mathematics, the Black-Scholes formula itself requires knowledge of probability theory just to understand how to use it. Now, if we want to reach beyond simply understanding how to use the formula, and attempt to understand where it comes from and why it has anything to do with the value of an option, then we need to work a little harder. This is the goal of Chapters 4 and 5.

In Chapter 4, we explain the key idea in all option valuation: the idea of a self-financing, replicating hedging strategy. This is illustrated by means of a simple analogy with a coin-tossing game, which contains surprisingly many of the elements of real option valuation.

Once this is understood, we explain what the Black-Scholes hedging strategy is and why it is a self-financing replicating hedging strategy. The key ingredient here is the "delta" of an option—the rate of change of the option's value with respect to stock price. We give an approximate formula for the delta with which we can see almost immediately that the Black-Scholes formula is self-financing and replicating—that is, that the Black-Scholes formula really is the value of the option.

Chapter 4 continues our study of Black-Scholes with a discussion of hedge parameters for options. Hedge parameters measure the rate of change of an option's value with respect to the variables affecting that value: stock price, time until expiration, interest rates, and volatility. Once these are understood, we provide six simulated hedging runs for European call options using the Black-Scholes methodology. In each simulated run, a stock price path is generated using a simulated "Black-Scholes" environment, and a European call option is hedged based on the Black-Scholes option pricing formula. We plot all the hedge parameters throughout the life of the option and keep track of the total cost of hedging. That is, we see how an imaginary trader "does" using the Black-Scholes formula.

These simulated hedging runs illustrate graphically how the Black-Scholes hedging strategy works and how hedge parameters change throughout the life of an option for a variety of different scenarios.

In Chapter 5, we also give more information on the Black-Scholes formula, explaining the concept of risk-neutral valuation. We also explain how

Black and Scholes originally derived the formula and give a new derivation based on risk-neutral valuation that is simpler than other derivations.

Beyond Black-Scholes
Chapters 6–11 move "beyond Black-Scholes." There are three central goals in this part of the book. The first is to understand the binomial model of option valuation and its application to barrier options. The next goal is to explain how to implement the implied volatility trees and implied binomial trees models. Lastly, we want to understand why we need these models. That is, we want to understand the need for moving "beyond Black-Scholes."

Chapter 6 focuses on what binomial trees are and how to construct simple binomial trees that closely model geometric Brownian motion. In addition, we discuss how to build binomial trees with a built-in dividend schedule, as well as the advanced topics of Arrow-Debreu prices and reading a stock price distribution from a binomial tree. Chapter 7 discusses how to value European and American call and put options on binomial trees.

Dividing the study of binomial trees into two separate chapters emphasizes a central point of how option pricing should be envisaged. First, build a model for stock price movements that is acceptable in the appropriate market. Next, use that model to price options. This point of view is particularly relevant in today's world equity markets, in which we have seen significant changes in the nature of price movements since 1987.[4] In particular, there has been a well-documented degradation in the effectiveness of the Black-Scholes model. It is this fact that led to implied theories of option pricing.

Implied Trees
Chapter 9 shows how to build "implied volatility trees," trees that are built to be consistent with the current prices of all traded options on a single underlying.[5] The implied volatility trees model can be thought of as a way of dealing with the "volatility smile." Such a model provides a picture of the market's view of future volatility movements in all possible future price scenarios for the underlying. This "collective" view of volatility can have significant impact on the valuation of many options, particularly American and barrier options.

---

[4]For more on this, see Chapter 8.

[5]This model was introduced by E. Derman and I. Kani. See Derman and Kani (1994a) and (1994b).

The original Derman-Kani model only worked with input options that are European. This imposed a significant limitation on the usefulness of the model, as most traded options are American style. Recently, the author of this book introduced an improvement of the Derman-Kani model that allows us to build implied volatility trees with input options that are *either* European or American. Chapter 9 shows how to incorporate the original Derman-Kani method with its extension to American options into a single system for building implied trees. This provides a way of extending the applicability of the original Derman-Kani method without giving up any of its useful features.

Chapter 10 explains the implied binomial trees model of options pricing.[6] This model is similar in spirit to the implied volatility trees model, but it is quite different in the details.

While the Derman-Kani model takes as its inputs the prices of traded options and provides a binomial tree as its "output," the implied binomial tree model takes as its input a probability distribution and returns a binomial tree. To be more precise, we fix a future date and specify a probability distribution for the stock on that date.[7] From these data, Rubinstein tells us how to build a binomial tree whose terminal distribution approximates this distribution.

What ties together the Derman-Kani model and the Rubinstein model is the fact that option prices themselves can be used to deduce a (risk-neutral) probability distribution for future stock prices, while the Derman-Kani method uses option prices to build a binomial tree, which in turn implies a risk-neutral price distribution. Rubinstein's model has two distinct components. First, produce a probability distribution; second, build a binomial tree with that terminal distribution.

Rubinstein's model is flexible in that its two steps are quite distinct. That is, it is possible to introduce into the model probability distributions *other* than those inferred from the market. Specifically, if an investor or trader has particular market views and wants to price options with those views in mind, then this investor or trader can use Rubinstein's model by modifying the market's view to meet his or her own views. Once this is done, this new distribution can be "fed" into the Rubinstein model to produce option values "consistent" with the investor's or trader's views. In fact, in Chapter 10 we give a simple method for taking a given probability distribution and deforming it to a new distribution with specified shape.

---

[6]This model was invented by M. Rubinstein. See Rubinstein (1994) and Rubinstein (1995a).

[7]Specifically, this should be a risk-neutral probability distribution.

In order to understand the motivation for the implied volatility tree and implied binomial trees model, we have to take a detour in Chapter 8 to study implied volatility in detail. Implied volatility is the volatility of a stock implied (via the Black-Scholes formula) by the price of an option. Since there are many different options on a given stock, one can ask if all of these implied volatilities are the same. The answer generally is no, and the collective way in which volatility varies across all options is known as the volatility smile.

Once the smile is studied, we digress a bit and discuss some possible alternative models for pricing options that were introduced before the implied volatility trees model. These models fall into two categories: stochastic volatility models and jump-diffusion models. We give a brief outline of these models and what possible advantages they offer.

Chapter 11 explains how to take any binomial tree and price barrier options on that tree. Once this is done, the methods of implied volatility trees and implied binomial trees can be combined with the pricing methods of Chapter 11 to value barrier options "in the presence of the smile."

Acknowledgments

Originally, I intended to write a small, single-purpose book explaining the ins and outs of the Black-Scholes option pricing formula. Halfway through the project, the opportunity arose to work at Goldman Sachs & Co. in their Quantitative Strategies Group. I am grateful to everyone in that group for sharing their knowledge and discussing option pricing with me.

In particular, I would like to thank Emanuel Derman and Mark Zurack for making the Quantitative Strategies Group open and accessible to me during my stay at Goldman Sachs. Iraj Kani taught me a great deal about option pricing, and many of the ideas in this book can be implicitly attributed to our discussions and his work with Emanuel Derman. I would especially like to thank Iraj and Emanuel for the many useful and enlightening conversations about option pricing. I would also like to thank Michael Kamal, Joe Zou, and Sylvan Roy, who read parts of the book and made useful comments, as well as spent a great deal of time discussing option pricing with me. Additionally, I thank Deniz Ergener and Brian Carrihill for their support and interest.

Many people were instrumental in the development of this book. Let me thank Chuck Epstein (Investing On-Line), who managed the project from its infancy, and Suzanne Cosgrove, who edited the first draft (in some places twice).

A number of people read all or part of the manuscript and gave important suggestions. I would especially like to thank Ira Kawaller (at the Chicago Mercantile Exchange) for reading a great deal of the manuscript and encouraging me that this project was worthwhile. In addition, I would like to thank Alex Bergier (Goldman Sachs), Marcus Hancock (Smith Barney), John Liew (Goldman Sachs), and Lisa Goldberg (BARRA, Inc.) for carefully reading the text and making comments. Marcus Hancock deserves special thanks for many hours of discussion concerning the practical aspects of options trading.

Several people read the entire draft late in its development and made many important suggestions, pointing out in many cases what undoubtedly would have been embarrassing errors. In particular, I would like to thank Israel Nelken (Harris Investment Management and Super Computing Consulting), Brian Ostrow (Nations Banc-CRT), and Tim Weithers (Nations Banc-CRT). Also, I am especially grateful to Christoph Rüther (Goldman Sachs, Frankfurt) for discussing the manuscript in detail and making specific suggestions for improvements.

In addition, I would like to thank Peter Carr (Cornell University), David Shimko (J. P. Morgan), and Bob Whaley (Duke University) for some useful conversations that contributed to the content of this book. I especially thank Mark Rubinstein (Berkeley and LOR) for taking the time to discuss implied binomial trees in detail with me. The chapter on this subject was greatly influenced by these conversations.

Several people took their time to point out errors and typos after the book was printed. I would like to thank Vincent Orrico, Joe Palovich, Don Chance, S. Bates, and Dmitri Betaneli for this.

I would also like to thank Ralph Rieves, my editor, for making sure this project continued to develop smoothly from the time Irwin took it over until its eventual publication.

Lastly, I would like to thank THE MATHWORKS for supplying me with copies of MATLAB, which was used to produce all of the graphs and charts in this book, except for those provided by Goldman Sachs & Co. (Figures 8.5.1 and 9.9.1).

1

STOCKS, OPTIONS, AND FUTURES

This book is about the methods and concepts of option valuation. Specifically, we will study the valuation of *equity options,* although the basic ideas for other options, such as foreign exchange options, are quite similar and will be pointed out along the way.

While option pricing is a theoretical subject, the motivation and intent of the work is wholly practical. Thus, while there are many simplifying assumptions and unrealistic economic scenarios in this book, the bottom line is that the ideas and methods presented here are the foundations of what is actually used in real trading environments.

The purpose of this introductory chapter is to acquaint the reader with the types of securities and derivative securities that will be covered in this book and the ways in which they will be presented. The focus here, as in the entire book, is on the way we take options, stocks, and other securities and represent them mathematically.

This chapter introduces the basic securities used in this book and discusses the major economic assumptions we will make in order to produce option pricing formulas. Lastly, we introduce our basic economic tool: the no-arbitrage hypothesis. This principle is at the heart of all our analysis, and we therefore acquaint the reader with it as early as possible in our study.

1.1   A PRELIMINARY DEFINITION OF OPTIONS

We are going to define options twice in this chapter. To begin, we will give a preliminary definition, useful for those who know absolutely nothing about options and need some idea in order to understand the motivation for the rest of the chapter. Later, once we have some more definitions at hand, we will give a more detailed account.

Options are contracts that give their holders the right to buy or sell an *underlying asset* at a fixed price (we will define precisely what we mean by an underlying asset in a moment).

There are many variants to this basic theme, which will be discussed later, but for now we concentrate on the two main types of options: calls and puts. A call option gives the holder the right to buy "something" at a fixed price, and a put option gives the holder the right to sell "something" at a fixed price. The question we want to focus on right now is, buy or sell what? This brings us to the definition of an underlying.

What Is an Underlying?

We begin with a basic example. We start with a stock, taking as its price the last price paid for it on an exchange. A call option on this stock is the right to buy the stock at a fixed price, called the *strike price*. Similarly, a put option is the right to sell it at a fixed price, also called the strike price. Later, we will talk about the details of this arrangement, but right now we want to stay focused on the relationship between the stock and the option.

Let's refine our example a little. Suppose we have a stock, XYZ, currently selling for $100, and we have an option to buy XYZ in three months for $100. This means in three months we can *exercise* the option and purchase XYZ for $100, regardless of its real price. If, for example, in three months, XYZ is selling for $110, we can still use the option to buy it for $100. In this case, the holder of the contract will profit $10 from exercising the option (excluding any taxes and transaction costs).

Likewise, if XYZ is selling for $90, we can still buy it for $100 by using the option. Of course, since XYZ is selling for $90, we are better off not using the option and instead purchasing it directly on an exchange. In this case, no profit can be realized from exercising the option, but losses associated with it are limited as well (because the holder is not obliged to exercise).

The main point of this example is that the value of XYZ (the underlying) combined with the strike price of the option is what determines the eventual profits from owning the option. From this, we arrive at our first principle. The underlying of an option can be any asset at all, as long as it has a value upon which both sides of the contract can agree. For example, the underlying can be a commodity, such as gold or silver, or a foreign currency, such as the U.S. dollar–yen exchange rate.

In all of these cases, one can specify an options contract on a particular underlying by specifying whether it is a call or a put and what the strike price is. Additional parameters, such as when the option can be exercised, must also be specified, but we will discuss those later.

Options and Option Pricing

With all of this said, we can now give a preliminary idea of what this book is about. First of all, we want to show that in many cases we can use theoretical methods to determine the value of an option. In this context, *value* has a very precise meaning; it is what the contract is intrinsically worth. This is in contrast to the price of the option, which is what someone actually pays for it. What this distinction really means will take more time to unravel, but for now we want to stress the point of this book:

This book is about determining the value of an option.

Since, as it stands, "options" covers a lot of ground, we are going to pare the field down a little. Rather than studying all options, we are going to focus on options on primarily two types of underlyings: stocks and stock indexes. We choose these two underlyings for two reasons. First, they are easier to understand than options on interest rates (another whole topic); second, they encompass all of the principles of options pricing. Thus *equity options* are the best subject for learning the principles of option pricing.

In order to accomplish our goal, however, we will have to study a variety of other financial instruments, including zero-coupon bonds and futures contracts.

1.2 STOCKS

The goal of the next few sections is to introduce how we deal with stocks, stock indexes, and zero-coupon bonds. The emphasis is not on markets or trading but on the aspects of these instruments important for option pricing. We begin with stocks.

Stocks

We assume the reader is familiar with what stocks are and how they are traded in the market. The *spot price* of a stock is the price at which it can be currently bought *or* sold. This is the first simplifying assumption in the theory of options pricing:

> *The spot price of a stock is assumed to be the same whether it is being bought or sold.*

We are stating, in opposition to reality, that there is a well-defined prevailing market price of any stock for which one can purchase (or sell) shares. Moreover, we will assume throughout this book that one can purchase any number of shares at the prevailing market price. That is, we do not allow for the possibility of *market impact,* wherein entry into certain markets can affect prices in those markets. Nor do we allow for *liquidity issues,* in which case desired stocks are not available at any price.

Later, when we study the Black-Scholes option pricing formula and option pricing in general, we will discuss how to "hedge" an option. Hedging is the process by which one attempts to eliminate the risk associated with a position in a contract. The hedging procedure will demand that the hedger frequently buy and sell shares at the prevailing market price and, moreover, that these purchases will often be of *fractional* numbers of shares. In all cases, the assumptions that the shares are available at the market price are critical to the validity of the formula.

It should be noted that the above assumptions are by no means trivial. They are serious and, in some cases, highly detrimental to the validity of the option pricing theory we develop later. We make the assumptions not because we want to but rather because we have to. In order to build a theory that is simple enough to use in practice, it is necessary to eliminate some difficulties that complicate theoretical analysis.

Notation for Stocks

We now discuss some of the notation used in stock price modeling and option pricing. The usual situation is one in which we are trying to price some option on a stock;[1] what this means and which type of option is involved are not important at this time.

The stock itself is represented by some letter, usually S, or sometimes by a nonexistent ticker symbol such as XYZ. That is, we will frequently speak in phrases like "some stock S" or "some stock XYZ" whose current price is $100.

To model the stock, we need to be able to talk about its price at various times. For example, we might want to say something about the price of S on December 20, 1995. Usually, however, we want to discuss the price of the

---

[1] Options are defined in Section 1.5.

stock on some date *relative* to another date. This is because typically there is a very specific range of dates in which we are interested: for example, the life span of an option on the stock.

For example, we might have an option on S that was written on July 26, 1995 (the initial date), and the present date might be December 26, 1995. In such cases, we are mainly interested in the amount of time that has expired from the initial date to the present date.

Suppose we want to track the price movements of some stock, XYZ, over a two-year period starting July 26, 1995. Then, we write t_0 (read "t sub zero") for the initial date (July 26, 1995), and other dates are denoted by a letter other than t_0. For example, some later date might be denoted by t_1 (read "t sub one"); in this case, t_1 might be December 26, 1995. What we are generally interested in is the amount of time that expires from t_0 to t_1. This amount of time is denoted by $t_1 - t_0$, which signifies the difference in time from time t_0 to t_1.

We keep track of time this way because the amount of time between two dates will always figure into the option pricing formulas we study, similar to the way the duration of a loan figures into the amount of interest paid. Time is usually expressed in units of one year; in the above example, since the difference in time from July 26, 1995, to December 26, 1995, is five months, or 5/12 years, we write $t_1 - t_0 = 5/12$.

How Many Days Are There in One Year?

An important question to the implementation of option pricing models is how many days are there in one year? The problem is, while there are 365 days in a year, only approximately 250 of them are *trading days*. So, for example, from one Monday to the next there are seven *calendar days* while there are five *trading days*. But, seven calendar days represent 7/365 or 0.0192 of a year, while the five trading days represent 5/250 or 0.02 of a year. In other words, the same interval of time represents two different fractional parts of a year, depending on whether we count trading days or calendar days.

Now the question is, do we use calendar days or trading days to measure time? The answer is, it depends on the situation. In certain instances, such as the computation of compound interest, the choice is forced on us by the various rules regulating these computations. For example, if a bank account computes compound interest daily for all calendar days, then the choice is clear. In other instances, it is an open question whether to use all days or just trading days. For us, the most crucial place where this is true is in the study of stock volatility.

We will see later that it is a theoretically open question whether stock volatility is affected during off hours. If our model states that only trading affects stock volatility, then we should use only trading days. On the other hand, if we believe events that take place beyond the usual trading hours affect volatility, then we should use some other measure, perhaps all days. This will be discussed in more detail later.

The Return on a Stock

When discussing stock prices, we are mostly interested in the return on the stock from one date to another (which is another example of why we look at the difference between times). For example, if we invest $100 per share in XYZ at time t_0 and sell it at time t_1 for $110, we want to know what rate of return the stock earned.

By rate of return we will always mean the *continuously compounded rate of return* on the stock over a fixed period of time. We will need to know what this is specifically when modeling stock prices, and the mathematics of this rate of return is reviewed in Chapter 2.

Dividends

Some stocks pay dividends, and dividends are an important ingredient in option pricing. The dividends paid on a stock and the schedule by which they are paid out have an important impact on the value of an option. Later, we will study the impact of dividends on options in a systematic way. For now we review what dividends are and how they affect the price of a stock.

The date on which buyers of a stock are no longer eligible to receive the next dividend payment is called the *ex-dividend date* of the stock. When a stock *goes ex-dividend,* basic economic theory says that its market value will drop by exactly the amount of the dividend payment.[2]

The original Black-Scholes option pricing formula assumed that stocks paid no dividends throughout the life of the option. This assumption can be relaxed to obtain option pricing formulas on dividend-paying stocks. There are several different approaches to modeling the payout of dividends, and each is taken into account in option pricing in a different way. We shall discuss these approaches later, mainly in the context of option pricing. For now, we will just give an idea of the direction in which these models may be taken.

---

[2]There has been a large amount of research into what is known as the *ex-dividend behavior* of stock prices. In general, it has been observed that stock prices do not actually drop by precisely the dividend payment. See the references at the end of this chapter for more information on this subject.

Two Types of Dividend Models

There are broadly speaking two types of dividend models: (1) deterministic and (2) stochastic.

Deterministic dividend models start with a "best guess" of what the future dividend payments will be presented in the form of a schedule. This schedule can be simple, such as a list of dates and dividend yields or dollar amounts (for example, a 1 percent dividend every year on a particular date), or more complicated, involving dividend payments as a function of both spot price and time. Another approach assumes that dividends are paid out continuously over time, so that the expected growth rate of the stock is diminished by exactly the dividend yield.

Stochastic dividend models introduce an element of randomness into the dividend yield. They essentially say that, while the exact form of the dividend yield cannot be known today, we can say something about the random characteristics of the dividends. These models are much like stock price models themselves, which never make precise statements about the actual future value of the stock.

Both methods of handling dividends lead to option pricing formulas that go beyond Black-Scholes. In this book, we shall only discuss the deterministic models. To read more about dividends in the Black-Scholes model, see Chapter 4, Section 4.9.

1.3   STOCK INDEXES AND FOREIGN CURRENCIES

A stock index is a composite of a variety of stocks in a single "basket." For example, the Standard & Poor's 500 (S&P 500) index is a composite of U.S. stocks accounting for about 80 percent of the total market capitalization of the New York Stock Exchange. The exact proportions of the stocks in the index are chosen based on market capitalization.

Every stock index has an "index level," which is a measure of the relative value of the index. The relative value of the index relates to the day-to-day changes in value of its composite stocks. If an index rises from a level of 200 to 210, this represents a 5 percent increase in value. For example, on November 10, 1995, the S&P 500 closed at an index level of 581.

Assumptions about Stock Indexes

We will make several assumptions regarding stock indexes. First of all, given a stock index, we will assume there exists a corresponding stock index fund in which an investor can purchase shares. Ownership of these shares gives the investor the right to receive dividend payments that occur while the investor owns the shares. When we speak of the spot or cash price of an index, we will mean the spot price of such a fund. Moreover, this fund is assumed to be completely liquid. The fund is denominated in index points, and the investor can buy any fractional number of shares he or she wants. Moreover, the investor can take short positions in shares of the fund. For simplicity, we denominate all dividend payments in index points as well.

Example
An investor buys 10 shares of an S&P 500 fund on November 10, 1995. The investor now owns 5,810 "index points." A 1 percent dividend yield is therefore worth 58.10 index points to the investor.

Similarities with Stocks
As with stocks themselves, we will assume there is a spot or cash value at all times for the index and that there is no bid-ask spread. In reality, since the underlying stocks of the index have a bid-ask spread, so should the index. However, since we assume there is no bid-ask spread for the stocks, we also assume there is no bid-ask spread for the index. The spot price in this context is the index level. We will ignore any possible market impact and liquidity issues.[3]

Stock indexes and, consequently, option valuation for stock indexes can be modeled using exactly the same techniques as for stocks. Thus, when we refer to a spot price, we will mean either the spot price of a stock or index. In many cases it will not be necessary to distinguish between a model for a stock and a model for an index. Sometimes, for example in the case of dividends, one type of model does work better for a stock versus an index. The price movement models that we study in detail, along with the method of implied volatility trees, are valid for both stocks and indexes.

Dividends and Stock Indexes

The main *practical difference* between the way stocks and indexes are handled with regard to theoretical option pricing is in dealing with dividends. We have already mentioned that, in the absence of other contributing factors, when a stock goes ex-dividend the spot price drops in value an amount equal to the value of the announced dividend. Because an index is

---

[3] We will also ignore any exchange rules such as the down-tick/up-tick rule.

composed of many stocks, there are a far greater number of ex-dividend dates as compared with an ordinary stock. For example, the Standard and Poor's 500 (S&P 500) has stocks paying dividends throughout the entire year, while the Japanese Nikkei 225 index has a large number of stocks paying out dividends all in the same month, but the dividend yields themselves are quite small. Clearly, the way one models the dividends of these two indexes will be quite different.

If the dividend yield is too large to be ignored but the payments are relatively spread out, the dividend yield can be approximated by a continuous dividend payment (more on this below). On the other hand, some indexes behave more like stocks with a large number of ex-dividend dates.

The main point is that modeling the dividend structure of both stocks and indexes is a practical issue that depends both on the expected size of the payouts and when the payouts are likely to be made, and must be estimated from historical data.

Dividends and Options

The business of estimating dividends is serious and difficult. The points that we would like to keep in mind are: (1) dividends impact the price of options, and (2) dividend payments cannot be predicted, but rather they must be estimated based on historical trends. For any given option pricing problem, a method of modeling dividends must be chosen and the dividends (or yields) must be estimated. With this information in hand, we will demonstrate in Chapter 4 how dividends affect the price of options.

We will now look at the continuous dividend yield model by studying dividend reinvestment. Next, we will apply these ideas to the study of foreign currencies; we will see that owning a foreign currency is identical to owning a security that makes a continuous dividend payment and reinvesting all of the dividends.

Dividend Reinvestment

Let's start with an investor who purchases shares in a stock index (via a fund, as described above) and uses all dividend payments to purchase more shares of the fund.

For the purpose of clarity, we will assume that dividend payments are made in percentage of the index. For example, if an investor owns 100 "shares" of the S&P 500 and the current level is 600, then a dividend payment of 5 percent allows the investor to purchase 5 more "shares" of the S&P 500 (i.e., 5 percent of 100 shares is 5 shares). From another point of view, the dividend payments can be thought of as being made in index points. With this, a 5 percent payment is worth 30 index points per share of index owned.

This is analogous to thinking about a 5 percent payment on a stock selling for $600 per share. In this case, the dividend payment per share is $30, and if someone owns 100 shares of this stock, then he or she can purchase 5 more shares with the dividend payment.

How Dividend Reinvestment Really Works

We are going to discuss what *dividend reinvestment* looks like when we use a continuous dividend yield model. This forces us to understand exactly what a continuous dividend yield really means. In particular, we will learn that if we buy one unit of a security paying a continuous dividend yield at a rate q, then in time Δt we will have

$$e^{q\Delta t}$$

units of the index. The letter e here is the natural exponential and is studied in detail in Chapter 2.

To understand this, we'll begin by looking at the case in which there are only a finite number of dividend payments, all equally spaced over a period of time and equal in amount. The approach taken here mimics our basic study of compound interest in Section 2.1 of Chapter 2. The only difference between compound interest and the present situation is that here we do not know what the market level will be when future dividend payments are made, and because we do not know the market level, we cannot know what the cash value of a dividend payment will be.

For example, suppose we assume a dividend yield of q percent *per annum*. If dividend payments are made at times $t_1, \ldots, t_N$ during the year, then we model each payment as q/N times the current market level. This means we believe a good model for the dividend behavior of our index is that N times during the year the stock goes ex-dividend, and each dividend payment's value is equal to a factor of q/N times the market level at that time.

Fortunately, since we are reinvesting the dividends, the market level of the index is absolutely irrelevant. All we care about is how much of the index we receive, and our model tells us that—we get exactly "q/N" of it.

Example

For example, suppose the current date is January 9, 1996, the S&P 500 is at 600, and we own one unit of it. Assume the dividend yield is 5 percent *per annum,* with four payments. Each payment is then $0.05/4 = 0.0125$ times the current market level. How much of the S&P 500 will we obtain from dividend reinvestment?

The first payment is on April 9, 1996. Suppose the level at this time is 625. The payment is then $0.0125 \cdot 625$, (or 7.81). This information is *not important* if we are reinvesting. Why? Because we know we are getting 1 1/4 percent of the level of the S&P 500 from the dividend payment. If we reinvest all of the dividend payment, then we use the proceeds to purchase exactly 1 1/4 of a percent of one unit of the S&P 500.[4]

After each dividend payment we receive 1 1/4 percent (1.0125) of as much S&P 500 as we own at that time. Since we started with one unit, we will have $1 + 0.0125 = 1.0125$ units after the first payment. After the second payment we will have $1.0125 \cdot 1.0125 = 1.0252$. After the third, we will have $1.0252 \cdot 1.0125 = 1.0380$, and finally, after the fourth, we will have $1.0380 \cdot 1.0125 = 1.0510$.

Note that this is analogous to computing compound interest: There were four dividend payments, each of $q/4$ times the index level. At the end of the fourth payment (one year later) we have $(1 + q/4)^4$ units of the index.

If there are N payments instead of four, then at the end of the N payments we will have $(1 + q/N)^N$ units. If dividends are paid *continuously* and reinvested into the index, we will have e^q units at the end of a year.

More generally:

Suppose we own x shares of a stock index with a continuous dividend yield of q, and we hold the index for a time Δt, reinvesting all dividends during that period. At the end, we will have $xe^{q\Delta t}$ units of the index.

Foreign Currencies

Foreign currencies play an important role in world financial markets. Both currency futures and currency options are actively traded on many exchanges. All of the models in this book can be used to model "currency-based" securities, provided we know how to interpret things properly.

This section will make two things clear:

1. A foreign currency can be viewed as a "security" with a spot price equal to the cost of buying one unit of the foreign currency in dollars.[5]

2. The foreign currency "pays" a continuous dividend yield equal to the foreign risk-free rate of interest, and these dividend payments are "automatically" reinvested in the currency.

---

[4]Note how we use the assumptions of our theoretical models here: we can buy any number of units of the security, there are no transaction costs, and there is no bid-ask spread. Moreover, we are assuming the level at which we can buy is exactly the same as the level when the dividend payment is made. In reality, there will be slight differences.

[5]Or, if your base currency is something other than dollars, for example pounds or yen, then the spot price is the cost of one unit of the foreign currency in the base currency.

The first item is easy to understand. Suppose we purchase a certain number of yen in today's market; the cost of this purchase may then be stated in price-per-yen. For example, suppose the current price of yen is $0.01, or 1 cent (that is, we can buy one yen for $0.01). As the spot exchange rate fluctuates, so does the price-per-yen. If the price "rises" to $0.011, then we can sell back our yen (that is, we can buy U.S. dollars with the yen), and gain a 10 percent return on our investment. If we originally bought 100,000 yen for $100, then we can buy back $100,000 \times 0.011 = 1,100$ U.S. dollars at the new rate. Similarly, if the spot exchange rate drops, we lose money on our investment, because closing the investment requires buying back U.S. dollars at a less favorable rate.

Now let's examine where the analogy with dividend payments comes in. If we buy yen with U.S. dollars we assume we hold the yen in a deposit (for example, a foreign bond) that pays the risk-free rate of the foreign government. For example, suppose the Japanese risk-free rate is 1 percent (continuously compounded). If we buy 1,000 yen and invest them at the Japanese risk-free rate for one year, then at the end of the year we will have $e^{0.01}100 = 101.05$ yen.

In general, if we buy x units of the currency at time t and invest them at the foreign risk-free rate, r_f (read "r sub f" for risk-free rate, foreign) then at time T we will have $xe^{r_f(T-t)}$ units of the foreign currency. That is, despite the dollars we might gain or lose due to the spot price fluctuation, the number of units of our investment increases at a rate equal to the foreign risk-free rate. This is identical to the situation in which we purchase x units of a stock index paying a continuous dividend yield of q with all dividends reinvested.

With this understood, we may value securities based on foreign exchange provided we know: (1) the risk-free rate for the domestic currency (e.g., if the domestic currency is U.S. dollars, then we must know the U.S. risk-free rate) and (2) the risk-free rate for the foreign currency. In this case the foreign risk-free rate is equivalent (mathematically) to a continuously reinvested dividend yield.

Economic Assumptions in Foreign Currencies

To view foreign currency as a dividend-paying stock index, an important economic assumption must be made: the foreign risk-free rate of interest is constant. In reality, this is far from true, and the inconstant nature of the foreign risk-free rate creates difficulties in pricing futures and options contracts on the foreign currency. We can quite easily see why this is so. If the foreign risk-free rate fluctuates over time, then the statement that, in time Δt, the number of units of the currency grows by a factor of $e^{r_f \Delta t}$ is false.

1.4 RISKLESS ZERO-COUPON BONDS

A riskless zero-coupon bond is a bond that pays no coupons and has no default risk. Such a bond has a maturity date on which it can be redeemed for its par value, or nominal amount. For example, a bond maturing on January 5, 1999, with a par value of $1,000 may be redeemed on January 5, 1999, for $1,000. Prior to that date the bond makes no payments.

It is important not to think of a riskless zero-coupon bond as riskless in the sense of investment. Such bonds still have risk if interest rates fluctuate. As interest rates rise, the market value of a bond falls. Thus, if we intend to sell a riskless zero-coupon bond *before* its maturity we expose ourselves to *interest rate risk.*

Despite this reality, in our models we always assume that there is a single rate of interest on which bonds of all maturities can be bought and sold in any amounts. As with stocks and indexes, we assume there are no market impact and liquidity issues. The interest rate at which riskless zero-coupon bonds can be bought and sold will be referred to as the *risk-free rate of interest.* This of course is part of the *constant interest rate assumption,* which we will see later in studying the Black-Scholes formula.

The value of a riskless zero-coupon bond is computed by discounting its par value by the risk-free rate of interest.[6] We will always perform this discounting using continuously compounded interest.

For example, if the risk-free rate of interest is 5 percent, then a riskless zero-coupon bond maturing in one year with a par value of $100 will be worth $95.12 today. That is, we have $100, discounted by $e^{-0.05}$, which is $100 \cdot e^{-0.05}$.

To summarize, we assume we can always borrow and lend at the risk-free rate of interest. That is, we assume we can invest all available cash at the risk-free rate and that we can borrow whenever we like at the risk-free rate.

Later, when we study the Black-Scholes formula and other option pricing techniques, we will see that to hedge an option we must be able to purchase and sell riskless zero-coupon bonds of arbitrary par values and arbitrary maturities. This assumption amounts to assuming that one can

---

[6]For a review of investment mathematics, see Chapter 2.

keep arbitrary amounts of money in both long and short positions invested at the risk-free rate.

1.5 DERIVATIVE SECURITIES

A derivative security is a financial instrument whose value depends on the price of an underlying asset. The term derivative security is broad and lays claim to many different types of financial instruments. In this book we focus on two of the most common sorts: options and futures.

Options

Broadly speaking, there are two types of options: puts and calls. Both are contracts that give the owner the right to do something. A call option on a security S (in this book a stock or index) gives the owner the right to buy S subject to the conditions of the option contract. A put option gives the owner the right to sell S also at a set price. An option contract is flexible; its holder is not obligated to purchase or sell anything. From a theoretical point of view, it is assumed that an investor will only exercise an option if it is favorable to do so. This is important, because, in reality, investors may do whatever they wish, even if it is illogical or irrational. In theoretical models, investors are bound to act rationally. We will see that this plays a key role in valuing derivative securities.

To exercise an option is to exercise the right to buy or sell the underlying instrument. Options come in two basic styles with regard to exercise rights: American and European. American options may be exercised at any time during the life of the option contract, while European options may only be exercised at expiration. There are also so-called *Bermuda options,* which can be exercised on some, but not all, dates before expiration.[7]

In reality, there are many technicalities to buying and selling options. They can be bought and sold on an options exchange, or they can be custom made in *over-the-counter* deals (done privately, but usually facilitated by an investment bank). In theoretical option pricing, however, the option contract is reduced to a certain set of data. The following are specified in the contract and are considered in theoretical option pricing:

---

[7]This terminology is apparently derived from the fact that Bermuda is somewhere between America and Europe.

Underlying instrument	the instrument that may be bought or sold
Contract size	the number of shares of the underlying the contract involves
Strike price	the price at which the underlying instrument may be bought if the option is exercised
Settlement date	the date on which money is received for the contract
Expiration date	the date on which the option expires (also called expiry)
Style	American, European, or Bermuda
Premium	the price paid for the contract

Examples

Consider an option with the following terms:

Underlying: XYZ

Size: 100 shares

Strike price: $100

Settlement date: 7/26/95

Type: call

Expiration date: 7/26/96

Style: European

These data describe a call option on XYZ struck at $100, settled on July 26, 1995, and expiring July 26, 1996. The option is European, so it can only be exercised on the expiration date. Therefore, on July 26, 1996, the owner of this contract has the right (but not the obligation) to purchase 100 shares of XYZ for $100 per share. From a theoretical point of view, this is all of the information about the option needed to value the option.

Exotic Options

We have now described the basic types of options and their variants. Options that fit into the above types (i.e., American or European puts and calls) are often called *plain vanilla* options due to their ubiquity in the derivatives world and in order to distinguish them from their newer *exotic* cousins.

Exotic options are merely variants of plain vanilla options. They range from very simple options (e.g., a digital call, which pays $1 if, on the expiration date, the spot price of the underlying is greater than the strike price, and nothing otherwise) to complicated options, such as Asian options, whose payoffs depend on the average value of the underlying over the life of the option.

Exotic options are usually born of the particular needs of hedgers, investors using the instruments to manage financial risk. Their structures are only limited by the creativity of the traders, researchers, and clients who develop them. In Chapter 11 we will study and learn how to price one type of exotic option in detail: barrier options.

1.6   THE VALUE OF AN OPTION

This book is about option valuation—developing formulas that are supposed to tell us how much an option is worth. First, however, we must make a convincing argument that such a notion makes sense. Certainly not all assets can be valued using straightforward formulas. What is it about options that makes them susceptible to such an analysis? To investigate this we will work backward, starting at the expiration of the option.

There is one time when it is easy to value an option—at expiration. Consider a call option struck at K on an underlying selling for S. What is the value of the call option if we are moments from expiration?

Since the stock may be bought for $\$K$, and sold for $\$S$, then if the underlying spot price is greater than the strike, the owner of the call can recover $S - K$ dollars by exercising the option and buying the underlying for $\$K$ and selling it for $\$S$. (Of course, for this to be valid we must make assumptions about liquidity and market impact. We shall discuss these in Section 1.9.) On the other hand, if the option is out of the money (the value of the underlying is lower than the strike price), then it is cheaper to buy the underlying directly in the market than to use the option. Therefore, a rational investor will not exercise the right to purchase the stock for the strike price, and the option expires worthless. This is an example of what we call optimal exercise. We summarize this by writing

$$C_{exp} = \max(S - K, 0),$$

where C_{exp} denotes the value of C at expiration. This is read, "C_{exp} is equal to the greater of $S - K$ and zero."

Conversely, if we consider a put option also struck at K on the same stock, then its value at expiration is $\max(K - S, 0)$. The same logic applies. If the spot is less than the strike, then the underlying may first be bought for $\$S$ and immediately sold for $\$K$ by exercising this option. Figure 1.6.1 displays a graph of "payoff at expiration" for European call and put options.

F I G U R E 1.6.1

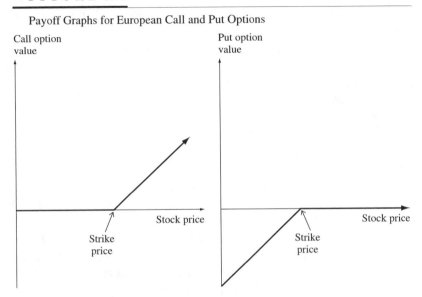

Payoff Graphs for European Call and Put Options

The Option Premium and Fair Value

The cost of purchasing an option contract is called the *option premium.* Every option has a premium, and premiums are determined in one of two ways. If there is a market for a particular option, for instance if it is traded on an exchange in a standardized format, then the premium for the option is set by the market itself. If the option is sold over the counter, then its premium is an agreed upon price between buyer and seller. In either case, the principle is the same. There are two parties, the buyer and the seller, and they both agree upon the price for which the contract is to be bought and sold.

In the theory of option pricing, we do not study the option premium itself but rather its *fair value,* also known as the *theoretical value.* The distinction is important.

Fair value can be thought of as roughly the "production cost" of the option. It is the value at which the option can be sold, say, by a trader writing the deal, so that neither a profit is made nor a loss incurred in the transaction. Its premium, the amount for which it is sold, is a different matter.

This is analogous to a manufacturer who can produce a certain product for a given price but sells it for a higher price in order to make a profit. We shall see that the option itself can be "produced" through a precise system of hedging, and we will identify the total cost of this "production" at the start of the hedging. This is the cost of the option to whomever undertakes selling it. The determination of the premium is then a practical (not theoretical) matter.

The difference between fair value and premium can be understood by means of a simple example. Suppose a fair coin is flipped. If the coin lands heads up, you receive $1; otherwise, you receive nothing. How much is this bet worth? On the one hand, one might say it is worth $0.50, because the probability of the coin landing heads side up is exactly one-half. This would then be the fair value. The real value of the bet, however, depends on the perspective from which you look at it. If we are the ones offering the bet (i.e., we are flipping the coin and paying the dollar if it lands heads up), then we want to build into our price some sort of profit. Thus, we might charge $0.53 in an attempt to make, on average, a $0.03 profit per flip. This is the premium for the bet.

One issue that arises in determining the option premium is the difficulty in managing the risk associated with writing the option. Theoretical option pricing models tell us the fair value of an option, but the writer of the option must decide how difficult it will be to hedge the option within a reasonable band of its fair value. Perhaps the underlying stock is thinly traded, or the data used in the pricing are unreliable. To account for such discrepancies, the writer may tack on an extra amount to the premium due to the difficulty in managing the option's risk.

The issue of premium versus fair value is one place in option pricing where theory and reality meet. It is here where a detailed understanding of the assumptions that go into a model are crucial. Without this understanding and an identification of what it entails for theoretical values, it is difficult to properly manage the risk associated with an option.

Market Priced Options

If an option is traded on an exchange, it has a price, just as there is a price for a stock traded on the New York Stock Exchange. The point of option pricing, and in particular the Black-Scholes formula, is to determine fair values for options *independent* of their exchange-traded prices.[8] The point here is volume: If an option is traded in fairly high volumes, we assume there are mechanisms at work that force the price of the option toward its theoretical fair value. We will discuss this in greater detail later.

---

[8]An important exception to this example is the theory of implied volatility trees, which takes as its starting point the prices of all exchange-traded options on a particular underlying, and then uses this information to price other options, not traded on an exchange. This is studied in Chapter 9.

Also, since many options, for example exotic options and over-the-counter vanilla options, are not traded on exchanges, one needs an assessment of their worth in order to have a benchmark of how much to charge for them. Moreover, option pricing theory goes even beyond just giving pricing formulas. It also provides vital information on hedging the option by allowing the writer of the option to calculate *hedge parameters.* Hedge parameters give a precise *theoretical* prescription for hedging the option and provide a profile of the riskiness of the option.[9] This will be discussed in Chapter 4.

For a stock option, the premium breaks into two components: *intrinsic value* and *time value.* Intrinsic value is the value that the option would have if immediately exercised. In the case of a call option, this is $\max(S - K, 0)$, and in the case of a put, it is $\max(K - S, 0)$, as we discussed in the case of the value of an option at expiration. The time value is whatever is left over.

Example
Suppose we have an option with the following data:

  Spot price of underlying: $105

  Type: call

  Strike price: $100

  Style: European

  Premium: $14.55

Then we have

  Intrinsic value: $5

  Time value: $9.55

The intrinsic value is $5, because if the option were exercised today, one could profit $\max(105 - 100, 0) = 5$ dollars by buying XYZ for $100 and then selling it for $105. Notice that the time value accounts for almost two-thirds of the option premium. One of our goals is to understand the meaning of this value.

Moneyness
An option is said to be *in the money,* if immediate exercise has positive value. The property of being in the money does not depend on whether the option is American or European—it is purely a statement about the relationship between the spot of the underlying and strike of the option. Thus, a call option is in the money if the spot price of the underlying is

---

[9]We say "a theoretical prescription" for hedging because in practice this theory does not adequately translate into practice.

currently greater than the strike price ($S > K$). Likewise, a put option is in the money if the spot price of the underlying is currently less than the strike price ($S < K$).

An option is said to be *out of the money* if exercising it would *not* yield cash. Thus, a call option is out of the money if the spot price of the underlying is currently less than the strike price ($S < K$). Likewise, a put option is out of the money if the spot price of the underlying is currently greater than the strike price ($S > K$).

An option is said to be *at the money* if the spot and strike are currently equal. We can also say that options are *near the money*. This is a loosely defined term that means the strike and spot are not too far apart.

Forward Contracts

A forward contract is a binding agreement between two parties wherein the first party agrees to deliver a certain asset, for a certain price (the delivery price), on a certain date (the delivery date).

For example, a forward contract on a share of stock might be specified as follows:

Asset	one share of XYZ
Delivery date	7/26/96
Delivery price	$100

In principle, a forward contract can be written on any asset whatsoever, and the pricing principles we will develop later work equally well for all of them, provided our economic assumptions hold. In reality, the assumptions we will use only hold for those assets that are held primarily for investment purposes.

In general, our pricing principles rely heavily on assumptions about the nature of investor behavior. Our primary assumption is that if there is a riskless cash profit to be made, investors will take advantage of it. In reality, forward contracts can be written on assets held for purposes other than investment.

The Payoff on a Forward Contract

Suppose a forward contract is written on the S&P 500. The delivery price will be an index level of 600. In order to convert index points to cash, we use a multiplier of $50 per index point. In other words, we value each index point at $50, so that the delivery price of the contract is 600 *times* $50, or $30,000.

Now suppose party B sells the forward contract to party A. That is, party A agrees to "buy" the index from party B on the delivery date at a price of 600 (times the multiplier of $50).

If the index is at a level of 610 on the delivery date, then party B has to acquire the index at 610 and then sell it to party A at the agreed upon level of 600. Excluding transaction costs and fees, this amounts to a loss of 10 times the multiplier of $50, or $500.

On the other hand, party A receives the index at a level of 600 and can sell it on a market at a level of 610, thereby making a profit of $500.

Because of this, the two parties can agree ahead of time to settle the contract in cash. Since party A will make a profit (buying the index below market value) if the index is less than 600 on the delivery date, party B can simply pay party A his or her profit directly. Conversely, if the index level is above 600 on the delivery date, then party A will suffer a loss and can pay this loss directly to party B. In this way, we see that a forward contract is very similar to a bet between parties on the future price of an asset.

In more detail, the two parties can agree that if the index level is below 600 at delivery, then party A pays party B the difference between the delivery price of 600 and the index level times the multiplier of $50. Conversely, if the index level is above 600 party B pays party A the difference of the index level times 600 and 600 times $50. This is called *settling in cash*.

In general, if the delivery price of a forward contract is written F and the spot price on the delivery date is S_d, then the payoff of the asset is $S_d - F$. If $S_d > F$, then the buyer of the forward contract will buy the asset at F (from the seller of the forward contract) and sell it at S_d, making a profit of $S_d - F$. On the other hand, if $S_d < F$, $S_d - F$ is negative and the transaction is a loss for the buyer of the forward contract.

Futures Contracts

Futures contracts are based on the same principle as forward contracts: They are binding agreements to exchange assets on a future date. The major difference between the two is that futures contracts are standardized and are traded on exchanges through clearinghouses that act as intermediaries between both sides. There are important financial differences between futures and forwards. The differences arise from *margin requirements* and *marking to market.* In order to understand these concepts, it helps to understand the structure of futures trading.

Futures Trading: The Clearinghouse

Futures contracts are traded through a clearinghouse. When two parties enter into a futures contract, they trade the contracts on an exchange and a clearinghouse acts as an intermediary.

If party A wants to sell a futures contract and party B wants to buy the same contract, then the clearinghouse will buy the contract from party A and simultaneously sell it to party B. As an intermediary, the clearinghouse assumes the default risk from both sides of the trade. That is, if either party defaults on its obligation to the other, the clearinghouse guarantees the obligation will be met.

In order to protect itself from this default risk, the clearinghouse demands a deposit from both sides of a trade in the form of *initial margin* and updates this initial margin according to how the futures price fluctuates throughout the life of the contract in a process called *marking to market.*

Fortunately, the clearinghouse only needs to protect itself from price changes in the underlying, not changes in the actual price of the underlying. To understand this, consider the following example.

In this example, party A and party B enter into a futures contract, and this contract is processed through a clearinghouse. Here are the specifications of the contract:

Current date	April 1, 1996
Delivery date	December 31, 1996
Delivery price	$1,000
Current price	$900

Suppose that party A is in the *long position;* that is, party A agrees to buy the underlying on the delivery date for $1,000. The asset is currently worth $900, so if the price does not rise, he or she will have to purchase the underlying for $100 above market value on the delivery date. If this happens and party A defaults (i.e., does not purchase the underlying), then the clearinghouse will have to buy the asset from party B for $1,000 and incur the $100 loss. Therefore, when the contract is engaged, the clearinghouse is potentially at risk $100 (and not $1,000).

To protect itself from this risk, the clearinghouse can ask each party to leave an initial margin of some fixed amount. This is usually done through a *margin account.* Suppose in this case each party is asked to give a $100 deposit. This initially protects the clearinghouse from default risk, but what if the price of the asset fluctuates?

Suppose the price of the asset rises at some point to $910. Then party A, the long position, has "made" $10, because the potential loss from the futures position was reduced from $100 to $90. Meanwhile, party B, the short position, has correspondingly "lost" $10. Both of these gains and losses are fictitious in a sense, because it is only at the delivery date that any actual financial transactions take place. Nevertheless, at the end of each day each party's margin account is adjusted to reflect the losses or gains incurred in that day's trading. This is called *marking to market.*

In this example, party A's margin account is increased by $10, reflecting the $10 gain, and party B's account is reduced by $10, reflecting the loss. Note that, overall, the balance of both accounts remains fixed—the gain experienced by party A is exactly mirrored by the loss experienced by party B.

Futures Contracts in Option Pricing

Futures contracts are important in the study of option pricing for several reasons. First and foremost, from a practical standpoint futures can often act as a substitute for an underlying security. The most important case in which this substitution occurs is in the hedging of options on stock indexes.

In general, you cannot buy a stock index. The stock index funds we mentioned above are not sufficient for the purposes of hedging stock index options. By contrast, there are very liquid markets for futures contracts on the S&P 500 (and for most stock indexes). This, combined with lower transaction costs (compared with trading in the stocks composing the index), make futures contracts an ideal substitute for the spot product.[10] Moreover, we will see that there is a very sound theoretical relationship between the price of a futures contract on an asset and the cash price of the asset, making the substitution of the futures contract for the cash instrument quite reasonable.

Later, when we study the Black-Scholes formula and other option pricing methodologies, we will be interested in how to use the theory to hedge an option. Ordinarily this is accomplished by taking some position in the underlying along with a bond position and paying close attention to the relationship between the spot price and the terms of the options

---

[10]Sutcliffe (1993) notes that transaction costs can be broadly viewed as commission, bid-ask spread, and market-impact and taxation. A study by Norman and Annandale (1991) for the LIFFE index shows that trading costs in shares versus index futures are almost ten times as great.

contract. Of course, this only makes sense if one can purchase the underlying security. In the case of indexes, this is impossible, but because there are liquid futures markets, one can use futures contracts plus the knowledge of the relationship between the spot price and the future price to hedge the option.

As a result, from a theoretical standpoint, there is little difference between hedging with the underlying versus hedging with a futures contract in the underlying. This concept will be covered in more detail at the end of the chapter when we discuss the theoretical price of a forward contract.

1.7   SECURITY POSITIONS

In theoretical option pricing, investors may freely buy and sell securities, and as we have indicated in the case of stocks and indexes, we always assume the price at which one can buy a security is equal to the price at which one can sell it. Thus, in the theory of option pricing, *there is no bid-ask spread.*

Next we will discuss the different positions an investor can hold, and we will represent these positions *mathematically* in terms of their contribution to a portfolio of securities.

The Long Position

We say an investor is *long* a security if he or she owns it. We always assume that an investor can be long any security in any number of shares or any amount. What this means is that, in theoretical option pricing, we never discuss the issue of whether one can actually make the transactions, let alone at the market prices. We briefly discuss the meaning of these issues and how they affect the theory.

Liquidity and Market Impact

Liquidity issues relate to the amount of trading there is in a security. Whenever one wants to buy a security, there must be a seller. Conversely, whenever one wants to sell a security, there must be a buyer. In certain situations, such as a fast-rising market, sellers are difficult to find. Moreover, certain stocks are generally thinly traded.

If one wishes to buy a significant number of shares of a security, then this can have an impact on the price per share itself. These issues have important consequences for option pricing. However, they are strongly influenced by real-world conditions that are hard to estimate and therefore hard to include in option pricing models. It is extremely difficult, for example, to predict the market impact of a large trade, because it depends on very specific details of the given market on the given day of the trade. For this reason, in basic option pricing models, market impact and liquidity issues are entirely ignored.

The Value of the Long Position

If an investor constructs a portfolio consisting of long positions in three stocks with current prices S_1, S_2, and S_3, then the value of this portfolio is $S_1 + S_2 + S_3$. If the investor has ten shares of the first stock, five of the second, and eight of the third, then the value of the portfolio is

$$10 \cdot S_1 + 5 \cdot S_2 + 8 \cdot S_3.$$

More generally, we might represent the number of shares by algebraic symbols. For example, the investor might have λ_1 shares of the first, λ_2 shares of the second, and λ_3 shares of the third (read, respectively, lambda sub one, lambda sub two, and lambda sub three). Here, each number λ_1, λ_2, and λ_3 is *positive* (i.e., greater than zero), reflecting a positive number of shares. The value of such a position is

$$\lambda_1 S_1 + \lambda_2 S_2 + \lambda_3 S_3.$$

This abstraction is necessary, because we will be forced to speak in such abstractions when we discuss hedging options. For example, there is a number, Δ (read delta), associated with every option, and to hedge the option we need to buy or sell Δ shares of the underlying. The value of this purchase or sale is Δ times the market value of the underlying.

The Short Position

Selling a security short means borrowing the security and then selling the borrowed security in the open market. This requires the short-seller to buy back the security at a later date in order to return it. Usually these transactions take place by means of a broker.

A short-seller is required to pay to the lender of the security any income from the security. The situation we are interested in is that in which an investor sells a stock short, and the stock goes ex-dividend. In this case, the short-seller must pay the amount of the dividend (times the number of shares) to the lender of the security.

We say an investor is *short* a security if he or she has sold the security short. Just as with buying securities, we assume that an investor can short any stock or stock index he or she wishes and may do so at the prevailing market price.

Moreover, we assume that the investor can hold this position as long as he or she wishes (in reality, the investor can be *short squeezed* and be required to give back the securities). Furthermore, and this is important, we assume the investor has immediate use of all proceeds from the short selling. That is, when the security is borrowed and then sold in the open market, we assume the proceeds from this sale are available in full to the short-seller. In reality, the short-seller is required to keep a margin account against possible adverse upswings in the stock price (this is yet another illustration of the gap between theory and reality).

Mathematically, short selling is much easier to represent than what actually goes on. The point is, if we are short a security, then this represents a debt that must be repaid by buying back the security at a later time. Therefore, if we are short a stock currently selling for S, then the value of this position in our portfolio is $-S$. That is, it lowers the value of our portfolio by S.

Put another way, if we have a portfolio consisting of a variety of stocks, some long and some short, we can ask how much someone would be willing to pay for the entire portfolio (and this question, as always, is asked in the theoretical sense, and ignores the usual liquidity and market impact issues). Suppose we have two stocks, one long and one short, with spot prices of S_1 and S_2, respectively. An investor purchasing this portfolio assumes the long position, worth S_1, but also assumes the debt associated with the short position. This debt, if currently liquidated, would cost the investor S_2. Thus, he or she subtracts this from S_1 and then is only willing to pay $S_1 - S_2$ for the portfolio.

Profit from the Short Position
An investor profits from a short position in exactly the *opposite* way as in the long position: A drop in the security price results in a profit, and a rise results in a loss. (This is true, except that we have to take into account dividend payments. This will be discussed in the next section.) To see this, just remember how we compute the value of a short position.

Consider a short position in a stock whose initial value is S. The value of that position is then $-S$, in that the investor owes an amount equal to the current value of the stock. Suppose the value of S later rises by ΔS to $S + \Delta S$. Then the value of the short position is now $-(S + \Delta S) = -S - \Delta S$. Thus, the value of the position has dropped by ΔS, and the investor has lost $-\Delta S$. Conversely, if the value of S drops by ΔS, then the value of the short position moves to $-(S - \Delta S) = -S + \Delta S$, and the value has *risen* by ΔS.

The Short Position and Dividends[11]

We saw above that an investor in a short stock position profits from a drop in stock price. While this is generally true, there is one important exception. Since the short-seller must pay the owner of the stock any dividends paid on the stock, he or she does not profit from the drop in price due to the stock going ex-dividend.

This means that the true value of a short position depends not only on the value of the stock but also on the dividend payments and the ex-dividend dates throughout the life of the short sale position. This matters, in particular, in figuring the total losses or gains an investor incurs while holding a short position. What is the total profit or loss from a short position held from time t_0 to time t_2 in which the stock goes ex-dividend at some time t_1?

To compute this, let's follow the transaction through from start to finish. At time t_0 the stock is borrowed by the short position and sold for a price of S_{t_0}. This is a *gain* of S_{t_0}. We assume that this profit is invested at the risk-free rate.[12] Next, at time t_1 the stock goes ex-dividend, and the owner of the short position makes a payment of $\$d$ to the owner of the stock. This is a *loss* of $\$d$. We assume the cash to make this payment was taken from a risk-free investment. Finally, at time t_2 the stock must be bought back from the market at a price of S_{t_2}. This is a loss of S_{t_2}. Therefore, the total profit or loss from this short sale (value 0 at time t_2) is

$$e^{r(t_2-t_0)}S_{t_0} - e^{r(t_2-t_1)}d - S_{t_2}.$$

Example

Assume the risk-free rate is 5 percent. On July 26, 1995 (time t_0), an investor sells XYZ short for $100. Three months later, on October 26, 1995 (time t_1), the stock goes ex-dividend for a payment of $1. Three months after that, on January 26, 1996, the short position is closed out, and the stock is bought back for $90. The total profit from this investment is:

$$e^{0.05(6/12)}100 - e^{0.05(3/12)}1 - 90 = \$11.52.$$

The first factor, $e^{0.05(6/12)}100$, represents the initial profit from the short sale, valued forward to six months later when the position is closed out. The next term, $-e^{0.05(3/12)}1$, represents the dividend payment of $1 valued three months forward to the day the position is closed out. The last term, $-\$90$, represents the cost of buying back the stock to close out the position.

---

[11] In this section, we assume the reader is familiar with compound interest and present value. For a review of these subjects, see Chapter 2.

[12] Technically speaking, this is not true. However, we make this assumption to simplify the analysis.

Option Positions

Just as with stocks, investors can take long and short positions in options. Moreover, we assume the price at which one can buy and sell the contract is the same; that is, we do not consider the bid-ask spread in studying options.

When an investor takes a short position in an options contract, this person is said to be *writing* the option. The short position is quite different from the long position in terms of the risks and rewards involved.

Being long an option gives one the right (but not the obligation) to buy or sell the underlying according to its type. On the other hand, being short an option is an *obligation* to *cover* the position. That is, the writer of an option *must* sell the underlying to (in the case of a call) or buy the underlying from (in the case of a put) the long option holder.

Short Option Positions

Let's examine the short option position in more detail, starting with the call. The writer of a call option has the obligation to sell the underlying to the long position at the strike price.

For example, suppose we write a call option on XYZ with a strike price of $100. Then we have to sell XYZ to the long position for $100 irrespective of the market price of XYZ on the date of exercise. Because of this, the potential losses from the short position are unlimited. No matter how great the market price of XYZ becomes, we have to be prepared to sell it at $100 a share. If the market price rises to $200 a share, then we have to sell XYZ for a $100 loss per share. Equivalently, if we do not already own it, we have to acquire XYZ for $200 a share, and then sell it for $100 a share. This amounts to a $100-per-share loss.

Now let's consider the short put position. In this case, the losses are limited, but still potentially large. If the price of the underlying drops below the strike, then the short option position is liable to suffer losses. However, since the short position cannot drop below $0.00, these losses are limited to the strike price per share. For example, if we write a short put on XYZ with a strike price of $100, then the maximum loss per share is $100.

1.8 ARBITRAGE AND THE BASIC PROPERTIES OF OPTIONS

The main economic principle that lies at the heart of all theoretical option pricing is that of *arbitrage*. Arbitrage theory in equity option pricing rests on certain basic assumptions about the nature of stock and option markets. When assets are traded or exchanged, sometimes opportunities arise to make riskless profits; such opportunities are known as arbitrage opportunities. A typical example of an arbitrage profit opportunity is that in which the same asset is traded on two different exchanges at two different prices. In principle, this discrepancy can be exploited to make a risk-free profit.

Notice that there are several built-in assumptions in this scenario: the investor must be able to sell on one exchange and immediately be able to use the proceeds to buy on the other. Such assumptions go toward the fundamental hypothesis that markets are efficient and frictionless. We will not need to go into the details of what efficient markets are or what the term even means. Rather, we shall take as our starting point the fundamental assumption that there are no arbitrage opportunities available. In doing so, of course, we are sweeping a great many assumptions under the carpet. Nevertheless, we have our fundamental assumption:

> *There is never a scenario in which a selection of assets is priced in such a way that some simultaneous purchase and/or sale of these assets may result in a riskless profit.*

This is called the *no-arbitrage* hypothesis. It is a powerful tool in pricing options and will be used to deduce several basic facts about option prices.

Arbitrage Arguments

There is a standard way in which we will construct arbitrage arguments. We will state it here as a basic principle and then give several illustrations of its use below. The basic arbitrage argument works as follows.

Two investments, investment A and investment B, are available at time t_0. Moreover, one can take a long or a short position in these investments. That is, there are investors who will buy the investments and there are investors who can sell them.

Assume that the investments will be liquidated and yield the same profit or loss at time t_1 *no matter what.* Moreover, assume that the costs of maintaining the investments (payments, etc.) are equal throughout the life of the investment (from time t_0 to time t_1). Then, in the absence of arbitrage opportunities, the initial costs of investment A and investment B must be the same.

One point: It is crucial that we know at time t_0 that the value of the investments at time t_1 will be the same and that the costs throughout the life of the investments will be the same. This is the key point which makes it all work. It is not enough to know this after the fact. For example, if we purchase two stocks, S_1 and S_2, today (time t_0), and they happen to have the same value at time t_1 (some later time), this means nothing as far as arbitrage arguments are concerned because we did not know with certainty at time t_0 that this would happen.

The economic reasoning behind the basic arbitrage argument is straightforward. If investment A differs in price from investment B, then an investor can sell short the more expensive investment and use the proceeds to buy the cheaper of the two, thereby yielding an immediate gain. Since all costs and the eventual profits from the investments are the same, this initial gain is a risk-free profit. On the other hand, the no-arbitrage assumption states this is impossible. Therefore, investment A and investment B must be the same price.

A Second Type of Arbitrage Argument

It is sometimes necessary to look at arbitrage arguments from an even more general point of view. The following discussion is an expanded version of the arbitrage arguments above.

Suppose we have two investments, investment A and investment B. As above, we assume the investments are to be closed out at some future time t_1. This time, however, assume that the costs incurred in maintaining investment A along with the value of A at time t_1 are *less* than the corresponding costs plus the value of investment B at time t_1. The conclusion in this scenario is then an obvious one: investment A must currently be worth less than investment B.

We will use this sort of argument in deriving the conclusion that it is never optimal to exercise an American call option on a non-dividend-paying stock early. Our first application of arbitrage argument relates to the relationship between put and call prices.

1.9   PUT-CALL PARITY FOR EUROPEAN OPTIONS

Put-call parity expresses a fundamental relationship between the value of a European put and a European call option of the same strike and expiration on the same stock. Let S be the spot price of a stock or index, let C be the value of a call option struck at price K, and let P be the value of a put option with the same strike and expiration as the call. We then have the fundamental relation, called *put-call parity:*

$$C - P = S - e^{-r(T-t)}K,$$

where

$T - t =$ time until expiration of the option
$r =$ the risk-free rate of interest

That is, the value of the call minus the value of the put is equal to the value of the stock minus the present value of K.

To see why this is true we will use our basic arbitrage argument. We have two investments:

1. Buy the call option and sell the put option. Value: $C - P$.

2. Go long the stock and sell a riskless, zero-coupon bond maturing at time T to K. Value: $S - e^{-r(T-t)}K$.

Neither of these investments incur any costs during their lifetime. Let's examine their values at time T, starting with investment one, the long-call, short-put investment.

Since the call and the put have the same strike, at expiration either the call will be in the money or the put will be in the money—but never both. Write S_T for the value of the stock at time T. If the call is in the money, the payoff is $S_T - K$, since the position is long. On the other hand, if the short put is in the money, then its payoff is $-(K - S_T) = S_T - K$. That is, since the position is short, its payoff is the negative of the usual $K - S_T$. In other words, the payoff on the put-call portfolio is $S_T - K$, independent of the stock price at time T.

The second investment, the stock-bond portfolio is comparatively easy to value. At time T, the bond will have matured to a value of K, and therefore the long-stock, short-bond position will have a value of $S_T - K$.

We see that both investments have the same value at time T and, moreover, cost nothing to maintain. Therefore, our basic arbitrage argument tells us the investments must have the same initial value. That is,

$$C - P = S - e^{-r(T-t)}K$$

value
of investment 1

value of investment 2

How the Arbitrage Is Carried Out

At this point we've derived a theoretical relationship between the value of the put and the call. The next step is to demonstrate that any deviation from this relationship does, indeed, constitute an arbitrage opportunity.

Let's assume there is a price discrepancy and we have

$$C - P > S - e^{-r(T-t)}K.$$

How do we turn this into a riskless profit? In our description of the basic arbitrage argument we stated that this is done by selling the more expensive investment short and then buying the cheaper one with the proceeds. Let's assume $S - e^{-r(T-t)}K > 0$. This means, in particular, that the value of the long-call, short-put portfolio, $C - P$, is also greater than zero. That is, we assume that the call has a higher premium than the put.

In this case, we can sell the put-call portfolio (we can short the call and buy the put) and simultaneously buy the stock-bond portfolio (we can buy the stock and sell the bond). This transaction will yield a profit (the difference between $C - P$ and $S - e^{-r(T-t)}K$).

Now we wait until expiration. Because we have a short position in the put-call portfolio, we will have a loss or gain of $K - S_T$ at expiration (a loss if $K - S_T < 0$ and a gain if $K - S_T > 0$). We are short the call; if it expires in the money, we will owe $S_T - K$ to the long call position. This represents a loss of $K - S_T$. On the other hand, we are long the put; if it expires in the money, we will have a gain of $K - S_T$. In summary, the put-call portfolio has value $K - S_T$ at expiration.

Meanwhile, the status of the stock-bond investment is that the bond has matured, and the stock-bond portfolio's value is $S_T - K$. If this is positive, then we can sell the portfolio and use the proceeds to pay what we owe on the short-call position (that is, since $S_T > K$ the call will be exercised and we will owe $S_T - K$ to this position). If it is negative, it represents a loss, and we can use the gain from the long-put position to pay this loss. The net expense is always zero, and therefore the gain made from the initial investments at time t_0 is a riskless profit.

Example

We have the following scenario:

$$C = \$8.60$$
$$P = \$3.50$$
$$S = \$100$$
$$K = \$100$$
$$T - t = 1.0$$
$$r = 0.05\%,$$

where $T - t$ represents the time until expiration and r denotes the risk-free rate of interest. Then we have

$$C - P = \$5.10$$
$$S - e^{-r(T-t)}K = \$4.88.$$

We see that the put-call portfolio is more valuable than the stock-bond portfolio. Therefore, selling the call and buying the put yields a profit of \$5.10, while buying the stock and selling the bond costs \$4.88. Thus, both transactions net a profit of \$0.22. At expiration, holding the short-call, long-put portfolio is monetarily exactly equal to holding the long-stock, short bond portfolio, so no more money is introduced and the \$0.22 is a riskless profit.

Why This Does Not Work for American Options

The above procedure relies on selling the call option and buying a put option and waiting until expiration, while simultaneously buying S and selling a bond maturing to K at expiration. The argument works because, at expiration, the value of this transaction is always zero (the put-call portion *cancels* the stock-bond portion). If, however, the options are American, then one of the options could be exercised early. If this occurs, then we can no longer expect the net values of the transaction to be zero at expiration.

Example

We use the same notation as in the previous example, except now we assume that the options are American and that, six months from exercise, the call is exercised when the stock is selling for $103.00. Let's analyze what happens.

Since we are short the call, we owe $3.00 to the long-call position. To finance this $3.00, we sell $3.00 more of bond at the risk-free rate, so that at expiration we will owe $103.00 ($100.00 from the original bond we sold plus $3.00 more).

Let's suppose the stock price falls back to $100.00 at expiration. Now we are long the stock (worth $100.00) but short the bond, which leaves us in debt $3.00. Thus, we owe $3.00 at expiration, and the arbitrage has failed.

1.10   THE ECONOMICS OF PUT-CALL PARITY

There was an important interplay between interest rates, and short selling, that we used in order to actually carry out the arbitrage in put-call parity. Let's examine exactly what assumptions we had to make in order to derive put-call parity.

Liquidity of Markets

First of all, we had to be able to construct the long-put, short-call portfolio, and we had to be able to buy the stock. This is a liquidity assumption. That is, we implicitly assumed that all of these securities were available in the marketplace at the time we needed them *and* at their fair market values.

Ability to Borrow

Next, because the portfolio was priced less than was predicted by put-call parity, it was necessary to borrow cash in order to purchase the portfolio (we borrowed by selling bond). We had to be able to borrow exactly the amount necessary to finance the portfolio for a term exactly equal to the remaining life of the call and put options, all at the risk-free rate. Thus, in order for put-call parity to hold, it is necessary to be able to borrow at the risk-free rate any amount for any desired period of time.

Short-Selling with Full Use of Proceeds

We assumed that if the put-call portfolio were overpriced (i.e., if $C - P$ were greater than $S - e^{-r(T-t)}K$), then we would sell the call short and buy the put. For example, if $C - P = \$5.10$ as in the example, then we would use these profits to buy the stock-bond portfolio. Not only is this an assumption about liquidity (that is, we are assuming we can receive the risk-free rate on any investment we want for any term we want), more importantly, it is an assumption about short selling.

To perform this transaction risklessly, we proceed as follows:

1. Sell the call. Profit: $8.60.
2. Buy the put. Cost: $3.50. Remaining funds: $5.10.
3. Sell the bond. Profit: $95.12. Remaining funds: $100.22.
4. Buy the stock. Cost: $100.00. Remaining funds: $0.22.

Of course, this is only possible if we have full use of proceeds after each sale. Without this, it is necessary to sometimes use outside cash to fund the transactions.

Conclusions

If any of the above economic assumptions fail to hold, there is an arbitrage opportunity *in theory,* but in reality, there may not be one. The distinction arises because of the practicality of carrying out the transactions that would lead to the riskless profits. It is often the case, for instance, that transaction costs exceed the expected level of profit and therefore make the arbitrage transactions not worthwhile.[13]

The reality is that the assumptions do not hold precisely, and there are indeed cases where put-call parity does not hold.[14] In general, however, the deviations from put-call parity are less than the costs necessary to exploit them.

Generally, the economic assumptions above are necessary to make arbitrage arguments work. One must be able to take various positions (long and short), depending on what circumstances dictate. Without these assumptions, the arguments break down, and we cannot assume that the arbitrage price relationships exist. On the other hand, these assumptions help

---

[13]Given any arbitrage price relationships, considerations such as transaction costs create a "band" around the no-arbitrage price within which arbitrage opportunities are not worthwhile to pursue. This is called the "no-arbitrage band." See Sutcliffe (1993).

[14]There have been several academic papers studying the validity of put-call parity; see Gould and Galai (1978) and Klemkosky and Resknick (1980).

to explain why the theoretical price relationships that we derive do not hold exactly. This is a constant theme in option pricing theory. A model gives an exact relationship, but this precision cannot be achieved in practice. Nevertheless, the theoretical relationship provides an important guide as to what the real relationship will be.

We just used arbitrage arguments to derive put-call parity. As a second example of the application of arbitrage arguments, we will show that an American call option on a non-dividend-paying stock is never optimally exercised before expiration.

1.11 EARLY EXERCISE OF AMERICAN OPTIONS

American options can be exercised at any time during their lives. The question is, does it ever make sense to do this? We shall now show:

For an American call option on a non-dividend-paying stock, it is never optimal to exercise early.

We demonstrate this by using an arbitrage argument.

First of all, let's specify exactly what we mean by "never optimal to exercise early." We say that early exercise is optimal if the value of exercising immediately ever exceeds the value of holding the option. That is, at each time in the life of an option we can compare the value of immediate exercise to the theoretical value of holding the option one moment longer. If the value of immediate exercise (the intrinsic value) exceeds the theoretical value of holding, then it is optimal to exercise.

This formulation is not very useful in its present incarnation because it seems unlikely that we could ever know precisely the value of holding the option. However, by means of an arbitrage argument, we can show abstractly that the intrinsic value of an American option is never greater than the value of the option itself.

The Arbitrage Argument
Start with an American call option on a non-dividend-paying stock. Pick a random time t during the life of the option and assume the option is in the money at that time. Consider the two separate investments:

1. Exercise the option at the time t.
2. Hold the option until its expiration and exercise it.

Let's consider what each of these investments will be worth at time T. To finance the first investment, we sell a bond maturing at time T and use the proceeds to purchase the stock for K. Thus, at expiration we have the stock and owe $e^{r(T-t)}K$ (the value of the bond at maturity). Total value: $S_T - e^{r(T-t)}K$.

On the other hand, holding the option until expiration is worth $\max(S_T - K, 0)$. If the option expires in the money, then it is worth $S_T - K$; otherwise, it is worth nothing. But, if interest rates are positive (that is, if $r > 0$), then we always have

$$S_T - e^{r(T-t)}K < \max(S_T - K, 0)$$

Note the left-hand side of this equation represents the value of exercising the option viewed at time T, while the right-hand side represents the value of holding the option until expiration. Therefore, by our second arbitrage argument, the value of investment 1 (exercising the option) is worth less than the value of investment 2 (holding the option). Note the dependence of our argument on positive interest rates. That is, we've proved what we set out to prove: it is never optimal to exercise early; that is, $S_t - K < C_t$, where S_t is the value of the stock at time t, and C_t is the value of the option.

What Happens If the Stock Pays Dividends?

One might ask where and why the argument breaks down when the stock pays dividends. We shall see that the arbitrage argument presented above for proving the relationship $S_t - K < C_t$ fails if the stock goes ex-dividend during the life of the option.

To show $S_t - K < C_t$, we have to form a portfolio consisting of the call and a riskless zero-coupon bond with par value $e^{r(T-t)}K$ (and a maturity date equal to the expiration of the call) and then short the stock. The value of this portfolio at time t is $C_t + K - S_t$.

We argue that if $S_t \geq C_t + K$ we could sell the stock short and use the proceeds to buy the option and the bond with some money remaining. Then the amount left over, denoted Π (i.e., $\Pi = S_t - C_t - K$), is always profit.

Suppose at time t_1 during the life of the option the stock goes ex-dividend. Then, on the ex-dividend date, the spot price immediately drops by an amount, d, equal to the dividend payment.

Let's get our bearings straight: We are carrying a portfolio consisting of a bond (maturing to $e^{r(T-t)}K$), a call option (C), and a short stock (S). The problem is, since we are short the stock, we must make a payment of $\$d$ to the owner of the stock. We do have some cash to make this payment: the profit, Π, from the original transaction, which is now worth $e^{r(t_1-t)}\Pi$. The question is, do we still make a riskless profit from the transaction? The answer is no.

We have to consider several situations. First, we consider the case in which our initial profit, Π, does not cover the dividend payment (that is, $e^{r(t_1-t)}\Pi < d$). Then, first of all, we must make the dividend payment on the ex-dividend date. We would like to be able to do this without the use of additional funds, but because $e^{r(t_1-t)}\Pi < d$, this is impossible. Therefore, we must add cash into the investment. Now the question is, can we recapture this money? The answer depends on how the option expires. If it expires in the money, the answer is no.

Suppose the option expires in the money. Then, the following happens:

1. The bond matures to its par value of $\$e^{r(T-t)}K$.

2. We exercise the option, purchasing the stock for $\$K$.

3. We return the borrowed stock (closing out the short position).

Are the profits from this transaction sufficient to recapture the loss incurred on the ex-dividend date? In general, the answer is no.

In a similar manner, we may show that if the option expires out of the money, but not too far out of the money, we will not profit from the above transactions.

What we have seen is that the introduction of the dividend payment makes the *guarantee* of a profit from the relationship $S - K \geq C$ impossible. In other words, there are times when it is optimal to exercise the option. But when?

When Is the American Call Optimal to Exercise?

We have the following principle:

> *The only dates on which it will ever be optimal to exercise an American option are those dates immediately prior to ex-dividend dates.*

The reason for this is simple. At all times not directly before dividend dates, we have the relationship

$$S_t - K < C_t, \tag{1.10.1}$$

where $S_t - K$ represents the intrinsic value of the option and C_t represents the value of the call. Why is this so?

We saw above that dividends spoil Equation (1.10.1) because the arbitrage that makes the relationship hold is spoiled on the ex-dividend date by our having to make a payment equal to the value of the dividend to the stock lender. Therefore, as long as we retain the "option" to exercise, we do not have to worry about making the payment. We retain this "option" right up until the last possible moment before the stock goes ex-dividend.

Using this observation, it is possible to derive an analytic (i.e., Black-Scholes style) option pricing formula for American call options on stocks with known dividends (that is, when all the ex-dividend dates and dividend payments are known). This is carried out in Whaley (1981).

1.12   VALUING FORWARD CONTRACTS

In this section, we use arbitrage arguments to find the theoretical value of forward contracts.

Forward Contracts on Assets with No Payments

Suppose we currently have a long position in a forward contract on a financial class asset such as a stock index. Is there any value to this position? Let's fix some notation:

where

S = current value of asset
F = delivery price
t = current date
T = delivery date
r = risk-free rate

We will use our arbitrage arguments to show that the value of the long position in this forward contract must be $S - e^{-r(T-t)}F$. Consider two investments:

1. A portfolio consisting of a long position in the asset and a short, riskless, zero-coupon bond maturing to F at time T. Current value: $S - e^{-r(T-t)}F$.
2. A long position in the forward contract.

Neither position has any maintenance costs. Investment 1 is worth $S_T - F$ on the delivery date. On the other hand, investment 2 is also worth $S_T - F$ at expiration. Why?

At expiration, the holder of the long position in the forward contract must buy the asset at F, but he or she can then sell it at S_T. Buying at F incurs a cost of F, while selling at S is a gain. The total value of the transaction is $S_T - F$.

Since the two investments have no maintenance costs and are worth the same at expiration, our arbitrage arguments say that they must be worth the same today. This proves that the current value of the forward contract is $S - e^{-r(T-t)}F$.

Forward Contracts on Assets with Continuous Dividend Yield

In the above analysis, we stated that neither portfolio (that is, neither the long-stock, short-bond portfolio nor the forward contract) had any maintenance costs. That is, during the time between settling the contract and delivery, no losses or gains were experienced in either investment. The situation changes when the underlying asset of the forward contract makes payments.

We now show how to value forward contracts on dividend-paying stocks, stock indexes, and foreign currencies. The latter does not, strictly speaking, make dividend payments. However, as we saw in Section 1.3, owning a foreign currency is analogous to owning a security that makes a continuous dividend payment (at a rate equal to the foreign risk-free rate) in which all dividends are reinvested in the asset. We start with stocks and indexes.

Assume the current date is t, and consider a stock or index paying a continuous dividend yield of q. Consider a forward contract for one unit of the stock or index with delivery date T and delivery price F. If the current price of the stock or index is S_t, what is the current value of the long position in this contract?

To answer this, we use an arbitrage argument. Write C_F for the value of the forward contract today and r for the risk-free rate of interest. Consider two investments made today:

1. $e^{-q(T-t)}$ units of the index, with all dividends reinvested. Current value: $e^{-q(T-t)}S_t$.

2. A long position in the forward contract, plus a long, riskless, zero-coupon bond maturing at time T to F. Current value: $C_F + e^{-r(T-t)}F$.

At time T, investment 1 "matures to" one unit of the index. This was explained in our discussion of dividend reinvestments: The amount of index holdings we have grows at a continuously compounded rate of q.

At time T, investment 2 also "matures to" one unit of the index. The bond matures to F, which is the delivery price of the index, and can therefore be used to purchase one unit of the index.

Since both investments are equal in value at time T, their values today (time t) must be the same. Therefore, we have: $e^{-q(T-t)}S_t = C_F + e^{-r(T-t)}F$, and the value of the forward contract today is given by:

$$C_F = e^{-q(T-t)}S_t - e^{-r(T-t)}F, \qquad (1.11.1)$$

where we recall

$$C_F = \text{the value of the forward contract today}$$
$$S_t = \text{the value of the index today}$$
$$F = \text{the value of the delivery price}$$
$$q = \text{the continuous dividend yield}$$
$$r = \text{the risk-free rate of interest}$$
$$T - t = \text{time between today and delivery date}$$

Forward Contracts on Assets with Lumpy Dividends

In this section, we assume we have a forward contract on a stock, currently worth S, settled at time t, with delivery at time T and delivery price F. Moreover, we assume that the stock makes dividend payments D_1, D_2, ..., D_n, with ex-dividend dates t_1, ..., t_n (and all ex-dividend dates occur between times t and T, or within the life of the contract).

The value of this contract is related to all the usual things, including the length of the contract and the risk-free rate of interest (r), but there is one new ingredient—the present value of all the dividends. We write D for this, and it is equal to

$$D = \sum_{k=1}^{n} e^{-r(t_k - t)} D_k.$$

That is, D is computed by adding up each dividend payment discounted to time t by the risk-free rate.

Now consider the following two investments:

1. Purchase one share of the stock for $\$S$, and borrow $\$D$. Total cost: $\$(S - D)$.

2. Purchase one forward contract on the stock deliverable at time T for $\$F$. Borrow F today at the risk-free rate of interest. Total cost: $\$Fe^{-r(T-t)}$.

[handwritten margin notes: Purchase one forward contract: cost = C_F. Borrow F today: cost = -F.]

We want to compare these two investments over the period of time from now (t) to the delivery date of the forward (T). In the first scenario, the investor uses the incoming dividend payments to make payments on the loan (where $\$D$ was borrowed), so by the time of the delivery date, the loan is entirely paid off. In the second scenario, the investor is not entitled to any of the dividend payments since he or she does not take delivery until time T.

At time T, both investments yield one share of the stock; moreover, both incur no costs from time t to time T. Therefore, their initial values must be equal, and we have

$$C_F + Fe^{-r(T-t)} = S - D.$$

Thus, the value of the forward contract is

$$C_F = S - D - Fe^{-r(T-t)}.$$

Foreign Exchange

Suppose we have a forward contract to buy one unit of a foreign currency at a rate of F in the domestic currency at time T. For example, if the domestic currency is U.S. dollars, then the contract specifies that the holder of the long position may purchase one unit of the foreign currency for $\$F$ at time T.

Write r for the domestic risk-free rate and r_f for the foreign risk-free rate, and suppose the current time is t. Write S_t for the current spot rate of the currency; that is, S_t is the rate at which we can buy the foreign currency in U.S. dollars. We want to find out the value, C_F, of the forward contract. By analogy with Equation (1.11.1), we have:

$$C_F = e^{-r_f(T-t)}S_t - e^{-r(T-t)}F. \qquad (1.11.2)$$

The Forward Price of an Asset

We now come to an important definition:

The forward price of an asset on some future date is the delivery price that makes the current fair value of a forward contract equal to zero.

Let's unwind this definition. There are three components: the current price of the asset, the delivery price, and the fair value of the forward contract. We have already seen that the value of the forward contract on an asset paying no dividends is

$$S - e^{-r(T-t)}F,$$

where F is the delivery price. The forward price is the delivery price, F, which makes the above expression zero. This is only possible if $S = e^{-r(T-t)}F$, or $F = e^{r(T-t)}S$.

If the asset pays a dividend rate of q, then the fair value is

$$e^{-q(T-t)}S - e^{-r(T-t)}F,$$

and the forward price is the value that makes this new equation zero.

What is the purpose of this definition? The idea is that two parties, party A and party B, want to exchange an asset S at a future date T but do

D I S P L A Y   1.11.1

VALUING FORWARD CONTRACTS

Forward Contracts

Notation:

    t = current time

    T = delivery date

    S_t = spot price of a stock, stock index, or foreign currency

    r = risk-free rate of interest

    q = continuous dividend yield of stock or stock index

    r_f = risk-free rate of foreign interest

    C_F = value of forward contract on S with delivery date T and delivery price F

    F = delivery price

    D = present value of all dividend payments during life of contract

Value of a forward contract

$C_F = e^{-q(T-t)}S_t - e^{-r(T-t)}F$ (stock or index with continuous dividend yield)

$C_F = S - D - e^{-r(T-t)}F$ (lumpy dividends)

$C_F = e^{-r_f(T-t)}S_t - e^{-r(T-t)}F$ (currency)

Forward prices

Forward price $= e^{(r-q)(T-t)}S_t$ (stock or index with continuous dividend yield)

Forward price $= e^{(r-r_f)(T-t)}S_t$ (currency)

Forward price $= e^r(S_t - D)$ (lumpy dividends)

---

not want to exchange any cash now. The only way to make this palatable to both sides is to ensure the agreement has no (monetary) value to either party now. Put another way, if neither party is paying to enter the agreement, then neither party should be able to immediately profit from the agreement (say, by immediately selling their position to another party). The only way to make the agreement have no fiscal value is to choose the delivery price via the above equations, making the value of the contract zero.

We usually write F for the forward price of an asset, and it can be thought of as the fair value of the asset on a given future date. Note that the terminology "fair value" is ambiguous—the definition of forward price refers to a specific date, while the term "forward price" does not. In general, we can speak in terms like "June forward price" or the "six-month forward price" to clarify what we mean.

The Forward Price of a Stock Index

Now consider a stock index paying a continuous dividend yield of q. If the current time is t, let's compute its forward price at time T. We want to find the delivery price F such that the current value of the contract is zero. From Equation (1.11.1), we want

$$C_F = e^{-q(T-t)}S_t - e^{-r(T-t)}F = 0.$$

This implies that $F = e^{(r-q)(T-t)}S_t$. This means the forward price is the current price "grown" at the risk-free rate minus the dividend yield. Intuitively this makes sense. The future value grows at the risk-free rate, but some of this value is continuously being lost through the dividend yield.

The Forward Price of a Foreign Currency

Suppose we have a foreign currency selling for a spot price of s_t (denominated in the domestic currency), the foreign risk-free rate of interest is r_f, and the domestic risk-free rate of interest is r. The value of a forward contract on the currency is

$$C_F = e^{-r_f(T-t)}S_t - e^{-r(T-t)}F,$$

where F is the delivery price, t is the current date, and T is the delivery date. To make $C_F = 0$, we must have

$$F = e^{(r-r_f)(T-t)}S_t.$$

All of the formulas related to forward contract are summarized in Display 1.11.1.

COMMENTS AND
SUGGESTED READINGS

There are many books on the basics of the stock market and options. Books with a view toward option pricing include Hull (1993), Cox and Rubinstein (1985), and McMillan (1986). McMillan is especially good for the practical aspects of options. For a treatment of the no-arbitrage hypothesis, see Varian (1987).

For basic treatments of futures markets, see Duffie (1989), Fink and Feduniak (1988), and Sutcliffe (1993). For information on futures on stock indexes, see Sutcliffe (1993) and Fabozzi and Kipnis (1984) and (1989). For information on some of the "real world" issues in futures markets, see Kawaller (1992). For a description of the leading international stock indexes, see Sutcliffe (1993) and Appendix 1A; see Chapter 2 for a list of existing markets in stock index futures. For a list of "world exchanges," see Hull (1993).

For a discussion of the use of stock index futures as a substitute for the underlying index, see Sutcliffe (1993) and Fabozzi and Peters (1989).

For information on dividend yields versus dividend schedules in stock indexes, see Sutcliffe (1993) and the references therein. For a specific example of the structure of the dividend yield of an index, see Robertson (1990) or Sutcliffe (1993, p. 76). For a detailed analysis of the dividend structure of the S&P 500 index and its effect on option prices, see Campbell and Whaley (1992).

In the text, we alluded to the differences between forwards and futures. For information on the difference between forward and futures *prices,* see Cox and Rubinstein (1985) and French (1983). For a study of the relationship between the S&P 500 futures price versus its spot price, see Kawaller, Koch, and Koch (1988). For more on exotic options, see Nelken (1995).

Option pricing has found its way into corporate finance. The fundamental idea here is to consider certain assets as options and to value them as such. Tom Copeland, Tim Koller, and Jack Murrin of McKinsey & Company, Inc., explain this as follows:

> A company that has the option to shut down and restart operations, or to abandon them, is more flexible and therefore more valuable than the same company without these options . . . .
> In practice, we have applied option pricing to a variety of situations where the value of flexibility was critical. In one case, the option value of a large mineral lease was 100 percent higher than its simple net present value. Al-

though the mine was only marginally profitable at the time, the option to defer development until the mineral price rose made the value much higher than indicated by net present value analysis.[15]

For a basic introduction to option pricing in financial decision making, see Copeland, Koller, and Murrin (1990). For a more advanced and complete treatment, see Dixit and Pindyck (1994).

---

[15]From *Valuation: Measuring and Managing the Value of Companies,* Copeland, Koller, and Murrin (New York: John Wiley & Sons, 1990), pp. 343–344.

2

⑥ FUNDAMENTAL MATHEMATICAL CONCEPTS

The mathematics of the Black-Scholes formula is certainly more advanced than anything Wall Street had seen prior to its introduction in 1973. Robert Merton, a Harvard Business School professor and a key developer of the rigorous mathematical foundations of options pricing, remarked on the changes that took place *after* the introduction of Black-Scholes:

> I got the biggest kick out of hearing those options traders routinely talk about ... differential equations and stochastic differential equations. Who would have thought people would be talking like that....
>
> People had no choice. They couldn't deal with it the way they dealt with over-the-counter. There is no other way to deal with the complexity of the option. The models made sense intuitively and seemed to work.[1]

In this chapter we lay down the mathematics necessary for understanding the presentation of Black-Scholes in this book. In fact, it is not necessary to understand stochastic differential equations to comprehend how and why the Black-Scholes works. All one needs to understand is basic probability theory. In fact, one does not have to understand all of basic probability theory, just certain key parts.

2.1 THE EXPONENTIAL, COMPOUND INTEREST, AND NATURAL LOGARITHMS

In working with the Black-Scholes options pricing formula and related formulas, we rely heavily on exponentials, natural logarithms, and the

---

[1] From *Capital Ideas,* Peter L. Bernstein (The Free Press, 1992), p. 227.

present value of assets. This section is a review of the basic rules of exponentials and compound interest and is intended as an easy reference to be used throughout the book.

We begin by explaining the concept of continuously compounded interest. This leads naturally to the definition of the exponent, and from there we move to natural logarithms. Once we have done this, we explain how to convert between ordinary compound interest and continuously compounded interest.

Simple Interest

If we put $1 in a bank deposit for one year at 10 percent interest, at the end of the year we receive $1.10. We compute this by adding 0.10 times $1 to the $1 we started with. That is, we have: $1 + 0.10 \cdot 1 = 1.10$.

If we put $10 in a bank deposit for one year at 10 percent interest, at the end of the year we receive $11.00. We compute this by adding 0.10 times $10 to the $10 we started with. That is, we have $10 + 0.10 \cdot 10 = 11.00$.

Note that we can factor out the original deposit in both cases to obtain a more readable expression. For example, $10 growing in one year to $10 + 0.10 \cdot 10$ can be written: $10(1 + 0.10) = 10 \cdot 1.10$.

If we have any sum of money, S, and we invest it at 10 percent annual interest for one year, then we will have $S + 0.10 \cdot S = S \cdot 1.10$ at the end of the year. Note that we multiply the starting sum (S) by a *multiplier* of 1.10 to obtain the new balance.

The point is, regardless of the sum we start with, we have 1.10 times that initial sum at the end of the year. Now we can replace the specific interest rate of 10 percent (0.10) with any interest rate, r, to obtain our first formula. If we make a bank deposit of S for one year at an annually compounded interest rate of r percent, then at the end of the year the money will have grown to $S(1 + r)$.

Time Periods Other Than One Year

Now suppose we invest $10 in a bank deposit for three-quarters of a year at 10 percent interest *per annum* prorated for the time deposited. Then after the three-quarters of a year we will have $10 + 0.10 \cdot 0.75$, or, $10.75. That is, because the interest is prorated for the period of time we actually keep the money invested, we only receive three-quarters of the 10 percent ($0.10 \cdot 0.75$) we would receive if we kept the money in for an entire year.

Compound Interest

Suppose the interest is compounded twice a year. This means that six months after we deposit our money, the interest *up to that point* is computed (with the rate prorated to a six-month rate) and added to the initial deposit. For example, suppose we deposit $100 at 10 percent compounded twice annually. After six months, we will receive 5 percent on our $100—that is, we receive *half* of the annual interest rate of 10 percent. Therefore, we will have $100 + 100 \cdot (0.10/2) = 100(1 + 0.10/2) = 105.00$ after six months.

For the next six months we receive interest on the $105.00. Thus, after one year we will have: $105.00(1 + 0.10/2) = 110.25$. Note that we obtain this sum by multiplying 100 by $(1 + 0.10/2)$ *twice*. First we compute $100(1 + 0.10/2)$, and then we multiply this value (105) by $(1 + 0.10/2)$. That is, we really compute $100(1 + 0.10/2)(1 + 0.10/2) = 100(1 + 0.10/2)^2$.

Now suppose the interest is compounded three times annually. This means that we divide the year into three equal periods, and at the end of each period we compute the interest paid on the amount of money in the deposit at that time.

Since the year is divided into three equal parts, in each part we receive an interest rate equal to one-third of the annual rate. If the annual rate is 10 percent, for example, then after each one-third of a year, we receive 10/3 percent.

If our initial deposit is $100, then after one-third of a year we will have $100(1 + 0.10/3) = 103 \ 1/3$. For the next third of a year we earn interest on the $103 1/3. That is, we will have $103 \ 1/3(1 + 0.10/3) = 106.7774$. For the last third of the year we receive interest on this sum, so that at the end of the year we have $106.7774(1 + 0.10/3) = 110.3366$. Note that we took the initial sum ($100) and multiplied it by $(1 + 0.10/3)$ three times. That is, we computed $100(1 + 0.10/3)^3$.

With these examples in mind, we now state the general rule.

The General Rule for Compound Interest
If we make a deposit of S at an annual rate of r and the interest is compounded n times, then at the end of one year we will have

$$S\left(1 + \frac{r}{n}\right)^n.$$

This is just an expanded version of what we have already seen. For example, in the discussion above we computed the sum to which $100 grows after one year at 10 percent, compounded three times per year. In that case we had: $S = 100$, $n = 3$, and $r = 0.10$.

There is one thing to note: The formula has almost nothing to do with S, the value of the deposit. That is, what the formula says is, "take the initial sum (S) and multiply it by the factor $(1 + \frac{r}{n})^n$." The factor itself does not change. If we start with \$1, we multiply by $(1 + \frac{r}{n})^n$. If we start with \$100, we multiply by $(1 + \frac{r}{n})^n$. We call this number, $(1 + \frac{r}{n})^n$, the *multiplier* for compounding.

Computing the Multiplier Numerically

Let's do an experiment. We'll compute the factor $(1 + \frac{r}{n})^n$ for an interest rate of 5 percent ($r = 0.05$) when $n = 1$, $n = 10$, $n = 50$, $n = 100$, $n = 500$, $n = 1,000$, $n = 10,000$, and $n = 1,000,000$. That is, we'll compute compound interest for compounding 1 time, 10 times, 50 times, 100 times, 500 times, 1,000 times, 10,000 times, and 1,000,000 times per year. We summarize this data in Table 2.1.1.

Let's examine the data in Table 2.1.1. There are several observations to make. First, the numbers keep getting larger. That is, the more frequently we compound, the larger the multiplier, and therefore the more money we get. More importantly, however, is the observation that, as the number of times we compound increases, the amount by which the multipliers change gets smaller and smaller.

For example, when we move from compounding once ($n = 1$) to compounding 10 times ($n = 10$), the multiplier goes from 1.05 to 1.05115013204079. The *change* is 0.00115013204079, or roughly 1/1,000. When we go from compounding 1,000 times to 10,000 times, the multiplier increases from 1.05126978233189 to 1.05127096496793, an increase of only 0.000001182636040, roughly 1/1,000,000. Moving from 10,000 to 1,000,000 (a much larger change than 1,000 to 10,000) produces a change in the multiplier of only 0.000000130007980, roughly 1/10,000,000.

T A B L E   2.1.1

Compound interest

Compounded n times	Multiplier
1	1.05000000000000
10	1.05114013204079
50	1.05124483243475
100	1.05125795994804
500	1.05126846837676
1,000	1.05126978233189
10,000	1.05127096496793
1,000,000	1.05127109497591

With these observations, it is natural to guess that, as we increase the number of times we compound, the magnitude of the changes in the multiplier continues to decrease. What we find, and also what we can prove mathematically, is that there is a well-defined number, that represents what would happen if we compounded the interest *continuously*. Put another way, since the changes in the multiplier decrease as we increase the frequency of compounding, it is reasonable to assume that there is a single number to which the multiplier moves.

To get a sense of this, look back at Table 2.1.1. Note that all of the multipliers begin with 1.05. All but the first begin with 1.051. All but the first two begin with 1.0512. The last two begin with 1.05127. We wonder if all multipliers with $n > 1,000,000$ begin with 1.05127. In fact, they do. For example, if $n = 10,000,000$, we have $(1 + 0.05/n)^n = 1.05127109592516$.

As we increase the frequency of compounding, the multipliers agree in successively more digits. Therefore, it is reasonable to assume that they will agree in more and more places. Once the multipliers agree in a certain number of places, increasing the number of periods (of compounding) will not change the agreement in those places.

Therefore, we can define a single number whose places are composed of all the places which are fixed in the above procedure. For example, we say that the first five places of our continuous compounding are 1.05127 because we see that no matter how many times we compound beyond, say 10,000, the first five places of the multiplier will be 1.05127 (see Table 2.1.1). If we want to know more places, we can just compute $(1 + 0.05/n)^n$ for a larger n. In this way, we are building a unique number called the *limit* of $(1 + 0.05/n)^n$ as n grows larger and larger.

The Exponential and Continuously Compounded Interest

The "limit" of $(1 + r/n)^n$ as n grows infinitely large is written e^r, read "e to the r." This is called the *exponential of r*. When $r = 1$, we have e^1. This is written e, and it is approximately equal to 2.71828182845905.

As we have seen, e^r represents the multiplier for compounding an "infinitely large" number of times. We think of this as continuous compounding, because any finite number of places in the decimal expansion of the multiplier represents compounding some number of times. For example, $e^{0.05} = 1.05127\ldots$. We know that 1.05127 represents compounding at approximately 1,000 times. We can write $e^{0.05}$ more accurately: $e^{0.05} = 1.051271096376$.

Interest Rate Conversions

In this book, when we say interest rate, we mean continuously compounded interest rate. If, for example, we say the risk-free rate of interest is r, we mean the continuously compounded risk-free rate of interest. Unfortunately, many interest rates are quoted with other types of compounding in mind. In this section, we show how to convert from simple compounded rates to continuously compounded rates. Display 2.1.1 presents the answers. The table uses natural logarithms, which are defined later in this section.

To see how to arrive at the formulas in Display 2.1.1, we need some general formulas. Suppose we make a bank deposit of $1, and the bank promises an interest rate of r_1, compounded n times *per year*. Moreover, suppose we withdraw our deposit after a time Δt. We want to know how much our money has grown. Let's do an example.

Example

Suppose the interest is compounded four times annually. That is, suppose $n = 4$. If we withdraw our money after two years (i.e., $\Delta t = 2$), then we can easily see how much our money has grown. In the two years, our money is compounded eight times, and we receive an interest rate of $r_1/4$ each time it is compounded. Therefore, our $1 grows to

$$\left(1 + \frac{r_1}{4}\right)^8$$

in two years.

Now, what if Δt is not an even number of compounding periods? For example, what if Δt is seven-eighths of a year? In this case, there are several options. In seven-eighths of a year, interest is compounded three times. At the time the money is withdrawn, not enough time has elapsed to compute a fourth compounding. On the other hand, some time has passed, and therefore we are entitled to some money.

The answer is to raise $(1 + r_1/n)$ to a *fractional power*. In other words, we receive $(1 + r_1/4)^3$ for the "true" compounding. This accounts for the interest earned on three-fourths of a year. Now, seven-eighths is exactly halfway between three-fourths and one, so we give half a period more compounding, which is $(1 + r_1/4)^{1/2}$. Then the total amount of compounding is

$$\left(1 + \frac{r_1}{4}\right)^3 \cdot \left(1 + \frac{r_1}{4}\right)^{1/2} = \left(1 + \frac{r_1}{4}\right)^{3\,1/2}.$$

Notice what has happened: We raised the "multiplier" (that is, $1 + r_1/4$) to reflect the amount of time that has passed.

DISPLAY 2.1.1

HOW TO CONVERT SIMPLE INTEREST RATES TO CONTINUOUSLY COMPOUNDED INTEREST RATES

Interest Rate Conversions

We have

r continuously compounded annual rate
r_1 rate compounded n times annually
Δt a period of time

Problem: Given r, compute r_1.
In time Δt, \$1 grows to

$$\left(1 + \frac{r_1}{n}\right)^{n\Delta t}$$

when compounded n times annually.
   In time Δt, \$1 grows to

$$e^{r\Delta t}$$

when compounded continuously.
   If we know r_1, a formula for r is:

$$r = n\log\left(1 + \frac{r_1}{n}\right)$$

If we know r, a formula for r_1 is:

$$r_1 = n(e^{r/n} - 1).$$

This motivates our general formula. In time Δt, \$1, compounded at an annual rate r_1, n times per year, grows to:

$$\left(1 + \frac{r_1}{n}\right)^{n\Delta t}.$$

Now computing interest rate conversions is a simple matter. We ask, at what continuously compounded rate of interest, r, do we have to deposit \$1 for it to grow to the same amount compounded n times at the annual rate r_1? This question amounts to the equation:

$$e^{r\Delta t} = \left(1 + \frac{r_1}{n}\right)^{n\Delta t}.$$

The left-hand side is the amount \$1 grows to at the continuously compounded annual rate of r. The right-hand side is the amount \$1 grows to at the annual rate of r_1 when compounded n times per year. We can solve these equations for either r_1 or r to obtain the answers given in Display 2.1.1.

Rules for the Exponential

There are a variety of rules for manipulating exponentials. We will discuss these rules now, and they are summarized in Display 2.1.2.

We have the following four rules of exponentials.

$$e^0 = 1$$
$$e^x e^y = e^{x+y}$$
$$(e^x)^y = e^{xy}$$
$$e^{-x} = \frac{1}{e^x}$$

These rules will be used in simplifying expressions having to do with compound interest.

The Natural Logarithm

Almost as important as the exponential is the natural logarithm. The natural logarithm function is the *inverse function* of the exponential. This means that if we apply the log function to the exponential function of a number, we get back the number we started with. We will always write log x for the natural logarithm of a number x (some authors use ln x).[2]

The two fundamental relations between logarithm and exponential always hold:

$$\log e^x = x \quad \text{and} \quad e^{\log x} = x.$$

The natural logarithm is basic to investment mathematics, as we shall see below.

There are three basic properties of the natural logarithm.

$$\log 1 = 0$$
$$\log xy = \log x + \log y$$
$$\log x^y = y \log x$$

The Return on an Investment

Suppose we have a stock S that has a spot price of S_t at time t. If at time $t + \Delta t$ the spot price of the stock is $S_{t+\Delta t}$, then the *annualized continuously*

---

[2] Some calculators write log to mean natural logarithm, and some write log to mean "logarithm base 10." In this book we only care about natural logarithm. A simple check to ensure that you are using natural logarithm with your calculator is to test the key by finding the log of 2.718282. If the key is natural logarithm, it will return 1 to at least seven digits accuracy, i.e., 1.0000000. If the key is not natural logarithm, it will return something completely different.

D I S P L A Y   2.1.2

RULES OF EXPONENTIALS, LOGARITHMS, AND COMPOUND INTEREST

Rules for the exponential

$$e^0 = 1$$
$$e^x e^y = e^{x+y}$$
$$(e^x)^y = e^{xy}$$

Rules for the logarithm

$$\log 1 = 0$$
$$\log xy = \log x + \log y$$
$$\log x^y = y \log x$$

$$e^{\log x} = x$$
$$\log e^x = x.$$

Return on investment

$\frac{1}{\Delta t} \log S_{t+\Delta t}/S_t$ = continuously compounded return on an investment purchased for S_t at time t and worth $S_{t+\Delta t}$ at time $t + \Delta t$.

$S_t e^{r\Delta t}$ = value of an investment at time $t + \Delta t$ that was purchased at time t and yielded a continuously compounded return of r.

---

compounded return r on S is given by the following equation:

$$r = \frac{1}{\Delta t} \log(S_{t+\Delta t}/S_t). \tag{2.1.1}$$

The equation makes sense because if S_t grows at a continuously compounded rate of r for a time Δt, then it grows to $S_t e^{r\Delta t} = S_{t+\Delta t}$.

Note the reason that the return is annualized: We assume time is in yearly units. Therefore, dividing by Δt is equivalent to finding the rate of return *per year*.

The number r is the *continuously compounded return*, because if we put B dollars in the bank today at a continuously compounded rate of interest r for a time Δt, then in time Δt the B dollars grow to

$$e^{r\Delta t} B.$$

Example

Suppose someone invests $100 in a share of stock on January 1, 1996, and then sells the stock on July 1, 1996, for $110. What was the annualized continuously compounded rate of return on that investment? We will use Equation (2.1.1) to compute this.

We call January 1, 1996, time t_0. The amount of time that expires during the investment period is six months, so $\Delta t = 0.50$ (i.e., one-half of a year). Thus, we have:

$$S_{t_0} = \$100$$
$$S_{t_0} + \Delta t = \$110$$
$$\Delta t = 0.50$$

Using Equation (2.1.1) directly, we compute that the continuously compounded return, r, is

$$r = \frac{1}{0.50} \log(110/100) = 0.19062.$$

That is, the annual rate of return on that investment was 19.062 percent.

2.2 PROBABILITY THEORY

In this section we study the probability theory necessary for understanding the Black-Scholes formula and the other models in this book. Our goal is to give an intuitive picture of what probability theory is, and how it can be useful for describing things which happen "randomly." Later we will present the necessary formulas and equations for use in option pricing.

The most basic concept we need to discuss is a *random event,* or *random variable.* We introduce its meaning with an example.

If we flip a coin, we regard the outcome, heads or tails, as "random." The term "random event," or "random variable," is a mathematically precise way of tying together the two important elements present in the flip of a coin (and, as we shall see, in all random events)—the possible outcomes and their probabilities.

First of all, we do not know ahead of time whether the outcome will be heads or tails. However, we do know what possible outcomes can occur, and we can make sense of the probability of each outcome. Let's make this more precise.

First, it is clear we know all of the possible outcomes of the flip ahead of time. In this case, there are only two: heads and tails. In addition, we know the probability of each outcome. The probability of heads is 50 percent, and the probability of tails is 50 percent (if, of course, the coin is "fair").

But what does it really mean that the probability of an event is 50 percent? It's the relationship between many flips that interests us. If we flip the coin 10 times or 100 times (that is, if we repeat the random event), how many heads versus how many tails will we see?

A probability of 50 percent means that, for a large number of flips, we can expect *close to* 50 percent of the flips to be heads and 50 percent to be tails. As we increase the number of flips, the likelihood of approaching 50 percent increases. There are more mathematically precise ways of defining probability, but we would like to keep our discussion on an intuitive level, so for now we maintain the basic notion above.

The Definition of a Random Event

A random event is an event (e.g., the flip of a coin) for which we know the following data:

1. All possible "outcomes" of the event (e.g., the possible outcomes of a flip of a coin are heads and tails) that can happen.
2. The probability of each "outcome" (e.g., the probability of heads is 50 percent).

In certain cases, the term random variable is preferable to random event, but nevertheless describes exactly the same thing. A random event adequately describes phenomena like flipping a coin (or rolling dice) in which something "happens" and for which there are direct results. Sometimes, however, we will model "events" in which the outcomes can simply be one number in a given range of numbers (for example, think of the roll of a die: the outcomes are the numbers 1, 2, 3, 4, 5, and 6). The result is therefore a variable (this means nothing more than the result varies over a range of numbers), and for each value of the variable we know the probability of that value: a random variable. A first encounter with this definition may be a bit puzzling. We will now spend some time clarifying its meaning.

Later in this book we will be interested in building models for stock price movements. In this case, we model the price of or the return on a stock as a random variable. In the case of modeling prices, we will want a variable that ranges over all positive numbers. That is, the possible prices the stock can achieve, as represented by the random variable, are all possible positive numbers. In the case of stock returns, the variable ranges over all numbers (i.e., we allow negative returns, such as -20 percent, as well as positive returns, but we do not allow negative stock prices). Note: We all know stocks cannot trade at some prices; for example, a stock cannot sell for $2.4139841341. This does not even make sense. Then why model stock prices with random variables that can take on any values? The answer, as we shall see, is simplicity and ease of analysis. We will return to this later.

One technical point: Only one outcome of a random event or random variable can occur at a time. Outcomes are therefore considered to be *mutually exclusive*. This is important, because we often want to ask what the probability of one of several outcomes is. For example, suppose a die is rolled so that the possible set of outcomes is 1, 2, 3, 4, 5, and 6, with probabilities of 1/6 each. Then we can ask, what is the probability that 1 or 4 will be rolled? The answer, due to mutual exclusivity, is 1/6 + 1/6 = 1/3. That is,

> *If we want to know the probability of one of several outcomes occurring in a random event, then this probability is just the sum of the probabilities of each outcome.*

The set of possible outcomes is often called the *range* of the random event, and the collective information about all probabilities is called the *distribution* of the event or variable.

Example

We now give a new example of a random event. The simplest random event is the flip of a coin. In this case there are two possible outcomes (heads and tails); the probability of heads is 50 percent and the probability of tails is 50 percent. Let's give this random event a name. We'll call it X. We can call it anything we like, but usually random events (and random variables) are given names with capital letters.

Now let's combine X with itself several times to form a new random variable. We do this by "modeling" three successive flips of a coin. In other words, we assume that we flip the same coin three times. Moreover, we'll agree that each flip has no influence on the outcome of any other flip. That is, we assume the flips are *independent*. Writing H for heads and T for tails, the possible outcomes for our new random event are:

$$HHH, HHT, HTH, THH, HTT, THT, TTH, TTT.$$

In this picture, HHH represents three successive heads, HHT represents two heads, followed by a tails, etc. The probability of each flip is 1/8. This follows since each flip is independent of the other, which implies that each outcome has the same probability as all of the other outcomes.

More on Random Events

There is one subtlety regarding random events that can lead to confusion later. First, it is important to understand that the set of possible outcomes is defined by whomever is looking at the random event, not the random event itself. This is important, because we use random events to model specific phenomena. Let's examine this.

In the die example, one could say the outcomes of the event are "the roll is an even number" and "the roll is an odd number." In this way, we define a new random event with only two outcomes. Part of it is the same as the old event, that is, it still involves the roll of a die, but the outcomes are different. In this case, the probability of each outcome is 1/2.

There are three additional concepts we need to understand regarding random events. They are,

1. The expected value of a random event.
2. The variance and standard deviation of a random event.
3. When two random events are independent.

We will study these concepts by introducing a very simple version of the binomial model of stock price movements, which will be studied completely in Chapter 6; for now we will give a trimmed-down version useful for studying probability theory.

The Binomial Model of Stock Movements

We will model a stock S, whose current spot price is S_0. Time in this model is divided into discrete bits (e.g., one day, or one week, or one year), and at the end of each *time period,* we look at the spot price to see how it has changed.

In this model, the "event" is the change in spot price at the end of a time period. In the binomial model, we hypothesize that when the stock price changes, it either rises by a fixed multiple or drops by a fixed multiple; for example, the 'up' multiple is 1.10, and the 'down' multiple is 0.90. In this case, if the current spot is $100, the new spot will either be $90 or $110.

If the up multiple is u, the down multiple is d, and the spot is S_0, then the set of possible outcomes of the event are as follows:

$$uS_0 \quad \text{and} \quad dS_0.$$

Notice that we have not completely described the random event because we have not said what the probability of each outcome is. Ordinarily in this model, we write p for the probability of the outcome uS_0 and call it the *up transition probability.*

A word about p: When we spoke of the probability of heads in a coin flip, we said a probability of 50 percent means, roughly, that if we flipped the coin an infinite number of times, one-half the flips would be heads. The probability p can therefore be thought of in the same vein. We let p be a number between zero and one. For example, if p is 0.62, then this means that if this event occured an infinite number of times, the price would rise 62 percent of the time.

What is the *down transition probability?* That is, what is the probability that the stock price will drop at the end of a time period in our random event? The answer is $1 - p$. The rationale is that every time the event occurs, *something must happen*—the stock price either rises or falls. Consequently, the sum of all the probabilities must be 1.

If the price does not rise, then it must fall. This is a basic property of the model. Thus, if the price rises 62 percent of the time, then it must fall the rest of the time, or 38 percent of the time.

Example

Let's summarize the binomial model we just described. The spot price of some stock is $100, the up ratio is 1.1, and the down ratio is 0.90. Moreover, let's assume that the up transition probability is 0.62. The possible outcomes are as follows:

1. The spot price rises to $110.
2. The spot price drops to $90.

The probability of the first outcome is 62 percent, and the probability of the second outcome is 38 percent. This is all there is to defining a random event: identifying the outcomes and their probabilities.

We can now pursue two important themes in probability theory. First, how can we use the information built into the random event to characterize it, and second, what is its relationship with other random events? In the first direction, we will study the mean and variance of a random event; in the second, we will discuss independent random events. However, before discussing either, we need to address a fundamental point.

The Probability of Something That Only Happens Once

The hardest aspect about random variables to understand is that they are *idealized* models of reality. That is, we sacrifice a precise model of reality for the facility of dealing with precise mathematical objects. As such, random variables have several advantages over the real thing. For example, we can *simulate* real events an unlimited number of times. We can discuss 1 trillion flips of a coin or answer questions like, how many times do we expect to get zero if we spin a roulette wheel 1,000 times?

In the case of stock price models, random variables create an interesting problem. We are trying to apply terms such as *probability* to events that only happen once. We can ask, for example, what is the probability that XYZ will be $100 or greater between now and next year? We know in reality that between now and next year happens only once, and the price either *will* or *will not* surpass $100. Therefore, the first question we must address in this discussion is, what do terms like probability mean when considering events that only happen once?

The answer is we simulate, via a model, the probability distribution of random variables such as the flip of a coin. For instance, suppose there is a game where player A flips a coin and player B pays $1 to player A if the coin comes up heads and nothing otherwise. How much should player A pay player B to play this game? That is, what is the fair value of the game?

To evaluate this, we have to ask, what is the probability the coin will come up heads? In the game, the coin will only be flipped once. But this does not stop us from pretending the coin is flipped some large number of times and going through the exercise of computing the probability.

The point is, it does not matter whether or not we can actually flip the coin more than once. Even if we say we will play the game once and never again, there is nothing preventing us from computing the probability that the coin will come up heads. Stock price models work in the same way. Time only happens once, but that does not stop us from creating a model and asking questions about probability, which in reality only makes sense when things happen repeatedly.

The Expected Value of a Random Event

Let's continue with the binomial stock price model we started above and ask, what is the average value of the new spot price? Let's clarify what this means.

Suppose we could let the stock price follow our model 1,000 times. Then, accordingly, approximately 62 percent of the time, the spot price would move up to $110, and 38 percent of the time, the price would move down to $90. What's the average price? To compute this, assume the price moves up *exactly* 62 percent of the time. (How can we justify this? Because, if we did this an *infinite* number of times, it would go up exactly 62 percent of the time.) Out of 1,000 times, 620 would be *up* moves and 380 would be *down* moves. The average is computed as follows:

$$\frac{620 \cdot \$110 + 380 \cdot \$90}{1,000} = 0.62 \cdot \$110 + 0.38 \cdot \$90 = \$102.40.$$

Let's make a few observations about this computation. First of all, the left-hand portion of the equation,

$$\frac{620 \cdot \$110 + 380 \cdot \$90}{1,000},$$

is the average value computed in the usual way we compute averages. The middle portion,

$$0.62 \cdot \$110 + 0.38 \cdot \$90,$$

was obtained by dividing 1,000 into each portion; that is, $620/1000 = 0.62$, and $380/1,000 = 0.38$. 0.62 is the up transition probability, and 0.38 is the down transition probability. The equation, translated into words, says:

> *The average value of the new spot price is the up transition probability times the up price plus the down transition probability times the down price.*

This is exactly the definition we are looking for. If a random event has more than two outcomes (e.g., a more complicated stock model in which there are, say, ten or twenty possible stock prices), then the expected value of the event is the sum over all possible outcomes, multiplied by the probability of each outcome. We give the precise, technical definition of expected value in Display 2.2.1.

Example

Suppose we have a discrete time stock price model, like the binomial model, except there are five different stock prices at the end of each period: the price can go down by 20 percent, down by 10 percent, stay the same, rise by 10 percent, or rise by 20 percent. Moreover, suppose the probability that the stock falls 20 percent is 15 percent, falls 10 percent is 20 percent, stays even is 30 percent, rises 10 percent is 20 percent, and rises 20 percent is 15 percent. If the current spot price is $100, then the possible new prices are $80, $90, $100, $110, and $120. These are summarized in Table 2.2.1.

Notice Table 2.2.1 actually describes two random variables. The first is the one-period return on the stock price; for example, if the price falls by 20 percent, then the one-period return is minus 20 percent. The second random variable is the new price itself. That is, for each outcome, the stock price moves to a new price; thus, for a minus 20 percent return, the new price (and therefore the outcome) is $80.

We will compute both the expected one-period return and the expected value of the stock after one period. First, we compute the expected return. Following the definition of expected value, we add up all the different possible returns, each multiplied by its probability, to obtain the following:

$$(-20\% \cdot 0.15) + (-10\% \cdot 0.20) + (0\% \cdot 0.30)$$
$$+ (10\% \cdot 0.20) + (20\% \cdot 0.15) = 0\%.$$

Thus, the average expected return on the stock is zero. Remember what this means. Using our model, on average we would see a zero percent expected return on the stock.

D I S P L A Y   2.2.1

THE DEFINITION OF EXPECTED VALUE

If S is a random event with possible outcomes

$$S_1, S_2, \ldots, S_N$$

for a total of N outcomes with probabilities

$$p_1, p_2, \ldots, p_N, \qquad p_1 + p_2 + \ldots + p_N = 1,$$

with the property that

$$p_i \text{ is the probability of outcome } S_i,$$

then the expected value of S, written $E[S]$, is given by the formula

$$E[S] = p_1 S_1 + p_2 S_2 + \ldots + p_N S_N.$$

T A B L E   2.2.1

Possible price changes, associated prices, and probabilities (Current spot price = $100)

Price Change	New Price	Probability
−20%	$ 80	15%
−10%	$ 90	20%
0%	$100	30%
10%	$110	20%
20%	$120	15%

With this in mind, it seems reasonable that the expected value of the stock price would be $100. That is, since the current spot price is $100 and the average expected return is 0 percent, the average new price should be the same as the current spot price. Computing the expected value of the stock price, we obtain

$$\$80 \cdot 0.15 + \$90 \cdot 0.20 + \$100 \cdot 0.30 + \$110 \cdot 0.20 + \$120 \cdot 0.15 = \$100.$$

The fact that the expected return on the stock in this model is 0 percent is only one aspect of this model. Other, quite different, models also have an expected return of zero. For example, if we have a binomial model in which the price can rise or fall by 80 percent and each outcome has a 50 percent probability, then, clearly, this model also has an expected return of zero. The difference is that this second investment *seems* much more risky.

This example clearly indicates the need for a measure of how much the actual returns vary on average from the expected return. For example, in the risky model described above (plus or minus 80 percent returns), the deviation from the mean return is quite large (because the actual returns are always plus or minus 80 percent while the average return is 0 percent), while the model in Table 2.2.1 varies from the mean considerably less: 30 percent of the time there is actually a zero percent (mean) return.

In the language of probability the concept we are looking for is the *variance* of the random event. To define this precisely, we will use some notation that is fairly common in the world of finance. Let's write S_0 for the current spot price and S_1 for the spot price at the end of one period; S_0 is the initial value, and S_1 is the outcome of the event. Right now we regard S_1 as a random variable. That is, we do not know what its value is, we only know its possible values and their probabilities.

We write $E[S_1]$ for the expected value of S_1; currently, S_1 is an unknown value, but the expected value is already known. We use this to define variance and also *standard deviation,* the more common measure of variability.

Example of Variance
Let's consider two different models of stock price movements simultaneously. They are listed in Table 2.2.2. Each example has an expected value of 8 percent, but we can see by looking at the possible returns of each model that Model 1 is less risky than Model 2. This will be mathematically explained using variance.

Variance measures the average dispersion from the expected value in each model. The dispersion from the mean is nothing but the difference between the expected return and the actual return. For example, in Model 1 there is a possible minus 12 percent return. This differs from the expected return by 20 percentage points.

To compute variance, we look at the square of each outcome's difference from the expected return. This is a new random variable (each outcome is "produced" from an outcome of our variable by squaring its difference from the expected value). The expected value of this new variable is the variance. Variance is formally defined in Display 2.2.2.

When we compute variance, we square the difference between each outcome and the expected value. This leaves us with a number whose units

T A B L E 2.2.2

Two different models with the same
expected value

Model 1		Model 2	
Return	**Probability**	**Return**	**Probability**
−12%	37.50%	−20%	49.09%
20%	62.50%	35%	50.91%
Expected Values			
Model 1		Model 2	
8%		8%	

D I S P L A Y 2.2.2

THE GENERAL FORMULA FOR STANDARD DEVIATION

Let S be a random event with outcomes

$$S_1, S_2, \ldots, S_N,$$

and probabilities

$$p_1, p_2, \ldots, p_N,$$

and expected value μ, that is,

$$E[S] = \mu.$$

The standard deviation of S, written $Var[S]$, is given by the formula

$$Var[S] = p_1(S_1 - \mu)^2 + p_2(S_2 - \mu)^2 + \ldots + p_N(S_N - \mu)^2.$$

We also have the equivalent formula

$$Var[X] = E[X^2] - \{E[X]\}^2.$$

The standard deviation of S is given by the formula

$$\sigma[S] = \sqrt{Var[S]}.$$

are "squares of percents." In order to bring us back to units of percents, we can take the square root of variance. This is the familiar concept of standard deviation. The standard deviations in Model 1 and Model 2 are computed in Display 2.2.3.

Notice that the standard deviation of Model 2 is much greater than the standard deviation of Model 1. This is now a mathematically precise version of the intuitive statement that Model 2 is more risky than Model 1.

A Useful Formula and Some Notation
Sometimes it is useful to view the mathematics of probability theory in abstract notation. We briefly do this for variance now.

We let X be a random variable. We then write $E[X]$ for the expected value of X, $Var[X]$ for its variance, and $\sigma[X]$ for its standard deviation. In this notation, the variance is given by the formula:

$$Var[X] = E[(X - E[X])^2].$$

Let's unwind this definition. The expression on the right-hand side starts with $X - E[X]$. This is a random variable whose outcomes are given by the outcomes of X minus $E[X]$. Next we square this. This is yet another random variable, the outcomes of which are the square of the outcomes of $X - E[X]$. Lastly, we have the definition that $Var[X] = E[(X - E[X])^2]$. This says that the variance is the *average squared dispersion from the mean of X*.

For future reference, we give the following useful formula:

$$Var[X] = E[X^2] - \{E[X]\}^2.$$

This is useful, because if $E[X] = 0$, this says that

$$Var[X] = E[X^2].$$

Until now, we've discussed certain *numerical aspects* of random events, in particular their means and standard deviations. The next question is how do different, possibly related, random events influence each other's probability distributions? This introduces the notion of *independent random events*, which we will discuss next.

Independent Random Events

Let's return to the example of a binomial model of stock price movement, only this time we'll consider price movements over more than one time period.

Thus, at the current time, the spot price might be $100; after one period, the price might rise or fall 10 percent, and after the second period, this

D I S P L A Y 2.2.3

THE COMPUTATION OF THE STANDARD DEVIATIONS OF MODEL 1 AND MODEL 2

Standard Deviation in Model 1

$$\sqrt{(-12\% - 8\%)^2\, 0.375 + (20\% - 8\%)^2\, 0.625} = 15.49\%.$$

Standard Deviation in Model 2

$$\sqrt{(-20\% - 8\%)^2\, 0.4909 + (35\% - 8\%)^2\, 0.5091} = 27.50\%.$$

---

might happen again. The question we have to ask is:

Does what happens in the first period influence what happens in the second period?

Those of you who have studied efficient market theory will recognize that this is a difficult question to answer. However, at the moment we are mainly interested in establishing a simple mathematical definition.

Each one period piece of the binomial model is a random event: the price either rises by 10 percent or falls by 10 percent. We'll denote the up transition probability (the probability of a price rise) by the letter p. If this up transition probability is p regardless of what happens the time before, then the events are called *independent*. If what happens in the previous period has an effect on the transition probabilities of the next period, then the events are called *dependent*.

One of the basic assumptions of all the stock models we deal with is that stock price movements from one moment to the next (or, in the case of a binomial model, from one time period to the next) are independent. This will be discussed in greater detail in Chapter 3.

The Probability of Independent Events

Let's consider the binomial model of price movements again. Remember, in this model we assert that price movements from one period to the next are independent and identically distributed. That is, at any given time, the probability that the price will move up is exactly the same as at any other time.

Suppose we have a two-period model, and the probability of an up movement is p. What is the probability of two successive up movements? The answer is $p \cdot p = p^2$. The general rule is that if we have several independent events occurring in succession, with probabilities $p_1, p_2, \ldots, p_N$, then the probability of all of them occurring just once is $p_1 \cdot \ldots \cdot p_N$.

Example

Now we will illustrate the computation of the probability of several independent events. Suppose we have a three-period binomial model of price movements in which the probability of an up movement is always 65 percent. The adjoining figure illustrates what this model

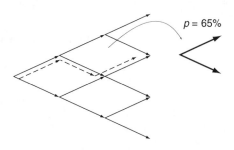

looks like. Also, a *price path* through the tree is depicted. What is the probability of traversing this path? Note that the path is composed of three segments: an up move, a down move, and an up move. The probability of an up move is 65 percent, and the probability of a down move is 35 percent. Therefore, our rule states that the probability of traversing the path is: $0.65 \cdot 0.35 \cdot 0.65 = 0.1479$. That is, of all the stock price paths in our three-period tree, there is a 14.79 percent chance the stock will travel the path depicted.

With this said, we need to keep one thing in mind: We have merely computed the probability of traversing the path depicted. Note that there are two other paths ending at the same node as the depicted path. In other words, we have *not* computed the probability of ending at the second highest node. To compute this, we have to compute the probability of traversing all three paths. To do this, we simply add up the probability of traversing each path.

Formulas for the Mean and Expected Value

Display 2.2.4 gives formulas for working with mean and standard deviation that we will occasionally use throughout the book.

2.3 THE NORMAL DISTRIBUTION

The normal probability distribution is the most important of all distributions. It is of primary importance in stock price modeling, and it is used in the Black-Scholes options pricing formula as a model for the distribution of future returns on a security. The normal distribution will be used repeatedly throughout this book, and therefore its study is crucial in what follows.

D I S P L A Y 2.2.4

SOME BASIC FORMULAS FOR MEAN AND STANDARD DEVIATION

Notation:

$$X = \text{A random variable}$$
$$Y = \text{A second random variable}$$
$$E[X] = \text{expected value of } X$$
$$Var[X] = \text{variance of } X$$
$$\sigma[X] = \text{standard deviation of } X$$

The following formulas occur frequently in probability. Let α be a constant. Then,

$$E[X + Y] = E[X] + E[Y]$$
$$E[\alpha X] = \alpha E[X]$$
$$\sigma[X] = \sqrt{Var[X]}$$
$$Var[\alpha X] = \alpha^2 Var[X]$$
$$\sigma[\alpha X] = \alpha \sigma[X]$$

Until now, we have studied random events, but we have limited our examples to events with a finite number of outcomes, such as the binomial model of price movement, where each time the spot moves, it can only move to one of two possible new values. We know in reality that stock prices can take on more than two values. In order to understand how we model security price movements, it is necessary to understand random events that can have an infinite number of possible outcomes. In probability theory, these are called *continuous random variables*. Before discussing these, we make a general comment about the use of continuous random variables.

Why Continuous Random Variables?

We know that in reality stocks do not take on an infinite number of values. Why, then, do we want to use continuous random variables to model them?

Our mathematical tools for dealing with continuous random variables are quite sophisticated. Continuous random variables exist within the realm of calculus and partial differential equations, mathematical branches that are highly developed.

By modeling random events with continuous random variables, we give ourselves access to a great deal of mathematical machinery that can simplify computations and elucidate difficult mathematics (indeed, the Black-Scholes formula would not be possible without such mathematical machinery). The sacrifice, of course, is that we know stock prices and stock returns are not "continuous." That is, there are only a finite number of possible stock prices, and every price between two prices cannot be achieved.

Despite this, the hope is, and experience tells us, these assumptions are "not too bad." That is, while they are not perfect, the gain made in terms of mathematical efficiency and power often wins out over the losses incurred by making the continuity assumption.

We now begin our study of random variables.

Continuous Random Variables

Conceptually, a continuous random variable is the same as a random event (studied above), except the set of possible outcomes is not limited to some finite set of values (e.g., heads and tails), but varies continuously. For example, in modeling security returns, we shall discuss the geometric Brownian motion model of security price movements (Chapter 3), which has as one of its assumptions that the return on a security in a fixed period of time can be any real number.

In the language of probability theory, then, the "event" we are studying is the return on a stock between now and some future date. The set of "outcomes" of the "event"—the return on a security—is represented by the set of real numbers. That is, we assume it is any real number.

Above we studied random variables with a finite number of outcomes. Matters are more difficult in the situation where the number of outcomes is infinite: We can no longer sensibly talk about the probability of a single outcome.

In the "finite" case (e.g., the flip of a coin), each outcome has a definite probability (e.g., the probability of heads is 50 percent). We might try to do the same thing in the continuous random variable case. Unfortunately, this cannot make sense mathematically. Simply put, there are too many possible outcomes for each one to have a positive probability. Imagine, for example, we are modeling the one-year returns on a stock index. We ask, what is the probability that the return will be 10 percent? If we compute that this has some very small probability, such as 0.000005 percent, then the problem is that there are numbers *very close to 10 percent,* such as 10.000000001 percent, 10.000000002 percent, etc. What are the probabilities of these returns?

The point is, if we assign a positive probability to each outcome and try to sum them up, the net result is always infinite. Therefore, we cannot make sense of the probability of a single outcome.

The way we handle this mathematically is to only consider ranges of events, such as all the returns between 10 percent and 11 percent and moreover use the mathematically expedient convention of saying that a single event has zero probability! We can always make sense of computing probabilities of outcomes such as "the return will be between 10 and 11 percent." Therefore, when we think of continuous random variables, we can still think in terms of outcomes and probabilities, but rather than focusing on single outcomes, we restrict our attention to ranges of outcomes.

Expected Value and Standard Deviation

A continuous random variable has an expected value and standard deviation, just like the finite random events we studied above. Intuitively, their meanings are exactly the same as in the case of finite variables. Even the formulas describing them have the same intuitive meaning, but they involve calculus, which is used to make sense of adding up an infinite number of possible events.

If we had a probability distribution used as a model to describe the future returns on some stock, then the expected value would mean the value one could expect on average, just as in the finite case. The standard deviation would again describe the dispersion of the outcomes about the mean of the random variable.

How We Model Continuous Random Variables

We now discuss the relationship between actual events (i.e., actual stock returns) and the random variables used to model them. Suppose we wanted to model the flip of a coin. First, we write down what the event is—in this case the flip of a coin. Next, we say what the possible outcomes are. There are two, heads and tails. Lastly, we try to deduce the probability of each outcome. This can be done by performing an experiment. For example, we flip 1,000 coins and see how many heads come up and how many tails come up. We use this to give an estimate of the probability of heads and tails.

We would like to carry out the same analysis to model events with an infinite number of possible outcomes, such as to find a model for stock returns, but we cannot deal with an infinite number of events and try to deduce the probability of each one. We explain the standard procedure of building a histogram via a procedure known as *binning*.

Binning is a process in which we divide all the possible outcomes of an event into a finite number of groups. For example, suppose we want to model "market returns" over the last 25 years. We divide stock returns into ranges, grouping all stocks with returns between 0 percent and 5 percent, 5 percent and 10 percent, etc. Then, a bar graph is constructed to show the relative number of stocks that had returns in each of the specified ranges. The resulting graph is known as a *histogram*. Figure 2.3.1 shows four sample histograms.

These histograms clearly give an idea of what the probability of a range of outcomes is. For instance, if the histogram bins are in the ranges of 0 percent through 1 percent, etc. (i.e., if the bin size is 1 percent), then one could compute the probability of a return being in that range by taking the total number of stocks sampled and dividing it by the number of stocks in that range. For example, suppose there are 150 stocks in total and 16 fall into the 0 to 1 percent range. That is, 16 in 150 stocks fall into the 0 to 1 percent range, or 10 2/3 percent. Therefore, we say that the probability of a stock falling into this range is 10 2/3 percent.

Note that in Figure 2.3.1, the curve that defines the top of each histogram is "bell-shaped." This curve often closely resembles a mathematical curve known as a *normal density curve*.[3] Normal density curves are characterized by two parameters: mean and standard deviation. Figure 2.3.2 displays two different sets of normal curves. The two curves in the left-hand graph have the same standard deviation (variance) but different means.

In a normal density curve, the *x*-axis represents the "events" of the random variable. For example, if we are modeling stock returns, the values on the *x*-axis represent possible stock returns. To understand what this means, examine the histograms in Figure 2.3.1.

The *y*-axis of a normal curve is harder to describe. By comparison, the *y*-axis has an obvious meaning in a histogram: It represents the number of "events" that fall into a particular range. On the other hand, we derive most of the relevant information in the histogram by examining the relative height of each bar. That is, we are really interested in what percent of all events fall within a certain range. Because of this, we could divide the height of each bar by the total number of events. For example, if there are 1,200 stock returns modeled in Figure 2.3.1, then we could divide each

---

[3]The normal density curve is determined by the graph $y = \frac{1}{\sigma\sqrt{2\pi}}e^{-x-\mu/2\sigma^2}$, where μ is the mean and σ is the standard deviation of the random variable.

F I G U R E 2.3.1

Four histograms

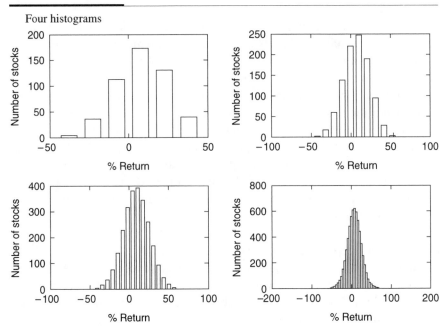

F I G U R E 2.3.2

Each graph above has two normal density curves in it. The left-hand figure contains two normal densities with the same variance but different means. The right-hand figure contains two normal densities with the same mean but different variances.

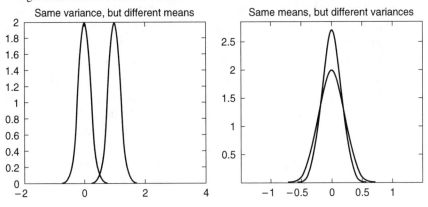

tower's height by 1,200. In doing this, the general shape of the histogram does not change.

The same basic fact holds for normal curves. First of all, the total area under a normal curve is always equal to one, which is analogous to the situation with a discrete random variable in which the probabilities of all events add up to one.

Next, in a normal distribution, for any range of values on the x-axis, we consider the area under the curve within those values. For example, if the x-axis represents returns, we can look at the area under the curve between 2 and 6 percent (see enlarged portion of Figure 2.3.3). This area is some number less than one and represents the percentage of returns between 2 and 6 percent. From another point of view, we can imagine the area under the curve as being composed of many infinitely thin histogram bars. This is illustrated in Figure 2.3.3.

The Mean and Standard Deviation

The mean of a normal distribution is its average or expected value. As with all types of random variables this is a useful characterization of the distribution. Unlike other random variables, however, the mean of a normal curve has the nice property of being the "half-way" point of the normal curve: 50 percent of the events are greater than the mean, and 50 percent are less than the mean. For example, if the mean event is a 5 percent stock return, then 50 percent of returns are greater than the mean, and 50 percent are less than the mean.

Graphically, the mean of a normal curve is the place on the x-axis below the peak of the curve. It is the average value of the "event" it is modeling. The standard deviation is a measure of the dispersion around the peak, analogous to the dispersion around the mean we saw with discrete random variables.

To see visually what standard deviation means, examine Figure 2.3.2 again. The curves on the right represent two normal curves with the same mean but different standard deviations. The thinner curve has more area near the peak of the curve. As we move "away from the mean," that is, if we examine events that are not near to the mean, the curve quickly gets near the x-axis. This, in turn, means there is less area under the curve in regions away from the mean, which means there is less probability of these events occurring. Therefore, the probability of events near the mean is large. This is a low standard deviation.

The higher standard deviation curve is fatter. Less area is concentrated near the mean. Intuitively, this means the events are more spread out, and we have less precise information of where they are most likely to be.

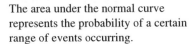

F I G U R E 2.3.3

The area under the normal curve
represents the probability of a certain
range of events occurring.

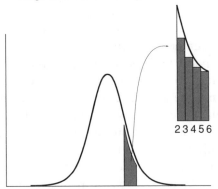

For example, imagine that the two curves on the right in Figure 2.3.2 represent probability distributions for the future returns of two different stocks. The low standard deviation stock is more likely to have a return near the mean, whereas the high standard deviation stock has less of a probability of a return near the mean. So, even though they both have the same average rate of return, one is much riskier than the other.

2.4 CUMULATIVE NORMAL DISTRIBUTION FUNCTION

The normal distribution is the most frequently encountered probability distribution partly because it is the easiest with which to work and make computations. For example, it is often the case that a model employs the normal distribution even when it is known that the data is not exactly normally distributed. Despite this, more accurate models are often so difficult to implement that the normal distribution is used in any case.

The reason that the normal distribution is "easy to work with" is because it yields nice and easy-to-use formulas for the probabilities of events. To understand these formulas, we first need to study the *standard normal distribution*.

The Standard Normal Distribution

The standard normal distribution is the normal distribution with a mean of 0 and a standard deviation of 1. Any normal distribution can be *transformed* into a standard normal distribution in a very simple way.

Suppose X is a continuous, normally distributed random variable with mean μ and standard deviation σ. Then, the random variable

$$\frac{X - \mu}{\sigma} \qquad (2.4.1)$$

is a normally distributed random variable with mean zero and standard deviation one. Let's examine this more closely.

Since X is a random variable, it has a possible set of outcomes (e.g., if X represents the return on some stock, then the stock price will be different on a future date, and the rate of return on the stock may be computed). If X has a particular outcome, say, for example, 0.20 (i.e., the return is 20 percent), then the outcome of our new random variable, $(X - \mu)/\sigma$, is obtained by computing $(0.20 - \mu)/\sigma$. That is, to get an outcome of $(X - \mu)/\sigma$, we merely start with an outcome of X, subtract μ, and then divide the result by σ (we give an example of the usage of this formula in stock price models below).

Since the average outcome of X is μ, it is clear that the average outcome of $X - \mu$ is 0. This follows from the formula

$$E[X - \mu] = E[X] - \mu.$$

Since the standard deviation of X is σ, its variance (which equals the square of the standard deviation) is equal to σ^2, and the variance of $X - \mu$ is also σ^2. This follows from the formulas in Display 2.2.4. Why is this?

Intuitively, this can be seen by studying Figure 2.3.2. In the left-hand figure, we see two normal densities with the same variance and different means. Notice that the curves have exactly the same shape, but one is simply shifted over from the other. This translates mathematically into the statement that if the right-hand curve represents a random variable X, then the right hand curve represents the random variable $X - \mu$, where μ is the size of the shift. In conclusion, shifting does not affect variance.

Now we claim the variance of $(X - \mu)/\sigma$ is 1. This follows from the formula $Var[X/\sigma] = (1/\sigma^2)Var[X]$. Recall that $Var[X]$ means "variance of X." Since standard deviation is the square root of variance, we see the standard deviation of $(X - \mu)/\sigma$ is also one.

Standard Cumulative Normal Distribution

Before discussing the standard cumulative normal distribution function, we must note that every distribution has a "cumulative distribution function." This function is very simple and answers the question: For a given number

x what is the probability that an outcome is less than or equal to x? When the distribution in question is the standard normal distribution, then the cumulative distribution function is called the standard cumulative normal distribution.

For example, suppose we have a model for the movement of the spot price of a stock or index that states that the one-year return on this stock is normally distributed with mean 10 percent *per annum* and standard deviation 20 percent *per annum*. This says the *expected* return on the stock is 10 percent, but the dispersion of the return around 10 percent is 20 percent.

If we had a formula for the cumulative normal distribution function (for mean 10 percent and standard deviation 20 percent), we could compute the probability that the return is less than x for any percent x.

In general, the way we obtain such formulas is by using the *cumulative normal distribution function*. To explain this, we first introduce some notation. For any number x, we write

$$N(x) = \text{cumulative normal distribution function of } x.$$

Since this is specifically for the standard normal distribution, we have to proceed in two steps: 1) transform the distribution to the standard normal distribution, and 2) use the cumulative normal distribution function. Since this may be confusing, we give an example of how this works.

Example

Suppose we have a stock, as above, whose one-year returns are normally distributed with mean 10 percent and standard deviation 20 percent. That is, we have a model for our stock that states the *possible returns* between now and one year from now are normally distributed with mean 10 percent and standard deviation 20 percent. What is the probability we will have a return of less than 0 percent; that is, what is the probability we will suffer a loss?

Solution: Write X for the one-year return on our stocks. Now, form a new random variable, Y, with mean 0 and standard deviation 1. We have

$$Y = \frac{X - 0.10}{0.20}.$$

Equivalently,

$$X = 0.20 \cdot Y + 0.10.$$

Now,

$$X \leq 0.00 \Leftrightarrow 0.20 \cdot Y + 0.10 \leq 0.00 \Leftrightarrow Y \leq -0.10/0.20 = -0.50.$$

In words, the probability X (the returns) will be less than zero is equal to the probability Y will be less than -0.50. Therefore, the probability $X \leq 0$

D I S P L A Y 2.5.1

POLYNOMIAL FORMULAS FOR THE CUMULATIVE NORMAL DISTRIBUTION FUNCTION

Formula 1

Accuracy: 4 decimal places.

$$N(x) = \begin{cases} 1 - Z(x)(a_1 t + a_2 t^2 + a_3 t^3), & x \geq 0 \\ 1 - N(-x) & x < 0. \end{cases}$$

where $t = \frac{1}{1+px}$, $Z(x) = \frac{1}{\sqrt{2\pi}} e^{-x^2/2}$ and

$a_1 = 0.4361836$ $\qquad p = 0.33267$

$a_2 = -0.1201676$

$a_3 = 0.9372980$

Formula 2

Accuracy: 6 decimal places.

$$N(x) = \begin{cases} 1 - Z(x)(b_1 t + b_2 t^2 + b_3 t^3 + b_4 t^4 + b_5 t^5) & x \geq 0 \\ 1 - N(-x) & x < 0 \end{cases}$$

where $t = \frac{1}{1+px}$, $Z(x) = \frac{1}{\sqrt{2\pi}} e^{-x^2/2}$ and

$p = 0.2316419$ $\qquad b_1 = 0.319381530$

$b_2 = -0.356563782$ $\qquad b_3 = 1.781477937$

$b_4 = -1.821255978$ $\qquad b_5 = 1.330274429$

is $N(-0.50) = 30.85$ percent. The next question is, how do we compute $N(-0.50)$.

In the next section, we give four formulas for the standard cumulative normal distribution function. Once we have these formulas, we can compute the cumulative normal distribution for any continuous random variable simply by transforming it into the standard normal distribution and applying the formula for the cumulative normal distribution. Later we shall use this technique to compute the probability that a European call option expires in the money.

2.5 FOUR APPROXIMATE FORMULAS FOR THE STANDARD CUMULATIVE NORMAL DISTRIBUTION

The mathematics derived so far has been a language for modeling reality. In Chapter 3 we are going to give the model for stock price movements used to derive the Black-Scholes formula. This model will involve the nor-

D I S P L A Y 2.5.2

RATIONAL FORMULAS FOR THE CUMULATIVE NORMAL DISTRIBUTION FUNCTION

Formula 1

Accuracy: better than 2.50×10^{-4}.

$$N(x) = \begin{cases} 1 - \frac{1}{2}(1 + c_1 x + c_2 x^2 + c_3 x^3 + c_4 x^4)^{-4} & x \geq 0 \\ 1 - N(-x) & x < 0, \end{cases}$$

where

$$c_1 = 0.196854 \qquad c_2 = 0.115194$$
$$c_3 = 0.000344 \qquad c_4 = 0.019527$$

Formula 2

Accurate to within 1×10^{-7}

$$N(x) = \begin{cases} 1 - \frac{1}{2}(1 + d_1 x + d_2 x^2 + d_3 x^3 + d_4 x^4 + d_5 x^5 + d_6 x^6)^{-16} & x \geq 0 \\ 1 - N(-x) & x < 0, \end{cases}$$

where

$$d_1 = 0.0498673470 \qquad d_2 = 0.0211410061$$
$$d_3 = 0.0032776263 \qquad d_4 = 0.0000380036$$
$$d_5 = 0.0000488906 \qquad d_6 = 0.0000053830$$

mal distribution, and the Black-Scholes formula in turn uses the standard cumulative normal distribution function. Therefore, to be able to use the Black-Scholes formula, one must have available a way to compute the cumulative normal distribution function.

In this section, we give four "approximate" formulas for the cumulative normal distribution function. The formulas are generally very accurate. They deviate from the actual cumulative normal distribution function only in very high decimal places. Since our purpose is to eventually use the formulas for options pricing, the slight deviations from the real formula make absolutely no difference.

The formulas are meant for programming into spreadsheets, pocket calculators, or computer implementations. As they only involve basic mathematics, they are extremely fast. These formulas are divided into two groups: polynomial and rational. The polynomial formulas are a bit more complicated and harder to use, and involve a term with an exponential and are found in Display 2.5.1. The rational formulas are simpler to use and program and are found in Display 2.5.2.

2.6 PROPERTIES OF THE CUMULATIVE NORMAL DISTRIBUTION FUNCTION

The cumulative normal distribution function is a central part of the Black-Scholes formula, so it is important to have a good grasp of its basic properties. Many of its properties are intuitive and can be explained quite easily. We now present a list of the main important features of the cumulative normal distribution function.

Limiting Behavior

The cumulative normal distribution $N(x)$ is close to zero for numbers x that are very small, and it is close to one for numbers x that are very large. This is easy to see: For very small numbers (e.g., $x = -1,000,000$), $N(x)$ is the probability that a normally distributed random variable is less than or equal to x. For such x, the probability that such a variable is less than x is almost negligible.

Likewise, for large positive x, the probability that a normally distributed random variable is less than or equal to x gets increasingly close to 100 percent as x gets larger.

Symmetry Formula

Is there a relationship between $N(x)$ and $N(-x)$? The answer is yes. We have

$$N(x) = 1 - N(-x).$$

FIGURE 2.6.1

The symmetry formula for the cumulative normal distribution function

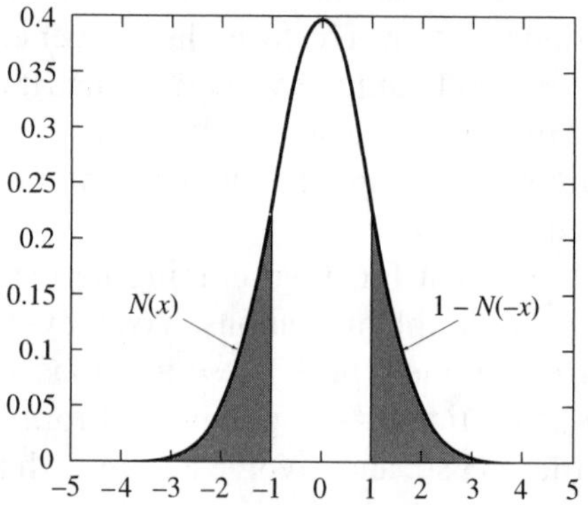

This can be reasoned as follows. The probability of being less than x is equal to $N(x)$. Now we ask, What is the probability of being greater than x? This is obviously $1 - N(x)$. But because the normal curve is symmetric about its mean, the probability of being less than x is the same as the probability of being greater than $-x$. That is, $N(x) = 1 - N(-x)$. This is explained graphically in Figure 2.6.1.

Mean Formula
We have the following formula:

$$N(0) = 0.50.$$

This says that the probability of being less than zero (for a standard normal distribution) is exactly the same as being greater than 0. This is easily seen, because $N(0) = 1 - N(-0) = 1 - N(0)$, which implies that $2N(0) = 1$, so that $N(0) = 1/2$.

3

⑥ THE GEOMETRIC
BROWNIAN MOTION
MODEL OF
PRICE MOVEMENTS

A model for stock price movements means many things to many people. In the theory of option pricing, a stock price model is, roughly speaking, a mathematical description of the relationship between the current price of a stock and its possible future prices. This relationship can be stated in probabilistic terms, or in a more precise form. Burton G. Malkiel, author of the famous book *A Random Walk Down Wall Street,* describes a stock price model that he asked his students at Yale to create:

> For each successive trading day, the closing stock price would be determined by the flip of a fair coin. If the toss was a head, the students assumed the stock closed 1/2 point higher than the preceding close. If the flip was a tail, the price was assumed to be down 1/2.
>
> The chart derived from random coin tossing looks remarkably like a normal stock price chart . . . I showed [one of the charts] to a chartist friend of mine who practically jumped out of his skin. "What is this company?" he exclaimed. "We've got to buy immediately. This pattern's a classic. There's no question the stock will be up 15 points next week."[1]

The "chartist" friend Malkiel refers to is a person who makes stock price charts and observes and interprets "patterns" in the charts. Malkiel's point is that randomly generated stock charts can look suspiciously like real ones. The geometric Brownian motion model is a souped up version of the

---

[1]From *A Random Walk Down Wall Street,* Malkiel (1985), p. 131.

simple coin-tossing model above. It posits that prices fluctuate based on random events that are no more predictable than the toss of a coin. The lesson with Malkiel's chartist friend above is a good example of how apparent patterns in the stock market can be consistent with a model of random stock price movements such as geometric Brownian motion.

What Is the Perfect Model?

The perfect model would be *predictive*—it would tell you the future price of a stock based on its present value and possibly some auxiliary data. The stock price models employed in options pricing are not predictive but *probabilistic*. That is, they do not make precise statements about what the future stock price will be, but instead, they assume a distribution of future prices derived from historical data, current market conditions, and possibly other relevant data.[2]

The geometric Brownian motion model states that future returns on a stock are normally distributed, and the standard deviation of this distribution can be estimated from historical data. The purpose of this chapter is to explain exactly what this means, and what it has to do with real stock prices. We study this model here because it is a key ingredient in the Black-Scholes formula. Also, we have to know how to use and calibrate the model, as the standard deviation we put into the model is important for the Black-Scholes formula.

The above mentioned standard deviation has another, more familiar name: *volatility*. Thus, the geometric Brownian motion model makes mathematically precise what we intuitively think of as the amount of fluctuation, or *riskiness*, inherent in a stock. For this reason, a good place to start our study of geometric Brownian motion is with a discussion of volatility and risk.

3.1 VOLATILITY AND RISK

Intuitively, price volatility is a measure of the amount and intensity of price fluctuation. The more volatile a stock's price, the more often and intensely

---

[2]The distribution we assume is what we mean when we say we are modeling a stock. How we come up with this distribution is the very essence of stock price modeling. In this chapter, we describe the geometric Brownian motion model, which, roughly speaking, assumes that stock returns are normally distributed and that we can obtain the standard deviation of this distribution from historical data. In Chapter 9, we discuss a way of inferring this distribution from market data on option prices.

it fluctuates. This is inversely proportional to the amount of information we have about the stock's future price: The more volatile a price is, the less easily one can pinpoint where it will be on a future date. Now consider the other extreme: a savings account that yields some fixed rate of interest. This has absolutely no volatility. If you know the balance of the account and the interest rate, then you can predict the balance of the account at any future date with 100 percent accuracy. Conversely, if we invest the balance in a more risky asset such as a stock, our ability to predict the "balance" declines as a function of the increasing riskiness of the asset. Part of our goal is to make this rather loose statement more precise.

Figure 3.1.1 displays an example of the relative riskiness of two different assets. This figure includes two examples of stock *sample paths.* On the left-hand side are five sample paths of a low volatility stock over a 90-day period, and on the right-hand side are five sample paths of a stock with high volatility.

The tendency of the high volatility stock to fluctuate wildly results in its price being much less predictable than the lower volatility stock. This can be seen intuitively from the sample paths: The low volatility prices remain in a much tighter range of prices relative to the high volatility ones.

F I G U R E 3.1.1

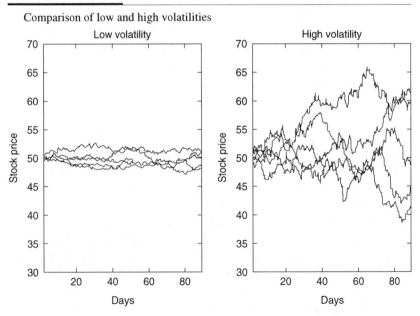

Comparison of low and high volatilities

The low volatility paths after 90 days lie in a range from 47.5 to about 52.5, while high volatility paths lie in a range from about 42 to 62.

These observations lead us to equate volatility with riskiness. The less accurately we can predict the future price of a stock, the more we regard it as risky. Therefore, if we can quantify the "amount" of volatility a stock possesses, then we can measure its riskiness.

A very simple measure of the volatility of a stock is the standard deviation of short-term returns on the stock. That is, we can measure how much the daily return on the stock deviates from its average daily return. The point is, we can compute this for a real stock.

To compute this, we measure the one-day returns on the stock (that is, the percent change in its value from one day to the next) over some period of time (e.g., six months) and then compute the mean and standard deviation of these values. We'll go through such a computation in a little while (see "Sample Computation of Volatility," page 106) but for now let's discuss some possible flaws in this point of view.

Overnight returns are one thing, but what about long-range price behavior? Perhaps the price fluctuates from day to day, but how does this relate to its long-range behavior? What if, for instance, it exhibits almost no long-term fluctuation? Is this possible?

If this is the case, then a large standard deviation of overnight returns might mislead one into thinking a stock is more risky than it actually is.

The geometric Brownian motion model says that this is not the case. It examines the relationship between the long- and short-range price behavior of the stock. In particular, the model posits that the short-range "volatility" of the stock (given by the standard deviation of overnight returns) is a perfect predictor of the long-range standard deviation of returns (e.g., one-year returns). We examine what this means in detail now.

3.2 THE MODEL

The name *geometric Brownian motion* has its origins in a physical description of the motion of a heavy particle suspended in a medium of light particles. The light particles move around rapidly, and as a matter of course, occasionally randomly crash into the heavy particle. Each collision slightly displaces the heavy particle; the direction and magnitude of this displacement is random and independent from all the other collisions, but the nature of this randomness does not change from collision to collision (in the language of probability theory, each collision is an independent, identically distributed random event). The geometric Brownian motion model takes this situation and, using some mathematics, derives that the displacement of the particle over a longer period of time must be normally distributed, with mean and standard deviation depending only on the amount of time that has passed.

This is a fantastic observation, because it implies that we can measure the average amount of displacement and the standard deviation of this displacement over some short period of time, and this same measurement will apply to longer periods of time. Therefore, if the particle's movement is very volatile over the short run, it will be proportionally volatile (in a sense to be made precise below) over the long run. Put another way, the randomness of the short-run behavior will not somehow be smoothed out over the long run.

The geometric Brownian motion model for particles fits real-world observations of "Brownian motion particles" and thus can be regarded as a mathematical explanation for this behavior. Now, surprisingly, stock prices have many characteristics in common with Brownian motion particles. In fact, M. Osborne (see Osborne, 1964), the man who introduced Brownian motion into the study of stock market prices, originally studied the stock market as a "macroscopic" example of Brownian motion.

To see the relation, imagine prices as heavy particles that are jarred around by lighter particles, trades. Indeed, each trade moves the price slightly. This comparison is not perfect, however, because price changes have one feature absent from Brownian particles: Prices change in proportion to their size (a so-called *geometric change*). That is, the expected percentage change in the stock price is the same regardless of its value. This means that the expected price change will depend on the current price of the stock. For instance, if a stock's expected return is 10 percent *per annum,* then the stock at $100 has an expected price change of $10, while the same stock at $50 has an expected change of $5. These are different *absolute* price changes but equal *percentage* price changes.

What this suggests is that Brownian motion is better adapted to model stock returns—that is, percentage changes in stock prices—than absolute price changes. Theories based on percentage changes rather than absolute changes are called *geometric.* Conversely, theories based on absolute changes are called *arithmetic.*

What the Model Describes

The geometric Brownian motion model describes the probability distribution of the future price of a stock. The basic assumption of the model is as follows:

*The return on a stock price between now and some very short time later
(Δt) is normally distributed. The mean of the distribution is μ times the
amount of time (μΔt), and the standard deviation is σ times the square
root of the amount of time (σ √Δt).*

We see that this stock price model depends on two parameters: μ and σ.
The parameter μ is called the *instantaneous expected return,* and σ is
called the *instantaneous standard deviation,* or the volatility of the stock.
In general, both are expressed in annualized terms.

Example

Suppose the instantaneous standard deviation of returns is computed to be
0.4187 percent per day. We imagine that this is computed by looking at one-
day returns on the stock for a series of days, computing the standard deviation
of the sample, and annualizing this value by multiplying by the square root
of the number of days in one year, that is,

$$0.4187\% \cdot \sqrt{365} = 8.00\%.$$

In other words, the standard deviation, expressed in percent *per annum,* is
8.00 percent.[3]

The Model in More Detail

The model starts by eliminating all the discreteness in security price movements. Stocks are traded continuously, and prices move continuously (i.e.,
there is no minimum time between trades whatsoever and no minimum or
maximum price fluctuation). For example, in this model a stock price could
theoretically move from \$1 to \$1,000,000 a share overnight, although we'll
see that the model assigns a *very* small probability to such an outcome.

Next, note the model only discusses what happens in a very short period of time. This goes back to our discussion of how we measure volatility.
We look at short-term returns on the stock (e.g., one day) and try to say
something about them (i.e., find their mean and standard deviation), and
then we use the model to make a general statement about the long-term
rate of return and standard deviation. Here's how we do that.

Conclusions of the Model

The conclusions of the model are:

*If S is a stock with spot price S_t at the current time t, and S follows a geo-
metric Brownian motion with instantaneous mean μ and instantaneous*

---

[3]In reality, an important question to ask is, how many days are there in a year? Since stocks
only trade approximately 250 days per year, we sometimes use this many days in the model.

standard deviation σ, then the return on S between now (time t) and a future time T is normally distributed with

1. *Mean* $(\mu - \frac{\sigma^2}{2}) \cdot (T - t)$
2. *Standard deviation* $\sigma \sqrt{T - t}$

These conclusions have two consequences. First, the standard deviation of returns increases in proportion to the square root of time. This means if we estimate the short-run standard deviation of returns (short-term volatility, e.g., overnight returns or weekly returns), then we can say the long-run standard deviation varies as the square root of time times the short-run volatility. This was observed as early as 1900 by Louis Bachelier, a French economist and mathematician (see Cootner, 1964), and is somewhat as we would expect. As time passes, the amount of fluctuation in stock price is sure to increase.

Second, the expected rate of return changes in proportion to time but not in proportion to the instantaneous rate of return. Instead, it changes in proportion to $\mu - \frac{\sigma^2}{2}$; that is, the instantaneous rate of return lowered by $\frac{\sigma^2}{2}$. We'll discuss why this is so in a moment, but first let's see some of its consequences. This phenomenon is an interesting consequence of the geometric Brownian motion model.

What it says is that short-term returns *alone* are not a good predictor of long-term returns. To properly understand long-term returns, we must also understand the volatility of the stock. Volatility tends to depress the expected returns below what the short-term returns suggest. We now explain why this is the case.

Why Returns Are Less than Expected

Let's examine why the presence of volatility lowers expected returns. We can see this easily by looking at a very simple example. Let's begin with a bank deposit of $100 that earns an annual interest rate of 10 percent (compounded once per year) over four years. In this situation, the deposit grows in a very simple manner, as is displayed in the adjoining figure. There is no uncertainty in the growth and therefore no volatility.

Now let's introduce volatility. Suppose at the end of each year there is a 50 percent chance that in addition to

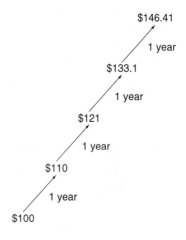

$146.41
  1 year
$133.1
  1 year
$121
  1 year
$110
  1 year
$100

whatever interest is earned, the price will rise by an additional 5 percent and a 50 percent chance that it will drop by 5 percent. In other words, the price movement will have two components: a *deterministic* component, equal to the interest earned; and a *random* component, equal to the contribution of the random 5 percent up or down movement. Suppose the actual outcome is that the first year, there is a 5 percent drop; the second year, a 5 percent rise; the third year, a drop again; and the fourth year, another rise. This is depicted in the adjoining figure. Note the end result. In the first process, where there is no volatility, the deposit grows to $146.41. In the second, where we introduce volatility, the deposit only grows to $145.68. The pattern of the volatility was straightforward. In the first year, it added 5 percent to the deposit; in the second, it subtracted 5 percent; and so on. It seems that the volatility jumps should have canceled themselves. In fact, this is not what happened.

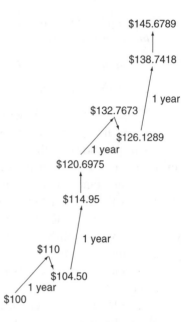

In our simple example, there were two possible random "jolts" that could occur at each time step. Either the price could jump up by 5 percent or jump down by 5 percent. Thus, the set of possible returns is distributed symmetrically about zero. This symmetry leads us to believe that the volatility will play no role in the expected returns. However, it clearly does. Why?

We can see the answer by noting what happens when a 5 percent positive return is followed by a 5 percent negative return. A 5 percent positive return multiplies the current amount by 1.05. Similarly, a 5 percent negative return multiplies the current amount by 0.95. Therefore, a positive return followed by a negative return multiplies the current amount by $1.05 \cdot 0.95 = 0.9975$. That is, a positive return followed by an equal (but opposite) negative return results in a slightly negative return!

Relation with Brownian Motion

The Brownian motion model says that in short time periods, stock prices are "jolted" by trades that result in small price fluctuations. The price fluctuations are seen in short-period returns. The returns are random variables that are normally distributed with expected value zero; that is, the probability of a particular range of returns is given by the area under a normal curve with the peak at zero.

If we delve a little deeper into the mathematics, we can show that price changes in Brownian motion can be decomposed into two components: a *deterministic* component and a *stochastic, or random,* component. This is much like the example of the deposit above. In that example, the deterministic component is the guaranteed 10 percent compounding each year. The stochastic component is the plus or minus 5 percent "jump" experienced each year on top of the guaranteed 10 percent.

Brownian motion works in exactly the same way. It is as if a stock following a Brownian motion is a bank deposit earning a continuously compounded return (the deterministic component) altered by a random amount (the stochastic component). The deterministic component is the instantaneous rate of return specified in the geometric Brownian motion model—we called it μ.

The stochastic component has one very important feature: It is normally distributed with an expected value of zero. The standard deviation of the stochastic component controls "how much" volatility there is on top of the deterministic component. This is the volatility of the stock—we called it σ.

The fact that the expected value of the stochastic component is zero is crucial. It means that the deviation of short-term returns from μ is just as likely to be positive as it is to be negative. In fact, given any range of "deviation of returns," say 0.50 to 1 percent, it is just as likely for a short-term return to fall in the 0.50 to 1 percent range as it is to fall in the range from -0.50 to -1.00 percent. In other words, the stochastic component is symmetric about zero, just as the random "jump" was symmetric about zero in our simple example above.

The upshot is the same as in our simple example. The effect of a positive return of x (e.g., $x = 0.15$, or 15 percent) does not quite balance out the effect of a negative return of x. Mathematically this is expressed in the equation $(1 + x)(1 - x) = 1 - x^2$.

For example, consider the case in which $x = 0.15$ and $1 - x^2 = 1 - 0.15^2 = 0.9775$. This means a positive return of 15 percent followed by a negative return of 15 percent results in a negative return of 2 1/4 percent.

Now, suppose $x = 0.50$. Then, a positive return of 50 percent followed by the negative return of 50 percent results in a return of -0.50^2, or minus 25 percent.

A Heuristic Argument

We can now give a heuristic argument explaining why the long-term returns of a stock following a geometric Brownian motion are proportional to the short-term returns depressed by $\sigma^2/2$. In other words, we can explain why the long-term expected returns are proportional to $\mu - \sigma^2/2$ and not μ.

If a positive return of X is followed by a negative return of the same magnitude, this depresses returns by X^2. We saw this as a consequence of the fact that $(1 - x)(1 + x) = 1 - x^2$. We already stated that the stochastic component of returns in geometric Brownian motion is normally distributed with mean zero and standard deviation σ. If X is a random variable representing the stochastic component of Brownian motion, then we have

$$Var[X] = E[X^2] - E[X]^2 = E[X^2].$$

On the other hand, $Var[X] = \sigma^2$, and since $E[X] = 0$, the above equation implies $E[X^2] = \sigma^2$.

But X^2 has another meaning for us. It is the amount returns are depressed when a positive return is followed by an equal but negative return. In other words, we have shown that the expected amount by which returns are depressed when there is a "positive return followed by an equal but negative return" is σ^2. Therefore, the *average* amount the stochastic component depresses returns in a single move is $\sigma^2/2$, because X^2 itself represents the result of two price moves. This result is exactly what the geometric Brownian motion model tells us.

A Technical Remark

The above result is ordinarily derived as a consequence of a mathematical tool known as Itô's lemma. The above argument shows, however, that this property of geometric Brownian motion is actually quite simple.

Example

Suppose a stock follows a geometric Brownian motion with

$\mu = 10\%$ per annum
$\sigma = 20\%$ per annum.

This means that over short periods of time, the average rate of return is proportional to μ times the amount of time, and the standard deviation is proportional to σ times the square root of the amount of time.

For example, if we observed the average one-day returns and the standard deviation of one-day returns, respectively, we would find that they are approximately $(1/365) \cdot 0.10$ and $(1/\sqrt{365}) \cdot 0.20$, respectively. On the other hand, the two-year returns would be normally distributed, with mean $2(0.10 - 0.20^2/2)$ and $\sqrt{2}(0.20)$; that is, the expected two-year return is 16 percent, with standard deviation 28.3 percent.

The model predicts that the four-year returns are normally distributed, with mean $4(0.10 - 0.20^2/2)$ and standard deviation $\sqrt{4}(0.20)$; that is, the expected four-year return is 32 percent, with standard deviation 40 percent.

Scaling in Geometric Brownian Motion, Part I

Conclusions one and two of the Brownian motion model (pages 98–99) are also known as the scaling property of stock price movements.

To understand what this means, note that if a stock has an instantaneous rate of return of 10 percent ($\mu = 10$ percent) and a volatility of 20 percent ($\sigma = 20$ percent), then in one year, the expected rate of return on the stock is 8 percent $(0.10 - 0.20^2/2)$, while in two years, the expected rate of return is $2 \cdot 8.00$ percent $= 16.00$ percent. That is, the model scales the expected rate of return *proportionally* to the amount of time that passes and calculates volatility proportionally to the *square root* of the amount of time that passes.

This is just another way of saying that knowledge of the probabilistic properties of the very short-term behavior of a stock gives equally valid knowledge of the statistical properties of its long-term behavior. Bear in mind, of course, that this is an assumption of the model, not a proven fact about stocks. This also leads to an interesting way of testing the Brownian motion model. We will discuss this briefly, along with other tests of the model, at the end of this chapter.

3.3   CALIBRATING THE MODEL

The geometric Brownian motion model is supposed to provide a useful tool for studying the stock market. In fact, it does, provided we understand the two parameters of the model: the expected return, μ, and the standard deviation, σ.

The conclusions of the model tell us how to do this. We calibrate the model by computing its parameters (μ and σ) over very short time intervals, such as one-day returns, and then using the conclusions of the model to infer information about the long-term returns and volatility.

This method, unfortunately, is suspicious, because it states that the mean and standard deviation of a stock are invariant parts of the stock price that do not change over time. Clearly this is not the case with the expected rate of return on the stock. As we know, it is extremely difficult to predict with any certainty what the mean return of a stock is. Fortunately, only the instantaneous standard deviation is important for the purposes of option pricing, and this is less difficult to predict. Nevertheless, this *constant volatility assumption* is highly suspect, and should be watched closely as we proceed.

The Steps in Computing Volatility

We now show explicitly how to compute the volatility of a stock from historical data. This is crucial for our study of the Black-Scholes formula, as we will need to know the volatility of a stock in order to use the formula.

The main idea is to do what we have been saying all along: compute the standard deviation of short-term returns. This can be done in the following steps.

1. Fix a standard time period Δt (e.g., one day, one week, etc.), and express it in terms of years. For example, if we are using closing prices, then Δt is equal to one day, which, expressed in years, is $1/365$.

2. Collect price data on the stock for each time period; for example, collect the daily closing prices for 10 straight weeks.

3. Compute the return from the beginning to the end of each period. If the closing price on day i is denoted S_i and the closing price at day $i + 1$ is denoted S_{i+1}, then the one-day return is given by the formula:

$$r_i = \log(S_{i+1}/S_i),$$

where r_i means "return number i." Note that this is the *daily* return on the stock, and we have not annualized it.

4. Compute the average value of the sample returns. If the sample returns are $r_0, r_1, \ldots, r_N$, so that there are a total of $N+1$ returns, then the average return is

$$\bar{r} = \frac{1}{N+1}(r_0 + r_1 + \cdots + r_N).$$

5. Compute the standard deviation using the formula

$$\sigma = \frac{1}{\sqrt{\Delta t}}\sqrt{\frac{1}{N}\left((r_0 - \bar{r})^2 + (r_1 - \bar{r})^2 + \cdots + (r_N - \bar{r})^2\right)}.$$

$$(3.3.1)$$

The reason we divide by $\sqrt{\Delta t}$ in the formula for σ is because the standard unit of time in options pricing is one year.[4] All measurements, such as interest rates and volatilities, are expressed in units of one year. The expression for σ ignoring the $\frac{1}{\sqrt{\Delta t}}$ is the standard deviation of returns for the actual time period studied.

On Computing the Standard Deviation

Note that in computing the mean squared differences in step 5, we divided by N and not $N + 1$ as expected. The reason for this comes from statistical analysis. We are not actually computing the standard deviation in step 5, we are only estimating it. To understand why this is the case, consider what would happen if we employed a different (but equally valid) method of collecting prices than the one above (e.g., opening prices instead of closing prices). There is no guarantee that we would end up with the same value of σ. In fact, we would probably obtain a different answer. Yet there is no way to say which choice (opening or closing prices) is better. From our point of view, both seem like equally good choices.

The only thing we can hope for is that the average over all possible choices of our standard deviation estimates is equal to the true standard deviation. In other words, there are an infinite number of ways to estimate the standard deviation, using opening and closing prices being only two. If we somehow computed the average over all methods, we would like the answer to be the real standard deviation. If this is the case, then the method of estimation is called *unbiased;* otherwise, it is called biased.

A simple statistical analysis shows that when estimating standard deviation, if we divide by $N + 1$ in equation (3.3.1) instead of N, what we have is a biased estimator. Where does the bias come from? The answer is $\bar{r}$.

The key thing to remember is that the way to estimate the standard deviation of a set of data is to pick $N + 1$ samples from the population and then compute the average mean-squared deviation from the mean of the data. But what if we do not know the mean of the population? Then we have to estimate the mean first.

This is the state of affairs that equation (3.3.1) represents: $\bar{r}$ is *not* the instantaneous return. Rather, it is an estimate of the mean return. The way to remove the bias introduced by $\bar{r}$ is as we have done in equation (3.3.1): We divide by N instead of $N + 1$.

---

[4]We divide by $\sqrt{\Delta t}$ instead of Δt because we are assuming that σ is the instantaneous volatility, and according to the Brownian motion model, $\sigma \sqrt{\Delta t}$ is the volatility for a period of time Δt.

T A B L E 3.3.1

Closing Prices for 20 Consecutive
Days of a Stock with $\mu = 8\%$
and $\sigma = 20\%$

Day	Price	Day	Price
1	50	11	48.78
2	50.79	12	48.33
3	49.78	13	47.97
4	49.12	14	48.83
5	48.67	15	47.82
6	48.94	16	46.62
7	48.69	17	46.93
8	49.14	18	46.02
9	49.30	19	45.95
10	48.68	20	46.11

Sample Computation of Volatility

Table 3.3.1 is a computer-generated list of closing prices for 20 days of a stock following a simulated Brownian motion with an instantaneous return of 8 percent *per annum* (i.e., $\mu = 8\%$) and a volatility of 20 percent (i.e., $\sigma = 20\%$). Table 3.3.2 computes the daily returns for the closing prices shown in Table 3.3.1. We use the above procedure to estimate the stock's volatility. Let's see how close our estimate comes to the true one.

The Five-Step Procedure

We now follow the five-step procedure.

1. Choosing Δt: Since we are looking at closing prices, Δt is equal to one day. What is this numerically? In our example, we will let one day equal 1/365. Note, however, since there are only approximately 250 trading days in a year, 250 is a possibly more realistic number in real simulations.

2. Collect prices. These are collected in Table 3.3.1.

3. Compute the one-day returns. These are computed in Table 3.3.2. For example, r_1, the return from day 1 to day 2, is given by:

$$\log(50.79/50) = 0.0157,$$

or, 1.57 percent. Notice that we now have 19 one-day returns.

T A B L E   3.3.2

Computation of One-Day Returns for Closing
Prices in Table 3.3.1

Day	Prices	Return	Day	Prices	Return
1	50 50.79	1.57%	11	48.78 48.33	−0.93%
2	50.79 49.78	−2.01	12	48.33 47.97	−0.75
3	49.78 49.12	−1.33	13	47.97 48.83	1.78
4	49.12 48.67	−0.92	14	48.83 47.82	−2.09
5	48.67 48.94	0.55	15	47.82 46.62	−2.54
6	48.94 48.69	−0.51	16	46.62 46.93	0.66
7	48.69 49.14	0.92	17	46.93 46.02	−1.96
8	49.14 49.30	0.33	18	46.02 45.95	−0.15
9	49.30 48.68	−1.27	19	45.95 46.11	0.35
10	48.68 48.78	0.21			

4. Compute the average of the sample returns. We do this by
   summing up the one-day returns in Table 3.3.2 and dividing
   that total by 19. This is equal to minus 0.43 percent; that is,

   $$\bar{r} = -0.0043.$$

5. Compute the standard deviation of the one-day returns using
   equation (3.3.1). We do this in two steps:

   Step 1: Compute the mean-squared differences $(\bar{r} - r_i)^2$ for each
   value of $i = 1, 2, \ldots, 20$. For example,

   $$(\bar{r} - r_1)^2 = (0.0043 - 0.0157)^2 = 0.001296.$$

   0.0004

Step 2: Sum all of the mean-squared differences and divide by 18. We divide by 18 because there are 19 one-day returns and, therefore, 19 mean-squared differences. Note: There are 20 closing prices, and therefore 19 one-day returns.

After completing the above steps, we arrive at our answer: $\sigma =$ 24.07. This is the estimate of the volatility based on the data. The actual volatility was 20 percent. Recall that the closing prices were generated from a perfect Brownian motion with 20 percent volatility, yet our computation gives a volatility of 23.47 percent. What happened?

The discrepancy arises for several reasons, the main one being that we are not really computing the *instantaneous* standard deviation of returns. Rather, we computed the standard deviation of daily returns. This discreteness in our computation introduces error into our estimation of the volatility, so that when compared with the real estimate, we are slightly off. Despite this, however, many independent tests would yield an "average estimated volatility" much closer to the real volatility of 20 percent (this follows since our estimator of volatility is *unbiased*).

A Numerical Example of Brownian Motion

We now give a numerical example of the geometric Brownian motion model. We are going to compare the "riskiness" of two stocks, S_1 and S_2, one with low volatility and one with high volatility.

We do this by examining the likelihood of the stocks' one-year returns being greater than a certain prescribed amount. For example, we might want to know the probability that the stock price will change in either direction by more than 10 percent (continuously compounded) in one year. That is, we want to know the probability of either a return of greater than 10 percent or less than minus 10 percent. The table below describes these probabilities.

In this table, both stocks have an expected return of 12 percent, but the left-hand stock (S_1) has 10 percent volatility, while the right-hand stock (S_2) has 25 percent volatility.

Volatility = 10%		Volatility = 25%	
Change	Probability	Change	Probability
2.50%	89.67%	2.50%	92.52%
5.00	79.16	5.00	85.11
10.00	57.54	10.00	70.72
20.00	19.85	20.00	45.22
50.00	0.01	50.00	5.93

Explanation: The probability that S_1 (the left-hand stock) will experience change of greater than 2.5 percent is 89.67 percent, while the probability of the same-sized change for S_2 is 92.52 percent. More striking is the same question for a 50 percent change. For S_1, this probability is 0.01 percent; this is almost negligible. For S_2, this probability is 5.93 percent, which is much more likely. The conclusion is clear: Since changes of any size are more likely with a 25 percent volatility stock than with a 10 percent volatility stock, we can regard the former as more risky than the latter. The formulas for making these computations are given on page 110, Display 3.3.1.

3.4   THE DISTRIBUTION OF STOCK PRICES

The geometric Brownian motion model concludes that stock returns are normally distributed. But what about stock prices? That is, how do the possible future prices of a stock distribute themselves?

We find the answer to this question in the relation between stock prices and stock returns. Recall that if a stock has price S_{t_0} today (where t_0 is today's date) and its price at time T is S_T, then the annualized return from t_0 to T is given by:

$$\frac{1}{T - t_0} \log(S_T/S_{t_0}).\tag{3.4.1}$$

Remember, S_T represents the *future* price of the stock and is therefore a random variable. On the other hand, S_{t_0} is the current price of the stock and is *not* a random variable. Using the basic properties of logarithms, the above expression is equal to

$$\frac{1}{T - t_0} \log S_T - \frac{1}{T - t_0} \log S_{t_0}.\tag{3.4.2}$$

Equation (3.4.2) represents, of course, the same random variable as equation (3.4.1). They are both random variables representing a future return on S. Let's suppose these returns have the data

$\mu = 10\%$
$\sigma = 15\%$.

That is, suppose the stock has an expected return of 10 percent, with a standard deviation of 15 percent. Let's write X for this random variable, so

D I S P L A Y 3.3.1

HOW TO COMPUTE THE PROBABILITY THAT RETURNS WILL HAVE AN ABSOLUTE VALUE GREATER THAN A FIXED PERCENT

Suppose we have a stock S following a geometric Brownian motion with short term returns μ and volatility σ. We want to know the probability of change of absolute value greater than $\alpha\%$ (continuously compounded) in the stock price over one year.

The geometric Brownian motion model says that returns are normally distributed with

$$\text{mean} = \mu - \sigma^2/2$$
$$\text{standard deviation} = \sigma$$

Let Y be a normally distributed random variable with mean $\mu - \sigma^2/2$ and standard deviation σ. We need to compute.

$$Pr(Y \le -\alpha) \quad \text{and} \quad Pr(Y \ge \alpha).$$

We know the variable X defined by

$$X = \frac{Y - (\mu - \sigma^2/2)}{\sigma}$$

is normally distributed, with mean 0 and standard deviation 1. We have

$$Pr(Y \le -\alpha) = Pr(\sigma X + \mu - \sigma^2/2 \le -\alpha).$$
$$Pr(Y \ge \alpha) = Pr(\sigma X + \mu - \sigma^2/2 \ge \alpha).$$

Therefore, $Pr(Y \le -\alpha) = Pr(X \le \frac{-\alpha - \mu + \sigma^2/2}{\sigma})$, and likewise $Pr(Y \ge \alpha) = Pr(X \ge \frac{\alpha - \mu + \sigma^2/2}{\sigma})$. But the right-hand sides of the above equations are

$$N\left(\frac{-\alpha - \mu + \sigma^2/2}{\sigma}\right) \quad \text{and} \quad N\left(-\frac{\alpha - \mu + \sigma^2/2}{\sigma}\right),$$

where $N(\cdot)$ is the cumulative normal distribution function. The probability of a change of absolute value greater than α is given by the sum of these probabilities and is equal to:

$$N\left(\frac{-\alpha - \mu + \sigma^2/2}{\sigma}\right) + N\left(-\frac{\alpha - \mu + \sigma^2/2}{\sigma}\right).$$

Returns and price distribution of a stock with 15 percent volatility and 10 percent returns

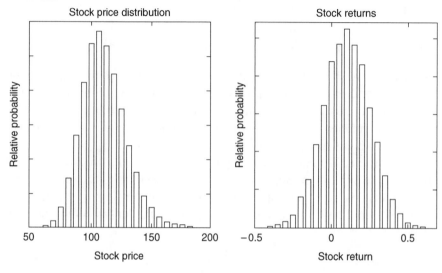

that we have

$$X = \frac{1}{T - t_0} \log S_T - \frac{1}{T - t_0} \log S_{t_0}.$$

Now, since $\frac{1}{T-t_0} \log S_{t_0}$ is a constant (i.e., *not* random), we can form the new random variable

$$X + \frac{1}{T - t_0} \log S_{t_0}.$$

This new variable is still normally distributed, but its mean is now the mean of X *plus* $\frac{1}{T-t_0} \log S_{t_0}$. Lastly, let's multiply the new variable by $\frac{1}{T-t_0}$, so that we have:

$$(T - t_0)X + \log S_{t_0} = \log S_T.$$

The left-hand side of this equation is a normally distributed random variable. Its mean is the mean of X times $(T - t_0)$ plus $\log S_{t_0}$. In particular, this says that the natural logarithm of the future stock price is normally distributed. Such a random variable is called *log-normal.*

This derivation proves that a stock following a geometric Brownian motion has future prices that are log-normally distributed. For this reason, some articles on options pricing refer to geometric Brownian motion as a *log-normal process.* Moreover, some authors will refer to the assumption that a stock follows a geometric Brownian motion as the *log-normal hypothesis.*

3.5 BROWNIAN MOTION AND CALL OPTIONS

As an illustration of the usefulness of the geometric Brownian motion model of stock price movements, we will compute the probability that a call option on a stock following the geometric Brownian motion model will expire in the money. This formula will be used in one of our derivations of the Black-Scholes formula, which is found in Chapter 5.

Suppose C is a European call option on S, a stock, struck at K, with time $T - t$ to expiration. Suppose also that the instantaneous expected rate of return on S is r and the standard deviation (volatility) is σ. Computing the probability that C expires in the money is equivalent to computing the probability that

$$S_T \geq K, \tag{3.5.1}$$

where S_T is the value of the stock at expiration.

To do this, we will apply two things we have already learned. First, we use the fact that the expected (mean) return on S from time t (current time) to time T (expiration date) is $(T - t)(r - \sigma^2/2)$.

Next, we use the transformation of a normally distributed random variable to a normally distributed random variable with mean 0 and standard deviation 1 to transform the random variable representing the return on S from time t to T to a random variable with mean 0 and standard deviation 1.

Let's begin. The return on S from time t to time T is given by

$$\log(S_T/S_t),$$

where S_t is the spot price of S at time t and, likewise, S_T is the spot price of S at time T. Note that S_T is a *random variable* representing the future, unknown price of S. Therefore, the return $\log(S_T/S_t)$ is also a random variable. This variable is normally distributed, with mean $(T - t)(r - \sigma^2/2)$ and standard deviation $\sigma \sqrt{T - t}$ (again, implied by the geometric Brownian motion model). Therefore, the random variable given by

$$\frac{\log(S_T/S_t) - (T - t)(r - \sigma^2/2)}{\sigma \sqrt{T - t}} \tag{3.5.2}$$

The Geometric Brownian Motion Model of Price Movements **113**

is normally distributed, with mean 0 and standard deviation 1. We know this because we simply subtracted the mean from $\log(S_T/S_t)$ and divided by the standard deviation.

To make use of these facts, we transform equation (3.5.1) so that the left-hand side is the same as the above equation. This leads to the new inequality,

$$\frac{\log(S_T/S_t) - (T - t)(r - \sigma^2/2)}{\sigma\sqrt{T - t}} \geq \frac{\log(K/S_t) - (T - t)(r - \sigma^2/2)}{\sigma\sqrt{T - t}}.$$

$$(3.5.3)$$

This equation was obtained a step at a time by first dividing both sides of equation (3.5.1) by S_t, taking logarithms, subtracting $(T - t)(r - \sigma^2/2)$, and finally, by dividing by $\sigma\sqrt{T - t}$.

Equation (3.5.3) is close to the equation we want. The left-hand side is normally distributed, with mean 0 and standard deviation 1. Thus, it describes the probability that a normally distributed random variable of mean 0 and standard deviation 1 is greater than or equal to the value of the right-hand side, which is:

$$\frac{\log(K/S_t) - (T - t)(r - \sigma^2/2)}{\sigma\sqrt{T - t}}.$$

Since our aim is to use the cumulative normal distribution function, we want an expression with a "less than or equal" in it (because the cumulative normal distribution function computes the probability of being less than a value). Therefore, we negate equation (3.5.3) and obtain:

$$\frac{\log(S_t/S_T) + (T - t)(r - \sigma^2/2)}{\sigma\sqrt{T - t}} \leq \frac{\log(S_t/K) + (T - t)(r - \sigma^2/2)}{\sigma\sqrt{T - t}}.$$

$$(3.5.4)$$

To complete the derivation, it is enough to note that the left-hand side of the above equation is a normally distributed random variable with mean 0 and standard deviation 1. Why? Because it is the negative of equation (3.5.2), which is also a normally distributed random variable with mean 0 and standard deviation 1. With this said, equation (3.5.4) means that for the original statement to be true (i.e., $S_T \geq K$) then the random variable on the left-hand side of equation (3.5.4) must be less than or equal to the value on the right-hand side.

The probability the inequality holds true is exactly given by the cumulative normal distribution function of the right-hand side. We conclude:

D I S P L A Y   3.5.1

THE PROBABILITY A CALL OPTION WILL EXPIRE IN THE MONEY

Let S be a stock, and C a call option, with the following data:

$$t = \text{current time}$$
$$T = \text{expiration date of } C$$
$$K = \text{strike price of } C$$
$$S_t = \text{current price of } S$$
$$S_T = \text{terminal price of } S$$
$$r = \text{instantaneous rate of return of } S$$
$$\sigma = \text{standard deviation of returns of } S$$

The probability that C will expire in the money is

$$N\left(\frac{\log(S_T/K) + (T-t)(r - \sigma^2/2)}{\sigma\sqrt{T-t}}\right)$$

$$Pr(S_T \geq K) = N\left(\frac{\log(S_t/K) + (T-t)(r - \sigma^2/2)}{\sigma\sqrt{T-t}}\right). \qquad (3.5.5)$$

This is summarized in Display 3.5.1.

A Different Formulation

An equivalent expression for equation (3.5.5) is

$$Pr(S_T \geq K) = N\left(\frac{\log(e^{r(T-t)}S_t/K) - (T-t)\sigma^2/2}{\sigma\sqrt{T-t}}\right). \qquad (3.5.6)$$

The expression is obtained by a straightforward manipulation of the numerator of equation (3.5.5). First we note that

$$(T-t)r = \log e^{(T-t)r}.$$

Then, we note

$$(T-t)(r - \sigma^2/2) = (T-t)r - (T-t)\sigma^2/2$$
$$= \log e^{(T-t)r} - (T-t)\sigma^2/2.$$

Finally, we obtain:

$$\frac{\log(S_t/K) + (T - t)(r - \sigma^2/2)}{\sigma \sqrt{T - t}} = \frac{\log(S_t/K) + (T - t)r - (T - t)\sigma^2/2}{\sigma \sqrt{T - t}}$$

$$= \frac{\log(e^{r(T-t)}S_t/K) - (T - t)\sigma^2/2}{\sigma \sqrt{T - t}}.$$

3.6 GEOMETRIC BROWNIAN MOTION: FACT OR FICTION?

Geometric Brownian motion is central to the Black-Scholes option pricing formula and is therefore at the center of modern option pricing. In this section, we briefly examine some of the empirical evidence *against* the model. We do so because such a critically important element of a model should not be used without careful scrutiny. There are several ways to test how closely Brownian motion models reality.

The nature of the tests we mention here focus on stock returns. That is, the tests examine directly whether the data fits the hypothesis by looking at market returns over various periods of time. Later we shall see (in Chapter 8) that another way of attacking the problem is equally important and provides cogent evidence against the model. We will look at the implications of the model for options markets themselves and demonstrate inconsistencies with observed market behavior.

The exposition below follows Peters (1991).

The Distribution of Returns Hypothesis

The geometric Brownian motion model makes two conclusions about stock price movements. First, it says returns are normally distributed. What does the data say?

Studies of stock market returns reveal an important fact: Large movements in stock prices are more likely than a normally distributed stock price model predicts. Put another way, the geometric Brownian motion model predicts that large price swings are much *less likely* than is actually the case.

Statistically speaking, stock returns exhibit what is known as *leptokurtosis:* The likelihood of returns near the mean and of large returns is greater than geometric Brownian motion predicts, while other returns tend to be less likely.

Turner and Weigel (1990 and 1992) examine returns on the S&P 500 from 1928 through 1990 and find, according to Peters (1991), that the occurrence of downward jumps three standard deviations from the mean is three times more likely than a normal distribution would predict. This means that if we used the geometric Brownian motion to compute the historical volatility of the S&P 500, we would find that the normal theory quite seriously underestimates the likelihood of large downward jumps.

Jackwerth and Rubinstein (1995) observe that in the geometric Brownian motion model (what they refer to as the log-normal hypothesis), the crash of 1987 is an impossibly unlikely event:

> Take for example the stock market crash of 1987. Following the standard paradigm, assume that stock market returns are log-normally distributed with an annualized volatility of 20% . . . On October 19, 1987, the two-month S&P 500 futures price fell 29%. Under the lognormal hypothesis, this is [has a probability of] 10^{-160}. Even if one were to have lived through the 20 billion year life of the universe and experience this 20 billion times . . . , that such a decline could have happened even once in this period is virtually impossible.[5]

Other studies examining stock returns can be found in Fama (1965a) and Friedman and Laibson (1989).

Scaling in Brownian Motion, Part II
We alluded earlier to another way of testing the geometric Brownian motion model. If this model holds, then stock returns should be proportional to elapsed time and standard deviation of returns should be proportional to the square root of elapsed time. This is a basic conclusion of the model and is called the *scaling property* of Brownian motion.

A study of this conclusion is taken up by Turner and Weigel (1990) and Peters (1991). Turner and Weigel find that monthly and quarterly volatilities are higher than annual volatility and, conversely, that daily volatilities are lower than annual volatilities. That is, this research suggests that stock returns do not scale as they are supposed to.

---

[5] From "Recovering Probability Distributions from Contemporaneous Security Prices," Jackwerth and Rubinstein (1995).

COMMENTS AND SUGGESTED READING

The application of the geometric Brownian motion model to stock price movements was introduced in Osborne (1959). An idea similar to geometric Brownian motion was introduced in Bachelier (1900), but this work was largely ignored, and Osborne rediscovered the idea independently.

> Believing that he was exploring uncharted territory [in Osborne (1959)] he includes only two references to other works.... Despite his attention to Brownian motion, he had never heard of Bachelier....[6]

For more on Bachelier, see Cootner (1964), Merton (1995), and Sullivan and Weithers (1994). For more on Osborne, see Bernstein (1992).

An excellent and elementary mathematical treatment of the Brownian motion model involving calculus can be found in Hull (1992) or Chance (1994). A more advanced treatment may be found in Merton (1990).

Implicit in the geometric Brownian motion model is the concept that prices follow a "random walk." That is, future price movements are determined by present conditions alone and are independent of past movements. This hypothesis is under continuous and intense scrutiny. For a lively and entertaining discussion of this theory, see Malkiel (1985). For a basic discussion of this theory, including evidence that the stock returns are not normally distributed, see Peters (1991) and Brealey (1983).

The presentation here on computing volatility is standard and can be found in almost all texts. A more detailed account can be found in Figlewski, Silber, and Subrahmanyam (1990). A basic exposition on estimating volatility may also be found in Clark (1994) or Leong (1993). Besides the simple method for calculating volatility discussed here, there is also the so-called GARCH method. An overview of the GARCH method may be found in Engle (1993).

There are many more studies of volatility than we can refer to here. See the references within each article for additional sources. For a study of S&P 500 volatility, see Harris (1989). For an analysis of market volatility, see Jones and Wilson (1989). For a study on the nature of stock market volatility, see Merville and Pieptea (1989).

---

[6]From Bernstein (1992), pp. 103–104.

4

⑥ THE BLACK-SCHOLES FORMULA

This chapter is devoted to studying the Black-Scholes options pricing formula for European put and call options. We will explain not just what the terms of the formula mean but also how and why the formula works. The basic principle behind the formula is explained nicely by Fischer Black himself.

> Suppose there is a formula that tells how the value of a [European] call option depends on the price of the underlying stock, the volatility of the stock, the exercise price and maturity, and the interest rate.
>
> Such a formula will tell us ... how much the option value will change when the stock price changes by a small amount within a short time. Suppose that the option goes up about $0.50 when the stock goes up $1.00, and down about $0.50 when the stock goes down $1.00. Then you can create a hedged position by going short two option contracts and long one round lot of stock.
>
> Such a position will be close to riskless. For small moves in the stock in the short run, your losses on one side will be mostly offset by gains on the other side. ...
>
> As the hedged position will be close to riskless, it should return an amount equal to the short-term interest rate on close-to-riskless securities. This one principle gives us the option formula.[1]

This principle gives the writer of the option a method of perfectly hedging the risk of covering the option on the expiration date. This *hedging strategy*

---

[1] From "How We Came Up with the Option Formula," Black (1989).

arises from studying the Black-Scholes formula and we will discuss it in detail later. Thus, the Black-Scholes formula has two components: an option and a strategy to hedge the option.

We find the relationship between the option and the hedging strategy in the total cost of hedging, and this is what makes the Black-Scholes formula so remarkable:

The total cost of hedging an option is known before hedging begins.

That is, the cost of setting up the hedged position, plus any additional costs incurred in maintaining it, can be computed ahead of time. Therefore, the Black-Scholes formula turns the seemingly risky venture of writing an option into a (cost-wise) predictable affair.

It should be emphasized that the rather clean picture painted above is too simple to carry out in the real world of options trading. It would be possible, however, if *all* the assumptions that go into the formula were correct. Theory, unfortunately, is a far cry from reality. Nevertheless, the Black-Scholes way of thinking about options pricing is still the best way known to understand it, and the values derived by the formulas are still important theoretical "benchmarks" for understanding what goes into the value of a call or put. Moreover, the ideas of options pricing laid down in Black-Scholes lead to new insights into better ways to value options. These insights will be discussed in Chapter 8, once the formula is thoroughly understood.

Before beginning a serious study of Black-Scholes, it is extremely important that one has a basic grasp of the two main principles behind pricing options. First, and most important, is the idea of a *self-financing replicating hedging strategy*. Second, is the fact that the value of an option does not depend on the expected value of the underlying stock. Instead, the key characteristic of the underlying stock that concerns us is its volatility. This fact is surprising, if not counterintuitive, because the extent of the payout on an option depends on the extent to which the stock price rises (in the case of a call) or falls (in the case of a put). We begin with a discussion of self-financing, replicating hedging strategies.

4.1 SELF-FINANCING, REPLICATING HEDGING STRATEGIES

The principles behind theoretical option pricing are surprisingly simple and can, for the most part, be explained by means of a simple example, which serves as an analogy for writing and hedging options.

Leave a trail of genius.

Marriott.
HOTELS & RESORT

Visit Marriott.com and book your next stay.

In the following example, there are two parties, the casino and the gambler. The casino offers a simple game to any and all gamblers: The gambler pays a fee to play the game. This consists of making a bet on three flips of a coin (in fact, any number of flips would be fine, but for the purposes of this example, we choose three). The coin is flipped successively three times. If it lands heads three times, then $1 is paid out to each gambler who has made a bet. On the other hand, if any of the flips lands tails, then all gamblers lose their bets and the game is over.

The question is, from the casino's point of view, what is the fair value of the bet? Since the casino wishes to offer the bet to all comers and its ultimate aim is to turn a profit, it should know its operating costs, or the average costs it will incur in offering the bet ahead of time. This is found in the fair value.

Once the casino has determined the fair value ("operating costs") of the bet, it can decide on a mark-up that delivers their desired level of profit.

The Fair Value of the Bet

There are eight possible outcomes to this three-flip game:

$$HHH, HHT, HTH, HTT, TTT, TTH, THT, THH.$$

Here, HHH means *heads, heads, heads;* THH means *tails, heads, heads*; and so forth. Each combination of tails and heads is equally likely, and only in the case of HHH does the casino pay anything, because in every other combination there is at least one tails. Therefore, there is a one-in-eight chance of having to pay $1 and a seven-in-eight chance of having to pay nothing. Thus, since the payout is $1, we deduce the correct premium to charge is $0.125, or 12 1/2 cents.

Notice that we have just "priced" the bet for the casino. In other words, given the input data describing all possible scenarios, we came up with a fair value of the bet.

We did this in two steps. First, we computed the probability the casino would have to make a payout, and then we multiplied this probability by the value of the payout (that is, the probability of making a payout is one-in-eight, and the size of the payout is $1). Intuitively, this is the "correct" fair value of the bet, but what drives this intuition? Here is one possible answer.

We assume if the casino plays this game enough, then on average, they will make a payout (one dollar) one in eight times, while collecting a premium every time. Now, if we assume that each premium is $0.125, then the premiums collected should cover all the payouts.

Of course, the casino does not actually make a payout every eighth play of the game. Rather, we can expect that if we tally up the number of games played and the number of payouts made in the long run, the ratio of games to payouts will be approximately one in eight. The casino could, however, have long streaks where it never has to make payouts or, perhaps, even longer streaks where it makes payouts frequently. The laws of probability do not exclude these things from happening. As a consequence, the casino must have enough cash available to cover its unlucky streaks. If they do, then our pricing methodology works perfectly. If not, another method has to be sought.

For example, consider what happens if a high-stakes gambler arrives at the casino and wants to play the game, but he requests a $100,000 payout. The gambler knows the odds and is willing to pay the premium of $12,500 (one-eighth of $100,000) for a chance at a $100,000 payout. If the casino makes three flips of the coin and they all land heads side up, he will receive $100,000; otherwise, he walks away $12,500 poorer. The casino checks its cash reserves and realizes it cannot cover the bet; if the three flips in the game all land heads, the casino will be out of luck and out of business. Thus, though they want to please every customer by offering any payouts requested, they cannot please this one because they just cannot afford to take the risk.

Luckily, the casino comes up with an idea that allows the gambler to have his bet and the casino to cover the risk without going bankrupt. The casino realizes that any time there is a flip of a coin, it can make a bet on that flip (that is, it can bet whether it lands heads or tails) for any amount of money and receive the fair value of the bet—a $1 bet has a payoff of $2, $100 has a payoff of $200, etc. The casino can make these bets in one of two ways: It can offer bets on heads (instead of tails) to other gamblers, or can take bets with a "bet broker."

Suppose, for example, the casino wants to bet $500 on heads, that is, it wants to wager $500 that the flip will turn up heads on the next bet. The casino then contacts a bet broker and pays the broker $500 for a chance to win $1,000 on the next bet. If the coin does land heads, the broker will pay the manager $1,000. Otherwise, the casino loses its $500 "premium."

More on Hedging

Returning to the issue of hedging the risk of the $100,000 bet, the casino knows it must somehow have $100,000 ready to pay the gambler if all three flips of the coin land heads. On the other hand, if any one of the three flips lands tails, it doesn't need anything. The casino handles this by contacting a bet broker and betting $12,500 that the first flip of the three-flip game will land heads. This is the manager's initial bet. Note two things: 1) The casino has already received $12,500 from the gambler and, therefore, does not need to wager its own money with the bet broker. Rather, it is simply passing the gambler's money along; and 2) If the first flip lands heads, the casino doubles its money.

As it turns out, the first flip lands heads. This has two consequences: First, the casino wins $12,500 from its bet with the broker, so that the winnings plus the initial premium total to $25,000. Next, the manager places a $25,000 bet on the second flip of the coin, again on heads.

The second flip lands heads, which means there is only one flip standing in the way of a $100,000 payout. Does this worry the casino? No, because it just won $25,000 from the last flip, bringing its total capital (from the bets) to $50,000. Now the casino uses this to bet $50,000 that the last flip will be heads. Now it's in a no-lose situation.

If the last flip comes up heads again, the casino doubles its $50,000 to $100,000—exactly the payout it needs to cover the bet. On the other hand, if the flip is tails, this is not a tragedy, because the high-stakes gambler is entitled to nothing, and the entire sequence of bets was financed by the original $12,500 premium. We conclude that the casino is "fully hedged."

So, in fact, it barely matters to the casino whether the high-stakes gambler wins or loses. In fact, it is inclined to hope he wins—it's good for business to have a few big winners. In any case, the casino does not have to take any position as to the outcome of the three flips. In all cases, the casino's risks are the same.

The procedure followed by the manager is what is known as a *hedging strategy,* and the one above is of a special sort. It has the following two important properties:

1. The strategy is *self-financing.* That is, the first step is financed by the premium, and each successive step is financed by the previous step. For example, the manager used the $12,500 premium to place a bet that the first flip would land heads. After winning the first bet, he then bet $25,000 that the second flip would be heads. The second bet was financed by the winnings from the first bet (which were, in turn, financed by the premium).

2. The strategy is *replicating.* That is, the manager was covered, in every scenario, against the risks inherent in offering the bet. Put another way, there are two relevant outcomes to the game: the coin lands heads three times, and the coin lands tails at least

once. In the former case, the casino owes the gambler $100,000; in the latter, the casino owes nothing. In both cases, the strategy returns exactly the right amount of money. If the coin lands heads three times, the strategy returns $100,000; otherwise, it returns nothing.

What This Has to Do with Option Pricing

The above example contains many of the aspects of full-fledged option pricing theory. First of all, a European option can be viewed as a bet on the future price of the underlying. Depending on what the price of the underlying is on the expiration date, a payout must be made according to the terms of the option. In addition, there are two sides to every option: the short position, analogous to the position of the casino (which sold the bets and was therefore short), and the long position, analogous to the gambler's position (who bought the bet and was therefore long).

Thinking about option pricing from the point of view of the short position, only one thing matters at expiration: being able to cover the payout.

If the option expires in the money, then the short portion is obligated to make a payout, while if it is out of the money, nothing is required. With the coin-tossing game, we showed that if enough assumptions were met about the "coin tossing world" (e.g., the existence of the bet broker who takes all bets, etc.), then the risk associated with the bet could be completely hedged away. This hedging was accomplished by means of a bet broker who would take all bets, thus widely distributing the risk concentrated in the casino through a variety of smaller bets.

One can imagine that the broker sells individual bets to all takers. That is, the casino makes a $12,500 bet on heads with the broker, and therefore the broker has to take the opposite position 12,500 times: He has to make 12,500 individual $1 bets on tails.

If there is a liquid market for these bets, then the broker can sell them individually, or in small lots. It is therefore the gambler and the marketplace who assumed the risk in the coin-tossing game. The broker acted as an intermediary, distributing the risk the manager did not want to take himself to a liquid market, which is eager to participate in the gambling.

The Analogy with Options Markets

What is the analogy with options markets? First, the gambler is analogous to the long-position holder of an options contract. He or she is betting that after three flips, a particular outcome will occur and that there will be a particular payout if it does. Similarly, the long-position holder of an option believes the price of the underlying will rise above the strike price, resulting in a payout.

What is the role of the casino in all of this? The casino acts as a trader who is short the option. It assumes the risk of making the payout if the "particular outcome" (e.g., three heads) does happen. The short-position holder (the trader) also assumes the same sort of risk: If the option expires in the money (if the underlying price is greater than the strike price), a payout must be made.

What about the bet broker? The bet broker assumes the role of a "market maker." Remember his role: The casino wanted to bet on heads (take a long position in the underlying), so it went to the broker. The broker "bought" these bets by agreeing to pay $12,500, $25,000, and $50,000 respectively for each bet on heads if the next flip lands heads. This broker does not actually want to take a position in heads or tails. Therefore, he simply finds parties (gamblers) willing to take the opposite side of the bet. That is, he "sells" these bets to gamblers willing to pay $1 if the coin lands tails.

As one can already see, we have produced a theoretical model that concludes that one can hedge away all the risk in the coin-tossing game for a premium of $12,500. Hedging is accomplished by means of a dynamic strategy that involves placing a "side bet" on heads and continuing to bet on heads as the game proceeds. If this strategy is carried out, and all the various assumptions are met, then all the risk is washed away. Of course the gap between theory and reality always lies in whether the assumptions are actually met.

Next, we examine exactly what assumptions went into the hedging strategy and then ask 1) to what extent these assumptions hold up, and 2) what the impact of relaxing these assumptions is on the hedging strategy?

Assumptions in the Coin-Tossing Game

First, the casino has to be able to play both sides of the bet. In covering the three-flip game, it is essentially "short" an option on flips. That is, the casino is on the side of taking the wager and therefore must be "long" flips (purchasing bets) in order to cover itself. Moreover, in order for the hedging strategy to work, the casino must be able to make wagers of $12,500, $25,000, and $50,000. In addition, the casino must be able to make bets of arbitrary sizes to cover bets with different payouts.

The "market" for bets provides the casino with an easy way to make bets as it needs them. We assumed, naturally, that there were always takers of these bets when the casino needed them (a liquidity assumption) and also that these bets were available at their fair market value. That is, if the casino makes a bet on heads for $200, then it expects a $400 payoff. This is a liquidity assumption as well as a *market impact assumption*. In essence, we are assuming that no matter how large a bet the casino wants, it can find takers at the fair market value. That is, we are assuming that large bets do not have any impact on the price of bets.

Next, let's examine why the hedging strategy is self-financing. It's self-financing in part because each time the casino wins a bet, it can immediately use the proceeds for the next bet. This is a "full use of proceeds" assumption. Without this assumption, for example, if there is some delay between winning a bet and being able to use the proceeds, then the question is, will the strategy still be self-financing.

What Happens If the Assumptions Fail?

Now, what if we relax some of our assumptions? Obviously, the hedging strategy will then fail to work perfectly. For example, if when the manager, in order to hedge, places a $12,500 bet on heads, the bet broker only offers a $24,000 payout, then the hedging strategy will fail to produce the $100,000 payout at the end of three flips, and the casino will not be fully hedged.

Generally speaking, there are two reasons we are not able to obtain the bets at their fair market value. First, there is the bid-ask spread. A broker buys bets and then sells them to the public. If the casino wants a $500 bet on heads, then the broker sells 500 $1 bets. In order to make a profit, however, he needs to buy the bets at a different price than the price at which he sells them. This is the bid-ask spread, and one can see that it does impact the price of the betting game (and in option pricing, the price of the option). Of course we could try to build a more sophisticated model to account for the spread, and this is exactly what we would have to do. For now, let's examine more assumptions.

Next, there is liquidity. For a variety of reasons, the market may not provide the necessary bets at a reasonable price. For example, the casino might not be able to find a $12,500 bet on heads at a reasonable price simply due to a lack of interested parties on the other side of the bet. In this instance, it has to either pay a great deal more than market value in order to lure potential bettors to bet against heads, or it has to play the three-flip game "naked," or unhedged. In either case, this liquidity issue cannot be ignored.

This concludes the introduction to option pricing. We now move on to the nuts and bolts of our study, beginning with the expected rate of return on a stock.

4.2   THE EXPECTED RATE OF RETURN ON A STOCK

The expected rate of return of an asset is both an intuitive quantity and a precise mathematical concept. Intuitively, the expected rate of return on a stock is what one believes the rate of return will be over a period of time. The expected rate, however, is only approximate, and there is risk involved. The risk is a measure of the degree of deviation from the rate of return that one expects. For example, a bank deposit has an expected rate of return equal to the interest it bears, and there is almost no risk.

Mathematically, expected return is defined as the expected value of the distribution (in the sense of probability theory) of returns on the stock. For example, if we believe the geometric Brownian motion model of price movements, then stock returns are normally distributed and the expected rate of return is equal to the mean of this distribution.

Expected Return and Forward Contracts

What is the relation between the expected rate of return on a stock and its forward price? Suppose we want to buy XYZ today for delivery one year from now and no dividends will be paid on XYZ during this time. What does the expected return on XYZ have to do with the value of this contract?

As we saw in Chapter 1, the forward price is equal to $e^{r(T-t)}S_0$, where S_0 is the current price, $T - t$ is the time until delivery, and r is the risk-free rate of interest. What this means is we can (in theory) lock in the future price of an asset today without knowing anything about the asset's expected return. All that matters is spot price, the risk-free rate of interest, and the time until delivery. Thus, in a sense, from the point of view of forward contracts, the expected value of the stock is equal to $e^{r(T-t)}S_0$.

Call Options

Consider a call option on some underlying versus a forward contract on the same underlying. The only difference between being long a call and long a forward contract is that in the case of the forward, the holder of the long position must buy the underlying regardless of the spot price on the delivery date.

In the case of the European call option, the long position will only exercise (purchase the underlying) if the option is in the money at expiration. This means that the long-call position will benefit from large upward movements in the price of the underlying but will not be penalized by large downward swings. Contrast this situation with the forward contract: Large upward swings benefit the long position, but large downward swings hurt it because, at delivery, the owner of the long forward position must then purchase the underlying at a price well above the current market value.

So, while forward contracts and call options are similar, they differ in the way volatility affects the value of the instrument. Intuitively, a forward contract's value is *not* affected by volatility because large upward swings enhance value, while large downward movements hurt value. On the other hand, a call option's value is enhanced by an increase in volatility due to the asymmetric effect it has on value upon exercise.

One of the great insights we derive from the Black-Scholes formula is that the value of an option depends on the volatility of the underlying but not on its expected return. That is, of the two key statistical aspects of stock prices (expected return and volatility), only volatility matters. This concept is called "risk-neutrality" and will be explained in greater detail in Chapter 5.

4.3 HEDGING

Any time you defray the risk of some investment by making another off-setting investment, you are *hedging* your risk. As with all investment strategies, there is a trade-off between risk and reward. In general, when you lower the risk of an investment, you do so at the expense of reward.

Setting up a hedge against the risk of an investment usually incurs some cost. Hedging is an investment, and the "return" on this investment is measured in part by how much the risk is lowered.

Suppose that you could construct a perfect hedge against the risk associated with an option. What would this mean? If you are *writing* a call option, you are exposed to the risk of the stock price rising above the strike price because you are obligated to deliver the stock at the strike price at expiration. In order to cover the call, you need, at expiration, cash equal to the difference between the prevailing market price of the stock and the strike price of the option—provided the former is greater than the latter.

To hedge against this risk, you want a counter-investment that pays you, at expiration, enough to cover the option you have written. Usually, this counter-investment is simpler in nature than the option itself. In Black-Scholes, we will see the hedge is a portfolio consisting of shares of the underlying stock and some riskless zero-coupon bonds. How much of each to put in the hedge is the key to determining the option's value.

A perfect hedge always pays exactly the amount necessary to cover the option and no more. The reason you don't want more is that you pay a premium for unnecessary extra coverage. For instance, one could cover the call completely by purchasing all the stock necessary to cover the option if it is exercised.

Though this strategy protects the writer from the risk of the option expiring in the money, it leaves the writer completely exposed if the option expires out of the money. In the latter case, the writer of the option is left holding an asset whose price may have dropped since purchase, and whose price ultimately did not exceed the strike price.

In a perfect hedge, the hedging instrument will behave exactly the same as the option itself. That is, if the option expires in the money, the hedge will be worth the amount necessary to cover the call. If the option expires out of the money, the hedge will be worth nothing. This is called *payoff replication,* and it is the cornerstone of the Black-Scholes option pricing formula.

Consider the key example of a European call. To hedge a European call option perfectly, one wants an instrument that pays exactly the value of the underlying stock or index minus the strike price at expiration *if* the option is in the money and that pays zero otherwise.

At this point, the question is, how does one create such a hedge? The answer is through a process known as *dynamic hedging*.

4.4 DYNAMIC HEDGING

Dynamic hedging is *the* most important concept in understanding the Black-Scholes methodology. It refers to a trading strategy carried out by maintaining, throughout the life of the option. The strategy has two key properties. 1) It replicates the payoff of the option, and 2) It has a fixed and known total cost. As a theory, dynamic hedging is a perfect way to understand options pricing, and it is therefore important for explaining what goes into an option's value.

Dynamic hedging is a process for managing the risk of options. The hedger maintains a counter-investment portfolio consisting of the underlying stock and a bond, one short and one long. For short-call options, the stock is held long and the bond is short; for short-put options, the opposite is true.

The hedging portfolio's value at any given time will always be equal to the value of the put or call option at that time. For example, in the case of a call option, at expiration the portfolio will be worth $S - K$ if the option expires in the money and nothing otherwise. Here, S is the value of the underlying (at expiration) and K is the strike price.

The amount of the bond and stock to hold in the portfolio is determined by the Black-Scholes formula, which takes as its inputs the current stock price, the strike price, the stock volatility, the risk-free rate of interest, and the time until expiration of the option. The portfolio obtained by this formula is called a *weighted portfolio* because the stock and bond are not held in equal proportions. The amount of stocks and bonds held are called the weights of the portfolio, and these weights are the main ingredients in the Black-Scholes formula.

Since Black-Scholes hedging is determined by the weights of the hedging portfolio and the formula depends on constantly changing parameters, the weights themselves are constantly changing. This means that the hedging portfolio, so defined, must be constantly updated in order to reflect the current outputs of Black-Scholes. For this reason, the portfolio is called a *dynamic* portfolio. A portfolio that does not conform to the current Black-Scholes weights is *out of balance*. The process of keeping the portfolio in balance is called *rebalancing*.

If the hedging strategy is performed correctly, that is, if it is kept in balance at all times, it has one important feature. The value of the portfolio will be equal to the value of the option at all times. In other words, Black-Scholes hedging strategy produces a *synthetic* version of the option. We'll see soon that this is a key fact.

Self-Financing Dynamic Hedging
The Black-Scholes hedging strategy requires the hedger of a short call to purchase a certain number of shares of the underlying stock and a certain amount of a riskless bond and then maintain this hedge according to a formula that changes over time. Later we will study these formulas in detail; right now we simply want to understand the different sorts of costs associated with hedging. There are two costs associated with this sort of hedging strategy: 1) set-up costs, the initial cash flows associated with buying the stocks and bonds, and 2) maintenance costs, the costs associated with re-balancing the hedge.

In addition, maintenance costs can be broken down into two types. First, there are *infusion of funds costs*. Since the hedging strategy generally requires shifting the relative amount of stocks and bonds in the portfolio, there may be a shift in value of the portfolio. This either requires an infusion of cash or releases cash from the hedge—an *infusion of funds cost*. The second kind of maintenance costs are *transaction costs*. These are the "real-world" fees and taxes associated with making the transactions, such as costs resulting from the bid-ask spread and the inability to execute trades at exactly the price specified by the strategy. In the theoretical study of option pricing, transaction costs are generally ignored, though it is impossible to ignore such costs in actual trading, despite the difficulty of properly estimating them.

A hedging strategy whose total to-date cost at any time (excluding transaction costs) is equal to set-up costs is called *self-financing*. In the beginning of this chapter, we gave a simple example of a self-financing hedging strategy with the coin-tossing game. In that example, any outcome (heads or tails) provided enough cash for the next transaction, while never providing more cash than necessary, that is, there were no infusion of funds costs. Dynamic hedging works on the same principle, but it is a bit more complex.

To better grasp the concept, let's begin by looking at an example of a portfolio that is *not* self-financing. Suppose we are hedging some option and have a strategy that requires us to buy 50 shares of a stock S at $20 per share and short a riskless bond for $700. The total cost of buying the stock and selling the bonds, $300, is called the *set-up* cost of the hedge.

The hedging portfolio is a weighted portfolio with 50 shares of S long and $700 of the bond short. The cash flows associated with purchasing the portfolio are as follows:

	Stock	Bond	Total
Set-up costs	−$1,000	$700	−$300

Setting possible transaction costs aside, the cost of initiating this hedge is $300. Now suppose the price of XYZ goes up to $22 per share and the hedging strategy requires buying four more shares of the stock (total cost = $88) and selling $60 worth of the bond (for now we will ignore where the hedging strategy comes from):

	Stock	Bond	Total
Amount	+4 shares	−$60	—
Costs	−$88	$60	−$28

To rebalance the portfolio, we must buy the four shares of stock and sell the bond, adding $28 to the value of the hedge. This is summarized as follows:

	Stock	Bond	Total
Set-up costs	−$1,000	$700	−$300
Rebalancing costs	−$88	$60	−$28
Total cost to date			−$328

Therefore this hedging strategy is not self-financing as it required a $28 infusion of funds.

In other situations, rebalancing can yield cash. For instance, if in the above scenario, rebalancing only required two shares of stock to be purchased, then the cost of the stock would have only been $44, and thus $16 cash would have been realized in this transaction. Despite the fact it yields cash, this is still called an infusion of funds cost.

In hedging, one ideally wants a situation, as in the coin-tossing example, where no funds are added or taken away from the hedge. This is the purpose of a self-financing hedging strategy.

Creating self-financing hedges for options relies on detailed knowledge of how sensitive the value of the option is with respect to the price of the underlying. This sensitivity is called the delta of the option, and its importance cannot be overestimated.

4.5   THE DELTA OF AN OPTION

The delta of an option is the rate of change of the option's value with respect to the underlying's price. This tells us the relative amount the option's value will change when the underlying's price changes. Roughly, if we know the delta, then we can predict how much the option's value will change when the underlying's price changes by a certain amount. This is the key to setting up a self-financing hedge for an option.

Option Value and the Underlying

An option's fair value depends on a number of factors, but most obviously, it depends on the price of the underlying. When the price of the underlying changes, the value of the option can be expected to change as well. We can measure this change in several ways. We can measure absolute change; that is, we can measure how much in dollars the price changes (e.g., if the price of a stock moves $1, then its absolute price change is also $1). We can also look at relative change.

When we look at changes in the value of an option, we are not interested in absolute changes but, rather, in changes relative to the underlying stock price. What we really want to know is the strength of the link between changes in the underlying's price and changes in the option's value. If the underlying price changes $1, what will the corresponding change in the option's value be?

At one extreme, let's examine a European call option which is deep in the money and near expiration. In that case, the option will almost surely expire in the money and yield a payout of $S - K$, where K is the strike price and S is the price of the underlying at expiration. Since the payout will be $S - K$, we can see that every dollar the spot price rises will be a dollar more paid out at expiration. Likewise, every dollar the spot price drops will be one dollar less paid upon exercise. Thus, there is a dollar-for-dollar relationship between movements of the spot price and movements of the option's value. In this case, the delta of the option is very close to one. In fact, the delta is not exactly one because of the small probability that the spot price will fall below the strike at expiration.

At the other extreme, consider a European call option that is deep out of the money and near expiration. In this case, the option will almost surely expire worthless; therefore, the current value of the option will be worth almost nothing. This means except for very highly unlikely large upward movements in the spot price, price shifts in the underlying will not change the value of the option. It will remain near zero no matter what. In this case, the delta of the option is close to zero: A $1 change in the price of the underlying results in almost no change in the value of the option.

Hedging

Notice that in both extremes—when the delta is near zero and when it is near one—we can see the best way to hedge the option. When the delta is near one, we buy one share of stock for every share of the short call we are hedging (i.e., if the option is written on 100 shares of the stock, then we purchase 100 shares to hedge it).

Conversely, when the delta is near zero, we can afford to write the call naked; that is, we do not need to hold stock as a hedge against the option risk because there is essentially no risk. This makes sense, because hedging the option is a form of protection against changes in the underlying's price that adversely affect the option position. From the perspective of writing the option, adverse changes mean any changes that increase the value of the option. However, when the delta is zero, the option's value is absolutely insensitive to changes in the stock price. We do not need to buy the underlying in order to hedge.

The subject of the delta is somewhat more subtle than the extreme cases above because some of the most crucial assumptions in the Black-Scholes model show up when studying it. Implicit in the "Black-Scholes world" is the assumption that there is only one factor of uncertainty in the value of an option: the fluctuation of stock price. In truth the uncertainty implicit in an option price is more complicated than this.

Sources of Uncertainty in an Option's Value

Stock price uncertainty is the lack of knowledge we have about future prices. We have already discussed our mathematical definition of this uncertainty, volatility. Now we discuss where this uncertainty comes from. Real world stock price uncertainty is more complicated than in the Black-Scholes world because the dynamics of stock price movements are more complicated than geometric Brownian motion. For example, in reality the volatility of the underlying can change unexpectedly, and changes in volatility will change the value of the option *even when the spot price does not change.*

There is also *jump risk* embedded in the price of an option. If there is a probability the underlying stock price will unexpectedly jump downward, then this risk is implicit in the price of the option. However, since this risk is not included in the stock price model (i.e., the geometric Brownian motion model does not account for possible stock price jumps), jump risk is not included in the Black-Scholes price of an option.[2]

This relates to the delta of an option, because if there are many sources of uncertainty in the value of the option, then changes in its value cannot be explained by changes in the underlying's price alone. For example, suppose we want to measure the delta of the option *a posteriori*. Later we will see that we can do this by looking at the stock price and option value at some time t_0, doing the same at a later time t_1, and then computing the relative change in the value of the option to the stock price at the two times.

Unfortunately, there are many reasons why this may not give an accurate estimate of the delta of the option. Underlying all of these is a single reason: The price of the option is not controlled by the price of the stock alone. For example, if the volatility suddenly "spikes up" between time t_0 and time t_1, then there will be a larger change in the value of the option than we would predict on the basis of stock price uncertainty alone.

In the Black-Scholes world, where stock prices are supposed to follow geometric Brownian motions with constant volatility, none of these difficulties arise. The option's value in our theoretical model changes for only two reasons: time change and stock price change. We will use this fact to give an approximation to the delta of the option by computing the actual rate of change in the value of the option with respect to the stock price.

---

[2]For more on this, see Chapter 8.

An Approximate Formula for the Delta of an Option

Suppose we have a call option C on a stock S. Write t_0 for the current time and t_1 for some time in the near future (e.g., t_1 could be tomorrow's date). We have the following notation:

C_{t_0} = Value of C at time t_0
C_{t_1} = Value of C at time t_1
S_{t_0} = Price of S at time t_0
S_{t_1} = Price of S at time t_1
r = Risk-free rate of interest

The delta of a call option is approximated by the equation[3]

$$\Delta_{t_0} = \frac{C_{t_0} - e^{-r(t_1 - t_0)} C_{t_1}}{S_{t_0} - e^{-r(t_1 - t_0)} S_{t_1}}. \qquad (4.5.1)$$

This equation is important, so we need to take it apart and examine it piece by piece. First, look at the numerator

$$C_{t_0} - e^{-r(t_1 - t_0)} C_{t_1}.$$

If this were simply $C_{t_0} - C_{t_1}$, then it would be the change in value of the call option from time t_0 to time t_1; however, there is the extra term $e^{-r(t_1 - t_0)}$ to explain. To understand it, recall that the delta is the rate of change of the price of the option with respect to changes in the stock price, assuming that all other variables are constant.

We already noted that in our model, only two variables change in value throughout the life of the option—the current time and the stock price (the option's value changes as well, but this is not a variable, it is what we are trying to compute). By looking at $C_{t_0} - e^{-r(t_1 - t_0)} C_{t_1}$, we are neutralizing the effect of changing time, since $e^{-r(t_1 - t_0)} C_{t_1}$ is the value of C_{t_1} at time t_0.

Similarly, looking at the denominator of equation (4.5.1),

$$S_{t_0} - e^{-r(t_1 - t_0)} S_{t_1},$$

we are looking at the change in the stock price from time t_0 to time t_1 by neutralizing the change in time. Lastly, the ratio of the two formulas is the rate of change of option value with respect to the stock price from time t_0 to time t_1, with the effect of time neutralized.

Example

Suppose that at time t_0, the value of S is \$50 per share and the value of C is \$2 per share, and on the next day, time t_1, the value of S is \$52 per share (a

---

[3]For an explanation of precisely what "approximately" means, see the discussion on pp. 137–140.

$2-per-share rise) and the value of C is $2.20 per share. Assuming that the risk-free rate of interest is 5 percent, let's compute the delta using equation (4.5.1).

First of all, we put the above data into the proper notation:

$$S_{t_0} = \$50$$
$$S_{t_1} = \$52$$
$$C_{t_0} = \$2$$
$$C_{t_1} = \$2.20$$
$$t_1 - t_0 = 0.002740$$
$$e^{-r(t_2 - t_1)} = 0.99986$$

Using equation (4.5.1) we find:

$$\Delta_{t_0} = \frac{2.00 - 0.99986 \cdot 2.20}{50 - 0.99986 \cdot 52} = \frac{0.199692}{1.99272} = 0.10021.$$

What does this mean? The numerator says that the time-adjusted change in the price of the option was approximately $0.199692, while the time-adjusted change in the stock price was $1.99272. The ratio says that for every $1 change in the stock price, there was an approximately $0.1002 change in the value of the option. Thus, the *rate* of change of option value to stock price is 0.10021 *dollars of option price per dollar of stock price*.

What Does Approximately Mean?

We have claimed equation (4.5.1) is an *approximate* formula for the delta. But what does this really mean? It means two things, one obvious and one less obvious.

The obvious part is that if we choose a time t_1 very close to time t_0 and apply equation (4.5.1), then we obtain values for the delta that are very close to the actual value of the delta at time t_0. Moreover, if we require an approximation to the delta of a certain given accuracy, then there is always a time t_1 close enough to t_0 so that our approximation is that given accuracy or better. In other words, we can "get" as close to the real delta as we want merely by choosing times t_1 sufficiently close to time t_0.

Less obvious is the following fact: Our approximate formula for the delta produces errors that "do not accumulate." Let's understand what this means. We will see in a moment that we will be repeatedly substituting the approximate value of the delta for the real value of the delta. Each time we do this, we produce a small error. The question is, do these small errors add up and make our approximation useless? The answer is no, and this will be one of the keys to making the formula work.

Hedge Parameters

The delta of an option is a *hedge parameter,* so named because, as we shall see, it gives vital information regarding how to hedge the risk of writing the option. One of the key contributions of Black and Scholes was to give formulas for the deltas of European call and put options, taking as input data stock price, strike price, volatility, the interest rate, and time until expiration.

Later, we shall see that to properly understand the risk of hedging an option, it is necessary to know how the option value changes with respect to all of the above inputs. Hedge parameters measure the rate of change of option value with respect to volatility and interest rates, among others. These parameters will be studied in Section 4.10.

Comments on the Approximate Formula

There are two important issues to discuss regarding the approximate formula for the delta: 1) What if the denominator of our delta formula is zero? and 2) How does the change in option value with the passage of time affect the approximate formula?

Both issues are serious and deserve attention. First, suppose that at time t_0, our stock price is S_{t_0}, and at time t_1, our stock price is $e^{r(t_1-t_0)}S_{t_0}$. Put another way, what if $S_{t_0} - e^{-r(t_1-t_0)}S_{t_1} = 0$? Then, naturally, our approximate formula is meaningless, as division by zero does not yield a real number.

This does not invalidate our formula, however, because according to the Brownian motion model, the probability that the stock price at time t_1 will be exactly equal to $e^{r(t_1-t_0)}$ times the price at t_0 is zero. This goes back to our discussion of continuous random variables in Chapter 2. The probability of any given "event" is always zero; only ranges of events matter in probability theory. Therefore, *theoretically* we can ignore the one price where the approximate formula for the delta is undefined because *theoretically* it never happens. Of course, in reality it can happen. At these times, our option's value has changed despite the fact that the stock price has only increased by the risk-free rate. How do we account for this?

First, option value does change with time, even when stock price does not and even in the Black-Scholes world. That is, even if we ignore such possibilities as changing volatility and jumps in stock price, the value of the option does change as time elapses. This will be discussed in section 4.10 of this chapter under the guise of the hedge parameter *theta.* Right now we must reconcile theta with our study of delta.

The problem is, on one hand we claimed that equation (4.5.1) is approximately the rate of change of option value with respect to stock price.

We already know that in making this approximation, we have let time change slightly and that there is an expected change in the value of the option due to this time change. This obviously affects our formula, but how?

The answer is surprisingly deep. First, suppose we used the following as our approximate formula:

$$\frac{S_{t_0} - S_{t_1}}{C_{t_0} - C_{t_1}}.$$

This would be wrong, because we are not accounting for the change in option value with respect to time. On the other hand, simply by discounting S_{t_1} and C_{t_1} by the risk-free rate, we perfectly neutralize the effect of theta. This is *very* difficult to see from the current picture. However, in Chapter 7, Section 7.8, we will use the binomial model of option pricing to prove that equation (4.5.1) is the correct approximate formula for the delta.

The Delta of a European Put Option

Until now we have only discussed the delta of a European call. As we have previously seen when discussing put-call parity, European calls and puts of the same strike and expiration are related by a simple formula. This relationship is reflected in the relationship between their deltas, which we state now:

Let C and P be a European call and put, respectively, with the same strike and expiration. If Δ is the delta of C, then the delta of P is $\Delta - 1$.

To verify this statement, one just has to recall put-call parity:

$$C - P = S - e^{-r(T-t)}K,$$

where C and P represent the value of the call and put, S represents the price of the underlying, K represents the strike price, r is the risk-free interest rate, and $T - t$ is time until expiration.

Now, if the price of S goes up by $1, then assuming put-call parity, the new value for $C - P$ is

$$(S + 1) - e^{-r(T-t)}K.$$

On the other hand, the price of the call changes from C to $C + \Delta$ (this is the point of Δ: A $1 change in the price of S results in a $\$\Delta$ change in the value of C). Suppose that the price of the put goes from P to $P + \delta$, where δ represents the delta of the put option. Then we have

$$(C + \Delta) - (P + \delta) = (S + 1) - e^{-r(T-t)}K,$$

which, after rearranging, becomes

$$(C - P) + (\Delta - \delta) = (S - e^{-r(T-t)}K) + 1.$$

Substituting $C - P = S - e^{-r(T-t)}K$, we obtain

$$(S - e^{-r(T-t)}K) + (\Delta - \delta) = (S - e^{-r(T-t)}K) + 1,$$

which implies:

$$\Delta - \delta = 1,$$

or in other words, $\delta = \Delta - 1$.

Why the Formulas are Approximate

It is important to remember that equation (4.5.1) for the delta of an option is only an approximation. In it we look at the rate of change of the option's value with respect to the stock price from time t_0 to time t_1. What makes the formula approximate is the fact that we compare the change in the option price to the change in the stock price over some small period of time. But, how small is small enough? The answer is, if we are interested in the delta at time t_0, then we want to look at times as close to t_0 as possible. This means that any time, no matter how close to t_0, can be bettered by choosing times even closer.

When we examine how the Black-Scholes formula is actually used, we will often treat equation (4.5.1) as if it were really the delta and not just a good approximation. This has the effect of making all the subsequent formulas derived from this approximation themselves approximations. Despite this, we can always make the formulas more accurate simply by choosing times closer together.

In general, no matter how close the times are together leaves us with something that is still an approximation. If we go all the way to the theoretical limit, where all times are infinitesimally close, we get a formula that is no longer approximate but is precisely correct.

This is important to keep in mind when studying the next sections on the Black-Scholes hedging strategy. When studying this strategy, we will always look at our positions by noting how the "cost" of the hedging strategy varies between two times. The values for the costs we obtain will always be approximate because of the approximation we use for the delta. How good the approximation is will depend on the amount of time between comparisons. The goal of the Black-Scholes hedging strategy is to produce a hedging strategy that is correct when hedging is performed continuously.

4.6 THE BLACK-SCHOLES HEDGING STRATEGY

So far we've given a bare-bones description of a method to hedge the risk in writing an option—produce a self-financing, replicating hedging strategy. Now it's time to explain the method behind the Black-Scholes formula. We will show that if we know the delta of a European call or put option, we can hedge this option and determine its theoretical value. Once this is understood, understanding the Black-Scholes formula boils down to understanding a formula for the value of the delta.

What is the Black-Scholes Formula?

The Black-Scholes formula is a formula for the value of a European call or put option. It takes as its inputs five parameters: the current time until expiration, the current price of the underlying stock, the risk-free rate of interest, the strike price of the option, and the volatility of the stock. Its output is the fair value of the option, which we refer to as the *Black-Scholes value* of the option.

The arguments used to derive the Black-Scholes formula depend on several important economic assumptions. These assumptions play a key role in determining the extent to which the Black-Scholes value of an option is the real value of the option. Understanding the role they play in the value of an option and identifying how relaxing these assumptions affects the validity of the formula is an important part of understanding the Black-Scholes method.

The nature of these assumptions is very similar to the sorts of assumptions we made in the coin-tossing example at the beginning of this chapter. Rather than giving a list of assumptions now, we will develop the theory by making the necessary assumptions along the way. These assumptions make everything work, and in the end, we shall catalog what assumptions we made, why we made them, and how relaxing them affects the theoretical value of the option.

The Preliminary Formula

Let C be a European call option on a stock or index S. The general form of the Black-Scholes formula for a European call option is very simple. We give that now as a *preliminary version* of the Black-Scholes formula:

$$\text{Current value of } C = \Delta_t S_t - e^{-r(T-t)} B_t, \qquad (4.6.1)$$

where $T - t$ is time until expiration and S_t is the current price of the underlying stock. Here Δ_t is the delta of the option at time t and B_t is the value of a certain riskless bond maturing at time T. The values for Δ_t and B_t are computed by two formulas whose inputs are the price of the stock, the strike price of the option, the time until expiration and the volatility of the stock, and the risk-free interest rate. The value B_t is equal to K (strike price) times the probability of expiring in the money. This will all be explained in detail later.

If P is a put option on S with the same strike and expiration as C, then the preliminary form of the Black-Scholes formula for P is

$$\text{Current value of } P = (\Delta_t - 1)S_t + e^{-r(T-t)}(K - B_t), \quad (4.6.2)$$

where Δ_t is the delta appearing in equation (4.6.1). Since the delta of P is equal to the delta of C minus one, the term $\Delta_t - 1$ in the above equation is nothing but the delta of P.

Obtaining the Formula

The above formulas are abstract—we don't know how to compute Δ_t and B_t. In addition, it is not apparent from equation (4.6.1) or equation (4.6.2) what, if anything, these formulas have to do with the value of a European option.

At this point we want to make one thing crystal clear:

Equations (4.6.1) and (4.6.2) are the key to understanding the Black-Scholes formula.

In order to pin down the relationship between the preliminary formulas and the price of an option we will

1. Show that equations (4.6.1) and (4.6.2) lead to self-financing, replicating hedging strategies for the call option C and the put option P, respectively.
2. Produce formulas for Δ_t and B_t.

These two problems are quite distinct. The first is simpler to understand and more at the heart of option pricing. It relates the formula to the price of an option.

The formulas for Δ_t and B_t can be derived using a variety of techniques, all of which rely on the geometric Brownian motion model of price movements. In this chapter, we will give the formulas for Δt and B_t. In Chapter 5, we will discuss how the formulas are derived.

Put-Call Parity in the Black-Scholes Formula

As an aside, let's see how the formulas for C and P relate to put-call parity. This will demonstrate that even in this form, these formulas contain important information about the value of an option.

Writing C_t for the value of the call (at time t) and P_t for the value of the put (at time t), we have:

$$C_t - P_t = \left(\Delta_t S_t - e^{-r(T-t)}B_t\right) - \left((\Delta_t - 1)S_t + e^{-r(T-t)}(K - B_t)\right)$$

$$= \left(\Delta_t S_t - e^{-r(T-t)}B_t\right) - \left(\Delta_t S_t - e^{-r(T-t)}B_t\right) - \left(-S_t + e^{-r(T-t)}K\right)$$

$$= S_t - e^{-r(T-t)}K.$$

Comparing this with the put-call parity relationship [equation (1.9)], we see this is exactly put-call parity.

The Black-Scholes Formula as a Hedging Strategy

If we want to use the Black-Scholes formula to compute option values and nothing more, then there is nothing much to discuss. However, the interesting and important part of option pricing theory is understanding intuitively what makes it tick. This leads to important insights into risks and hedging costs. To understand this, it is necessary to understand how the formula translates into a hedging strategy that replicates the payoff of the option. Once this is understood, our basic no-arbitrage hypothesis ensures that the value of the option is equal to the cost of the hedging strategy.

We will show how the preliminary Black-Scholes formula leads to a hedge for the short-call position (for a European call). The analogous strategy for puts will be obvious. Hedging is divided into two parts: 1) setting up the hedge, and 2) maintaining the hedge.

Setting Up the Hedge

To set up the hedge at time t, form a portfolio Π_t with the following elements:

1. Δ_t shares of S long.
2. A short, riskless, zero-coupon bond maturing at time T to B_t.

Clearly, the value of this portfolio is the value of the stock minus the present value of the bond. This is

$$\Delta_t S_t - e^{-r(T-t)}B_t,$$

which is the same as the Black-Scholes formula for the value of C. Therefore:

We begin hedging the short-call position by forming a hedge whose cash flows are equal to the Black-Scholes value of the option.

Once this hedge is set up, the next step is to maintain the hedge as time passes.

Maintaining the Hedge

At every time t, we have to hold Δ_t shares of S long and a bond maturing at time T to B_t short. In order to do this, we will have to continuously monitor the values of Δ_t and B_t, buying or selling shares in order to keep the portfolio *in balance*.

This is a dynamic hedging strategy, because at each time t, the values of Δ_t and B_t will generally differ from their previous values. Therefore, in order to keep the hedge in balance, adjustments have to be made at every moment in time. The costs of this rebalancing act are called *rebalancing costs,* and what concerns us is that to ensure the strategy is self-financing; we want the rebalancing costs at every step to be as close to zero as possible.

We make an important point:

Rebalancing costs do not include transaction costs.

One of our basic assumptions is that *there are no transaction costs* in hedging an option. Of course, this assumption is false, but nevertheless, as with the original Black-Scholes formula, we make this assumption for the simplicity it affords us.

Before discussing rebalancing costs further, we clear up the meaning of "Δ_t shares of S."

What Does "Δ_t Shares of S" Mean?

We have insisted that we hold Δ_t shares of S at time t, and we have seen that Δ_t is always between 0 and 1. Therefore, the question arises: What does it mean to buy Δ_t shares of S?

Our hedging strategy is designed to hedge the risk of a short call or put option on a single share of stock. In reality, a hedging strategy is used to hedge an option on some larger number of shares (e.g., in the U.S., a standard options contract is on 100 shares of the underlying). In this case, since Δ_t is always a number between 0 and 1, we see that it represents the percentage of the lot of shares that should be purchased.

For example, if C is an option on 100 shares of S and $\Delta_t = 0.55$, then the hedging strategy requires that we purchase 55 shares of S at time t. Although the entire hedging strategy, and consequently the Black-Scholes formula, is stated in terms of options on a single stock, practically speaking, it can only be carried out for larger numbers of shares.

Now that we have a general idea of what the Black-Scholes formula looks like and how it translates into a hedging strategy, we address the question of how to see that it is self-financing.

Showing the Hedging Strategy is Self-Financing

If we hedge a short option position using the Black-Scholes strategy, then we will always be in possession of a portfolio (consisting of a bond and a stock) whose value is equal to the current Black-Scholes value of the option C. This is clear from the original equations for the formula, (4.6.1) and (4.6.2), because these equations are true for any time t.

Using this observation, we shall now see that arbitrage considerations imply that the hedging strategy must be self-financing. Here is why: In hedging an option using Black-Scholes, we first initiate the hedge and then maintain it. Initiating the hedge has a certain cost, and according to the Black-Scholes formula, this cost is equal to the value of the option. Maintaining the hedge involves transactions of buying and selling bonds and shares of the stock. These transactions may or may not have net costs, which we have called *infusion of funds costs*. The total of all the costs of maintaining the hedge (excluding transaction costs) is the maintenance cost of the hedge. We therefore have:

total cost of hedging $=$ set-up costs $+$ maintenance cost.

On the other hand, the Black-Scholes formula says that at every moment in time, the hedging portfolio's value is equal to the value of the option. Holding the hedging portfolio is, financially speaking, identical to holding the option. Thus, if we set up the hedge at time t, the cost of this hedge should reflect the present value of all future cash flows associated with the hedge. This follows from basic arbitrage theory.

On the other hand, the Black-Scholes formula (along with its hedging strategy) says that the set-up costs of the hedging portfolio are equal to the value of the option. In summary:

set-up costs $=$ value of option $=$ total cost of hedging.

The first equality is due to the Black-Scholes formula, and the second equality reflects the arbitrage considerations we just explained.

Therefore, set-up costs equal the total cost of hedging, which implies that the maintenance cost of hedging must equal zero and the portfolio is self-financing. In conclusion, we have shown:

If the Black-Scholes formula holds, then the hedging strategy must be self-financing.

Discussion

The above argument may leave you a little cold. After all, we haven't really proved anything. We've only demonstrated that *if* the Black-Scholes formula is really a formula for the value of a European option, then its hedging strategy must be self-financing.

One can still wonder, Is it really self-financing? The problem is that the above arguments start with the assumption that the Black-Scholes formula really produces the value of the option, and then arrive at the conclusion that the hedging strategy is self-financing.

It would be more convincing if we started with the hedging strategy and then showed that it replicates the payoff of the option and is self-financing. This approach leaves no doubt as to what is happening, because if a hedging strategy replicates the option's payoff and is self-financing, then we know by basic arbitrage considerations that the set-up cost of the hedge (in this case, given by the Black-Scholes formula) is always equal to the value of the option.

4.7 HOW AND WHY THE BLACK-SCHOLES FORMULA WORKS

It is now time to understand exactly why Black-Scholes is self-financing. To unravel the Black-Scholes formula, start with a European call option C on a stock or index S struck today at K and expiring at time T. We assume that the current time is t_0 and the risk-free rate of interest is r. We are going to explain in detail how the hedging strategy works and show that the rebalancing costs are equal to zero.

The hedging strategy tells us to begin by setting up a portfolio at time t_0, purchasing Δ_{t_0} shares of S and shorting a riskless, zero-coupon bond maturing at time T (the expiration date of C) to B_{t_0}. At some later time t_1, the delta will be Δ_{t_1} and the bond value will have changed to B_{t_1}. At this point, we have to adjust the components of the portfolio to reflect this. What is the cost of this adjustment?

Rebalancing

Suppose that at time t_1 (a short while after t_0), we decide to rebalance the portfolio. At time t_1, the price of S is S_{t_1}, and we have to update the portfolio so that it has Δ_{t_1} shares of S and a short bond maturing to the new value B_{t_1}.

In order to rebalance, we essentially need to sell off the Δ_{t_0} shares of S and buy Δ_{t_1} shares back, for a net purchase (or sale) of $\Delta_{t_1} - \Delta_{t_0}$. This is all at a price of S_{t_1}. Likewise, we need to buy back the bond maturing to B_{t_0} and short a new one maturing to B_{t_1}.

The total cash flow is tabulated below:

Time	Amount Spent
t_0	$\Delta_{t_0} S_{t_0} - e^{-r(T-t_0)} B_{t_0}$
t_1 discounted to t_0	$(\Delta_{t_1} - \Delta_{t_0}) S_{t_1} - e^{-r(T-t_1)}(B_{t_1} - B_{t_0})$

There is only one problem with this. It does not take into account the risk-free rate of interest. We need to pick a single time and compare the value of all purchases *at that time*. In the present situation, we will evaluate all purchases at time t_0. This means the money spent at time t_1 must be discounted by a factor of $e^{-r(t_1-t_0)}$. We recalculate the above enumeration with this in mind and tabulate the results in Table 4.7.1.

The term $e^{-r(T-t_0)}(B_{t_1} - B_{t_0})$ in Table 4.7.1 comes from computing

$$e^{-r(t_1-t_0)} e^{-r(T-t_1)}(B_{t_1} - B_{t_0}) = e^{-r(T-t_0)}(B_{t_1} - B_{t_0}).$$

The Total Amount Spent

To compute the total amount of money spent on hedging at time t_0 *and* at time t_1, we add up the entries in Table 4.7.1. This works out to:

$$\left(\Delta_{t_0} S_{t_0} - e^{-r(T-t_0)} B_{t_0}\right) + \left(e^{-r(t_1-t_0)}(\Delta_{t_1} - \Delta_{t_0}) S_{t_1} - e^{-r(T-t_0)}(B_{t_1} - B_{t_0})\right).$$

Now, rearranging this a bit, we obtain

$$\Delta_{t_0}(S_{t_0} - e^{-r(t_1-t_0)} S_{t_1}) + e^{-r(t_1-t_0)}(\Delta_{t_1} S_{t_1} - e^{-r(T-t_1)} B_{t_1}). \quad (4.7.1)$$

This is the total amount of money spent in setting up the hedge at time t_0 and rebalancing at time t_1.

T A B L E   4.7.1

Total amount of money spent on hedging the call option C, taking into account the time difference between t_1 and t_0

Time	Amount Spent
t_0	$\Delta_{t_0} S_{t_0} - e^{-r(T-t_0)} B_{t_0}$
t_1	$e^{-r(t_1-t_0)}(\Delta_{t_1} - \Delta_{t_0}) S_{t_1} - e^{-r(T-t_0)}(B_{t_1} - B_{t_0})$

Although it is not yet apparent, we are about to see something very interesting. If in the above equation, we replace Δ_{t_0} with the approximate formula for Δ_{t_0} in formula (4.5.1), it has the effect of canceling out $S_{t_0} - e^{-r(t_1-t_0)}S_{t_1}$ in (4.7.1). This is carried out explicitly in Display 4.7.1. The result is that the total cost of hedging from time t_0 to time t_1 is approximately equal to:

$$(C_{t_0} - e^{-r(t_1-t_0)}C_{t_1}) + e^{-r(t_1-t_0)}(\Delta_{t_1}S_{t_1} - e^{-r(T-t_1)}B_{t_1}). \quad (4.7.2)$$

This formula is a key equation in understanding Black-Scholes and must be examined closely.

First of all, it consists of three terms: 1) the value of the option at time t_0; 2) the negative of the value of the option at time t_1 (adjusted for time value); and 3) the Black-Scholes formula for the value of the call at time t_1 (also adjusted for time value).

This is an important step in our understanding of Black-Scholes, for it says that

If the Black-Scholes formula holds at time t_1, it also holds at time t_0.

How do we know this is true? First, if Black-Scholes holds at time t_1, then the terms

$$-e^{-r(t_1-t_0)}C_{t_1} \quad \text{and} \quad e^{-r(t_1-t_0)}(\Delta_{t_1}S_{t_1} - e^{-r(T-t_1)}B_{t_1})$$

D I S P L A Y 4.7.1

DERIVING EQUATION (4.7.2)

We have the approximate formula for the delta:

$$\frac{C_{t_0} - e^{-r(t_1-t_0)}C_{t_1}}{S_{t_0} - e^{-r(t_1-t_0)}S_{t_1}}.$$

Substituting this into equation (4.7.1) we obtain:

$$\left(\frac{C_{t_0} - e^{-r(t_1-t_0)}C_{t_1}}{S_{t_0} - e^{-r(t_1-t_0)}S_{t_1}}\right)(S_{t_0} - e^{-r(t_1-t_0)}S_{t_1}) + e^{-r(t_1-t_0)}(\Delta_{t_1}S_{t_1} - e^{-r(T-t_1)}B_{t_1}).$$

This is immediately equal to:

$$C_{t_0} - e^{-r(t_1-t_0)}C_{t_1} + e^{-r(t_1-t_0)}(\Delta_{t_1}S_{t_1} - e^{-r(T-t_1)}B_{t_1}),$$

which is Equation (4.7.2).

are equal and cancel each other out (after all, the Black-Scholes formula is supposed to be the price of the option at time t_1). That is, if $C_{t_1} = \Delta_{t_1} S_{t_1} - e^{-r(T-t_1)} B_{t_1}$, then the only term left in equation (4.7.2) is C_{t_0}. This says that if we set up the Black-Scholes hedge at time t_0 and rebalance at time t_1, the total cost is the cost of the option at time t_0.

In the above setup, there is nothing special about time t_0 and time t_1 except that they are close enough together so that the approximate formula for the delta holds.

The essential ingredients in the argument (that if Black-Scholes holds at time t_1, then it holds at time t_0) are the Black-Scholes formula itself and the approximate formula for the delta. Therefore, as long as we have two times that are close enough together so we can substitute this formula for the delta, we can show that if the Black-Scholes holds at the later time, then it holds at the earlier time.

In particular, we can take time t_1 and some later time t_2 and show that if Black-Scholes holds at t_2, then it holds at t_1. Since holding at t_1 implies holding at t_0, we obtain that if Black-Scholes holds at time t_2, it holds at time t_0. Now we can use this observation to make the formula hold for times that are not close together.

Proof for Times Not Close Together
Now we can pick a whole sequence of times $t_0, t_1, \ldots, t_{N-1}, t_N$ where the time between t_i and t_{i+1} is never too great. Using the above arguments, we show that if Black-Scholes holds at time t_N, it holds at time t_{N-1}. Then, since it holds at time t_{N-1}, the same arguments imply that it holds at time t_{N-2}. Continuing in this way, we can finally show step-by-step that the Black-Scholes formula must hold at time t_0. In this way, we show that if the formula holds at any given time, then it must hold at any earlier time. In particular, we have shown: *if we demonstrate that Black-Scholes holds at expiration, then we have proved that Black-Scholes holds at every time.* This is important, so let's examine this statement closely.

Discussion
First, we observe that the above statement is what makes it possible to value European options. We know what the value of an option is at expiration, so all we have to do is check that the Black-Scholes formula agrees with the value of the option at expiration in both the case where it expires in the money and the case where it expires out of the money. But this is easy to do, because the payoffs of vanilla European puts and calls are so simple. We will check this explicitly in the next section, but for now suffice it to say they do hold.

Next, we have used the approximate formula for the delta in deriving the key statement above. Therefore, an obvious question is, What if the small errors in the delta add up to an unacceptably large error? The answer is, they don't. In other words, the approximate formula for the delta is a very nice approximate formula. Not only does it give a formula that is close to the real delta, but it can be used repeatedly without causing harm. How do we know this is true?

This is at the heart of the mathematics of the Black-Scholes formula. It follows, either by knowing that the formula is the value of the option and using the arbitrage arguments previously discussed, or by actually analyzing the exact nature of the errors produced in the approximate formula and showing in detail that they do not "get too large." We will not discuss these more technical points here.

Black-Scholes at Expiration

To show that the Black-Scholes formula holds and actually provides a self-financing, replicating hedging strategy, we have seen that it is enough to check that the formula holds on the expiration date of the option.

We have to examine both the case where C expires in the money and the case where it expires out of the money separately: $C_T = S_T - K$ if the option is in the money (K is the strike price), and it equals zero otherwise. Summarizing, we have:

$$C_T = \begin{cases} S_T - K & \text{if the option is in the money,} \\ 0 & \text{otherwise.} \end{cases}$$

On the other hand, the value of Δ_T is one if the option is in the money and zero otherwise. We have to compare the above with the value of the Black-Scholes hedge at expiration in order to verify

$$C_T = \Delta_T S_T - B_T.$$

But we have never said anything about the value of B_T. It is now clear that we don't have to. The above equation tells us exactly what B_T must be: B_T must equal K if the option expires in the money, and it must equal zero otherwise. That is,

$$B_T = \begin{cases} K & \text{if the option is in the money,} \\ 0 & \text{otherwise.} \end{cases}$$

With this stated, we have

$$\Delta_T S_T - B_T = \begin{cases} S_T - K & \text{if the option is in the money,} \\ 0 & \text{otherwise.} \end{cases}$$

That is, the Black-Scholes formula holds at expiration, which in turn implies that it holds at all earlier times. We are very close to having an option pricing formula. What is left is to provide formulas for Δ_t and B_t. These will be given in a moment, but first we digress on two points. First, we discuss one more time the fact that we used an approximate formula for the delta in order to prove that our hedging strategy works, and second we discuss the relationship between Δ_t and B_t for times other than expiration.

How to Make the Approximation Exact

The problem with the above computations is everything depends on the validity of the approximate formula for the delta (equation 4.5.1). However, by rebalancing the hedge more frequently, the approximation becomes closer to the exact value of the delta. The closer together between rehedging, the closer to exact the formula for the delta is. If, finally, we rehedge at times *infinitely* close together, the formula will be exact. That is, if we rehedged continuously, the formula for the delta would be 100 percent exact. Consequently, the hedging procedure would be 100 percent self-financing.

A fundamental assumption in the Black-Scholes formula is that we can trade continuously. We make this assumption precisely because of the above considerations. Without them, all the substitutions, etc., are only approximations. Now, in reality, we can never trade continuously. Therefore, the hedging strategy will not be perfectly self-financing. How close to self-financing it is will depend on how good an approximation to the delta we obtain.

The Relationship Between Δ_t and B_t

So far we only have an abstract understanding of the Black-Scholes formula. Soon we will give formulas for both Δ_t and B_t, but there is one important thing to understand before seeing these formulas: The formula for B_t is completely determined by the delta and the terminal condition that B_t be either K (if the option is in the money) or zero (if it is out of the money). This is an amazing fact that at first glance is not obvious at all.

To understand how this works, consider that we want the value of the hedging portfolio at every time to be equal to the value of the option. At a given time t, the value of the hedging portfolio is $\Delta_t S_t - e^{-r(T-t)} B_t$, where S_t is the price per share of S at time t.

If t_0 and t_1 are times that are very close together, then we will show that the following relationship between the "Δ" value and the "B" value must hold:

$$(\Delta_{t_1} - \Delta_{t_0})e^{-r(t_1 - t_0)}S_{t_1} = (B_{t_1} - B_{t_0})e^{-r(T - t_0)}. \qquad (4.7.3)$$

That is, small changes in the delta term completely determine what small changes in the B term must be. This fact, along with the terminal conditions on B, determine it completely.

To see that equation (4.7.3) holds, we exploit the relationships already developed, along with the requirement that the Black-Scholes formula holds at every time (in particular, at times t_0 and t_1); that is, we know:

$$\Delta_t S_t - e^{-r(T - t)}B_t = C_t.$$

We have to work through four lines of equations, making a few substitutions to obtain the desired result. Here are the equations:

$$
\begin{aligned}
C_{t_0} &- e^{-r(t_1 - t_0)}C_{t_1} + (\Delta_{t_1} - \Delta_{t_0})e^{-r(t_1 - t_0)}S_{t_1} \\
&= \Delta_{t_0}S_{t_0} - e^{-r(T - t_0)}B_{t_0} - (e^{-r(t_1 - t_0)}\Delta_{t_1}S_{t_1} - e^{-r(T - t_0)}B_{t_1}) \\
&\quad + (\Delta_{t_1} - \Delta_{t_0})e^{-r(t_1 - t_0)}S_{t_1} \\
&= \Delta_{t_0}S_{t_0} - e^{-r(T - t_0)}B_{t_0} - \Delta_{t_0}e^{-r(t_1 - t_0)}S_{t_1} + e^{-r(T - t_0)}B_{t_1} \\
&= \Delta_{t_0}(S_{t_0} - e^{-r(t_1 - t_0)}S_{t_1}) - e^{-r(T - t_0)}(B_{t_0} - B_{t_1}) \\
&= C_{t_0} - e^{-r(t_1 - t_0)}C_{t_1} + e^{-r(T - t_0)}(B_{t_1} - B_{t_0}).
\end{aligned}
$$

Examining the above equations, the main thing is to compare the first line and the last line, from which we obtain:

$$
\begin{aligned}
C_{t_0} &- e^{-r(t_1 - t_0)}C_{t_1} + (\Delta_{t_1} - \Delta_{t_0})e^{-r(t_1 - t_0)}S_{t_1} \\
&= C_{t_0} - e^{-r(t_1 - t_0)}C_{t_1} + e^{-r(T - t_0)}(B_{t_1} - B_{t_0}).
\end{aligned}
$$

The two terms $C_{t_0} - e^{-r(t_1 - t_0)}C_{t_1}$ on both sides cancel, and after multiplying both sides by $e^{r(t_1 - t_0)}$, we obtain:

$$(\Delta_{t_1} - \Delta_{t_0})e^{-r(t_1 - t_0)}S_{t_1} = e^{-r(T - t_0)}(B_{t_1} - B_{t_0}). \qquad (4.7.4)$$

This equation demonstrates that changes over a small period of time in the delta determine changes in the value of the bond over the same period of time. We see that this severely limits the possible choices for B_t.

In fact, combining it with the terminal conditions that $B_T = K$ or $B_T = 0$, according to the moneyness of the option, it can be shown that this leaves exactly one choice for the value of B_t at every time t. The value of the bond portion of the Black-Scholes formula is completely determined by the delta of the option. The conclusion to all of this is:

> *The theoretical value of a vanilla European call option is completely deter-mined by its delta, the risk-free rate of interest and the time to expiration.*

Summary

Let's review the main points covered so far. First of all, we have shown that the Black-Scholes formula gives rise to a hedging strategy for the short position of a vanilla European call. To show that the value of the hedging portfolio is equal to that of the option at every time, we need to: 1) know the delta of the option at every time, and 2) use the delta to determine the correct value of B_t at every time t. There is only one thing left to do: give formulas for Δ_t and B_t.

4.8   THE BLACK-SCHOLES FORMULAS FOR Δ_t AND B_t

Now that we understand the general idea of the Black-Scholes formula, let's actually see what it is. All we have to do is to give the formulas for Δ_t and B_t.

The formulas are given in terms of the cumulative normal distribution function, discussed in Chapter 2. They are:

$$\Delta_t = N(d_1), \quad d_1 = \frac{\log(S_t/K) + (r + \frac{\sigma^2}{2})(T - t)}{\sigma\sqrt{T - t}} \tag{4.8.1}$$

$$B_t = N(d_2)K, \quad d_2 = \frac{\log(S_t/K) + (r - \frac{\sigma^2}{2})(T - t)}{\sigma\sqrt{T - t}} \tag{4.8.2}$$

where

$$S_t = \text{price of stock per share at time } t$$
$$K = \text{strike price}$$
$$r = \text{risk-free rate of interest}$$
$$\sigma = \text{volatility of stock under geometric Brownian motion}$$
$$\text{model}$$
$$T - t = \text{time until expiration}$$
$$N(\cdot) = \text{cumulative normal distribution function}$$

Combining this with equation (4.6.1), we present the Black-Scholes formula for vanilla European call options on a non-dividend-paying stock:

$$C_t = N(d_1) \cdot S_t - e^{-r(T-t)}K \cdot N(d_2). \tag{4.8.3}$$

The Formula for Puts

We now give the formula for puts. There are several ways to go about this. The easiest is to use put-call parity, but keeping with our philosophy of viewing the formula as a hedging strategy, we use equation (4.6.2) instead.

Given any call option, there is a corresponding put option with the same strike and same expiration. If we have a call option C on a stock S with strike K and time until expiration $T - t$, then the formula for B_t, the value of P at time t, is

$$P_t = (N(d_1) - 1)S_t + e^{-r(T-t)}K \cdot (1 - N(d_2)).$$

To make this formula a little cleaner, we recall that the cumulative normal distribution function has the property

$$1 - N(x) = N(-x),$$

and obtain

$$P_t = -N(-d_1) \cdot S_t + e^{-r(T-t)}K \cdot N(-d_2). \qquad (4.8.4)$$

Sample Use of the Formula

Let's use the formula and value some options. First, consider a European call option on XYZ struck at $100 per share. Suppose that the option expires in one year, XYZ is currently selling for $100 per share, and the stock has a volatility of 15 percent *per annum*. Assume the risk-free rate of interest is 5 percent. In the notation of the Black-Scholes formula, we have:

S	$100
K	$100
$T - t$	1.0
σ	0.15
r	0.05

We compute

$$d_1 = \frac{\log(100/100) + (0.05 + \frac{0.15^2}{2})(1.0)}{0.15\sqrt{1.0}} = 0.4083$$

$$d_2 = \frac{\log(100/100) + (0.05 - \frac{0.15^2}{2})(1.0)}{0.15\sqrt{1.0}} = 0.2583$$

Then, using the formula for the cumulative normal distribution function, we have

$$N(d_1) = 0.6585$$
$$N(d_2) = 0.6019$$

Therefore, the Black-Scholes value of the call is

$$C = N(d_1) \cdot S - e^{-r(T-t)} K \cdot N(d_2)$$
$$= 0.6585 \cdot 100 - 0.95123 \cdot 100 \cdot 0.6019$$
$$= 8.595,$$

and the Black-Scholes price of the put is

$$P = (N(d_1) - 1)S + e^{-r(T-t)} K \cdot (1 - N(d_2)) = 3.725.$$

Now, let's verify that the put and call price satisfy put-call parity; that is, we want to see that

$$C - P = S - e^{-r(T-t)} K.$$

We have:

$$C - P = 8.595 - 3.725 = 4.87 \qquad S - e^{-r(T-t)} K = 4.87,$$

so that put-call parity is satisfied.

4.9 BLACK-SCHOLES WITH DIVIDENDS

Until now we have avoided introducing dividends into our study of option pricing. That is, we have considered only non-dividend-paying stocks. In reality, options on stocks and indexes paying dividends are common and extremely important.

In this section, we will give two different extensions to the basic Black-Scholes formula to account for dividends. Both depend on estimating the unknown future dividend payments of the underlying stock, but they differ in the way they model the dividends.

In the first model, a *dividend schedule* is produced for the stock. The dividend schedule is a list of ex-dividend dates and dividend payments. This approach, sometimes called the *lumpy dividends* approach, conforms to real stock dividend behavior.

In the second approach, we assume that the stock has a constant dividend yield; that is, the stock is continuously paying out dividends at a uniform rate. This approach, called the *continuous dividend yield* model, is a less accurate, but more convenient, pricing tool.

Lumpy Dividends

The term "lumpy dividends" refers to the fact that dividends are paid out sporadically, at discrete points in time. To price options assuming lumpy dividends we must create a list of ex-dividend dates and estimate the dividend payment for each date. This estimate is usually created from historical data and introduces a possible source of error into option pricing. We will not discuss methods of estimating dividends.

Following our basic arbitrage theory, we assume that on an ex-dividend date, the price of the stock drops by exactly the amount of the announced dividend payment. Therefore, because we have a dividend schedule, we know on what dates and by how much the stock price will go down.

Example of Lumpy Dividends

Suppose a European call option on XYZ is settled on January 1, 1996, matures on January 1, 1997, and that we have assumed the following *dividend schedule:*

Date	Payment
5/1/96	$0.80
8/1/96	$0.80

We want to examine how these dividend payments affect the price of the option. To study this, we will assume that the current price of XYZ is $100 per share and the strike price of the option is $100. We start by seeing that the option should not be considered at the money because by the time the option expires, the two dividends will have been paid and the stock price will have been impacted by the $1.60 in dividend payments. It is *as if* we are starting with a handicap: The stock price is reduced by a certain amount according to the dividend payments and their associated ex-dividend dates.

To see the precise nature of the price decrease due to dividends, let's compute the value of a forward contract on XYZ with delivery on January 1, 1997, assuming the risk-free rate of interest is 5 percent. If there were no dividends, then the value of the underlying in one year would be (from the point of view of a forward contract)

$$\$100 \cdot e^{0.05} = 105.13.$$

This is nothing more than the current value of the stock valued forward by the risk-free rate.

But there are dividends. On May 1, 1996 (the first ex-dividend date), the stock price will drop $0.80. This is the same as the stock price dropping $e^{-(4/12)\cdot 0.05}0.80 = 0.787$ today (we computed the present value of the dividend payment). Similarly, on August 1, 1996, the stock price will drop by 0.80, which is worth $e^{-(7/12)\cdot 0.05}0.80 = 0.777$ today. In thinking about the expected value of the stock on January 1, 1997, it is as if the stock price has already been reduced by $0.787 + 0.777 = 1.564$. Therefore, to compute the new expected value of the stock, we simply reduce the current value of the stock by $1.564 and then compute the expected value of this new total, which works out to

$$e^{0.05}(100 - 1.564) = e^{0.05} \cdot 98.436 = \$103.4829.$$

The meaning of this may be more clear from another point of view. We could borrow the present value of all the future dividend payments today ($1.564) and then buy the stock (total cost: $100 − $1.564). Then, as the ex-dividend dates occur, we could use the payments to pay back the loan. Therefore,

> The forward value of a dividend-paying stock on a future date is the forward value of today's value minus the present value of all future dividend payments.

We use this observation to produce an arbitrage argument for the value of an option on a stock paying lumpy dividends.

Arbitrage Argument for Valuing Options

Let's start with a stock, S, and a vanilla European call, C, on S settled at time t_0 and expiring at time T. Assume there is one ex-dividend date for S on t_1, some time between the settlement and expiration. Suppose, as usual, that the stock follows a geometric Brownian motion with volatility σ *per annum* and that the option is struck at K.

Next, consider a portfolio consisting of one share of S and a riskless, zero-coupon bond sold short, maturing at time t_1 (the ex-dividend date) to a par value of D (the amount of the dividend payment). Call this bond B and the stock-bond portfolio Π. Let C' be a call option on the portfolio Π with strike price K and expiration T. In other words, C' is an option to buy the portfolio for K at time T (the expiration date of C). We summarize these data as follows:

S = a stock paying a dividend, with ex-dividend date t_1
σ = volatility of S

D = value of dividend paid by S

t_0 = current time

t_1 = ex-dividend date of S

T = expiration date

C = call option on S

K = strike price

B = riskless, zero-coupon bond maturing on t_1 to D

Π = a portfolio consisting of S long and B short

C' = call option on Π with strike K and expiration T

We will prove the following:

1. C' can be priced and hedged using the Black-Scholes formula.
2. C and C' have the same value.

Pricing C'

We will give a rough argument that the portfolio Π follows a geometric Brownian motion and give its volatility. A more rigorous argument requires stochastic calculus, and will not be discussed here.

At every time t prior to the ex-dividend date t_1, the value of Π is given by

$$S_t - e^{-r(t_1 - t)}D,$$

where S_t is the value of S at time t and r is the risk-free rate of interest. The value of this portfolio behaves quite similarly to the value of S_t, except that at any given time t, its value is shifted downward by $e^{-r(T-t)}D$. Using a mathematical tool for studying the mathematics of Brownian motions known as Itô's lemma, we can show that the portfolio Π follows a process closely related to a geometric Brownian motion, but with a volatility equal at time t to

$$\sigma_t = \frac{S_t}{S_t - e^{-r(t_1 - t)}D}\sigma. \tag{4.9.1}$$

In other words, the volatility of Π is equal to the volatility of S times the ratio of the price of S to the value of Π. If the dividend yield is not too large, then these volatilities are very close and are often assumed to be the same.

Let's examine what happens to the portfolio Π on and after the ex-dividend date. To simplify matters, we will assume the dividend payment is actually received on this date (this is never the case, but the slight deviation between the ex-dividend date and the date of the dividend payment is negligible in this argument).

Under these assumptions, two things happen simultaneously on the ex-dividend date: First, the price of S drops by an amount equal to D. Next, the bond B matures, and an amount equal to D is paid by the short position. The net effect of these changes is, of course, zero, as they cancel one another out. That is, the combined effect of the bond maturing and the dividend being paid has zero effect on the value of Π. Finally, since the bond has matured, the portfolio Π is reduced to just the long position in the stock. Before continuing with the argument, let's examine an example of this.

Example

Suppose we have the following parameters:

$S = \$100$
$t_0 = $ January 1, 1996
$t_1 = $ July 1, 1996
$D = \$1$
$T = $ January 1, 1997

To form the portfolio Π on January 1, 1996, we buy one share of S, and short a bond B maturing on July 1, 1996, (time t_1) to $1. Assuming the 10 percent risk-free rate, the present value of $1 on January 1, 1996, is $e^{(1/2) \cdot 0.10} = \$0.95$. So, the current value of Π is $100 - 0.95 = 99.05$.

Suppose the stock price just prior to the ex-dividend date is $104. Then the instant before the stock goes ex-dividend, the portfolio Π, consisting of the long stock and short bond, is worth $103. When the stock goes ex-dividend, there are two consequences. First, the stock price drops $1 and (under our assumption) the owner of the stock receives $1. The stock's going ex-dividend lowers the value of portfolio by $1. At the same time, the bond matures, so the short position ceases to exist. The par value of the bond is paid using the dividend payment. This raises the value of the portfolio by $1. The net effect is that the portfolio is still worth $103.

From the time t_1 on, since the portfolio Π is simply the long stock position, it clearly follows the same process as the stock, a geometric Brownian motion. Thus, if we accept that before the ex-dividend date the portfolio Π behaves like a stock with volatility σ, then the portfolio Π can be treated as a stock worth the value of S minus the present value of all future dividend payments.

The above argument is easily generalized to the situation in which the stock has many ex-dividend dates. In this case we see

A stock S with many ex-dividend dates behaves at all times like a stock with no ex-dividend dates whose value is the spot price of S minus the present value of all future dividend payments (within the relevant period of time).

Here, "within the relevant time" means that we only consider dividend payments that will occur within the span of time we are considering. For example, when we are pricing options, this always means we only consider the ex-dividend dates that occur during the life of the option.

Pricing the Option

Now, it is clear that the option C' on Π can be priced using the Black-Scholes formula for a stock S' whose value is that of S minus the present value of all future dividend payments. The question is, does our new option C' have the same value as C? The answer is yes, and we can prove it with an arbitrage argument.

Clearly if C were cheaper than C', one could buy C, short C' and invest the proceeds. At expiration, all dividends on S will have been paid, so that the portfolio Π and the stock S will be identical at that time. Therefore the options C and C' are identical as well, the combined long and the short positions are riskless, and the initial proceeds are a riskless profit.

The conclusion is that a very good approximation for the value of an option on a dividend paying stock, S, is given by using the Black-Scholes formula on an imaginary stock with a volatility given by equation (4.9.1) and a price equal to the price of S *minus* the present value of all the dividends throughout the life of the option [written D in equation (4.9.1)]. This is summarized for a call option in Display 4.9.1. To value a put option, simply use the Black-Scholes formula for a put option instead of for a call option, employing the same substitutions.

Continuous Dividend Yield

Options on stock indexes can sometimes be modeled using an approach other than lumpy dividends. The central idea is that if an index is composed of a large number of stocks that pay dividends evenly throughout the year, then the total dividend yield of the index, which is a composite of the yields of the stocks making up the index, may be modeled, assuming the dividends are continuously paid.

The accuracy of the continuous dividend yield model depends on all the previously discussed factors, plus the accuracy of the additional assumptions regarding what the dividend yield is.

Example
Suppose that the current annual dividend yield of the S&P 500 is on average 2.6 percent and we are pricing a three-month S&P call option. Moreover, suppose we know that over the three-month life of the option, 153 of the

D I S P L A Y 4.9.1

HOW TO VALUE A CALL OPTION ON A STOCK THAT PAYS LUMPY DIVIDENDS

Let S be a stock paying lumpy dividends. Suppose that C is a call option on S with expiration T and strike K, and the risk-free rate of interest is r. Assume the current date is t_0. To value C, one proceeds in the following steps:

1. Produce a dividend schedule of ex-dividend dates and dividend payments within the life of the option; for example,

$$(t_1, D_1), (t_2, D_2), \ldots, (t_N, D_N),$$

where t_1 is the first ex-dividend date, D_1 is the first dividend payment, and t_2 is the second date, etc.

2. Next, form the present value of all the future dividend payments; that is, compute

$$D = e^{-r(t_1 - t_0)} D_1 + e^{-r(t_2 - t_0)} D_2 + \ldots e^{-r(t_N - t_0)} D_N.$$

3. Subtract the discounted dividend payments from the current stock price. If S_0 is the current stock price, compute

$$S^* = S_0 - D.$$

4. Assume S^* follows a geometric Brownian motion. If σ is the volatility of S, then

$$\sigma^* = \frac{S_0}{S^*} \sigma$$

is the volatility of S^*.

5. The value of C is the Black-Scholes formula substituting S^* for S:

$$C = S^* N(d_1) - e^{-r(T - t_0)} N(d_2) K$$

$$d_1 = \frac{\log(S^*/K) + (r + (\sigma^*)^2/2)(T - t)}{\sigma^* \sqrt{T - t}}$$

$$d_2 = d_1 - \sigma^* \sqrt{T - t}.$$

---

500 stocks will pay dividends and that these dividends are relatively evenly spaced. Then, in our model, we could use an annual dividend yield of 2.6 percent and assume this yield is continuous.

We will not give a complete derivation of the Black-Scholes formula with continuous dividends. The formula can either be viewed as a limiting case of the lumpy dividend formula, where the frequency of dividend payments is increased infinitely until "in the limit" one has a continuous dividend yield, or one can proceed directly, using a modification of the same derivation used by Black and Scholes. This was first done by Merton (1973).

Suppose that q is the annual continuous dividend yield of a stock index S, and let C (respectively, P) be a call (respectively, put) option on S with expiration T and strike price K. Also suppose that the settlement date is t and the value of S at time t is S_t. The Black-Scholes-Merton formula for the value of C_t is then:

$$C_t = N(d_1^*)e^{-q(T-t)}S_t - e^{-r(T-t)}N(d_2^*)K$$

$$d_1^* = \frac{\log(S_t/K) + (r - q + \sigma^2/2)(T - t)}{\sigma\sqrt{T - t}}$$

$$d_2^* = d_1^* - \sigma\sqrt{T - t}.$$

Similarly, the formula for a put option is

$$P_t = -N(-d_1^*)e^{-q(T-t)}S_t - e^{-r(T-t)}N(-d_2^*)K.$$

Notice that the formula for d_1^* differs from the formula for d_1 in the Black-Scholes formula only in the presence of $r - q + \sigma^2/2$ instead of just $r + \sigma^2/2$. Thus, if $q = 0$, that is, if there is no dividend yield, then $d_1^* = d_1$ and the Black-Scholes-Merton formula becomes the Black-Scholes formula for a non-dividend-paying underlying stock or index.

The Intuition behind the Formula

Where does the formula come from? We have already mentioned that we can derive the continuous dividend yield option pricing formula from the ideas used in understanding lumpy dividends. Ultimately, this amounts to replacing S with an instrument whose value at every time t is $e^{-q(T-t)}S_t$, where S_t is the value of S, and then valuing options on this instrument using the Black-Scholes formula.

The formula for d_1 (in Black-Scholes), using this new instrument, is

$$d_1 = \frac{\log(e^{-q(T-t)}S_t/K) + (r + \sigma^2/2)(T - t)}{\sigma\sqrt{T - t}}, \tag{4.9.2}$$

but since

$$\log(e^{-q(T-t)}S_t/K) = \log(e^{-q(T-t)}) + \log(S_t/K)$$
$$= -q(T - t) + \log(S_t/K),$$

equation (4.9.2) becomes

$$d_1 = \frac{\log(S_t/K) + (r - q + \sigma^2/2)(T - t)}{\sigma\sqrt{T - t}},$$

which is equal to d_1^*. A similar computation is used to show that computing d_2 as above yields d_2^*. Therefore, the Black-Scholes-Merton formula is obtained from the Black-Scholes formula by replacing the stock with the new instrument whose value is $e^{-q(T-t)}S_t$ at time t.

4.10   HEDGE PARAMETERS

In this section, we discuss the dynamic nature of an option's value. Stock price and stock price volatility, interest rates, and time until expiration are all important ingredients in the value of an option. It is therefore important to study the way an option's value is expected to change if one of the above variables changes.

We have already studied the most important hedge parameter, the delta. We saw that the delta of an option is crucial in hedging and valuing that option. We now study the way an option's value varies with respect to its other input variables, as well as how delta itself changes with respect to changes in the price of the underlying.

The five hedge parameters are summarized in the following exhibit.

Greek	Symbol	Meaning
Delta	Δ	The rate of change of the value of an option with respect to changes in the stock price
Gamma	Γ	The rate of change of the delta with respect to changes in the stock price
Theta	Θ	The rate of change of the value of an option with respect to time
Rho	ρ	The rate of change of the value of an option with respect to the risk-free rate of interest
Vega	ν	The rate of change of the value of an option with respect to volatility

What Hedge Parameters Really Tell Us

Now we know what hedge parameters are, but what do they really do for us? Here is the general picture.

Given an input to the Black-Scholes formula (e.g., volatility, σ, or spot price, S), there is a corresponding hedge parameter (vega or delta) that measures the rate of change of option value with respect to the input. A small change in the input value (written $\Delta\sigma$ or ΔS) and no change in other inputs results in a change in option value. For example:

$$\sigma = \text{input volatility}$$
$$C(\sigma) = \text{option value at volatility } \sigma$$
$$\Delta\sigma = \text{a small change in volatility}$$
$$\nu = \text{option vega at volatility of } \sigma$$
$$C(\sigma + \Delta\sigma) = \text{unknown value at volatility } \sigma + \Delta\sigma$$

Given the above data, we have the approximate formula for the value $C(\sigma + \Delta\sigma)$:

$$C(\sigma + \Delta\sigma) \approx C(\sigma) + \nu\Delta\sigma. \tag{4.10.1}$$

This says that the value of the option at an input volatility of $\sigma + \Delta\sigma$ is *approximately* equal to the value of the option at an input volatility of σ plus the vega times change in the volatility. In other words, for small changes in σ, we see directly from (4.10.1) what the change in option value is.

Sample Computation

We give a sample computation of the above formula, with the following input data:

$$\sigma = 15\%$$
$$S = \$100$$
$$K = \$100$$
$$T - t = 1 \text{ year}$$
$$r = 10\%$$
$$\Delta\sigma = 1\%$$

where S is the spot price, K is the strike price, $T - t$ is time to expiration, and r is the risk-free rate. What is the Black-Scholes value of a plain vanilla European call option with these data? We have:

$$C(\sigma) = \$11.67$$
$$C(\sigma + \Delta\sigma) = \$11.98.$$

The formula for the vega of a European call option will be given in the next section. Right now, we give the answer:

$$\nu = 30.30.$$

Formula (4.10.1) predicts:

$$C(\sigma + \Delta\sigma) \approx 11.67 + 30.30 \cdot 0.01 = 11.97. \qquad (4.10.2)$$

First, we see that, indeed, equation (4.10.1) provides a good approximation of the value of $C(\sigma + \Delta\sigma)$ for a 1 percent increase in volatility. We'll discuss exactly how to interpret this in general, but right now, the point is that this is how we want to interpret hedge parameters. They measure what small changes in an input variable "do" to the value of an option. This is what is meant by rate of change; it is contained within equation (4.10.1). By changing σ on the right-hand side of this equation, we change the value of $C(\sigma + \Delta\sigma)$. How much change takes place is directly proportional to how big the vega is. The bigger ν is, the greater the change for a given $\Delta\sigma$.

We now begin a detailed study of hedge parameters. We start by picking up where we left off above and we give a detailed account of vega, the rate of change of option value with respect to volatility.

Sensitivity to Volatility—the Vega

The *vega,* or *kappa,* of an option measures the relationship between stock volatility and option value. Before discussing vega itself, we will speak about the relationship between the value of an option and the volatility of the underlying. After that, we will discuss the rate of change of an option's value with respect to volatility. Lastly, we will warn the reader regarding the *correct* way to interpret vega.

Though it has a precise mathematical meaning, which is discussed in Chapter 3, the basic idea of volatility is quite simple. It measures the average size and intensity of fluctuations in the stock price. A high-volatility stock can be expected to have much greater fluctuations in price, on average, than a low-volatility one.

Option Value and Volatility

What is the relationship between the value of an option and the underlying's volatility? First, consider a vanilla European call option. Looking ahead to the expiration date, if the option expires in the money, then the higher the price of the underlying stock, the greater the payoff of the option. In other words, there is a "bonus" for large positive changes in the stock price because they result in larger payoffs on the option. On the other hand, if the option expires out of the money, then no matter how low the price of the stock, the option pays the same—zero. We see:

The more likely large changes in the underlying's price are, the more valuable the option is.

It does not matter that large fluctuations in the stock price can work against the long option position; the effect of large negative changes do not grow in proportion to the size of those changes. Once an option expires out of the money, nothing worse can happen.

Figure 4.10.1 illustrates this point. It displays graphs of (vanilla) European call option values versus spot prices for options on underlyings of different volatilities. Each graph contains plots for three options all stuck at $100: one on a stock with 100 percent volatility, one with 50 percent, and one with ten percent. Each point represents the value of a vanilla European call on an underlying of a certain volatility. The risk-free rate is set to zero.

The graphs illustrate two facts:

1. The effect of volatility on option value diminishes as time moves toward expiration.

2. The effect of volatility on option value is greatest at the money.

F I G U R E 4.10.1

Black-Scholes call value versus spot price for different volatilities and times to expiration. Each graph has three plots representing options on stock with volatility of 100%, 50% and 10%.

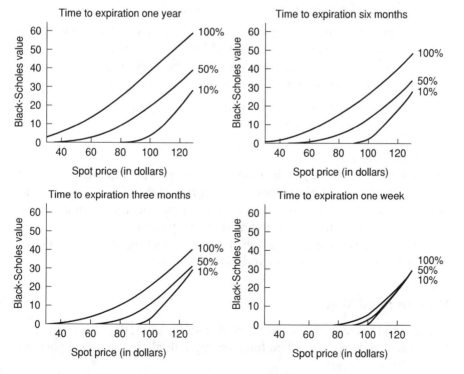

The latter point is most obvious with only one week until expiration. At that time, volatility has little effect on value except near the money.

Why Vega Is Important

The parameter vega is important because it gives us a measure of what happens if the volatility of the underlying changes. An assumption of the Black-Scholes model is that volatility does not change, so one might ask, then why bother to see what happens if it changes? The answer is that, in reality, volatility does change. This will be discussed in Chapter 8.

Since volatility does change, and since volatility is a key determinant of option value, we need to know how sensitive an option is to changes in its value. This is vega.

What Vega Means: Calls and Puts

Let's continue with our discussion of vega. What vega gives us is a simple rule-of-thumb to determine what a 1 percent change in volatility will "do" to the value of the option. This is given by equation (4.10.1). Here is the rule:

Suppose we know the value of any option (call or put). If v is the vega of this option, then a 1 percent change in volatility results in approximately a $\frac{v}{100}$ dollar change in the value of the option.

For example, if the vega of an option is 22.30, then a 1 percent change in volatility will result in approximately a 0.2230 dollar change in option value.

The second fact we need to consider is the relationship between the vega of a European call and a European put. This is simple:

The vega of a European put is equal to the vega of a European call of the same strike and expiration.

Graphs of Vega

Figure 4.10.2 displays a graph of the relationship of the European call (and therefore put) option vega versus the spot price of the underlying for a variety of times to expirations and volatilities in the underlying. In all cases, the risk-free rate of interest is assumed to be 0 percent.

Figure 4.10.3 displays a graph of the relationship of the European call (and therefore put) option vega versus time to expiration.

How to Read Vega

Examining Figure 4.10.2, we see that in all of the plots, the vega is greatest for at-the-money options. Therefore, we might think that an option position

F I G U R E 4.10.2

European option vega versus strike price for an option on an underlying worth $100. In each main plot, the three plots represent underlyings with volatilities of 10, 50, and 100 percent respectively.

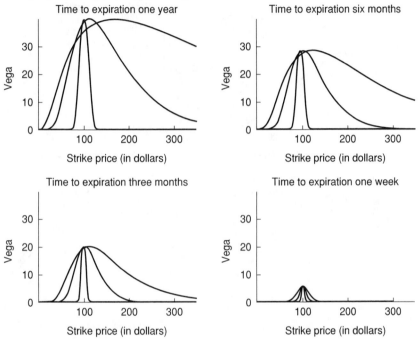

is most vulnerable to volatility changes at the money. In fact, nothing could be further from the truth.

The point is, when using hedge parameters, we have to ask ourselves what our real concern is: percentage price changes or absolute price changes. We illustrate this point with an example.

Example

Data on three call options with three months to expiration are provided in the following table, which we will explain below.

	Option #1	Option #2	Option #3
Spot	$100	$100	$100
Strike	$100	$110	$120
Vega	19.53	5.47	1.67
Value	$3.63	$0.53	$0.03
1% change in volatility	$0.19	$0.054	$0.016
	5.23%	10.19%	53.3%

F I G U R E 4.10.3

European option vega versus time to expiration price for call or put options at different strikes when underlying is $100. Each curve is labeled with the strike price of the option it represents.

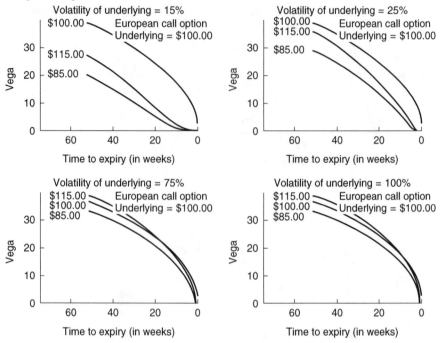

This table shows three options on the same underlying which has a volatility of 15 percent. From left to right, the options are at the money, out of the money, and deep out of the money. The risk-free rate is 5 percent. Each option has three months to expiration. The table shows the Black-Scholes vega and value of each option. The last two rows of the table explain what happens if there is a 1 percent change in volatility, first in absolute terms and then in relative terms.

In absolute terms, the at-the-money option is most sensitive to volatility changes. A 1 percent change in volatility results in a $0.19 change in option value for the $100 strike option. This amounts to a 5.2 percent change in premium (that is, $0.19 is 5.2 percent of the total value). A $110 strike option experiences a $0.054 change in premium for a 1 percent change in volatility. This is a 10.19 percent change in premium. Lastly, the $120 strike option experiences a $0.016 change in premium for a 1 percent change in volatility. This is a 53.3 percent change in premium.

In reality, the percent change in premium is what we care about. To see why, imagine investing $10,000 in either of the three options above. A 1 percent change in volatility changes the value of the first investment by 5.23 percent (a change of plus or minus $523), while a 1 percent change in volatility changes the value of our investment by 53.3 percent if we buy option 3 (a change of $5440). The point is that for a fixed dollar investment (e.g., the $10,000 investment) we will buy more shares of investment three than investment one. Thus, while changes in vega have a smaller effect on price per share of investment three, the overall effect on a fixed dollar investment is much larger.

Conclusions about Vega

The conclusion about vega is that we really want to look at the *normalized vega* of the option, which is the ordinary vega divided by the option premium. Note:

> *Normalized vega measures the percentage change in option value for a 1 percent change in volatility.*

Figure 4.10.4 displays a graph of normalized strike price versus normalized vega. The x-axis is strike price and the y-axis is normalized volatility. We can see from this graph that out-of-the-money options are in fact most sensitive to changes in volatility.

Time Decay—Theta

The rate of change of an option's value with respect to change in time is called the *theta* of the option. As time passes, an option's value will change, *even if the underlying's price remains the same.* We begin our study of theta by specifying exactly what the theta of an option is and what it measures.

What Theta Measures

When time changes during the life of an option, we think of it as moving toward the expiration date. We think of the amount of time between now and the expiration date as shrinking. Therefore, there is an ambiguity when speaking of time: Time increases as we move forward in time, while time to expiration decreases. Thus, whenever speaking of theta, it is important to know how theta is being measured. In this book, and in many other option pricing books, the convention is summed up in the following manner:

> *If Θ is the theta of an option, then when one day passes, the value of the option changes by approximately $\frac{\Theta}{365}$.*

F I G U R E 4.10.4

Vega normalized to measure the percentage change in option value for a 1 percent change in volatility. Each graph contains three plots with options of volatilities 15 percent, 25 percent, and 50 percent. The underlying has a spot price of $100.

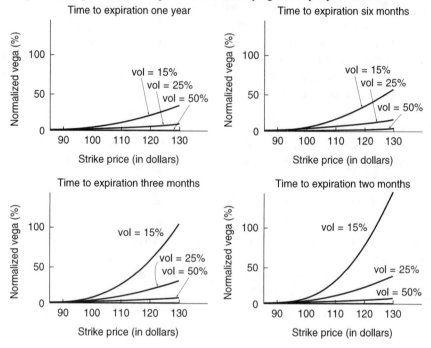

Let's look at this via an equation analogous to equation (4.10.1) for the meaning of vega. We start with the following data:

$$t = \text{today's date}$$
$$\Delta t = \text{a small change in time, measured in years (e.g., one day} = 1/365)$$
$$C(t) = \text{the value of an option at time } t$$
$$C(t + \Delta t) = \text{the value of an option on date } t + \Delta t$$
$$\Theta = \text{the theta of the option}$$

The theta of the option relates the value $C(t)$ to $C(t + \Delta t)$ by the formula:

$$C(t + \Delta t) = C(t) + \Theta \Delta t. \qquad (4.10.3)$$

This leads immediately to a conclusion:

A negative theta means that option value decreases with time, while a positive theta means that option value increases with time.

Example
We use equation (4.10.3) to clarify the meaning of theta. We start with the
following data:

$$S = \$100$$
$$K = \$100$$
$$T - t = 1 \text{ year}$$
$$r = 10\%$$
$$\sigma = 15\%$$
$$\Delta t = 1 \text{ day} = 1/365$$

where S is the spot price, K is the strike price, $T - t$ is time to expiration,
and r is the risk-free rate. What is the value of a plain vanilla European call
option with these data? We have:

$$C(T - t) = \$11.67$$
$$C((T - t) + \Delta t) = \$11.65.$$

Note that the first expression, $C(T - t)$, represents the call option value with
one year to expiration, while the second expression represents the call option
value with $T - (t + \Delta t) = (T - t) - \Delta t$, one year less one day to expiration.
The theta of the one-year option is:

$$\Theta = -8.8142.$$

Therefore, applying equation (4.10.3) yields:

$$C(t + \Delta t) = 11.67 + (-8.8142) \cdot (1/365) = 11.65.$$

In the above expression, 1/365 represents one day, and we see that theta
provided an excellent approximation for the one-day change in option value.

Theta and Spot Price
Figure 4.10.5 displays the relationship between European call option theta
and the spot price of the underlying. In these graphs, the risk-free rate is
set to zero. Notice that the values are always negative. This is an important
fact:

The theta of a European call option is always negative.

This means that if all other inputs to an option's value stay constant, the
value of the option will naturally decrease as time passes. This is why theta
is often called the *time decay* of the option. The term *time decay* is not quite
accurate for European put options.

Figure 4.10.6 displays the relationship between the value of a European put option and spot price. In these graphs, the risk-free rate is set to
10 percent.

F I G U R E 4.10.5

Theta of a European call option versus spot price. Each graph has three plots representing the thetas of options on underlyings with the volatilities of 10%, 50% and 100%.

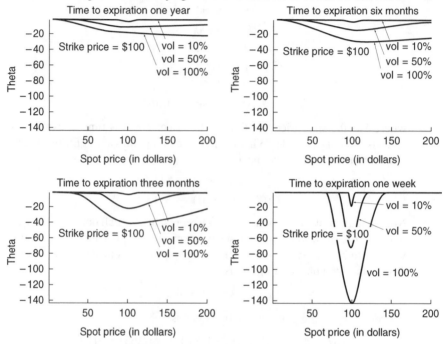

Note that the value of theta is positive for some in-the-money options. One thing to note is that theta can only be positive if the risk-free rate is positive (in particular, non-zero). In fact, the theta of a European put option on a non-dividend-paying stock can always be described as follows:

$$\Theta_p = \Theta_c + rKe^{-r(T-t)},$$

where Θ_p and Θ_c are, respectively, the thetas of a put and a call of the same expiration and the same strike, $T - t$ is the time to expiration, r is the risk-free rate, and K is the strike price. We see that if $r = 0.0$, then $\Theta_p = \Theta_c$. When the risk-free rate is positive, the theta of the put rises in relation to the call option in proportion to the present value of the strike price.

Theta and Time to Expiration
Figure 4.10.7 displays the theta of European call options versus time to expiration. In the graphs, the call option is struck at $100, the risk-free rate

F I G U R E   4.10.6

Theta of a European put option versus spot price for stocks of various volatilities

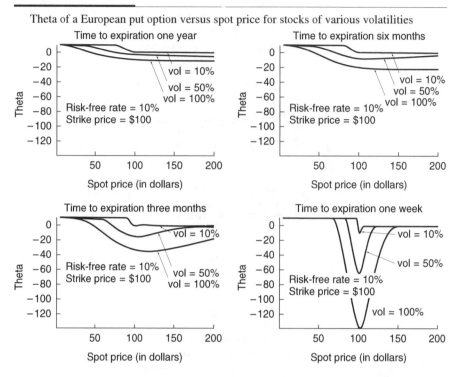

of interest is 0 percent, and the underlying is assumed to have 15 percent volatility. Figure 4.10.8 displays similar graphs for European put options.

Why Time Decay Exists

An important question arises when studying theta: Why does the value of an option change just because time changes? To answer this, let's consider an at-the-money option first. Suppose we have an at-the-money vanilla European call option on a stock and there are two weeks left in the option's life. Because there is some probability that the option will expire in the money, this option has value. (For example, the Black-Scholes value of a two-week at-the-money $100 strike vanilla call on an underlying with 15 percent volatility is approximately $1.27 when interest rates are 5 percent.)

Suppose that for the next two weeks, the price of the stock stays at exactly $100. At the end of the two weeks, the option will expire at the

F I G U R E   4.10.7

Theta of a European call option versus
expiration. Each plot represents a call
option struck at $100 on an underlying
of value $90, $100, or $115.

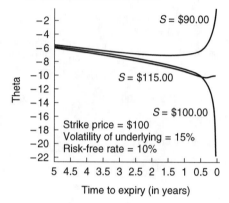

F I G U R E   4.10.8

Theta of a European put option versus
expiration. Each plot represents a put
option struck at $100 on an underlying
of value $90, $100, or $115.

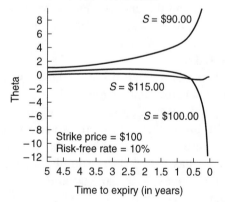

money, and therefore it will expire worthless. Thus, between two weeks before expiration and expiration, the value of the option has to decrease from
$1.27 to $0.00. A table displaying what this "decay" looks like follows, and
Figure 4.10.9 displays a graph of these data.

Days until expiration	Black-Scholes value
14	1.2693
13	1.2197
12	1.1684
11	1.1153
10	1.0600
9	1.0022
8	0.9415
7	0.8773
6	0.8089
5	0.7351
4	0.6543
3	0.5634
2	0.4569
1	0.3202

Now, here is the crucial point: Since we know the value of the option at two weeks to expiry is $1.27 and we know an at-the-money option is worthless at expiry, the price of the option must drop between two weeks until expiration and expiration. Why? Consider the alternative: The option value stays exactly the same and then suddenly "jumps" to zero just before expiration.

Time decay is important to understand because, unlike the variables controlling the other hedge parameters, time change is predictable. For in-

F I G U R E 4.10.9

Black-Scholes value versus time to expiration as an illustration of the time decay of an option's value

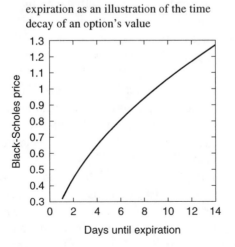

stance, stock price change is, according to the Brownian motion model, completely unpredictable. Therefore, knowing theta can be an important aid in figuring how the value of an option "depreciates" as time passes. That is, since the option's value changes even when its stock price remains the same, it is possible to separate the effect of time on the value of the option. Put another way, the change in the option's value can be decomposed into a deterministic component (controlled by time decay) and a random component (controlled by delta).

The Convexity of the Option—Gamma

The gamma of an option measures how curved a graph relating the underlying's price to the option value is. Equivalently, gamma is the rate of change of the delta with respect to the change in the stock price.

We study gamma because it increases our understanding of delta. Because we deal with delta dynamically, that is, as part of a hedging strategy, it is not enough to simply know what the delta is at any given moment. It is equally important to know how delta is going to change as the price of the underlying changes. This allows us to use gamma as a hedging tool.

Gamma and Hedging

Recall two features of the Black-Scholes hedging strategy: 1) We hold delta shares of the underlying, and 2) When the hedging portfolio becomes out of balance, that is, when we are no longer holding delta shares of the underlying, we bring the portfolio back into balance by buying or selling, so that we have delta shares of the underlying.

Since gamma measures the sensitivity of the delta to changes in the price of the underlying, the implications for hedging are clear. The larger gamma is, the more often the hedge must be rebalanced.

The gamma of an option is affected by all of the input variables of the Black-Scholes formula of an option. Of particular importance are the volatility of the underlying, the time until expiration, and the moneyness of the option. In particular, the closer the option is to being at the money, the greater the gamma will be.

Figure 4.10.10 displays graphs of the gamma of a European call option with respect to strike price, demonstrating the relationship between moneyness, time to expiration, volatility, and gamma. All the graphs represent the Black-Scholes gamma of a vanilla European call with spot price $100. The risk-free rate of interest is assumed to be zero, so the time value

Gamma versus strike price for vanilla European call options on underlyings with spot price $100 and various volatilities.

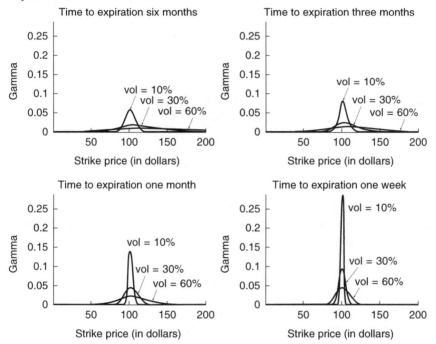

of money plays no role. Notice that for a given strike price, the greater the volatility, the greater the gamma. Also, note that the closer to expiration, the greater the gamma is near the money.

Figure 4.10.11 displays a graph of gamma versus time to expiration for a European call option. There are three plots. Each plot represents the gamma of a vanilla European call option struck at $100 on an underlying of value $100, $90 or $115. Notice that as we move closer to expiration (as we move to the right on the graph), the gamma always increases. This indicates that as an option moves toward expiration, it gets more difficult to hedge (this is most important when the option is new or at the money). Also, notice that gamma is always greatest at the money.

The Gamma of a Put versus a Call

Gamma measures how sensitive an option's delta is to changes in the underlying's price. The important fact is, for a given strike and expiration, vanilla European calls and puts have the same gamma. We can see why

FIGURE 4.10.11

Gamma versus time to expiration for a
vanilla European call option

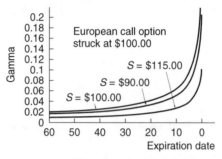

Time to expiry (in weeks)

this is so as follows. Suppose C is a European call and P is a put on the same underlying with the same strike and expiration. If we write Δ_c for the delta of the call and Δ_p for the delta of the put, then we know from put-call parity

$$\Delta_p = \Delta_c - 1.$$

The two deltas are related by a simple constant, and therefore if Δ_c changes by a certain amount, so will Δ_p. The conclusion is:

> *The gammas of a put and a call on the same underlying with the same strike and expiration are equal.*

Interest Rate Sensitivity—Rho

The rho of an option measures its sensitivity to changes in the risk-free rate. As we know, one of the inputs to the Black-Scholes formula is the risk-free rate of interest, and therefore as this rate changes, so does the option value. Thus rho is a measure of the risk in an option position due to changes in the risk-free rate.

Rho is always positive for European calls and always negative for European puts. So, as interest rates increase, the values of European call options rise, and the values of European put options fall. This makes intuitive sense since as interest rates rise, the forward value of a stock increases.

Figure 4.10.12 displays the rhos of European put options on stocks of volatility 60 percent, 30 percent, and 10 percent. Each graph represents a different time until expiration. All the options are struck at 100, and each

F I G U R E 4.10.12

Black-Scholes rho versus spot price for different volatilities and times to expiration.

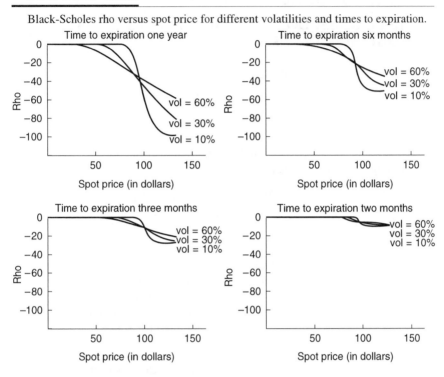

plot represents spot price versus rho. We can see from the graphs that the value of rho is most affected by volatility and largest far from expiration, and out of the money.

Charts

Display 4.10.1 contains a summary of the Black-Scholes formula for European calls and puts, along with formulas for the various hedge parameters discussed above.

The formulas can easily be programmed into a spreadsheet program, provided it has a tool for computing the cumulative normal distribution function $N(\cdot)$. If the cumulative normal distribution function is not available, then simply use one of the four formulas provided in Chapter 2, section 5 to write your own cumulative normal distribution function.

D I S P L A Y 4.10.1

THE BLACK-SCHOLES FORMULA AND HEDGE PARAMETERS

The Black-Scholes Formula

$$C = N(d_1)Se^{-q(T-t)} - e^{-r(T-t)}N(d_2)K \qquad \text{(call option)}$$

$$P = -N(-d_1)Se^{-q(T-t)} + e^{-r(T-t)}N(-d_2)K \qquad \text{(put option)}$$

$N(d_1)$ and $N(d_2)$ are the cumulative normal distribution functions of d_1 and d_2, where

$$d_1 = \frac{\log(S/K) + (r - q + \sigma^2/2)(T - t)}{\sigma\sqrt{T - t}}$$

$$d_2 = d_1 - \sigma\sqrt{T - t}.$$

C = value of the call
P = value of the put K = strike price of the option
t = current time r = risk-free rate of interest
T = expiration date q = continuous dividend yield
S = stock price σ = volatility of the stock

Hedge Parameters (for stocks paying continuous dividends)
Call options

Symbol	Name	Formula
Δ	Delta	$e^{-q(T-t)}N(d_1)$
Γ	Gamma	$\dfrac{N'(d_1)e^{-q(T-t)}}{S\sigma\sqrt{T-t}}$
ν	Vega	$S\sqrt{T - t} \cdot N'(d_1)e^{-q(T-t)}$
Θ	Theta	$-\dfrac{SN'(d_1)\sigma e^{-q(T-t)}}{2\sqrt{T-t}} - rKe^{-r(T-t)}N(d_2) + qSN(d_1)e^{-q(T-t)}$
ρ	Rho	$K(T - t)e^{-r(T-t)}N(d_2)$

D I S P L A Y 4.10.1 (*Cont.*)

THE BLACK-SCHOLES FORMULA AND HEDGE PARAMETERS (*CONTINUED*)

Put options

Symbol	Name	Formula
Δ	Delta	$e^{-q(T-t)}(N(d_1) - 1)$
Γ	Gamma	$\dfrac{N'(d_1)e^{-q(T-t)}}{S\sigma\sqrt{T-t}}$
ν	Vega	$S\sqrt{T-t} \cdot N'(d_1)e^{-q(T-t)}$
Θ	Theta	$-\dfrac{SN'(d_1)\sigma e^{-q(T-t)}}{2\sqrt{T-t}} + rKe^{-r(T-t)}N(-d_2)$ $- qSN(-d_1)e^{-q(T-t)}$
ρ	Rho	$-K(T-t)e^{-r(T-t)}N(-d_2)$

Notes

- $N'(x) = \dfrac{1}{\sqrt{2\pi}}e^{-x^2/2}$
- To obtain formulas for hedge parameters on non-dividend-paying stocks, set $q = 0$ in the above formulas.

COMMENTS AND SUGGESTED READING

The exposition of the Black-Scholes formula in this chapter is different than that found in other texts. There are many mathematical derivations of the formula, ranging from the elementary, such as Hull (1993) and Tompkins (1994), to the more advanced, which include Duffie (1992), Jarrow and Rudd (1983), Merton (1973b), and Wilmott, Dewynne and Howison (1993). The original derivation is in Black and Scholes (1973). Also see Bookstaber (1987) and Cox and Rubinstein (1985). For an interesting first-hand account of the Black-Scholes formula, see Black (1989). Also see Brenner (1983) and Natenberg (1994).

For a history of option pricing formulas, see Merton (1995) and Sullivan and Weithers (1994).

There have been many studies on the effectiveness of option pricing formulas, which include Black and Scholes (1972), MacBeth and Merville (1979), Chance (1986), and Sheikh (1991). The latter article examines S&P 100 index options using 14 months of transaction data and finds systematic deviations from Black-Scholes prices. Pricing biases in the Black-Scholes formula caused by errors in estimating parameters (e.g., the risk-free rate and volatility) are studied in Hammer (1989).

For a study of "alternatives" to the Black-Scholes formula, see Brenner (1983), Hull (1993), or Rubinstein (1985).

For information on the effect of taxes on option valuation, see Scholes (1976). For treatments of tax issues from the point of view of the optimal time to realize gains and losses, see Constantinides and Scholes (1980) and Constantinides and Ingersoll (1984).

For information on how hedge parameters are used by traders, see Cookson (1993) and Natenberg (1994). For a discussion of several more esoteric hedge parameters, such as "charm," see Garman (1992).

The addition of dividends into the Black-Scholes model was carried out by Merton (1973b). There have been many studies on the effect of expected dividend payments on the price of options.

Several other articles on option pricing relating to Black-Scholes are as follows. In Perrakis and Ryan (1994), a model is given for pricing options on thinly traded stocks. The authors compare their model prices to Black-Scholes prices. Two articles examining the gains and losses associated with imperfect dynamic hedging are Leland (1985) and Hodges and Neuberger (1989). For an article giving closed-form formulas for option values that include the possibility of default risk, see Rich (1996).

For a nontechnical study of the application of the Black-Scholes formula for executive stock options (and what may be wrong with it), see Young (1993).

A nontechnical study of the economic assumptions in the Black-Scholes formula and their relevance to option pricing "in the 1990s" is given in Putnam (1993).

5

⑥ MORE ON THE BLACK-SCHOLES FORMULA

In this chapter, we dig deeper into the Black-Scholes theory, addressing unanswered questions and introducing the theory of risk-neutral valuation, which plays a key role in option pricing and is indispensable for understanding the models to come later in this book.

5.1 QUESTIONS ABOUT BLACK-SCHOLES

If we are given a vanilla European call option, the questions we would like to address are:

1. How are the formulas for the Δ_t and B_t in the Black-Scholes formula obtained? That is, how is the Black-Scholes formula actually mathematically derived?
2. What is the relationship between the formulas for Δ_t and B_t and the geometric Brownian motion model?
3. What are the economic assumptions underlying Black-Scholes?

Here, Δ_t is the delta of the option and B_t is the value of the "bond" component of the Black-Scholes formula. There are several ways to obtain the formulas for Δ_t and B_t. The way Black and Scholes did it was to solve a *differential equation* relating the value of the option to its input variables.

To appreciate what this means, think about what we have done so far—we have shown that a formula for a European call option on a stock that follows a geometric Brownian motion must have the form

$\Delta_t S_t - e^{-r(T-t)} B_t$, where Δ_t is the delta of the call at time t and B_t is completely determined by Δ_t and the payoff structure of the option.

Let's recall how we studied the Black-Scholes formula. First, we observed that the changes in the components of the Black-Scholes hedging strategy (Δ_t and B_t) satisfy certain very precise relationships [see equation (4.7.3)]. Next, we examined the option's value on its expiration date and saw that Δ_t and B_t have to satisfy certain *boundary conditions* in order to replicate the option payout. These boundary conditions are determined by the payoff of the option. In the case of a European call, the payoff is $\max(S_T - K, 0)$, where S_T is the terminal stock price and K is the strike price.

Black and Scholes worked along these lines to obtain a differential equation for the value of the option. This equation relates the value of the option to the hedge parameter's delta, gamma, and theta, discussed in Chapter 4, Section 4.10. The equation is described as follows.

An option C (now, any option, not just a vanilla European call or put) on S is given, and its value is assumed to depend on three types of data: 1) stock model data, 2) option specification data, and 3) boundary conditions. Stock model data are based on the assumption that the underlying follows a geometric Brownian motion. The specific data are spot price, instantaneous rate of return, and volatility. Option specification data include time to expiration and strike price, while boundary conditions describe exactly how the option pays off. For example, the boundary condition for a vanilla European call can be summarized as:

> *A vanilla European call only pays off at expiration, and the payoff is* $\max(S_T - K, 0)$.

Let's describe boundary conditions in more detail.

Boundary Conditions

We have already seen the simple boundary condition for a vanilla European call option. Boundary conditions for more complicated options can be described as well. For instance, an American option's boundary is described in terms of what is known as its *early exercise boundary*. This is the boundary, delineated in coordinates of time and stock price, where it becomes more favorable to exercise the option than to hold it. For example, a point on the early exercise boundary for an American put would describe a time t and a stock price S such that at any price below S (at time t only), the option is optimal to exercise, and at any price above S (at time t only), the option is more valuable to hold than to exercise.

It is an interesting fact about option pricing that if we can describe this boundary precisely, then an exact formula for the value of an American option can be derived.[1]

Once an option and its boundary conditions are described, an equation is given relating the security to its various hedge parameters. The variables in the equation, however, do not represent numbers as in ordinary algebraic equations. Rather, they represent functions of time and stock price. Such an equation is called a differential equation. The Black-Scholes differential equation is given as follows:

$$\Theta_t + rS_t\Delta_t + \frac{1}{2}\sigma^2 S^2 \Gamma_t = rC_t, \tag{5.1.1}$$

where

Θ_t = the theta of the option at time t
S_t = value of S at time t
Δ_t = the delta of the option at time t
σ = the volatility of the stock
Γ_t = the gamma of the option at time t
r = the risk-free rate of interest
C_t = value of C at time t

Just as the variables in this equation are not numbers, neither is the solution. Rather, the solution is a formula for C_t, the value of the option. This formula relates the value of the security to the current stock price, and it has the correct boundary values, and of course is the Black-Scholes formula when the option is a vanilla European call or put.

The phrase *has the correct boundary values* means that wherever a boundary condition has been specified, the formula agrees with the specified boundary condition. For instance, in the case of a European call option, we know the value of the option *at the expiration date*—this is the boundary, and the condition is that the value of the option is equal to $\max(S_T - K, 0)$.

From this point of view, we learn something very interesting about options. If we believe the Black-Scholes differential equation, then all options have price behavior captured in the same way by their hedge parameters. The only difference between many options—European, American, or otherwise—is in their boundary conditions.

---

[1] A great deal of work has been done on describing the early exercise boundary of an American option, none of which has produced a completely satisfactory answer. See the notes at the end of the chapter for more on this.

How Differential Equations Are Solved

In practice, there are two types of solutions to differential equations: *closed-form solutions* and *numerical solutions.*

A *closed-form solution* is an actual formula that satisfies the differential equation for all possible values of the input parameters. For example, the Black-Scholes formula is a closed-form solution to the Black-Scholes differential equation. This type of solution is most desirable because it is easy to use and takes relatively little computer time to compute.

Conversely, a *numerical solution* is one that is produced on a computer and gives an approximate answer. This type of solution is less desirable than a closed-form solution because the solutions require a great deal of computation time, which is expensive in terms of computer time. Unfortunately, it is generally not easy to find closed-form solutions to partial differential equations, and numerical solutions often have to suffice. One exception is the case of European options.

In this case, Black and Scholes were able to explicitly solve their differential equation, and their solutions for European calls and puts are precisely the Black-Scholes formula. These solutions also give the formulas for the hedge parameters found in Display 4.10.1.

Where the Differential Equation Comes From

As we emphasized in the last chapter, the key to the Black-Scholes formula is in being able to perfectly replicate the payoff of the option using a certain number of shares of the stock combined with a certain amount of a riskless bond. This idea is *not* due to Black and Scholes. It was already known, for instance, to Thorp and Kassouf (1967).[2]

The main difference—and it is a huge difference—that distinguishes Black and Scholes' work from its predecessors is that they observed that a combination of "delta" long shares of the underlying and the short option is *riskless* over a very short period of time and therefore should earn a return equal to a riskless investment. The latter is obtained through simple arbitrage arguments. This is explained in Black's quote at the beginning of Chapter 4. We now proceed to demonstrate that the riskless hedge is actually riskless.

Proof That the Riskless Hedge Is Riskless

Consider a call option C with value C_{t_0} at time t_0 on a stock S with value S_{t_0}. Let Δ_{t_0} represent the delta of C at time t_0, and consider the portfolio of

---

[2]This is not a controversial topic; in fact, Black and Scholes refer to this fact in Black and Scholes (1972).

Δ_{t_0} shares of S long and C short. Its value at time t_0 is

$$\Delta_{t_0} S_{t_0} - C_{t_0}.$$

At time t_1, its value will change to

$$\Delta_{t_0} S_{t_1} - C_{t_1},$$

where S_{t_1} and C_{t_1} are the values of the respective instruments at time t_1. Be careful to note that this portfolio still has Δ_{t_0} shares of stock. The number of shares does not automatically change when the delta changes. That is, even though the delta (Δ_{t_1}) is different, the number of shares in the portfolio is still Δ_{t_0}.

Discounting this to time t_0, we obtain

$$e^{-r(t_1 - t_0)}(\Delta_{t_0} S_{t_1} - C_{t_1}).$$

Let's compute what the change in value of this portfolio from time t_0 to time t_1 was. By subtracting the value at time t_1 from the value at time t_0, we obtain

$$(\Delta_{t_0} S_{t_0} - C_{t_0}) - e^{-r(t_1 - t_0)}(\Delta_{t_0} S_{t_1} - C_{t_1}),$$

which simplifies to

$$\Delta_{t_0}(S_{t_0} - e^{-r(t_1 - t_0)} S_{t_1}) - (C_{t_0} - e^{-r(t_1 - t_0)} C_{t_1}). \qquad (5.1.2)$$

Now consider our "approximate" formula for the delta of C at time t_0, equation (4.5.1) in the last chapter:

$$\Delta_{t_0} = \frac{C_{t_0} - e^{-r(t_1 - t_0)} C_{t_1}}{S_{t_0} - e^{-r(t_1 - t_0)} S_{t_1}}.$$

Substituting this into equation (5.1.2), we obtain

$$\frac{C_{t_0} - e^{-r(t_1 - t_0)} C_{t_1}}{S_{t_0} - e^{-r(t_1 - t_0)} S_{t_1}}(S_{t_0} - e^{-r(t_1 - t_0)} S_{t_1}) - (C_{t_0} - e^{-r(t_1 - t_0)} C_{t_1}),$$

which is equal to

$$(C_{t_0} - e^{-r(t_1 - t_0)} C_{t_1}) - (C_{t_0} - e^{-r(t_1 - t_0)} C_{t_1}) = 0.$$

There is one important word of warning regarding the above equation. Since we used the approximate formula for the delta, the above equation represents something that is only approximately equal to zero. As time t_1 gets closer and closer to time t_0, the value of the above equation becomes exactly 0. The end result of this is that the Black-Scholes hedge, $\Delta_{t_0} S_{t_0} - C_{t_0}$ is what we call *instantaneously riskless*. That is, it is not riskless for any more than a single instance, less time than any positive amount of time. In other words, the portfolio does not change value: It is perfectly riskless.

This is a powerful observation, which Black and Scholes used to the optimal advantage. They observed that previous attempts at deriving an options pricing formula neglected to make this observation.

> What [Thorp and Kassouf] failed to pursue is the fact that in equilibrium, the expected return on such a hedged position must be equal to the return on a riskless asset.[3]

What Black and Scholes are getting at in this quote is that by arbitrage principles an asset that is riskless over a period of time, however short, must return the risk-free rate of interest over that period of time. Therefore the Black-Scholes hedge $\Delta_{t_0} S_{t_0} - C_{t_0}$ must have an *instantaneous rate of return* equal to r.

Once this observation is made, it is possible to easily derive the Black-Scholes differential equation. Such a derivation, however, requires the mathematics of stochastic differential equations, which is beyond the scope of this book. A simple exposition of this may be found in Hull (1993).

5.2 RISK-NEUTRAL VALUATION

The Black-Scholes differential equation reveals something about the nature of option pricing that is not intuitively obvious: The value of an option does not depend on the expected rate of return of the stock. We say that the Black-Scholes differential equation "reveals" this because nowhere in the equation does the term corresponding to rate of return appear. That is, since equation (5.1.1) uniquely determines the formula for the option, and none of the parameters in the formula depend on the expected rate of return, we deduce that the option formula itself is independent of the expected rate of return.

These observations led the financial economists Cox and Ross to develop an important tool known as the risk-neutral valuation method of security valuation.[4]

The method of risk-neutral valuation is a tool that is a mixture of economics and mathematics that allows one to more easily produce option pricing formulas.

---

[3]From "The Pricing of Options and Corporate Liabilities," Black and Scholes (1972), pp. 399–418.

[4]This concept was introduced in Cox and Ross (1976).

How Risk-Neutral Valuation Works

The main principle behind risk-neutral valuation is the observation that the value of an option on a stock does not depend on the expected return of the stock. This leads to a powerful technique for options valuation.

Cox and Ross reason as follows: First, if a stock follows the geometric Brownian motion model of price movements, then the Black-Scholes differential equation says that to avoid arbitrage opportunities, option values must equal the values predicted by the Black-Scholes formula. But these formulas should be valid regardless of the average investor's view toward risk. Why? Because the Black-Scholes differential equation does not include as an input the expected return of the underlying—the only measure of investors' risk preferences.[5]

More precisely, as long as a given "investment world" satisfies the basic assumptions of the Black-Scholes formula, the values given by the formula will hold. The latter assumptions are cataloged in Section 5.5 of this chapter.

Now the question is, is there an "investment world" where it is particularly simple to derive option pricing formulas? The answer is yes, and it is the world in which investors are completely neutral toward risk. Such a world, called a *risk-neutral world,* is characterized by the fact that investors require no risk premium for their investments. That is, they always demand *only* the risk-free rate of interest as their average expected return on an investment. There is only one world in which investors would have this view toward risk.

A world is risk-neutral precisely when the expected return on all assets is the risk-free rate of interest. Thus, one could say that the reason investors are neutral toward risk is because on average there is none.[6]

Returning to pricing formulas, we see that as long as our world satisfies the basic economic assumptions of Black-Scholes, the Black-Scholes prices hold in it as well. That is, if we use the Black-Scholes model in a risk-neutral world, we will obtain the same option values as we would in our own world.

---

[5]We note, however, that investors' risk-preferences do influence the price of the underlying, so that, strictly speaking, option prices are affected by risk preferences. The author thanks David Shimko for pointing this out.

[6]The term "risk-neutral" comes up a lot in option pricing theory. It should always be taken to mean "in a risk-neutral world," which in turn means "in a world where all assets have an expected rate of return equal to the risk-free rate of return."

Thinking about Risk-Neutral Worlds

What makes risk-neutral worlds unique is that they place all assets on a level playing field. In that the expected return on all assets is equal to the risk-free rate, we ask, What determines the price of an asset? There is only one possible answer: volatility.

In the "real world," we have to consider the relationship between risk (i.e., volatility) and reward (i.e., expected return) to price an asset. In a risk-neutral world, reward has been normalized; that is, the playing field has been leveled with respect to reward. Therefore, one can expect a *monotonic* relationship between the risk of an asset and its price. Put another way, the riskier an asset in a risk-neutral world, the less expensive it is. To see this, we just have to imagine two assets with the same price, the same expected rate of return, and two different volatilities. We make the basic assumption that an investor would choose to purchase the less volatile asset. Why? We assume this because we are speaking about an investor, someone who is purchasing the assets to earn a rate of return on his or her investment. All other things being equal, we take it as self-evident that such a person would always choose the least risky way to earn a given rate of return.

It is clear that risk-neutral worlds are the perfect economic tool for pricing options, for these "worlds" isolate risk as the most important determining factor in the price of an asset. This puts all assets on an equal footing with options, which the Black-Scholes equation shows are already "risk-neutral" assets of a sort. In the following section, we use the assumption of risk-neutrality to give a very quick derivation of the Black-Scholes formula.

A Risk-Neutral Derivation of Black-Scholes[7]

We now use the observations about risk-neutral worlds to derive the Black-Scholes formula. What we do is assume we are in a risk-neutral world, derive an option pricing formula, and then note, as we discussed above, that this formula holds in all worlds. Remember, the derivation that follows is intuitive, and only valid once it has been determined that the price of an option does not depend on the expected rate of return of the underlying.

We start by assuming that we have a call option C on a stock S struck at K with time until expiration $T - t$, so that today's date is t and the expiration date is T. We form the Black-Scholes riskless hedge, consisting of Δ_t shares of S long and C short. Call this portfolio Π. Its value at time t is given by

$$\Pi_t = \Delta_t S_t - C_t.$$

---

[7]This section is based on unpublished work of the author.

Since we are in a risk-neutral world, the expected value of Π at time T is equal to

$$e^{r(T-t)}(\Delta_t S_t - C_t). \tag{5.2.1}$$

This is true *because* of the risk-neutral assumption. We are regarding Π as an asset whose value at any time t is equal to $\Delta_t S_t - C_t$. In a risk-neutral world, the return on any asset, no matter how obscure, is given by the risk-free rate.

On the other hand, we can compute the expected value of Π a second way using the boundary values of Δ and C. If the option expires in the money, then its delta is one and the option value is $S_T - K$. Thus, in this case, Π will be worth $S_T - (S_T - K) = K$.

Conversely, if the option expires out of the money, then both Δ_T and C_T will be equal to zero and Π will be worth nothing. Therefore, Π has only two possible values at expiration: K (if the option expires in the money) or 0 (if the option expires out of the money). This means that the expected value of the portfolio at expiration will be $p \cdot K$, where p is the probability that C will expire in the money.

It is important to remember that to compute p, we need to know the distribution of returns on the stock from time t (now) to time T (expiration). In fact, we know this distribution. We assumed that the stock follows a geometric Brownian motion, so the returns are normally distributed, and we are in a risk-neutral world, so the expected rate of return is equal to the risk-free rate of interest. All that remains is to compute the volatility from historical data.

In Chapter 3 we computed p. Assuming that the volatility of S is σ and the risk-free rate is r, we have

$$p = N(d_2), \quad d_2 = \frac{\log(S_t/K) + (r - \frac{\sigma^2}{2})(T - t)}{\sigma\sqrt{T - t}}. \tag{5.2.2}$$

Combining this with the fact that the expected value equals $p \cdot K$ we see the expected value of Π at time T is equal to $N(d_2)K$.

We now have two expressions for the expected value of Π, given in equations 5.2.1 and 5.2.2. One says the expected value is $e^{r(T-t)}\Pi$, and the other says it is $N(d_2)K$. This means we have:

$$e^{r(T-t)}(\Delta_t S_t - C_t) = N(d_2)K.$$

At this point, we can just solve the above equation for C_t, and obtain:

$$C_t = \Delta_t S_t - e^{-r(T-t)}N(d_2)K.$$

Of course, at this point we do not have a formula for Δ_t. We will get to this in a moment, but admit that it involves a bit of differential calculus. However, since this is an important derivation, we include the proof for completeness. The uninterested reader may skip this proof without consequence.

Deriving the Formula for Δ_t

First, we write down a simple algebraic identity:

$$N'(d_2) = \frac{S_t}{K} e^{r(T-t)} N'(d_1), \qquad (5.2.3)$$

where $N'(x) = \frac{1}{\sqrt{2\pi}} e^{-x^2/2}$. This is verified with nothing more than algebra.

Now, we differentiate both sides of the equation

$$C_t = \Delta_t S_t - e^{-r(T-t)} N(d_2) K,$$

with respect to S_t and obtain:

$$\Delta_t = \Delta_t + \Gamma_t S_t - \frac{e^{-r(T-t)} N'(d_2) K}{S_t \sigma \sqrt{T-t}}.$$

Therefore,

$$\Gamma_t S_t = \frac{e^{-r(T-t)} N'(d_2) K}{S_t \sigma \sqrt{T-t}}.$$

Substituting equation (5.2.3), we obtain:

$$\Gamma_t S_t = \frac{N'(d_1)}{\sigma \sqrt{T-t}},$$

so that

$$\Gamma_t = \frac{N'(d_1)}{S_t \sigma \sqrt{T-t}}.$$

On the other hand, since

$$\frac{\partial N(d_1)}{\partial S_t} = \frac{N'(d_1)}{S_t \sigma \sqrt{T-t}},$$

we see that

$$\Delta_t = N(d_1) + \text{constant}.$$

We see immediately, however, that the constant must be zero in order for the boundary conditions to hold.

5.3 DELTA HEDGING

This section describes a variant of the Black-Scholes hedging strategy that works quite well in hedging the risk associated with writing a European call or put option and eliminates the need for trading the bond portion of the hedge. This has the practical advantages of reducing transaction costs, but it has the disadvantage of neither replicating the payoff of the option nor matching the total cost of hedging to the set-up cost of the hedge. Despite this, this hedging strategy does completely hedge the risk associated with writing the option.

Description of Delta Hedging for a European Call or Put Option

The following strategies are used to hedge short option positions. Let C be a call option on a stock S, and let Δ_t be the delta of the option at time t. Then, the delta hedging strategy is:

Hold Δ_t shares of S at time t.

If P is a put option with the same strike and expiration as C, then the delta hedging strategy is:

Sell $1 - \Delta_t$ shares of S at time t.

The Purpose of Delta Hedging

So, what good is delta hedging? Let's consider hedging the short position on a call option. That is, suppose we are writing an option and want to employ delta hedging. If we follow the hedging strategy, at expiration, we will have one share of S if the option expires in the money and no shares otherwise. To see this, remember that at expiration, the delta is one if the option is in the money, and it is zero otherwise. Conversely, if we are hedging the short position of a put option, at expiration we will be short one share of stock if the option expires in the money, and we will be short nothing otherwise.

In the case of the call, if the option expires in the money, we are required to sell the stock at $\$K$ per share, and if it expires out of the money, nothing is required.

If the option expires in the money, then we have the stock to sell, so we don't have to acquire it (i.e., we are covered). Therefore, the pertinent question is, Did we break even hedging the option? Put another way, we want to ask, What did it cost us to hedge the option? In this case, we hope it costs no more than the option premium plus the K we receive for the stock.

In the same vein, if the option expires out of the money, we possess nothing at expiration, but we also need nothing. Therefore, we are perfectly covered. Still, we have to ask how much the hedging strategy costs. In this case, we would like the strategy to have cost no more than the option premium.

What we need to do is compute the total cost of delta hedging. We will compute the costs in a moment, but right now we tabulate what they are. The costs are summarized in Table 5.3.1.

It is important to understand that we have to value the cost of hedging at a particular time. As hedging takes place, rebalancing costs occur at different times. The interest expense must be accounted for. Despite the seeming complexity of accounting for this, we will see that the costs come out the same every time, regardless of how the rebalancing costs are distributed.

We now explain why the costs arise as they do.

How Does Delta Hedging Work?
Understanding delta hedging is easy because much of the work was already done in studying the Black-Scholes hedging strategy.

Suppose the "delta hedge" is initiated at time t_0 and rebalanced at time t_1. Let's compute the approximate total cost of hedging between time t_0 and t_1. First, there is the initial cost of hedging, $\$\Delta_{t_0} S_{t_0}$, the cost of Δ_{t_0} shares of S at a cost of $\$S_{t_0}$ per share. Next, there is the rebalancing cost at time t_1, which is computed by looking at the cost of selling off the Δ_{t_0} shares and buying back Δ_{t_1} shares—all at $\$S_{t_1}$ per share. Lastly, we have to discount the cost of this purchase to time t_0, multiplying by a factor of $e^{-r(t_1-t_0)}$.

TABLE 5.3.1

The cost of delta hedging a call option on a stock S with strike price K and time until expiration $T - t_0$

Expires	Cost	Holding at Expiration
In the money	$e^{r(T-t_0)} C_{t_0} + K$	S_T
Out of the money	$e^{r(T-t_0)} C_{t_0}$	0

We tabulate these costs as follows:

		Valued at time t_0
initial cost	$\Delta_{t_0} S_{t_0}$	$\Delta_{t_0} S_{t_0}$
rebalancing cost	$(\Delta_{t_1} - \Delta_{t_0}) S_{t_1}$	$e^{-r(t_1 - t_0)}(\Delta_{t_1} - \Delta_{t_0}) S_{t_1}$

The total cost, discounted to time t_0, is the sum of the right-hand column of the above table:

$$\Delta_{t_0}(S_{t_0} - e^{-r(t_1 - t_0)} S_{t_1}) + e^{-r(t_1 - t_0)} \Delta_{t_1} S_{t_1}.$$

Now we substitute the approximate formula

$$\Delta_{t_0} = \frac{C_{t_0} - e^{-r(t_1 - t_0)} C_{t_1}}{S_{t_0} - e^{-r(t_1 - t_0)} S_{t_1}}$$

into the above equation and obtain that the total cost of hedging, valued at time t_0, is

$$C_{t_0} - e^{-r(t_1 - t_0)} C_{t_1} + e^{-r(t_1 - t_0)} \Delta_{t_1} S_{t_1}.$$

Now let T be the expiration date of C. Proceeding along the same lines as with Black-Scholes hedging, we can derive that the total cost of hedging between initiation (time t_0) and expiration (time T) is

$$C_{t_0} - e^{-r(T - t_0)} C_T + e^{-r(T - t_0)} \Delta_T S_T. \tag{5.3.1}$$

Substituting the terminal values for Δ_T ($\Delta_T = 1$ if the option is in the money, $\Delta_T = 0$ if the option is out of the money) and the possible values for C_T ($C_T = S_T - K$ if the option is in the money; $C_T = 0$ if the option is out of the money), we transform equation (5.3.1) into

$$C_{t_0} + \begin{cases} e^{-r(T - t_0)} K & \text{if the option is in the money,} \\ 0 & \text{if the option is out of the money.} \end{cases}$$

This is the total cost of delta hedging from time t_0 to time T, valued at time t_0. If we look at the values at time T, we obtain the values in Table 5.3.1. That is, we have shown that delta hedging perfectly hedges the risk of the short-call position.

5.4 A COMMON MISCONCEPTION ABOUT BLACK-SCHOLES

In this section, we discuss a common misconception about the Black-Scholes formula. Consider a plain vanilla European option C on a stock S

struck at K and expiring at some time T in the future. Here is one common way of looking at valuing C.

Since the payoff of C is $S_T - K$ if the option expires in the money, and zero otherwise (where S_T is the value of S at expiration), we can "decompose" the option into two fundamental pieces:

1. A long stock-or-nothing option struck at K; that is, an option paying S_T if it expires in the money, and nothing otherwise.
2. A short binary option struck at K with payout K; that is, an option that pays K if $S_T > K$ and zero otherwise.

Clearly, a portfolio consisting of these two options has the same value as a European call option because holding this portfolio replicates the payout of the call. We now separately discuss how to value each of these options.

The Binary Option

The value of the binary option may be deduced using a risk-neutral valuation argument similar to the risk-neutral derivation of Black-Scholes found in the previous section.

Following that argument, the value of the binary option is easy to see; it is

$$-e^{-r(T-t_0)} P \cdot K,$$

where $T - t_0$ is the time until expiration, r is the risk-free rate, and P is the risk-neutral probability that the option expires in the money. It makes sense, at least intuitively, that since $P \cdot K$ represents the expected value of a binary option, this is so because the binary option has only two payoffs: K (if the option is in the money) and zero (if the option is out of the money). Its expected value, then, is the probability of each outcome times the value of that outcome.

Now, if we accept the risk-neutrality assumption (that is, if we accept that the value of any security is the risk-neutral expected value of its payouts, discounted to today's date), then there is nothing more to say, and we move on to the cash-or-nothing option.

The Stock-or-Nothing Option

Having dispensed with the binary option's value, we use the same logic to value the cash-or-nothing option; its value is argued to be

$$e^{-r(T-t_0)} P \cdot S_{t_0}. \tag{5.4.1}$$

That is, the value of the cash-or-nothing option is equal to the present value of the risk-neutral probability of the stock expiring in the money times the current value of the stock. At first glance, this seems to make sense in that we are mimicking the argument for the binary option, only using the stock instead of the bond. Unfortunately, the situation is not so simple.

Discussion

The reasoning above leads some people to the erroneous conclusion that the Δ of a European call option is the risk-neutral probability of the stock expiring in the money. Moreover, it has lead to confusion regarding the Black-Scholes formula. For this reason, the matter deserves some attention.

First of all, equation (5.4.1) *is not* the expected value of a stock-or-nothing option. Why? To understand this, let's recall what expected value means.

Suppose we believe the stock, S, follows a geometric Brownian motion. Then, the expected value of the stock-or-nothing option is given, roughly speaking, as the "sum" over all possible payouts of the option times the probability of those payouts occurring. For such an option, the payouts are easy to describe. They are S_T if $S_T > K$ and zero otherwise. Therefore, to compute the expected value, we have to "sum" over all possible values of S_T that are greater than K and multiply that total by the probability of these values occurring.

This is, in fact, an easy exercise in calculus, and the correct value of the stock-or-nothing is

$$N(d_1)S_{t_0}, \qquad d_1 = \frac{\log(S_{t_0}/K) + (r + \frac{\sigma^2}{2})(T - t_0)}{\sigma\sqrt{T - t_0}}, \qquad (5.4.2)$$

where $N(\cdot)$ represents the standard cumulative normal distribution, r represents the risk-free rate of interest, and σ represents the volatility of S. Examining equation (5.4.2), we see that $N(d_1)$ is nothing but the delta of the European call. Thus, $N(d_1)$ is *not* the probability of expiring in the money; rather, it is related to the expected value of the entire stock-or-nothing option. Moreover, we saw from the Black-Scholes formula that $N(d_1)$ is indeed the delta of the call.

We can see this directly by using a hedging argument. We discuss this now.

A Hedging Argument

A simpler way to compute the value of the stock-or-nothing option is to use the same sort of hedging arguments employed in delta hedging a European call.

Write δ_{t_0} for the delta of the stock-or-nothing option at time t_0. That is, δ_{t_0} is the rate of change of the option value with respect to changes in the underlying.

We are going to make two observations:

1. We can use the delta of the stock-or-nothing option to hedge it.

2. δ_{t_0} is equal to the delta of the call option, C.

Let's recall that the stock-or-nothing pays S at expiration (T = expiration) if the option is in the money and nothing otherwise. Write $\mathscr{C}_{t_0}$ for the value of the stock-or-nothing option at time t_0. Then, an approximate formula for δ_{t_0} is

$$\delta_{t_0} = \frac{\mathscr{C}_{t_0} - e^{-r(t_0 - t_1)}\mathscr{C}_{t_1}}{S_{t_0} - e^{-r(t_1 - t_0)}S_{t_1}}.$$

Note that this is quite similar to the approximate formula for the delta of a European call option (therefore, we will not discuss it much).

Now, arguing as we did with European calls, we can see that as time nears expiration, the delta of $\mathscr{C}$ nears one if the option expires in the money, and is zero otherwise (just as the delta of the call). Moreover, if we hold δ shares of S at all times, this will perfectly hedge $\mathscr{C}$, the cash-or-nothing option.[8]

An Arbitrage Argument

Now, if we hold a portfolio at time t_0 consisting of δ_{t_0} shares of S long and $N(d_2)$ "shares" of a riskless, zero-coupon bond maturing to K short (where $N(d_2)$ is the term found in the Black-Scholes formula), then this portfolio will be worth

$$\delta_{t_0}S_{t_0} - e^{-r(T-t_0)}N(d_2)K. \tag{5.4.3}$$

On the other hand, if we make sure to hold δ_t shares of S and short $N(d_2)$ "shares" of the bond at all times t (where $N(d_2)$ is computed with the correct values of S_t and t), then this strategy is self-financing and replicates the payoff of the option. Therefore, equation (5.4.3) *is* the Black-Scholes formula, and in particular, δ_{t_0} must be equal to $N(d_1)$, the delta of the call option.

5.5 THE ECONOMIC ASSUMPTIONS BEHIND BLACK-SCHOLES

We have just produced two strategies for hedging the risk associated with a put or call option—the Black-Scholes hedging strategy and delta hedging.

---

[8]We will not do the calculations here, as they are exactly the same as those for European calls.

We now scrutinize these hedging strategies and the logic used to derive them to see what kind of economic world supports them. That is, we are going to catalog exactly what economic assumptions go into Black-Scholes.

Short Selling with Full Use of Proceeds
The Black-Scholes hedge for short European calls consists of a bond sold short and a certain number of shares of the underlying long. Conversely, the hedge for short puts consists of a certain number of shares of a stock sold short and a long bond position. In both cases, the value of the hedging portfolio is determined by the value of the long position and the value of the short position. In order for the hedging strategy to work, we have to be able to use the proceeds from the short sale to help finance the purchase of the long position. If this money is not available, then it has to be obtained elsewhere—either by borrowing or by removing that money from another investment. In either case, this changes the cost of hedging, and the hedging strategy will not be self-financing. We conclude:

> If we cannot short-sell and have full use of proceeds, the Black-Scholes hedging strategy will not be self-financing.

The Liquid Markets Assumption
Each time we rebalance the Black-Scholes hedge, we have to be able to buy or sell shares of the underlying stock and sell or buy a riskless, zero-coupon bond in the proportions required by the hedge. Moreover, these purchases must take place at exactly the same price we are using to compute the delta and bond. For example, if the underlying stock is selling for $100 per share, then we use this value as an input to the formula for the delta and to the formula for the amount of bond to hold. When we actually make the purchase, there is no guarantee that we will obtain the underlying for $100 per share.

The assumption that we can purchase the underlying for $100 is part of the liquid markets assumption. But what if we need to purchase many shares and the market for these shares is thin? First of all, a large purchase of an asset can potentially impact the market by raising the assets price; this is all the more serious in thin markets. For example, if the hedging strategy calls for purchasing 10,000 shares of the underlying (which could happen if, for example, in hedging a call option on 100,000 shares, the delta rises 0.1 between rebalancing) in a thinly traded market, the purchase might not be possible at the fair market value. The large number of shares relative to a poorly traded market might raise the price. In such a case, the cash flow of the purchase would not equal what is expected by the Black-Scholes formula. This would have the effect of raising the total cost of hedging the option beyond what is necessary for it to be self-financing. Likewise, if it is necessary to sell a large block of the asset to rebalance, the trade price of the asset may move down, again having a detrimental effect on the hedge.

The Black-Scholes formula itself does not take any of this into account. It is implicit in the formula that all trades can be made and are made at fair market value. An explanation of this from the trader's perspective is summed up in the following quote discussing hedge rebalancing.

> ...when to rebalance the hedge involves looking at how the market has traded in the past. Depending on that, a trader might decide to rebalance for only small changes in the delta...[in] liquid foreign exchange markets, where dealing costs are minimal, this means traders might rebalance once or even twice a day. For single-stock options, for which the underlying might be both illiquid and expensive to trade, it may be only once a week.[9]

The Constant Interest Rate Assumption

When hedging a European call option, we are constantly buying and selling bonds, as per the hedging strategy. In particular, the hedging strategy requires that we sell a bond of a particular *par value*. We compute the cost of this transaction by discounting the par value by the risk-free rate of interest. There is one large problem with this: The risk-free rate of interest is not constant, but the Black-Scholes formula assumes it is.

When the risk-free rate differs from the one assumed by the formula, the actual costs of the bond differ from the ones implicit in the formula. For example, if the hedging strategy requires us to buy a riskless one-year bond with a par value of $10,000, and if the risk-free rate is assumed to be continuously compounded at 5 percent, then the price of the bond according to Black-Scholes is $9,512. However, if at the time of the purchase the risk-free rate is 4 percent, then the actual cost of the bond is $9,608.

The impact of this difference is felt in the total cost of hedging. The Black-Scholes formula is self-financing when all of the assumptions underlying it are met. In particular, this means that all of the costs built into the formula have to be equal to the actual costs in carrying out the strategy. When this fails to be true, we can no longer be confident that the total cost of hedging will be equal to the Black-Scholes price.

The Continuous Trading Assumption

The Black-Scholes hedging strategy works if one can rebalance the hedge continuously. In reality, we do not do this. However, the more frequently

---

[9]From "Moving in the Right Direction," Cookson (1993), p. 22–26.

one rehedges, the more closely one can approximate the Black-Scholes price. This, of course, immediately leads us to the question of transaction costs.

The No-Transaction-Costs Assumption

Nowhere in the Black-Scholes formula are transaction costs taken into consideration. All costs are computed *as if* the total cost of the transaction is given by the market values of the instruments bought or sold. In reality, all transactions have costs that differ from market values due, at least, to bid-ask spread and often include broker fees, commissions, and exchange costs. For example, at a given time the Black-Scholes formula may indicate "buy eight shares at $53 per share." In reality it may be impossible for a trader to execute this trade at that time, and the trades may have to choose between buying fewer shares or paying a higher price. These costs move the real total cost of hedging away from the theoretical cost of hedging.

The No-Arbitrage Assumption

The Black-Scholes theory is predicated on the assumption that if you can hedge an option for a certain price, then this must be the price of the option. Any other price allows an easy arbitrage opportunity.

For this to be so, the economy must allow no-arbitrage opportunities, for such opportunities arise whenever there are two essentially equivalent assets being sold for different prices. Therefore, the no-arbitrage assumption is crucial. In reality there are arbitrage opportunities, especially in thinly traded markets.

The Geometric Brownian Motion Assumption

The Black-Scholes hedging strategy works because one can compute the delta of a European option. The formula for the delta only holds when the stock price movement has the statistical properties associated with a geometric Brownian motion. We should carefully note several things here.

First, the geometric Brownian motion model assumes that the underlying stock price path has constant volatility. If this is not the case, then fluctuations in volatility that are not correlated with stock change (random volatility changes) can cause changes in the option value *even when the stock price does not change*. This implies that we can make or lose money on a "delta-neutral" position when volatility changes unpredictably. The upshot is that one cannot be perfectly hedged if volatility is randomly changing.

Next, geometric Brownian motion assumes that stock price paths are continuous. That is, Black-Scholes assumes that stock prices do not jump.

In reality, prices do jump, and a "Black-Scholes"-hedged position will not be hedged against jump risk. Therefore, even the most meticulously maintained hedge is vulnerable to sudden jumps in the price of the underlying (for more on this see the simulated hedges at the end of this chapter).

Jim Gatheral, head of equity risk management at Merrill Lynch says:

> Black-Scholes assumes random walk. But the underlying returns are not normal and everyone knows that, so the deltas are going to be wrong.[10]

Why Study Black-Scholes at All?

After such a long list of impossible-to-satisfy assumptions, we have to wonder what the purpose of all this is. There are several answers.

First of all, the concepts behind Black-Scholes are *the* framework for thinking about option pricing. There is just no better paradigm available for option pricing. Next, the financial world is accustomed to thinking about option values in terms of "Black-Scholes-implied volatility." This is the volatility in the Black-Scholes equation that makes the Black-Scholes price equal the market price of the option. This will be studied in detail in Chapter 8, but here is what Richard Cookson has to say about it:

> So if Black-Scholes gives the wrong results, why use it? In the foreign exchange markets, option traders are forced to—at least when they deal with each other. The market is so standardized that traders quote Black-Scholes volatility to each other, not price .... [11]

The same is true in equity markets as well.

5.6   SIMULATED BLACK-SCHOLES HEDGING

The best way to see what Black-Scholes hedging is like is to see it in action. To that end, we have provided five simulated runs hedging 12-week call options. In each run, we tally all the costs of hedging an option the Black-Scholes way, and moreover, we provide graphs of the stock price path and all of the standard hedge parameters—delta, gamma, theta, vega, and rho—versus time, so that you can see how these parameters change throughout the life of the option.

The simulated hedging provides a variety of scenarios to examine. Some options expire in the money, and others expire out of the money. We have also varied the volatility of the underlying stock so that you can compare the effect of this on prices, hedging, and hedge parameters.

---

[10] From Cookson *loc. cit.*
[11] From "Moving in the Right Direction," Cookson (1993), p. 22–26.

Explanation of Tables and Graphs

Each simulated hedging has two parts. First, there are tables that tally all the costs associated with hedging the option. In all runs, the Black-Scholes hedge is rebalanced once a week and the costs are tallied along the way. The total cost of hedging *and* the Black-Scholes price are given so they can be compared. A second table is provided that gives the total cost of hedging if the hedge is rebalanced at intervals of two weeks, one week, and one day. This gives an idea of the effect of the frequency of rebalancing on the total cost of hedging.

Each row in a simulated hedging table describes one week in the life of the hedge. The extreme left column tells the number of weeks until expiration. The next column is the stock price. After that come "Delta" and "P," where "Delta" is computed as $N(d_1)$ in the Black-Scholes formula and represents the delta of the option, and "P" is calculated as $N(d_2)$ and is the risk-neutral probability of the option expiring in the money.

The last three columns are the costs of rebalancing the hedge, broken down into three parts: stock costs, bond costs, and total costs. Since we are hedging a call option, we have to buy the stock (stock cost) and short a bond (bond cost). Total costs are the stock cost plus the bond cost.

In all weeks but the first, the rebalancing costs represent the cost of getting the hedge back into balance. Notice that, most often, the proceeds from the sale of the bond come very close to canceling out the stock costs. When this happens, the hedge is behaving as it should and is self-financing.

When the hedge is set up (when there are 12 weeks until expiration), the rebalancing costs are really the set-up costs. Therefore, the top "total costs" entry in each table is the Black-Scholes price of the option. Subsequent entries in this column represent rebalancing costs.

The Figures

Accompanying each simulated hedge table is a set of nine figures, consisting of graphs related to the hedging of the option. The first three figures are bar graphs of the rebalancing costs of the option. Rebalancing costs are graphed for three different rebalancing frequencies: bi-monthly, weekly, and daily. The horizontal axis of each graph represents weeks until expiration, and the vertical axis represents the total cost of hedging.

We note that in general the more often the hedge is rebalanced, the smaller the rebalancing costs are, and moreover, the smaller the total cost of hedging is. This is to be expected, as the Black-Scholes theory tells us that if we rebalance continuously, the strategy is self-financing.

The next six figures in each set are graphs of the stock price, the Black-Scholes value of the option, and the various hedge parameters: delta, gamma, theta, and vega.

The figures accompanying each simulated hedge are extremely useful when studied, for they allow the reader to examine what happens to Black-Scholes value and the hedge parameters given moves in the underlying. Particular attention should be paid to the direction the parameters move, and how this relates to time to the expiration and moneyness of the option.

The Scenarios

There are five simulated hedging runs in all. The first three assume a constant volatility throughout the life of the option and therefore simulate hedging in the Black-Scholes world. The difference, of course, between the hedging simulation here and the Black-Scholes formula is that we only rebalance the hedge once a week, while the Black-Scholes theory requires continuous rebalancing. This accounts for the differences between the Black-Scholes price and the actual price of the option. These scenarios are given as follows:

Table	Initial Stock Price	Strike Price	Volatility	Expires
5.6.1	$50	$50	15%	in the money
5.6.3	$50	$50	15%	out of the money
5.6.5	$50	$50	15%	at the money

The next two scenarios assume a 15 percent stock volatility, except in each case, there are three volatility spikes throughout the life of the option. The spikes are large, one-day positive variations in the stock volatility. In these scenarios, we have included an extra plot with a picture of when the spikes occur and how large they are.

Table	Initial Stock Price	Strike Price	Volatility	Expires
5.6.7	$50	$50	15%	in the money
5.6.9	$50	$50	15%	out the money

Discussion

We introduce the volatility spikes in order to illustrate the effect on hedging of large, unpredictable changes in volatility over a short period of time. In each case, volatility rises from 15 percent to over 100 percent for a very brief while and then returns to 15 percent. We can see that in each case, the volatility spike has a devastating effect on the integrity of the hedge as well as the total cost of hedging.

COMMENTS AND SUGGESTED READING

There are many derivations of the Black-Scholes differential equation. The original derivation is in Black and Scholes (1973). This derivation is not completely rigorous (though their resulting formula is correct). For a simple, understandable derivation, see Hull (1993). A rigorous mathematical derivation is given in Merton (1973a).

Numerical solutions to partial differential equations are an important part of options pricing, but they are beyond the aims of this book. For an introduction to some of the basic methods, see Hull (1993) or Wilmott, Dewynne, and Howison (1993). An excellent, readable introduction to the sorts of differential equations found in option pricing is given in Farlow (1993).

The early exercise boundary of an American option is discussed in many places. See, for instance, Duffie (1992). For a method to approximate the early exercise boundary and a resulting pricing formula, see Barone-Adesi and Whaley (1987). This method is also described in Hull (1993) and Natenberg (1994).

The theory of risk-neutral valuation was introduced by Cox and Ross (1976) and has been widely accepted as an indispensable aspect of options pricing.

T A B L E 5.6.1

Hedging costs associated with a call option
Simulated hedging for a European call option, with rebalancing
taking place once per week. The option had strike price of
$50.00, the stock was assumed to have 15 percent volatility
per annum, and the risk-free rate of interest is 5 percent. Its
Black-Scholes price is $1.73.

				Rebalancing Costs		
Weeks until Expiry	**Stock Price**	**Delta**	**P**	**Stock Costs**	**Bond Costs**	**Total**
12	50.000	0.5777	0.5493	28.88	−27.15	1.73
11	49.375	0.5020	0.4745	−3.74	3.70	−0.04
10	49.375	0.4949	0.4688	−0.35	0.28	−0.07
9	51.125	0.7008	0.6788	10.52	−10.41	0.11
8	52.125	0.8074	0.7909	5.56	−5.56	−0.00
7	53.375	0.9096	0.9003	5.45	−5.43	0.02
6	52.000	0.8184	0.8047	−4.74	4.75	0.01
5	50.750	0.6725	0.6556	−7.40	7.42	0.02
4	51.500	0.7952	0.7832	6.32	−6.35	−0.03
3	52.625	0.9358	0.9311	7.40	−7.37	0.03
2	53.625	0.9931	0.9925	3.07	−3.06	0.01
1	52.875	0.9970	0.9968	0.21	−0.21	−0.01
0	53.125	1.0000	1.0000	0.16	−0.16	−0.01
Total cost						1.79

T A B L E 5.6.2

Total cost of hedging
the call option shown
in Table 5.6.1 for various
rebalancing schedules

Bimonthly	**Weekly**	**Daily**
1.86	1.79	1.58

F I G U R E 5.6.1

Hedging costs and hedge parameters associated with simulated hedging in Table 5.6.1

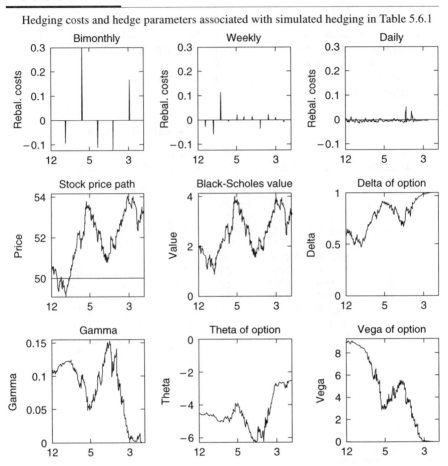

T A B L E 5.6.3

Hedging costs associated with a call option
Simulated hedging for a European call option, with rebalancing
taking place once per week. The option had strike price of
$50.00, the stock was assumed to have 15 percent volatility
per annum, and the risk-free rate of interest is 5 percent. Its
Black-Scholes price is $1.73

				Rebalancing Costs		
Weeks until Expiry	Stock Price	Delta	P	Stock Costs	Bond Costs	Total
12	50.000	0.5777	0.5493	28.88	−27.15	1.73
11	49.750	0.5457	0.5183	−1.59	1.53	−0.06
10	49.250	0.4796	0.4534	−3.26	3.21	−0.05
9	48.500	0.3748	0.3514	−5.08	5.06	−0.02
8	48.500	0.3600	0.3383	−0.72	0.65	−0.07
7	50.250	0.5950	0.5736	11.81	−11.69	0.12
6	51.625	0.7785	0.7631	9.47	−9.42	0.05
5	50.500	0.6333	0.6157	−7.33	7.33	0.00
4	51.000	0.7223	0.7082	4.54	−4.61	−0.07
3	49.250	0.3737	0.3601	−17.17	17.35	0.18
2	50.875	0.7487	0.7393	19.08	−18.92	0.16
1	50.250	0.6166	0.6087	−6.64	6.52	−0.12
0	50.000	0.5000	0.5000	−5.83	5.43	−0.40
Total cost						1.45

T A B L E 5.6.4

Total cost of hedging
the call option shown
in Table 5.6.3 for various
rebalancing schedules

Bimonthly	Weekly	Daily
1.24	1.45	1.27

F I G U R E 5.6.2

Hedging costs and hedge parameters associated with simulated hedging in Table 5.6.3

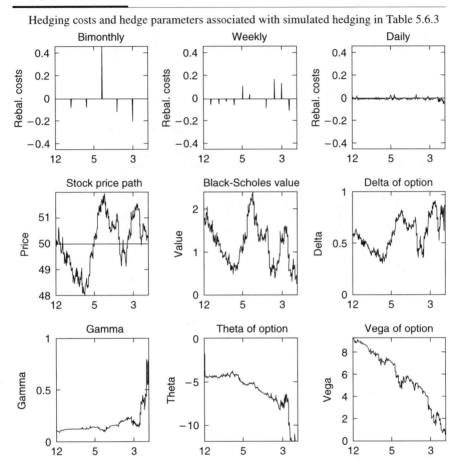

T A B L E 5.6.5

Hedging costs associated with a call option
Simulated hedging for a European call option, with rebalancing
taking place once per week. The option had strike price of
$50.00, the stock was assumed to have 15 percent volatility
per annum, and the risk-free rate of interest is 5 percent. Its
Black-Scholes price is $1.73.

Weeks until Expiry	Stock Price	Delta	P	Rebalancing Costs Stock Costs	Bond Costs	Total
12	50.000	0.5777	0.5493	28.88	−27.15	1.73
11	49.750	0.5457	0.5183	−1.59	1.53	−0.06
10	49.875	0.5560	0.5299	0.51	−0.57	−0.06
9	48.500	0.3748	0.3514	−8.79	8.85	0.06
8	49.000	0.4270	0.4041	2.56	−2.61	−0.05
7	49.250	0.4501	0.4284	1.14	−1.21	−0.07
6	50.000	0.5551	0.5349	5.25	−5.29	−0.04
5	48.500	0.2983	0.2824	−12.45	12.57	0.12
4	48.250	0.2283	0.2159	−3.38	3.31	−0.07
3	47.250	0.0702	0.0655	−7.47	7.50	0.03
2	46.375	0.0065	0.0060	−2.95	2.97	0.02
1	47.875	0.0210	0.0200	0.69	−0.70	−0.01
0	46.750	0.0000	0.0000	−0.98	1.00	0.02
Total cost						1.62

T A B L E 5.6.6

Total cost of hedging
the call option shown
in Table 5.6.5 for various
rebalancing schedules

Bimonthly	Weekly	Daily
1.74	1.62	1.77

F I G U R E 5.6.3

Hedging costs and hedge parameters associated with simulated hedging in Table 5.6.5

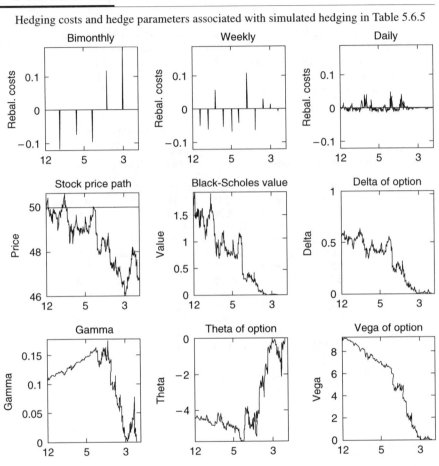

T A B L E 5.6.7

Hedging costs associated with a call option
Simulated hedging for a European call option, with rebalancing
taking place once per week. The option had strike price of
$50.00, the stock was assumed to have 15 percent volatility
per annum, and the risk-free rate of interest is 5 percent. Its
Black-Scholes price is $1.73.

Weeks until Expiry	Stock Price	Delta	P	Rebalancing Costs Stock Costs	Bond Costs	Total
12	50.000	0.5777	0.5493	28.88	−27.15	1.73
11	48.375	0.3851	0.3591	−9.31	9.41	0.10
10	47.000	0.2227	0.2036	−7.63	7.70	0.07
9	46.125	0.1303	0.1176	−4.26	4.26	0.00
8	47.625	0.2520	0.2336	5.79	−5.76	0.03
7	48.625	0.3603	0.3399	5.27	−5.28	−0.01
6	50.750	0.6668	0.6481	15.56	−15.32	0.24
5	52.125	0.8467	0.8355	9.38	−9.32	0.06
4	53.875	0.9719	0.9691	6.74	−6.66	0.08
3	54.625	0.9947	0.9941	1.25	−1.25	−0.00
2	53.875	0.9956	0.9952	0.05	−0.05	−0.00
1	53.625	0.9997	0.9997	0.22	−0.22	−0.00
0	53.125	1.0000	1.0000	0.02	−0.02	−0.00
Total cost						2.30

T A B L E 5.6.8

Total cost of hedging
the call option shown
in Table 5.6.7 for various
rebalancing schedules

Bimonthly	Weekly	Daily
2.94	2.30	1.99

F I G U R E   5.6.4

Hedging costs and hedge parameters associated with simulated hedging in Table 5.6.7

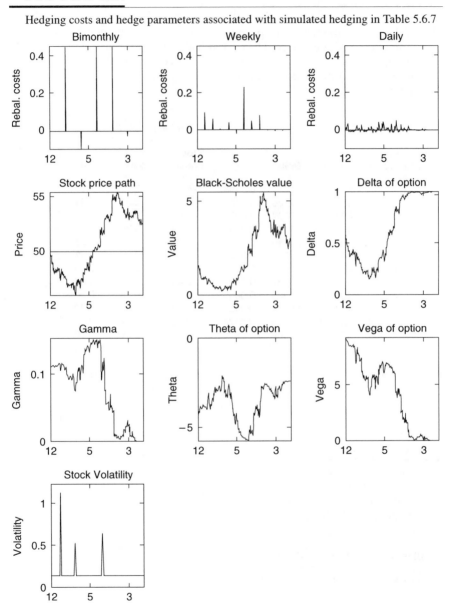

T A B L E 5.6.9

Hedging costs associated with a call option
Simulated hedging for a European call option, with rebalancing
taking place once per week. The option had strike price of
$50.00, the stock was assumed to have 15 percent volatility
per annum, and the risk-free rate of interest is 5 percent. Its
Black-Scholes price is $1.73.

Weeks until expiry	Stock price	Delta	P	Rebalancing Costs		
				Stock costs	Bond costs	Total
12	50.000	0.5777	0.5493	28.88	−27.15	1.73
11	49.500	0.5166	0.4891	−3.02	2.98	−0.04
10	42.375	0.0097	0.0081	−21.48	23.82	2.34
9	43.375	0.0174	0.0149	0.34	−0.34	−0.00
8	43.375	0.0119	0.0102	−0.24	0.23	−0.01
7	44.000	0.0148	0.0128	0.12	−0.13	−0.01
6	44.000	0.0088	0.0077	−0.26	0.26	−0.00
5	45.125	0.0187	0.0167	0.45	−0.45	−0.00
4	46.250	0.0389	0.0355	0.94	−0.94	−0.00
3	47.000	0.0524	0.0487	0.63	−0.66	−0.02
2	46.500	0.0084	0.0078	−2.05	2.04	−0.01
1	46.000	0.0000	0.0000	−0.39	0.39	0.00
0	45.000	0.0000	0.0000	−0.00	0.00	0.00
Total cost						3.97

T A B L E 5.6.10

Total cost of hedging
the call option shown
in Table 5.6.9 for various
rebalancing schedules

Bimonthly	Weekly	Daily
4.43	3.97	3.06

F I G U R E 5.6.5

Hedging costs and hedge parameters associated with simulated hedging in Table 5.6.9

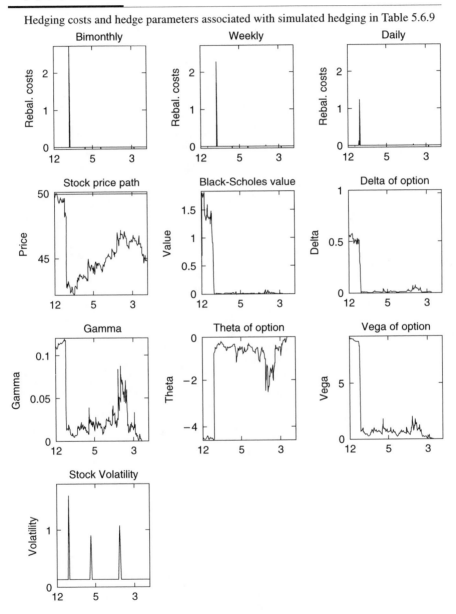

6

⑥ BINOMIAL TREES

In this chapter, we introduce the most versatile and widely used model for stock price movements and for options pricing—the binomial model. In 1979, the binomial model was introduced for options pricing by John Cox, Stephen Ross, and Mark Rubinstein in a paper entitled, "Option Pricing: A Simplified Approach." Not even they could have predicted how widespread and popular the model would become.

The model is simple and easy to understand, yet it is an extremely powerful tool for pricing a wide variety of options. To understand why this is so, remember that underneath the Black-Scholes model lies the geometric Brownian motion model of stock price movements. The validity of Black-Scholes option values depend in part on whether geometric Brownian motion is an accurate model for the underlying stock price movement.

The problem is, the geometric Brownian motion model of price movements is *not* a perfect model for stock price movements, especially with regard to option pricing.[1] How do we introduce a new model for stock price movements that is also better for option pricing? This is really two questions: First, what *is* a better model for stock price movements than geometric Brownian motion? Next, given such a model, how can we use it to price options?

In this chapter, we lay the foundations for moving "beyond Black-Scholes" by introducing the binomial model for stock price movements. This allows us to very precisely define what stock price movements look

---

[1] We will study this in detail in Chapter 8.

like by specifying what is known as the *local volatility* of the stock price movement, the volatility for each possible stock price at every time. We explicitly build a model for price movements by constructing a *binomial tree*. This tree specifies precisely all possible future stock prices and the associated probabilities of obtaining those prices.

Chapter 7 will show how to take a binomial tree and use it to value options. We'll begin with European put and call options, and then we will show how to modify the basic concept to price American options. Later, in Chapter 11, we show how to extend the basic concept once again to price barrier options on binomial trees. In addition, in Chapters 9 and 10 we will explain two methods that use binomial trees to "build a better stock price model."

In our study of binomial trees, we are dividing the task of pricing options into two distinct parts: stock price modeling and option pricing. In this chapter, we show how to build very general stock price models (using binomial trees). In the next chapter, we explain how to use a binomial tree to price options. This is important for our approach to option pricing, since we shall see in Chapters 9 and 10 that we can tailor stock price models to fit market conditions. Thus, it is sensible to separate the task of building the stock price model from the task of pricing the option.

Background

In their paper, Cox, Ross, and Rubinstein (1979) showed that the Black-Scholes formula could be deduced from their methods in a radically simple way. Moreover, this way of looking at Black-Scholes is extremely illuminating.

What we present here is a much more general model of stock price movements than what Cox, Ross, and Rubinstein examined, though they surely knew that such models exist. The binomial trees used in their paper were precise discrete time analogs of the continuous time geometric Brownian motion model, and therefore whatever advantages or disadvantages that model has also exist in the binomial model of Cox, Ross, and Rubinstein. We call the trees of Cox, Ross, and Rubinstein Cox-Ross-Rubinstein trees, or standard trees. The binomial trees discussed in this chapter, called *flexible trees,* are much less restrictive.

Conceptually, the difference between the standard trees of Cox, Ross, and Rubinstein and flexible trees is the difference between a model that allows only constant volatility (e.g., geometric Brownian motion) and a model that allows variable volatility. In standard trees, volatility is the same everywhere. That is, no matter what price path the stock takes, it will always have the same volatility. In flexible trees, volatility changes with time and spot price. That is, the volatility of the stock at any given time depends on both the time and the spot price.

6.1   CONTINUOUS VERSUS DISCRETE TIME MODELS

The binomial model of stock price movements is a *discrete time model,* as opposed to the geometric Brownian motion model, which is a *continuous time model.* Discrete time models divide time into discrete bits and only try to model prices at these times. For example, a price model that describes closing stock prices is a discrete time model. By contrast, continuous time models describe *all* times.

The geometric Brownian motion model is a continuous time model. Its advantage is its simplicity. At every moment of time you get a precise description of the probabilistic properties of the return on a stock. On the other hand, this very simplicity is the source of a certain inflexibility in the model: The stock's volatility has to be the same throughout the life of the option.

It is possible, of course, to modify Brownian motion to make it more flexible. This is done, unfortunately, at the expense of simplicity. It is very difficult to produce nice, easy-to-use formulas for option pricing with these more general models—in other words, nothing as elegant and simple as the Black-Scholes formula exists for these models.

What one needs is a different approach to building models. One needs models that are well-adapted to the problem of pricing options. Binomial trees are such a solution.

6.2   BINOMIAL TREES

The binomial tree model of stock price movements begins with the specification of a binomial tree. We wish to model a stock price over a certain period of time. The starting time of the tree is called the *initial time,* or *initial date.* The ending time is called the *terminal time,* or *terminal date.*

The period of time the tree covers is broken up into individual time periods, and the model says what the possible stock prices at the end of each time period are and to what new prices the stock can move from one time period to the next.

The tree is called a binomial tree because the spot price will either move up or move down at the end of each time period. How much the stock moves up or down is related to its volatility. Moreover, the tree specifies the probability that the price will move up or down at each node. This section devotes itself to making all of this precise.

Example

To get a feel for this, look back at the quote on page 93 discussing making stock charts by flipping a coin. The model in this experiment is a perfect example of a binomial tree. In this example, a stock was modeled using the flip of a coin. A stock starts on day 1 with an initial price of $50. At the end of each day, a coin is flipped: If it lands heads, the stock price moves up 1/2 point; if the coin lands tails, the price moves down 1/2 point.

In this model, each time period is one day and is clearly a binomial model because the stock price will either move up by 1/2 point or down by 1/2 point at the end of each time period; moreover, we know the probability of these moves: The probability of moving up or down is always one-half.

Figure 6.2.1 displays a picture of a binomial tree. There are four time periods (so that the tree is called a four-period tree), and the stock price changes four times. The current time is t_0, and the stock price is known to be $100 at this time. At the end of each period, the stock price will either move to the the "up" state or the "down" state. For example, in the figure, the price is at $100 at time t_0, while at time t_1, it can either rise to $102.53 or fall to $97.53.

The tree in Figure 6.2.1 is called a *recombining tree*. These are the only sorts of trees we study in this book. A recombining tree has the property that at any time, an up move followed by a down move is exactly the same as a down move followed by an up movement.[2] This is illustrated in the adjoining figure.

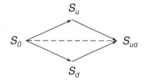

Each place in a tree where two lines cross is called a *node* of the tree. Each node represents a possible future price of the stock. For instance, in Figure 6.2.1 there are two nodes at time t_1, representing two possible stock prices: $102.53 and $97.53.

----

[2]Note this does not necessarily imply that the resulting price $S_{ud} = S_0$, that is, that an up movement followed by a down movement brings us back to where we started. Our trees can be much more general than this.

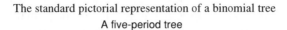

F I G U R E 6.2.1

The standard pictorial representation of a binomial tree
A five-period tree

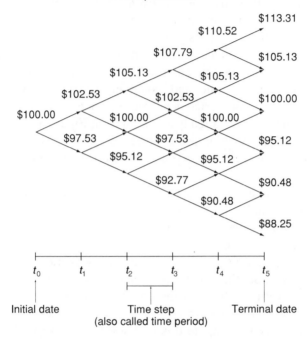

What does the model say about times between each period? Do the prices move up and down between periods, or alternatively, do they suddenly jump to their new states? The answer is, from the point of view of the model, it simply does not matter. As we shall see, all information about option pricing that we can deduce from the model is valid, regardless of what happens to the price between time periods.

Up and Down Ratios

At each node of a binomial tree, there are two possibilities for the movement of the stock price: The stock price will either rise or fall from the current time to the next. Suppose the stock price rises from S_0 to S_u. Then, the ratio $u = S_u/S_0$ is called the "up" ratio for the movement at that node. This is the amount by which S_0 is multiplied *if* the price rises. Conversely, if the price falls, then it will fall by the "down" ratio, d, given by $d = S_d/S_0$. Later, we will give precise formulas relating these ratios to the volatility of the stock and its expected rate of return.

Transition Probabilities

The probability that the price will move up from one node to the next is called the *up-transition probability* at that node. The probability of the price moving down is called the *down-transition probability*.

What binomial models make apparent about stock price models in general is that all future possibilities of the stock price are spelled out ahead of time. These models really are models for future price movements. Every possibility, those that happen, as well as those that do not, is mapped out ahead of time, and moreover, we can say exactly what the probability of each stock price occurring is, once we know all the transition probabilities. This is already apparent from Figure 6.2.1, though there we did not list the transition probabilities. This is true with the Brownian motion model as well, but it is much more difficult to clearly see in that case.

Naturally, no one actually expects stocks to behave as in a binomial model. Rather, what is hoped is that the model captures some of the essential probabilistic features of the underlying stock, at least enough for options pricing.

For example, we saw in the risk-neutral valuation derivation of the Black-Scholes model that a key determinant of a European option price is the risk-neutral probability that the option will expire in the money (i.e., the probability in a risk-neutral world). Naturally, the model provides a very concrete way to compute this probability, and we shall see that the binomial model also provides a way to compute this. In fact, all stock price models provide, at least in principle, a way to compute such probabilities. The question is, How valid are they? If a model provides unrealistic values for these probabilities, then option values produced using the model will be incorrect as well. In this case, one can say that on the whole, the model, viewed as a tool for option pricing, will not be useful.

As an example of what can go wrong, consider the constant volatility assumption of geometric Brownian motion—that is, the assumption that volatility is constant throughout the life of an option. If this assumption is false, then in computing the probability that the option will expire in the money, future changes in volatility will not be taken into account. If, for example, we can expect volatility to rise with increased stock prices and drop with decreased stock prices, then the probability that an in-the-money option will remain in the money is greater than the geometric Brownian motion model predicts. This inaccuracy will in turn be reflected in the option price.

Binomial trees fall into two broad categories: *standard trees* and *flexible trees*. Standard trees are the more well-known and popular trees and present a discrete time analogue of geometric Brownian motion. Flexible trees free us from almost all restrictions on the nature of the tree and allow us to very precisely control stock volatility. We will study both kinds of trees in this chapter, but we begin our discussion with standard trees.

Standard Binomial Trees

The up and down ratios and the transition probabilities of standard binomial trees are the same at every node. The length of each time period is also the same.

Since the ratios and probabilities never change, we can talk about the up and down ratio of the whole tree. For example, if a standard binomial tree has an up ratio of 1.1, then if the spot price at some node is $100, it will rise (if it rises) to $110 at the next time period.

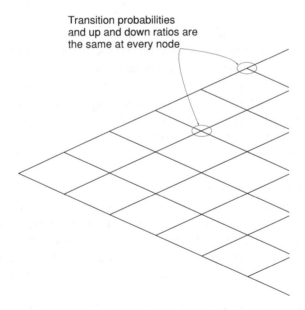

Transition probabilities
and up and down ratios are
the same at every node

Now, how do we guarantee the tree will be recombining? For a standard tree, this is automatic.

All standard binomial trees are recombining, because if the up ratio is *u* and the down ratio is *d*, then an up move followed by a down move is a move by a factor of ud. Likewise, a down move followed by an up move is a move by a factor of du, and naturally we have $ud = du$.

Centering the Tree

The term *centering* refers to what happens to the stock price when an up move is followed by a down move. What is the new spot price in relation to the original one? The ratio by which the spot price rises is called the *centering* of the tree.

In a standard tree, if the up ratio is u, then we often choose the down ratio to be $1/u$ so that an up move followed by a down move takes the spot price back to where it started. For example, if the up ratio is 1.1, then the down ratio can be chosen to be $1/1.1 = 0.909$. Then, if the price starts at $100 and moves up and back down, it first goes up to $110 and then falls back down to $100.

It is possible to choose the down ratio so that an up move followed by a down move brings you back to the forward price of the stock. That is,

$$ud = e^{2r\Delta t},$$

where u is the up ratio, d is the down ratio, r is the risk-free rate, and Δt is the length of the time period (the reason the 2 appears in the above expression is because an up move followed by a down move takes two time periods). Trees with such up and down ratios are said to be "grown along the forward," which refers to the fact that an up move followed by a down move takes the spot price to the forward price of the stock two periods later. In general, the choice of where to return the price after an up-down movement is called a *centering condition*.[3]

Why Trees Are "Geometric"

One might wonder why we don't consider trees in which the stock price rises or falls by a fixed amount; for example, every time the price rises, we could have it rise by $10. The reason is that this does not accurately reflect the way prices work. As we explained when discussing geometric Brownian motion, stock market models are geometric by nature. We discuss this further.

In general, a stock's expected return should not depend on its absolute price. Now, if a stock price rises $10 per year and its initial spot is $100, then in the first year, this is a 10 percent return (because the spot rose from

---

[3]This terminology is borrowed from "The Volatility Smile and Its Implied Tree," Derman and Kani (1994).

$100 to $110). However, in the second year, the same price rise ($10) would only be a 9.1 percent return (because the spot rose from $110 to $120), and in the third year, it would only be an 8.33 percent increase, and so on.

It would be more realistic to require the spot to rise by 10 percent per year in the model, so that it rises to $110 in the first year, while in the second year, it rises by $11 (10 percent of $110), to $121, which still represents a 10 percent increase.

Flexible Trees

Flexible trees[4] are so called because very few restrictions are placed on the up and down ratios and the transition probabilities of the tree. We only require one thing: that the tree be recombining.

The reason we look at flexible trees is because it is almost as easy to price options on flexible trees as it is to price options on standard binomial trees, but flexible trees allow us to model changes in volatility. This is crucial in advancing the theory of option pricing beyond Black-Scholes. We'll discuss a specific model for volatility in Chapter 9.

Where We Go from Here

The goal of the next few sections is to describe the finer properties of binomial trees in more detail. In the next section we discuss the relationship between a binomial tree and stock returns. This is important for understanding risk-neutral valuation of options on a binomial tree. After this, we move on to study the local volatility of a binomial tree. This "fine structure" of volatility is at the heart of modern option pricing, as it is becoming increasingly important to understand and be able to model stock price volatility very precisely.

After these two sections is a section giving two methods for building standard binomial trees. This section is important for the reader who wants formulas for actually programming a tree into a computer or a spreadsheet. We discuss two methods: the original Cox-Ross-Rubinstein method, and the equal probabilities method. Both methods are discrete time analogues of geometric Brownian motion, but have different features. We discuss the relative strengths of each model, as well as give several examples.

Once this is done, we tie together the two methods and give a very general framework for building binomial trees, which includes both of the above methods as a special case. The last several sections discuss advanced features of building binomial trees: binomial trees and dividends, binomial

---

[4]This terminology is due to E. Derman and I. Kani (Goldman Sachs).

trees with variable interest rates, and Arrow-Debreu prices, important for our discussions of implied volatility trees later in this book.

6.3 BINOMIAL TREES AND STOCK RETURNS

The rate of return of a stock represents the amount of interest (compounded continuously) earned on a stock over a period of time. The *expected rate of return* on a stock, on the other hand, is more difficult to define. In a stock price model, the terminology refers to the average return of the stock when "return" is regarded as a random variable.

The relation, then, between stock returns and binomial trees is that binomial trees are stock price models, and as such, they give us a probabilistic model of stock returns. We explain this now.

Stock Returns—The One-Period Model

First we consider the case of a one-period binomial tree. Figure 6.3.1 displays a one-period binomial tree representing a stock S with initial price S_0, up price S_u, and down price S_d, and computes that the expected value of S is

$$pS_u + (1 - p)S_d,$$ (6.3.1)

where p is the up-transition probability. This is called the *one-period expected value*. See the display in Figure 6.3.1 for an explanation of where this formula comes from.

Let's consider what we want to do with this information. We are building a stock price model. For a moment we'll take the approach we took in the geometric Brownian motion model and assume that we have a given rate of return as an *input to the model*. What does this mean? For Figure 6.3.1, it means that after one period, we want the average value of the stock to be equal to $S_0 e^{\mu(t_1 - t_0)}$, where μ is the expected rate of return *per annum* and $t_1 - t_0$ represents the amount of time (in years) between time t_0 and time t_1. That is, we want to ensure that *on average,* the value of the stock grows by a factor of $e^{\mu(t_1 - t_0)}$.

To make this work, it is enough to solve the expression in equation (6.3.1) for the value of p, which makes the expected value of the stock equal to $S_0 e^{\mu(t_1 - t_0)}$; that is, we must have

$$pS_u + (1 - p)S_d = S_0 e^{\mu(t_1 - t_0)}.$$ (6.3.2)

Solving for p, we obtain

$$p = \frac{S_0 e^{\mu(t_1 - t_0)} - S_d}{S_u - S_d}.$$ (6.3.3)

FIGURE 6.3.1

The expected value of a stock in a one-period tree

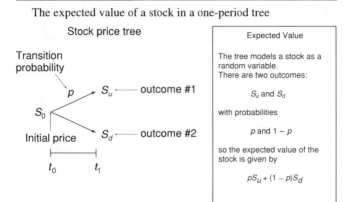

Stock price tree

Transition probability

p S_u ——— outcome #1

S_0

Initial price S_d ——— outcome #2

t_0 t_1

Expected Value

The tree models a stock as a random variable. There are two outcomes:

S_u and S_d

with probabilities

p and $1 - p$

so the expected value of the stock is given by

$pS_u + (1 - p)S_d$

To recap, if we have a given expected rate of return that we want a one-period tree to capture, we can ensure that the average rate of return (in the one-period tree) is equal to the given rate simply by setting the up-transition probability to the value given above. The next obvious question is, what happens in a multiple-period tree?

Multiple-Period Trees and Rate of Return

To understand expected returns in a multiple-period model, we have to consider two different scenarios: standard trees and flexible trees. The expected return in a standard tree is easy to describe. The expected return in a flexible tree is less easy to describe but, ultimately, much more important. We will discuss rate of return in standard trees now and relegate returns in flexible trees to Section 6.12.

Multiple-Period Standard Trees

To understand multiple-period trees, it is actually enough to understand a two-period tree. General trees work in exactly the same way. The two-period tree in Figure 6.3.2 displays the situation we need to study.

In this figure, we start with a stock with initial value S and a *standard binomial tree*. Remember what this means: there is a fixed up ratio and down ratio by which the stock price will move after each period. In this case, equation (6.3.2) reads:

$$pS_u + (1 - p)S_d = Se^{\mu(\Delta t)},$$

where again μ is the expected rate of return and Δt is the amount of time between periods. Now, however, we can cancel the three S's in this equation

FIGURE 6.3.2

Expected value in a two-period tree

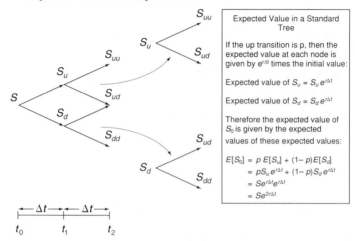

and obtain:

$$pu + (1 - p)d = e^{\mu \Delta t}.$$

Using this equation we may derive that the expected value of S after two periods is $Se^{2r\Delta t}$. The derivation of this expression is given in the display in Figure 6.3.2.

What we see is that after one period the expected value of the stock is $Se^{r\Delta t}$, while after two periods it is $Se^{2r\Delta t}$. The pattern is clear, and we have:

> In an n-period standard binomial tree, if the one-period expected value is $e^{r\Delta t}$ times the initial value, then the n-period expected value is $e^{nr\Delta t}$.

Let's notice a key point about the expected returns in a standard binomial tree. The expected *rate* of return is proportional to the number of periods. That is, if the one-period expected rate of return is $r\Delta t$, then the n-period expected rate of return is $nr\Delta t$. In other words, the long-term returns are proportional to the one-period returns.

6.4 BINOMIAL TREES AND VOLATILITY

Intuitively, volatility is a measure of the uncertainty of returns of a stock. This was discussed in detail in Chapter 3 on the geometric Brownian motion model. In this model, stock volatility was assumed to be constant; that is, the uncertainty of returns is the same at all times. In reality, things are more complicated. Stock volatility depends on spot price and time in a complicated, and not well understood, way.

Let's recall what stock volatility is in more detail and try to fit it into the context of binomial trees. First of all, volatility is the standard deviation of short-term returns of spot price. Recall that if the spot price is S_0 today and is S_1 at some later time, then the annualized return on S over this period of time is

$$\text{return} = \frac{1}{\Delta t} \log(S_1/S_0),$$

where Δt is the amount of time between observations.

Suppose the spot price of a stock or index at time t_0 is S_0 and the spot will either rise to S_u (the up price) or fall to S_d (the down price) at time t_1. Then there are two possible returns over the period of time from t_0 to t_1:

$$\frac{1}{t_1 - t_0} \log(S_u/S_0)$$

$$\frac{1}{t_1 - t_0} \log(S_d/S_0),$$

representing the returns respectively if the spot price rises or falls. Let the probability that the price will rise be p, and let the probability that it will fall be $1 - p$. The expected value of the rate of return from time t_0 to time t_1 is given by:

$$\frac{p}{t_1 - t_0} \log(S_u/S_0) + \frac{1 - p}{t_1 - t_0} \log(S_d/S_0). \tag{6.4.1}$$

The standard deviation of the return on the stock is given by the formula:

$$\sigma_{loc} = \frac{1}{\sqrt{t_1 - t_0}} \sqrt{p \cdot (1 - p)} \cdot \log(S_u/S_d), \tag{6.4.2}$$

where the symbol "σ_{loc}" stands for *local volatility*. Conceptually, local volatility represents the volatility—the amount of variation in the stock price—specific to the particular node of the tree we are studying. In Figure 6.4.1, we show a picture of what this means.

If a binomial tree is standard, then the up and down ratios, the transition probabilities, and the length of each time period are always the same. For example, consider a standard binomial tree with up ratio u. Then if at time t_0, the spot price is S_{t_0}, the two possible prices in the next period, time

FIGURE 6.4.1

Local volatility at a node S_{uu} is determined only by the up and down nodes in the next time period

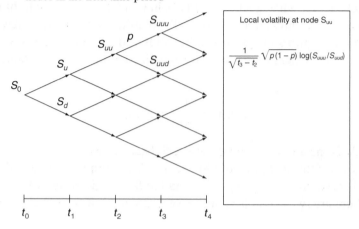

t_1, are $S_{t_0} \cdot u$ and S_{t_0}/u and the transition probability is p. Therefore, in the case of a standard binomial tree, equation (6.4.2) reads

$$\text{Local volatility} = \sigma_{loc} = \frac{1}{\sqrt{\Delta t}} \sqrt{p \cdot (1-p)} \log(u^2). \quad (6.4.3)$$

Since none of the terms in this equation depend on the particular node we computed out, we have:

In a standard binomial tree, the local volatility is the same at every node.

Sound familiar? This is exactly the constant volatility assumption of the geometric Brownian motion model of stock price movements. For this reason, the standard binomial tree is called a discrete time approximation of a geometric Brownian motion model.

We would like a way to relate the geometric Brownian motion model to the binomial model in some concrete manner. In particular, if σ is the historical volatility of a stock or index, then we want a formula for the up ratio, u, and the up-transition probability, p, so that the annualized local volatility of the tree is equal to σ and the expected return at each node is equal to whatever it is supposed to be. In other words, we want to build a discrete time analog of geometric Brownian motion. We give several different methods in the next section.

6.5 BUILDING A STANDARD BINOMIAL TREE

Suppose we want to model a stock or index with volatility σ. How would we go about it? First, we have to fix a total length of time that the model will span. This could be, for example, from the settlement date of some option to its expiration.

We will write T for the total amount of time we are modeling, expressed in years. Next, we have to pick the number of time periods, N, for our model and divide the total time T we are modeling into N equal-length pieces. We write Δt for the length of each period, and we have:

$$\Delta t = T/N.$$

Next, we write μ for the expected rate of return of the stock or index, expressed in the same units as T, and write σ for its volatility. We need a formula for u, the up ratio, and p, the up-transition probability, so that the model has expected rate of return μ and standard deviation σ. That is, the model should have the property that the expected return and local volatility, computed respectively using equations (6.4.1) and (6.4.2), are equal to μ and σ.

The first method for accomplishing this is due to Cox, Ross, and Rubinstein.[5] The second, called the "equal probabilities" approach, has the advantage that the local volatility is *exactly* equal to the desired input probability σ.

The Cox-Ross-Rubinstein Approach
Write σ for the volatility of the stock or index, Δt for the length of the time step, and μ for the expected annual rate of return of the stock or index.

Then, we have the formulas for Cox-Ross-Rubinstein up and down ratios and transition probability:

$$u = e^{\sigma \sqrt{\Delta t}}, \quad d = \frac{1}{u}, \quad p = \frac{e^{\mu \Delta t} - d}{u - d}. \tag{6.5.1}$$

Up to a very good approximation, these formulas make the local volatility at each node equal to σ and make the expected rate of return exactly equal to μ. The formulas are summarized in Display 6.5.1. In the next subsection, we give an example illustrating to what extent u gives a good approximation of σ.

---

[5] See "Option Pricing: A Simplified Approach," Cox, Ross, and Rubinstein (1979).

DISPLAY 6.5.1

THE PARAMETERS AND FORMULAS FOR THE STANDARD BINOMIAL MODEL

Parameters:

T = total time in years
N = number of periods
Δt = length of time period in years = T/N
σ = historical volatility, in percent *per annum*
μ = expected return of the stock or index in percent *per annum*
u = up ratio
d = down ratio

General formulas

$$\sigma_{loc} = \frac{1}{\sqrt{\Delta t}} \sqrt{p(1-p)} \log(u/d)$$

$$\Delta t = T/N$$

Cox-Ross-Rubinstein approach

$$p = \frac{e^{\mu \Delta t} - d}{u - d}$$

$$u = e^{\sigma \sqrt{\Delta t}}$$

$$d = 1/u$$

Equal probability approach

$$p = 0.5$$

$$d = \frac{2e^{\mu \Delta t}}{e^{2\sigma \sqrt{\Delta t}} + 1}$$

$$u = \frac{2e^{\mu \Delta t + 2\sigma \sqrt{\Delta t}}}{e^{2\sigma \sqrt{\Delta t}} + 1}$$

We have already seen that the value for p gives us the correct expected value of the stock. This was demonstrated in Section 6.3; see equation (6.3.2). Now we give a numerical example showing that the formula for the up ratio gives a volatility that is approximately correct. After the example, we explain exactly what "approximately correct" means.

Example

Figure 6.5.1 displays an example of a four-period binomial tree. All the formulas and computations are given directly in the figure.

Notice that the input volatility is 15 percent but the local volatility, computed from the tree itself, is 14.7 percent. This discrepancy arises because the Cox-Ross-Rubinstein approach only provides an approximation of the

FIGURE 6.5.1

Example of a standard, Cox-Ross-Rubinstein binomial tree

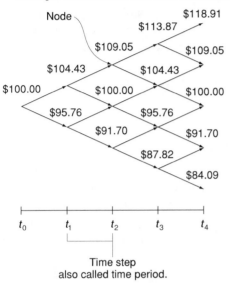

Standard Cox-Ross-Rubenstein Tree

Number of periods: 4

$\Delta t = .0833$ (one month) $\sqrt{\Delta t} = .2887$

$\sigma = 15\%$ (per annum) $r = 10\%$ (per annum)

$u = e^{\sigma\sqrt{\Delta t}} = 1.0443$ $d = 1/u = .9576$

$p = \dfrac{e^{r\Delta t} - d}{u - d} = .5853$ $\sigma_{loc} = \dfrac{1}{\sqrt{\Delta t}}\sqrt{p(1-p)} \cdot$

$\log(u/d) = 14.7\%$

Time step
also called time period.

correct local volatility. If we were to increase the number of periods significantly, we would get a much better approximation.

We calculated the volatility at each node of a standard tree using the Cox-Ross-Rubinstein formulas for a fixed length of time and a varying number of time periods to see how quickly the calculated volatility converges to the actual volatility. The tree modeled a one-year period of time; the expected return was equal to 5 percent and the volatility was equal to 15 percent. Below is a table showing the volatility calculation as we increase the number of periods:

Number of Periods	Local Volatility
10	14.95%
25	14.98%
100	14.99%
200	15.00%

What the above table illustrates is that even a tree with only a few periods (10) does a decent job of approximating the desired volatility (we wanted 15 percent and got 14.95 percent). As the number of periods increases, the accuracy of the approximation increases as well, so that by the time we use n 200 periods, the tree produces a local volatility of 15 percent accurate to at least two decimal places.

The Equal Probability Approach

There is a second, less well-known, approach to implementing the binomial model. This approach, called the "equal probability implementation," derives the model ensuring that the up and down transition probability at every node is equal to 50 percent. The formulas are summarized in Display 6.5.1.

To derive the formulas, note that we have two equations that must be satisfied:

$$pu + (1 - p)d = e^{\mu \Delta t}$$

$$\sqrt{p(1 - p)} \log(u/d) = \sigma \sqrt{\Delta t},$$

where p is the up-transition probability, σ is the volatility, μ is the expected rate of return, and Δt is the length of time in the time step. The first equation, called the *one-period forward equation,* specifies that the expected value of the stock for one time step is equal to the forward price (using an expected return equal to μ) for one period. The second equation is the local volatility equation.

Since we are requiring that $p = 0.5$, we may substitute this into the above equations and obtain:

$$u + d = 2e^{\mu \Delta t} \tag{6.5.2}$$

$$\log(u/d) = 2\sigma \sqrt{\Delta t}. \tag{6.5.3}$$

Now, exponentiating equation (6.5.3), we obtain

$$u/d = e^{2\sigma \sqrt{\Delta t}}, \tag{6.5.4}$$

that is, $u = de^{2\sigma \sqrt{\Delta t}}$. Substituting this into equation (6.5.2), we obtain

$$d = \frac{2e^{\mu \Delta t}}{e^{2\sigma \sqrt{\Delta t}} + 1} \tag{6.5.5}$$

and

$$u = \frac{2e^{\mu \Delta t + 2\sigma \sqrt{\Delta t}}}{e^{2\sigma \sqrt{\Delta t}} + 1}. \tag{6.5.6}$$

Figure 6.5.2 displays a binomial tree computed using the equal probabilities method. In the example, we use very high interest (30 percent) rates and a very low volatility (1 percent). The other parameters in the model are listed in the figure.

Example

Let's look at an example of computing the parameters for the equal probabilities method. This example is different than what we computed in Figure

F I G U R E 6.5.2

Example of a binomial tree computed using the equal probabilities approach

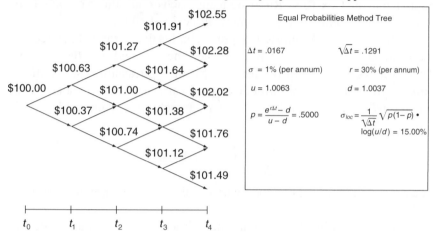

6.5.2. Suppose we have:

$\Delta t = 0.0833$ (1 month)
$\mu = 10\%$
$\sigma = 15\%$

Note that Δt. First, we compute d:

$$d = \frac{2e^{0.10 \cdot 0.0833}}{e^{2 \cdot 0.15 \cdot \sqrt{0.0833}} + 1} = 0.964737.$$

Next, we compute u:

$$u = \frac{2e^{0.10 \cdot 0.0833 + 2 \cdot 0.15 \sqrt{0.0833}}}{e^{2 \cdot 0.15 \sqrt{0.0833}} + 1} = 1.05199$$

Of course, according to our model, the up-transition probability is 50 percent ($p = 0.5$).

Let's use these numbers to compute the local volatility and see if we get back 15 percent:

$$\sigma = \frac{1}{\sqrt{\Delta t}} \sqrt{p(1 - p)} \log(u/d)$$

$$= \frac{1}{\sqrt{0.0833}} 0.5 \log(1.05199/0.964737)$$

$$= 0.149996.$$

Except for a small error (due to rounding in our computation of the exponentials), we get back the volatility with which we started.

Equal Probabilities versus Cox-Ross-Rubinstein

There are two issues to consider when comparing the equal probabilities approach to the Cox-Ross-Rubinstein approach of building a binomial tree: ease of implementation and accuracy of local volatility.

The Cox-Ross-Rubinstein approach builds the up ratio of the tree with the formula $u = e^{\sigma \sqrt{\Delta t}}$, where Δt is the time step and σ is the volatility. This formula, along with the formula for the up-transition probability p, builds a tree that has the correct expected value at each node and has *approximately* a local volatility of $\sigma \sqrt{\Delta t}$ at each node, computed with the formula:

$$\frac{1}{\sqrt{\Delta t}} \sqrt{p(1-p)} \log u^2.$$

The approximation is quite good when dealing with a large number of periods.

On the other hand, the equal probabilities approach builds a tree with exactly the correct volatility, even in low periods. However, there is an even more important reason to prefer the equal probabilities method, which we describe now.

Negative Probabilities and Trees

In certain trading environments, Cox-Ross-Rubinstein trees do not work. When the volatility of the stock is low and interest rates are high, the Cox-Ross-Rubinstein formula for the transition probability fails to give a usable answer. We illustrate this point with the example below.

Consider a binomial tree with the following data:

$\Delta t = 0.0192307$ (one week)
$\mu = 0.50$
$\sigma = 0.25$

Using respectively the equations for the Cox-Ross-Rubinstein and equal probabilities methods, we form the following one-step trees:

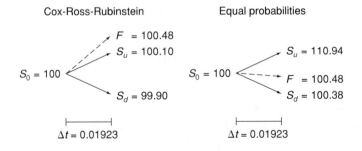

Cox-Ross-Rubinstein

$S_0 = 100$
$F = 100.48$
$S_u = 100.10$
$S_d = 99.90$
$\Delta t = 0.01923$

Equal probabilities

$S_0 = 100$
$S_u = 110.94$
$F = 100.48$
$S_d = 100.38$
$\Delta t = 0.01923$

Notice that we have included the position of the forward price, $F = e^{\mu \Delta t} = 100.48$, relative to the up and down prices. One can see from the figures that the Cox-Ross-Rubinstein method is in trouble because the forward price falls outside of the up and down prices. Since the forward price is equal to the one-period expected value of the stock price, we can see that even if the up transition probability were equal to one, the expected value would only be equal to S_u, still short of F. Thus, the Cox-Ross-Rubinstein picture cannot work. In fact, using the Cox-Ross-Rubinstein formula for the up-transition probability, we compute:

$$p = \frac{e^{\mu \Delta t} - u}{u - d} = 3.005632.$$

This is not a valid probability. All probabilities must fall between zero and one, that is, between 0 and 100 percent.

By contrast, the equal probabilities method cannot fail in this manner, because from the outset, we require that the up-transition probability be equal to 50 percent. This guarantees that the forward always lies between the up and down prices.[6] In this sense, the equal probabilities method is an indispensable alternative to Cox-Ross-Rubinstein.

6.6   THE MOST GENERAL STANDARD TREES

This section discusses the most general setup possible for generating standard binomial trees. Remember that in this section, we are speaking solely about standard trees. Therefore, all of the trees in this section have the same up ratios, down ratios, and transition probabilities at every node.

We begin by breaking the definition of the tree into three separate components.

Defining Characteristics
First we have the *input data* of the tree:

$\Delta t = $ the length of the time step
$\mu = $ the one-period expected return
$\sigma = $ stock volatility

Notice that we did not put "number of periods" as a defining parameter. Knowing the number of periods is, of course, important for building a tree,

---

[6]There is a way to modify the Cox-Ross-Rubinstein tree to avoid these "bad probabilities" by "growing the tree along the forward." For a description, see *Options, Futures and other Derivative Securities,* Hull (1992), section 14.6.

but we are interested in the intrinsic properties of the tree with regard to the stock model. The number of periods merely describes over what period of time we are modeling the stock. For example, if Δt is one month, then the number of periods just tells us how many months we are modeling.

The Parameters of the Tree

Next we have the parameters of the tree. These are as follows:

u = up ratio
d = down ratio
p = up-transition probability

Note that we do not put as a parameter "down-transition probability." This is because we always know that the down-transition probability must be one minus the up-transition probability. That is, if q is the down-transition probability, then $p + q = 1$, so $q = 1 - p$.

The parameters of the tree are what we use to make sure the tree has the correct defining characteristics. That is, we use the parameters u, d, and p to build a tree with the defining characteristics we want. This leads us to the last part of our analysis.

The Defining Equations of the Tree

Next, we have the defining equations of the tree. The defining equations relate the parameters of the tree to the defining characteristics, *plus* give the tree a little extra definition through its centering condition and its transition probability. The defining equations are:

$$pu + (1 - p)d = e^{\mu\Delta t} \qquad \text{(expected value equation)}$$
$$\sqrt{p(1 - p)}\log(u/d) = \sigma\sqrt{\Delta t} \qquad \text{(volatility equation)}$$
$$ud = e^{2c\Delta t} \qquad \text{(centering condition)}$$
$$p = \textit{fixed constant} \qquad \text{(probability condition)}$$

The first two equations were discussed in Sections 6.3 and 6.4, so we will only discuss the last two. The centering condition equation says, simply, an up move followed by a down move grows the stock by e^{2c}, where c is some fixed constant. For example, if $c = 0$, then we have $e^{2c\Delta t} = 1$, and

$$ud = 1,$$

or $d = 1/u$. This yields a Cox-Ross-Rubinstein-type tree.[7] On the other

---

[7]We say "type," because solving the constraint equations gives a slightly different formula for volatility than Cox-Ross-Rubinstein. The advantage of the C-R-R formula is its simplicity.

hand, if we have

$$ud = e^{2\mu \Delta t},$$

then we say the tree is "grown along the forward."

The last equation simply says that we are requiring the transition probability to be some fixed value, for example, $p = 0.5$, as in the equal probability approach.

Using the Equations

In using the equations of a binomial tree, there is one important *caveat:*

> There are only three input parameters, so we can only use three of the four equations at any time.

We have already seen this and its consequences twice: In the Cox-Ross-Rubinstein approach, we used the first three equations at the expense of having any control over the value of p. This has the consequence that in environments with low volatility and high interest rates, the situation can arise in which Cox-Ross-Rubinstein trees yield unusable results.

6.7   THE NUMBERING SYSTEM OF THE NODES

We need a standard way to refer to the nodes of the binomial tree.

When dealing with binomial trees, it is nice to have a way to refer to each node. We number each node systematically in order to better keep track of them. The numbering system is simple. Starting at the initial time, t_0, each node is numbered according to its time period and its height from the bottom. So, the left-most node (the spot price) is numbered (0,0), and the two nodes at time 1 are numbered, from the bottom up, (1,0) and (1,1).

Figure 6.7.1 shows an example of how the numbering system works.

6.8   RISK-NEUTRAL WORLDS AND BINOMIAL TREES

A binomial tree consists of two primary pieces of information: stock prices and transition probabilities. In option pricing, however, we generally do all of our pricing in a *risk-neutral world*. Remember: In a risk-neutral world, the expected appreciation of every asset is given by the risk-free rate of growth. When using binomial trees, we create a risk-neutral world by choosing the transition probabilities to ensure that the expected value is equal to growth at the risk-free rate. These are called *risk-neutral transition probabilities*.

FIGURE 6.7.1

The numbering system for a binomial tree

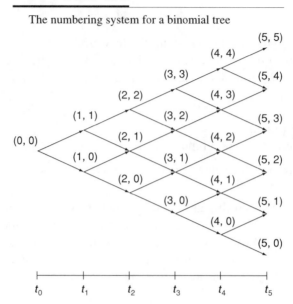

Until now, we have allowed the expected rate of return of the stocks we model to be equal to anything we want, and we denoted the expected rate of return by μ. In fact, in theoretical option pricing, we almost never use an arbitrary rate of return. Rather, we always use the *risk-neutral* rate of return. That is, we set the rate of return equal to the risk-free rate of interest.

The One-Period Forward Equation

Suppose we know that the spot price of some stock or index is S_0, and it can either rise in the next period to S_u or fall to S_d from now to the next time period Δt later. That is, suppose we have a one-period binomial model for the price of the stock.

Write p for the up-transition probability and r for the risk-free rate. Assume we are in a risk-neutral world; that is, assume the expected value of the stock is equal to its forward price one period later:

$$pS_u + (1 - p)S_d = e^{r\Delta t}S_0. \qquad (6.8.1)$$

This equation is called the *one-period forward equation*. The left-hand side of this equation is the expected value of the stock, assuming: 1) we are in a "binomial world" (that is, there are only two possible stock prices after time Δt), and 2) the up-transition probability is p. The right-hand side is the expected value of the spot price—assuming we are in a risk-neutral world, and it is also the forward price of the stock Δt from now.

Equation (6.8.1) can be solved for the value of p. We obtain:

$$p = \frac{e^{r\Delta t}S_0 - S_d}{S_u - S_d}. \tag{6.8.2}$$

Thus, we have obtained a formula for the *risk-neutral* probability that depends on the risk-free rate of interest and the values S_0, S_u, and S_d.

We can see from the setup that risk-neutral probabilities are precisely those probabilities that are compatible with the arbitrage free forward price of stock. Recall that in Chapter 1 we derived an arbitrage free price of a forward contract, and deduced that the forward price depends on nothing more than the amount of time (until delivery) and the risk-free rate of interest.

From this point of view, we see that equation (6.8.2) represents the "correct" formula for the up transition probability from the point of view of arbitrage free pricing of forward contracts. In the next chapter we will see that risk-neutral probabilities are also the correct probabilities for options pricing.

Terminology
From now on when we refer to a *risk-neutral binomial tree* we mean a binomial tree whose transition probabilities satisfy equation (6.8.2) at every node. That is, if we regard each node as the "vertex" of a one-period tree, with the node value equal to S_0, the up value equal to S_u, the down value equal to S_d, and the up transition probability equal to p, then equation (6.8.2) should hold.

Example Tree
In Figure 6.8.1, we give an example of a four-period flexible tree with the risk-neutral transition probabilities and the local volatilities all computed. Notice that the local volatilities change according to spot price and time.

6.9 FORWARD INTEREST RATES AND BINOMIAL TREES

For most real option pricing applications it is necessary to remove the "constant interest rate" assumption of the Black-Scholes formula and allow arbitrary interest rates. In this section, we examine what this means and how to implement a binomial tree with "varying interest rates."

F I G U R E 6.8.1

Example of a flexible binomial tree with all risk-neutral transition probabilities and local volatilities computed using the Cox-Ross-Rubinstein method.
In this tree, the risk-free rate of interest is 5 percent and each time period is one year, so that the tree as a whole represents four years.

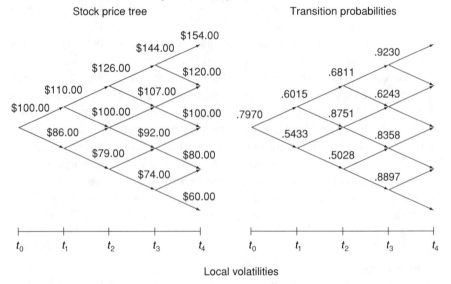

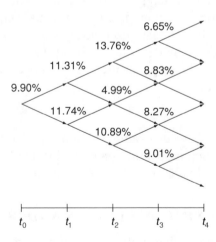

Local volatilities

Forward Interest Rates

Since each time step of a binomial tree represents some future time, the question is, what will it cost to borrow $1 for one time period in the future? This underlies the concept of a forward interest rate, which in all respects is similar to a forward contract on a stock. We'll make this clear with an example, but first we make a technical note regarding yield curves.

The Yield Curve

This section assumes knowledge about the yield curve. The yield curve tells us the rate of interest applicable to borrowing or lending for a particular amount of time. For example, if we want to borrow money (i.e., sell a bond), what is the interest rate we pay if we want the bond to mature in one year? Here, when we speak of the yield curve, we will mean something very precise:

> The yield curve tells us the riskless lending and borrowing rate for all maturities.

In other words, if we know the risk-free rate for loans of every possible maturation, then we can make a graph on which the horizontal axis is the time to maturity and the vertical axis is the interest rate for a bond maturing in the amount of time specified by the horizontal axis.

The point of this section is that if we know the yield curve (that is, if we know the riskless interest rate for every possible maturity), then we also know *forward interest rates*. Forward interest rates are the interest rates we will have to pay in the future. We'll explain this in a moment, but first we explain the relation of the yield curve to the Black-Scholes constant interest rate assumption.

The Yield Curve versus Constant Interest Rates

In the Black-Scholes model, we assumed constant interest rates. This means that the risk-free rate of interest is assumed to be constant now and at all future times. Where this is the case, we will see in a moment that this implies that all forward interest rates are constant as well, which in turn implies that the yield curve is flat, that is, that bonds of all maturities have the same interest rate. Figure 6.9.1 displays this discrepancy.

Forward Rates and Binomial Trees

Suppose we have a 10-step binomial tree with Δt equal to one year. Then we write t_0 for today, t_1 for one year from now, t_2 for two years from now, and so on. Let's write r_0 for today's one-year interest rate. That is, r_0 represents

FIGURE 6.9.1

The left-hand figure displays a hypothetical yield curve. Notice that interest rates rise for longer duration bonds. The right-hand curve is a flat, Black-Scholes constant rate yield curve.

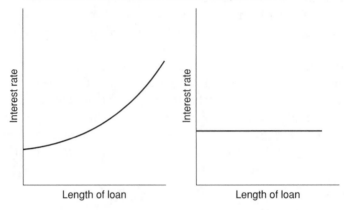

the risk-free rate of interest for bonds maturing in one year. This makes sense, and we can presumably obtain a value of r_0 from empirical data.

Now, let's consider the time step from t_1 to t_2, which represents the span of time between one year from now and two years from now. Write r_1 for the risk-free interest rate for one-year bonds purchased one year from now, r_2 for the risk-free rate for one-year bonds purchased two years from now, and so on. Our key observation is that we can deduce these values from the yield curve. We'll explain how to deduce r_1 from the yield curve and the no-arbitrage hypothesis. The argument is exactly the same as that used to deduce forward prices for stocks in Chapter 1.

The point is that the yield curve tells us today's risk-free rate for both one-year bonds and two-year bonds. We'll write i_1 for the short-term rate for one-year bonds and i_2 for two-year bonds.[8] Consider the following two investments:

1. A long position in a two-year, riskless, zero-coupon bond maturing to \$1.

2. A long position in a forward contract on a one-year, riskless, zero-coupon bond maturing to \$1, with delivery price F.

We are going to use these two investments to deduce the value of r_1, the one-year forward interest rate.

---

[8] We admit that this notation is somewhat awkward, as $i_1 = r_0$.

Let's suppose that the second investment costs nothing to get into today. In other words, the delivery price, F, is the (one-year) forward price of the one-year bond. Then, the *value today* of the second investment is given by $e^{-i_1}F$. Why? Because its value today is given by discounting its one future cash flow (the delivery price) to today.

Note what we have done: we have equated the two cash flows of the investments to today. The first investment has essentially one cash flow, today's value (that is, if we were to enter into the first investment today, then we would lay out its value today). The second investment also has one cash flow, but this cash flow occurs one year from now. Therefore, to equate the cash flows, we look value them both today.

On the other hand, both investments mature to the same value in two years, one dollar. Therefore, by the no arbitrage principle, both investments have the same value today. That is,

$$e^{-i_1}F = e^{-2i_2}.$$

The left-hand side of the above equation is nothing more than the delivery price of the second investment valued today. The right-hand side represents value of a two-year bond (maturing to one dollar) today. The above equation is the same as $F = e^{i_1 - 2i_2}$.

But we can infer the value of r_1, the one year forward rate, from F quite easily. Since F represents the forward price of a one-year bond, one year after delivery, the bond will mature to one dollar. This means, $e^{r_1}F = 1$, and $r_1 = -\log F$. Thus we have

$$r_1 = -\log F = 2i_2 - i_1.$$

The main point of this equation is that the one-year forward rate (for a one-year interest rate) is completely determined, via the arbitrage principle and the yield curve.

Now that we've dispensed with the above example, we move on to study how to deduce general forward rates from the yield curve. We shall see that the main principle remains the same.

General Forward Rates
Figure 6.9.2 displays the general scenario for forward rates. In this figure, we see two time steps, from t_0 to t_1 and from t_1 to t_2, and *three* risk-free interest rates, the interest rate for loans starting at time t_0 and maturing at time t_1, the interest rate for loans starting at times t_0 and maturing at time t_2, and the *forward rate* for loans starting at time t_1 and ending at time t_2.

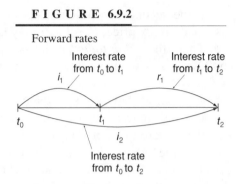

F I G U R E 6.9.2

Forward rates

This is the rate we can contract for today (time t_0) to purchase a bond at time t_1 maturing at time t_2. Applying the general arbitrage principle we used above, we can show the following general principle:

$$i_1(t_1 - t_0) + r_1(t_2 - t_1) = i_2(t_2 - t_0). \qquad (6.9.1)$$

Notice how this equation fits with Figure 6.9.2.

What We Do with Forward Rates

The main point is that if we start with a yield curve for riskless rates, we can infer from the curve all possible forward rates. In particular, if we have a binomial tree with times $t_0, t_1, \ldots t_N$ (that is, with nodes at time t_0, t_1, etc.) then we can infer the forward rate r_i from time t_i to t_{i+1}. In particular, we can start from the outset assuming we have exogenously given forward rates $r_0, r_1, \ldots, r_{N-1}$ for the time steps t_0 to t_1, etc. (where r_0 represents the risk-free rate today for loans maturing at time t). What we are about to show is that we can build a binomial tree assuming we have different forward rates for each time step. The only thing to verify is that the tree is still recombining. We do this now.

Trees with Varying Forward Rates

In this section, we verify the following principle:

> When building a binomial tree using the Cox-Ross-Rubinstein method, the equal probabilities method, or the general equations in section 6.6, we can use a different forward rate for each time step by recomputing the equations of the tree at each time step.

It is important to note that the resulting trees are no longer standard: We will see that the up and down ratios at each time step will change. Before seeing this, however, we need to see what conditions we need in order for

F I G U R E 6.9.3

When trees recombine, the ratio u/d
at time t_i is the same as the ratio
u'/d' at time t_{i+1}

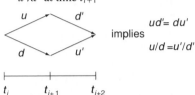

implies

$ud' = du'$

$u/d = u'/d'$

the tree to be recombining. To do this, we relax the standard of standard trees (all up and down ratios are the same) and instead require:

> Within each time step each up ratio is the same, each down ratio is the same, and the ratio of the up ratio to the down ratio is the same for all time steps.

Thus at each time t_i there is a given up ratio, say u_i, a given down ratio, say d_i, but their ratio u_i/d_i is the same at all times.

Let's illustrate this with a simple example. Figure 6.9.3 displays a piece of a binomial tree at three times t_i, t_{i+1}, and t_{i+2}, and we have:

$u =$ up ratio at time t_i
$d =$ down ratio at time t_i
$u' =$ up ratio at time t_{i+1}
$d' =$ down ratio at time t_{i+1}

Now it is clear that if the tree is recombining, then $ud' = du'$. This means that an up move followed by a down move is the same as a down move followed by an up move; this, however, is exactly the same equation as

$$u/d = u'/d'. \qquad (6.9.2)$$

With all of this noted, we will now go through the three different methods of producing trees and show specifically how to vary the interest rates at each time step for that type of tree.

The Cox-Ross-Rubinstein Method

In this method, the up ratio is given by $e^{\sigma \sqrt{\Delta t}}$ (where σ is the volatility of the stock and Δt is the length of a time step), and the down ratio is one over the up ratio. When we want to change forward rates, we can do so without changing the up and down ratio at each time step. What changes, however, are the risk-neutral transition probabilities.

Suppose we have the following notation:

r_i = forward rate from time t_i to time t_{i+1}

p_i = risk-neutral up-transition probability from time t_i to time t_{i+1}

Then we have

$$p_i = \frac{e^{r_i \Delta t} - d}{u - d},$$

where u is the up ratio and d is the down ratio. Thus, in a Cox-Ross-Rubinstein tree, to vary the interest rates we vary the transition probabilities but keep the up and down ratio as in the standard formulation.

The Equal Probabilities Method

In the equal probabilities method, the up- and down-transition probabilities are always equal to 0.5. This means that something else must be changed if we are to vary the interest rates. The answer, of course, is that the up and down ratios change because of equations (6.5.5) and (6.5.6). We have to allow a different up and down ratio for each time step. If we let

u_i = the up ratio from time t_i to time t_{i+1}

d_i = the down ratio from time t_i to time t_{i+1},

then we clearly have

$$u_i = \frac{2e^{r_i \Delta t + 2\sigma \sqrt{\Delta t}}}{e^{2\sigma \sqrt{\Delta t}} + 1} \quad \text{and} \quad d_i = \frac{2e^{r_i \Delta t}}{e^{2\sigma \sqrt{\Delta t}} + 1},$$

where we have substituted r_i (the forward rate from time t_i to time t_{i+1}) for the expected value, written μ in equations (6.5.5) and (6.5.6).

The only thing to do now is verify that the tree still recombines. We have observed that for this to be true, we have to show that the ratio of the up to the down ratio at every time step is the same. But this is immediate, because as we saw in the derivation of the equal probabilities method, at every time step we always have

$$u/d = e^{2\sigma \sqrt{\Delta t}}$$

[see equation (6.5.4)], that is, the up ratio over the down ratio is controlled by the volatility and the length of the time step.

6.10 BINOMIAL TREES AND DIVIDENDS

Binomial trees model stock price movements. Until now we have not taken into account stocks that pay dividends. In this section, we show how to build binomial trees in which the stock is assumed to pay dividends. In all cases, we assume we know when the future ex-dividend dates are and what the dividend payments will be.

We divide this into two separate problems:

1. Stocks that pay dividends as a percentage of spot price (easier); and

2. Stocks that pay fixed dollar amounts (harder).

Note both of these forms of dividends are *lumpy*; that is, the dividends arrive at discrete points in time.

We assume throughout that we have a known *dividend schedule*. This is nothing more than a list of ex-dividend dates and dividend payments, where the payments are either a percentage yield (case 1) or a fixed dollar amount (case 2). In all cases, to simplify matters we assume

> Ex-dividend dates occur on the binomial tree. That is, we assume that ex-dividend dates are actually dates represented by the tree.

For example, if the time steps of the tree are at times $t_0, t_1, t_2, \ldots$, then we assume that each ex-dividend date occurs at some of the times t_i.

Dividends as a Percentage of Spot Price

Here is the setup. Time step t_{i+1} is an ex-dividend date. On this date, a dividend of q percent of the spot price will be issued. Therefore, the spot price on that date will drop from $S_{t_{i+1}}$ to $S_{t_{i+1}}(1-q)$. Figure 6.10.1 displays a picture of this.

Here is how to build a tree with this dividend structure. Build the tree by forward induction. Start at time step t_0 with the spot price. Now, build each time step as usual (that is, build the tree with any method you like). When we reach a time step that is an ex-dividend date, we calculate each node as usual and then multiply each node by $1 - q$. That's all there is to it. This is already shown in Figure 6.10.1.

The question is, does this actually work? There are two things to check. First, is the tree still recombining? Second, is the tree still risk-neutral?

The tree is indeed still recombining. Remember, the tree is recombining if an up move followed by a down move is equal to a down move followed by an up move at every node. Changing all the nodes at a time step by a fixed ratio $(1-q)$ does not change the ratios of two "vertically adjacent" nodes at that time step. Therefore, the tree remains recombining.

FIGURE 6.10.1

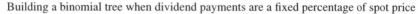

Building a binomial tree when dividend payments are a fixed percentage of spot price

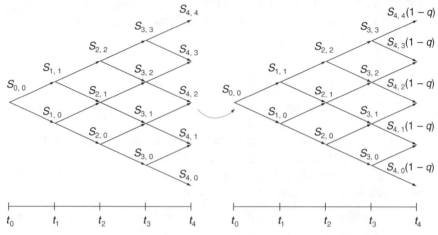

A more important question is whether there are arbitrage opportunities introduced by our method. Consider a node at time t_i with value S, where the up node is valued Su, the down node is valued Sd, and we have

$$pSu + (1 - p)Sd = e^{r\Delta t}S. \tag{6.10.1}$$

This is the standard one-period forward equation, which says that the expected value of the stock at any node is equal to growth at the risk-free rate. Put another way, it says that the expected value of the stock (at our node) is equal to the one-period forward price from the current node to the next time step.

Adding an ex-dividend date at time t_{i+1} on the one hand changes the up and down nodes to $Su(1-q)$ and $Sd(1-q)$. On the other hand, it changes the value of the one-period forward contract on the stock. The new value is $e^{r\Delta t}S(1 - q)$. Now, multiplying equation (6.10.1) by $(1 - q)$ on both sides, we obtain:

$$pSu(1 - q) + (1 - p)Sd(1 - q) = e^{r\Delta t}S(1 - q).$$

The left-hand side of this equation is the expected value of the stock, including the ex-dividend day price drop, while the right-hand side is the value of a one-period forward contract on our stock. Thus, the one-period forward equation still holds, and the conclusion is that the tree is still risk-neutral.

F I G U R E 6.10.2

A non-recombining binomial tree when the
dividend payments are a known dollar amount

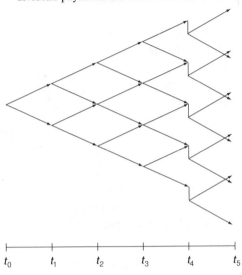

t_0 t_1 t_2 t_3 t_4 t_5

Binomial Trees with Known Dollar Dividends

We now describe how to build binomial trees when the dividend payments
are a known dollar amount. We cannot proceed as we did when the dividends were a known percentage of spot. That is, we cannot simply lower
each node at an ex-date by the dollar dividend amount. This does not work
because the resulting trees are not recombining, and we always want to
remain in the framework of recombining trees. The problem we face is
illustrated in Figure 6.10.2. In this figure, there are too many nodes at time
step t_5. We need a different approach.

The Basic Idea of How It Works

The basic idea of the approach is to combine two facts we already know.
First, we use the forward price of a stock that pays income. Let's suppose
we are modeling some stock S that has a future (known) dividend stream.
Recall that if S_0 is the spot price, r is the risk-free rate of interest, and $\mathcal{D}$ is
the present value of all dividends (with ex-dividends dates in the life of the
contract), then the forward price, F, with delivery at time T of the stock,
today is

$$F = e^{r(T-t_0)}(S_0 - \mathcal{D}),$$

where t_0 is today's date. What we want to do is use this to come up with a "dividend version" of the one-period forward equation derived in Section 6.8, equation (6.8.1).

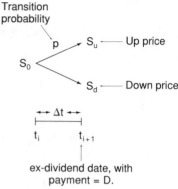

Stock price tree

To do this, we combine the forward price "with dividends," with the following constraint: In a one-period binomial tree, we demand that the expected value of the stock in one time step is equal to its forward price. That is, according to the above figure, we have

$$pS_u + (1 - p)S_d = F, \qquad (6.10.2)$$

where F is the forward price of S_0 at time t_i with delivery at time t_{i+1}. We call this the one-period forward equation *with dividends*. If time t_{i+1} is an ex-dividend date with dividend payment D, then this forward price is given by

$$F = e^{r\Delta t}(S_0 - e^{-r\Delta t}D), \qquad (6.10.3)$$

where Δt is $t_{i+1} - t_i$, and now $e^{-r\Delta t}D$ represents the present value the dividend payment with ex-dividend date t_{i+1}. Therefore, the one-period forward equation with dividends looks like:

$$pS_u + (1 - p)S_d = e^{r\Delta t}S_0 - D.$$

Now, we assume we know the values of S_u and S_d, the transition probability, and the value of D. With this information, we solve for the correct value for S_0, the vertex node. Combining equations (6.10.2) and (6.10.3), we obtain

$$S_0 = e^{-r\Delta t}(pS_u + (1 - p)S_d + D). \qquad (6.10.4)$$

There is an important assumption in equation (6.10.4) that we have to emphasize. We are assuming that S_u and S_d represent dividend-adjusted stock node values. That is, we are assuming that the price S_u and the price S_d reflect the price of the stock immediately *after it goes ex-dividend*. Thus, the addition of D in the right-hand side reflects adding the dividend back into the stock prices. This will be the key to building recombining binomial trees with dividends, which we do now.

How to Build a Recombining Tree with Lumpy Dividends

We now give the algorithm for building a recombining binomial tree with dividends when the dividend payments are known dollar amounts. The tree will be very useful later for pricing American call options. The key to building the tree is not to model the dividend payments themselves but, rather, to model the forward value at each node of an ex-dividend date.

We assume we have the following setup. We are modeling a dividend paying stock whose spot price today (time t_0) is S_0, and we want to build an N-period binomial tree with nodes at time $t_0, t_1, \ldots t_N$. Assume each time step is length Δt.

Let:

$$r = \text{the risk-free rate}$$
$$\sigma = \text{the volatility of the stock}$$

We proceed in the following steps.

1. Produce a dividend schedule $(D_1, 1), \ldots (D_N, N)$, where D_i is the dividend payment at time t_i. If t_i is not an ex-dividend date, then D_i is set to zero. For example, ($1.50, 3) indicates that there is a $1.50 dividend with ex-dividend date t_3,[9] and ($0.00, 2) means that t_2 is not an ex-dividend date.

2. Compute the present value of all future dividend payments in the schedule; this means we compute

$$\mathcal{D} = \sum_{i=0}^{N} e^{-ri\Delta t} D_i,$$

where r is the risk-free rate, i represents the i-th time step, and Δt is the length of the time step, so that $i\Delta t$ simply represents $t_i - t_0$, the amount of time from t_0 to t_i.

---

[9]Remember, we are assuming that all ex-dividend dates are represented on the tree, so we only have to specify at which time step the ex-dividend date occurs.

3. Build a risk-neutral binomial tree starting with a spot price of $S_0 - \mathcal{D}$, using σ as the volatility and r as the risk-free rate.[10]

4. Adjust the nodes for dividend payments. For each time t_i, compute the present value (at time t_i) of all dividend payments occurring *after* time t_i. That is, compute

$$\mathcal{D}_i = \sum_{j=i+1}^{N} e^{-r(j-i)\Delta t} D_j,$$

where $(j - i)\Delta t$ represents the amount of time from t_i to t_j. Add the value $\mathcal{D}_i$ to each node at time t_i.

That's it. When we have completed this procedure, we will have a tree that 1) has a spot price equal to S_0, and 2) models all dividend payments. We now build a sample tree to illustrate how the procedure works.

Example of How to Build the Tree
We will build a four-period binomial tree with nodes as follows: t_0 is today, t_1 is one year from now, t_2 is two years from now, etc., so that, Δt is one year. We assume that there is one dividend, with ex-dividend date t_2 and payment $1.00. We will build a Cox-Ross-Rubinstein tree with the following data:

$$\sigma = 15\%$$
$$r = 10\%$$
$$\Delta t = 1 \text{ year}$$
$$S_0 = \$100.00$$

Now we follow the four-step procedure above:

1. Compute the present value of all future dividends:
$$D = e^{-r(t_2 - t_0)}D_1 = e^{-0.10(2.0-0.0)1.00} = 0.8187.$$

2. Build the tree starting with a spot price of $S_0 - D$, but otherwise consisting of the data above. Thus, we build a tree with spot price of

$$100 - 0.8187 = 99.1813.$$

3. Next, we compute for each time step the present value of all dividend payments occurring after that time step. We have

---

[10]Note: It does not matter what method we use to build the tree, as long as it is recombining and risk-neutral.

$$\mathcal{D}_0 = \$0.8187$$
$$\mathcal{D}_1 = \$0.9048$$
$$\mathcal{D}_2 = \$0.00$$
$$\mathcal{D}_3 = \$0.00$$
$$\mathcal{D}_4 = \$0.00$$

These are computed as follows: $\mathcal{D}_0$ represents the present value at time step t_0 of all dividend payments occurring after time step t_0. There is only one dividend payment, occurring at time step t_2, so $\mathcal{D}_0 = e^{-2.0 \cdot 0.10} 1.00 = 0.8187$. Similarly, $\mathcal{D}_1$ represents the present value at time step t_1 of all dividend payments occurring after time t_1. So, $\mathcal{D}_1 = e^{-1.0 \cdot 0.10} 1.00 = 0.9048$.

On the other hand, there are no dividend payments after time step t_1, so $\mathcal{D}_2$, $\mathcal{D}_3$, and $\mathcal{D}_4$ are all equal to zero.

4. Raise the node value by the dividend payment. We raise all the nodes at time step t_0 by $\mathcal{D}_0$, all the nodes at time step t_1 by $\mathcal{D}_1$, etc.

Figure 6.10.3 displays two binomial trees, both representing stocks with 15 percent volatility and a risk-free rate of 10 percent. The first tree, however, represents a stock with no dividends, while the second tree represents a stock built with a $1 dividend payment at time t_2, as in the example.

What Does the Tree Model?

An obvious question is, What does the tree we build with the above procedure really model? After all, examining Figure 6.10.3 and comparing the right- and left-hand sides, we do not see a one-dollar drop at time step t_2, as we might expect from that ex-dividend date.

In fact, we are not trying to model the dividend drop on the ex-dividend date but, rather, the forward value of the stock at the time immediately before the ex-dividend date. For example, consider node $(1,1)$ (that is, the top node at time step t_1) of the right-hand tree. Let's compute the forward price of the stock at this node. If the price goes up, it moves to $133.88, while if it moves down, it moves down to $99.18. The risk-neutral transition probability is

$$p = \frac{e^{r\Delta t} - u}{u - 1/u} = \frac{1.1052 - 0.8607}{1.1618 - 0.8607} = 0.8120,$$

where u is the up-ratio for the tree. Thus, the expected value of the stock at node $(1,1)$ is

$$pS_u + (1 - p)S_d = 0.8118 \cdot 133.88 + 0.1882 \cdot 99.18 = 127.35.$$

FIGURE 6.10.3

Sample tree with dividends

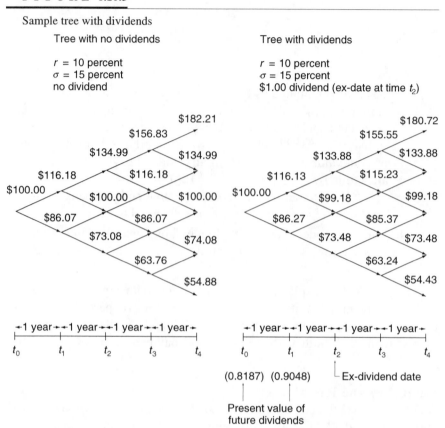

Tree with no dividends

r = 10 percent
σ = 15 percent
no dividend

Tree with dividends

r = 10 percent
σ = 15 percent
$1.00 dividend (ex-date at time t_2)

On the other hand, the forward price of the stock at node $(1,1)$ with delivery at time t_2 is given by equation (6.10.3), which in this case works out to

$$e^{0.10 \cdot 1.0}(116.1370 - e^{-1.0}1.00) = 127.35.$$

Here, the term $e^{-1.0}1.00$ is the present value of the dividend with ex-dividend date t_2. We see that the tree is risk-neutral at node $(1,1)$. That is, the forward price from node $(1,1)$ to one period later is equal to the expected value of the stock as computed via the tree. Moreover, this forward price includes the dividend payment in it.

The General Picture
The general picture works as follows. What we are really doing is dividing the stock's value into two components: the *dividend part* and the

non-dividend part. The dividend part is worth the present value of all future dividend payments in the dividend schedule, and the non-dividend part is the rest of the stock's value. If the dividend part is worth $\mathscr{D}$, then the presumption is that we can borrow $\mathscr{D}$ at time t_0 and use each dividend payment to repay the debt.[11] In this way, the total cost of purchasing the stock is its stock price *minus* $\mathscr{D}$, that is, the non-dividend part.

In the above tree-building procedure, we first build a tree with a spot price $S_0 - \mathscr{D}$. This has the feature that at the last date of the tree, all dividend payments have been made, and the resulting node values are those that reflect this. Once we build this tree, we have to add back the dividend part of the spot price at each time, making sure that equation (6.10.4) holds at each node.

To see if this is what really happens, suppose we have just completed step three of the procedure for building a binomial tree with dividends. In other words, we have computed the present value of all future dividends and we have built a binomial tree with the non-dividend part of the stock, but we have not adjusted the nodes for dividend payments. Suppose we have three nodes, S_0, S_u, and S_d, where S_0 is a node at time t_{i-1}, while S_u and S_d are nodes at time t_i, representing the up and down nodes from S_0.

Let p be the up-transition probability we used to build the tree. Then, at this point the following equation holds:

$$pS_u + (1 - p)S_d = e^{r\Delta t}S_0. \tag{6.10.5}$$

Now, to complete step four of the tree-building procedure, we will add $\mathscr{D}_i$ to S_u and S_d, while adding $\mathscr{D}_{i-1}$ to S_0. We are going to show that after this is done, equation (6.10.4) will hold.

To see this, we have to note that

$$\mathscr{D}_{i-1} = e^{-r\Delta t}(\mathscr{D}_i + D_i),$$

where D_i is the dividend payment for ex-dividend date t_i. In words, this equation means that the present value of all future dividend payments at time step t_{i-1} is the present value of all future dividend payments at time step t_i plus any dividend payment at time step t_i, all discounted to time t_{i-1}. Now, we will add $\mathscr{D}_i$ to nodes at time t_i and see what happens to equation (6.10.5):

---

[11]Once again, we see the notorious assumption that the dividend payment occurs on the ex-dividend date.

$$p(S_u + \mathcal{D}_i) + (1 - p)(S_d + \mathcal{D}_i) = pS_u + (1 - p)S_d + \mathcal{D}_i$$
$$= e^{r\Delta t}S_0 + \mathcal{D}_i$$
$$= e^{r\Delta t}S_0 + e^{r\Delta t}\mathcal{D}_{i-1} - D_i$$
$$= e^{r\Delta t}(S_0 + \mathcal{D}_{i-1}) - D_i.$$
$$= e^{r\Delta t}(S_0 + \mathcal{D}_{i-1} - e^{-r\Delta t}D_i).$$

Putting it all together, we have

$$p(S_u + \mathcal{D}_i) + (1 - p)(S_d + \mathcal{D}_i) + D_i = e^{r\Delta t}(S_0 + \mathcal{D}_{i-1} - e^{-r\Delta t}D_i).$$

$$(6.10.6)$$

To interpret this equation, note that there are three important terms: $S_u + \mathcal{D}_i$, $S_d + \mathcal{D}_i$, and $S_0 + \mathcal{D}_{i-1}$. These three terms represent, respectively, the dividend adjusted values of S_u, S_d, and S_0 (adjusted as per step 4 of the tree building procedure), and are the node values of our binomial tree at the end of the tree-building procedure.

On the other hand, D_i represents the dividend payment with ex-dividend date t_i. Examining the form of equation (6.10.6), we see that it is precisely the one-period forward equation "with dividends." The left-hand side is the expected value of the stock for S_0 from time t_{i-1} to time t_i. The right-hand side, on the other hand, is the forward price of S_0 from time t_{i-1} to time t_i.

6.11 ARROW-DEBREU PRICES

Each node of a binomial tree has an associated *Arrow-Debreu price*. Arrow-Debreu prices are an important part of advanced option pricing methods such as implied volatility trees, which we will discuss in Chapter 9. In this section, we define what Arrow-Debreu prices are and explain how to calculate them.

What Are Arrow-Debreu Prices?
To understand what Arrow-Debreu prices are, remember that each node of a binomial tree represents two things: 1) a future moment in time, and 2) a possible stock price at that time. The Arrow-Debreu price of a node is the value of a security that pays $1 if the stock price reaches that node and zero otherwise.

Recall that we number the nodes of a tree (i, j), where i represents time and j represents height from the bottom (see Figure 6.7.1). For example, node (i, j) represents a particular time t_i and a particular spot price S_{t_i}. To say that the spot price reaches node (i, j) means that at time t_i, the stock

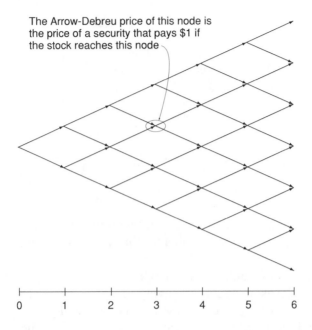

The Arrow-Debreu price of this node is the price of a security that pays \$1 if the stock reaches this node

price is equal to S_{t_i}. For example, in the figure above is a binomial tree. The Arrow-Debreu price of node (3,2) is the value of a security that pays \$1 if the spot price at time t_3 is at node (3,2) and nothing otherwise. Part of the aim of this section is to learn how to compute the Arrow-Debreu price of a node. This will be essential when we study implied volatility trees in Chapter 9. We begin with a two-step tree example.

Sample Computation

We now illustrate how to compute Arrow-Debreu prices. In the figure at the top of page 262 is a two-step binomial tree. The up branches are respectively labeled p_1, p_2, and p_3, indicating the up-transition probabilities (i.e., the probability that the stock price will move up is p_1 at time t_0, etc.). We will show how to compute the Arrow-Debreu prices of nodes (2, 2), (2, 1), and (2, 0). In fact, we will be satisfied with computing the probability of arriving at each of the nodes (2,2), (2,1), or (2,0). Once we can do this, the Arrow-Debreu price will be that probability multiplied by the discount factor from time t_0 to time t_2. To understand this example, let's first examine the Arrow-Debreu price of node (2,2) in the following figure.

What percentage of the time would the stock in the figure end up at node (2,2)? Since there is only one path to this node (the path in which the stock price rises after time t_0, and then rises again after time t_1), the

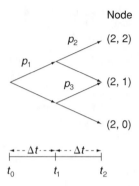

probability of ending up at node (2,2) is precisely the probability of moving up after time t_0 and then up again after time t_1. This probability works out to be $p_1 \cdot p_2$.

Since the probability of reaching node (2,2) is $p_1 \cdot p_2$, we know that if we were to invest in a security paying \$1 if the stock reaches node (2,2), then $p_1 \cdot p_2$ represents the fraction of time we would receive a payment of \$1 when investing in that security. Thus, *on average*, the payout of the Arrow-Debreu security of node (2,2) is \$1 $\cdot p_1 \cdot p_2 \cdot$. On the other hand, the value of the Arrow-Debreu security for node (2,2) is equal to its expected payout (\$1 $\cdot p_1 \cdot p_2$) discounted to time t_0: $e^{-r(t_2 - t_0)} \cdot p_1 \cdot p_2$.

We use these principles to compute the Arrow-Debreu price of node (2,1). We have to compute the probability that after two moves, the stock will end up at node (2,1). There are two possible paths that arrive at this node. We compute the probability of following each of the paths below.

Call the path that goes up and then down, path 1, and the path that goes down and then up, path 2. These are shown in Figure 6.11.1.

The way to compute the probability of reaching node (2,1) is to add the individual probabilities of reaching node (2,1) via the two different paths. These probabilities are:

$$\text{Probability of traversing path 1} = p_1 \cdot (1 - p_2)$$
$$\text{Probability of traversing path 2} = (1 - p_1) \cdot p_3$$

Thus, the probability of reaching node (2,1) is

$$p_1 \cdot (1 - p_2) + (1 - p_1) \cdot p_3.$$

Why is this the case? Because the probability of two distinct events occurring is simply the sum of the probabilities of each event occurring.

F I G U R E 6.11.1

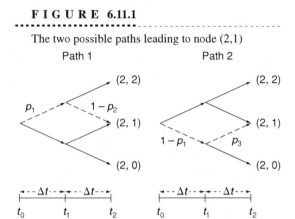

The two possible paths leading to node (2,1)

Path 1   Path 2

The Arrow-Debreu price of node (2,1) is therefore the above value discounted to time t_0:

$$e^{-r(t_2-t_0)} \cdot (p_1 \cdot (1 - p_2) + (1 - p_1) \cdot p_3).$$

The General Definition of an Arrow-Debreu Price

From this example, we see that an Arrow-Debreu price of a node is quite simple.

> The Arrow-Debreu price of a node is the probability of reaching that node discounted by a factor of $e^{-r(t_n-t_0)}$, where $t_n - t_0$ represents the time between today and the time where the node is.

If we try to compute the Arrow-Debreu price of a node many time steps out (e.g., at time step 10), we would run into a problem: As the number of time steps increases, the number of paths reaching a node at that time step increases rapidly. Practically speaking, this makes it complicated and time consuming to compute the probability of reaching a particular node.[12]

Fortunately, we are not interested in the general formula for the Arrow-Debreu price of a node. Rather, we want to know how to deduce Arrow-Debreu prices at a given time step from Arrow-Debreu prices of the previous time step.

An Iterative Procedure

Figure 6.11.2 displays the situation we want to consider. The Arrow-Debreu price of nodes (n, n) and $(n, n - 1)$ are labeled respectively $\lambda_{n,n}$

---

[12]This is particularly true when using flexible trees, where the transition probabilities change from node to node.

F I G U R E 6.11.2

A fragment of a binomial tree

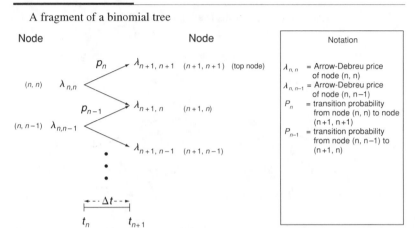

and $\lambda_{n,n-1}$, and similarly, the Arrow-Debreu prices of nodes $(n + 1, n + 1)$, $(n + 1, n)$, and $(n + 1, n - 1)$ are denoted $\lambda_{n+1,n+1}$, $\lambda_{n+1,n}$, and $\lambda_{n+1,n-1}$. The transition probabilities from nodes (n, n) to $(n + 1, n + 1)$ and $(n, n - 1)$ to $(n + 1, n)$ are p_n and p_{n-1}.

We will give formulas for the Arrow-Debreu prices of nodes $(n + 1, n + 1)$ and $(n + 1, n)$ in terms of this information.

Write Δt for $t_{n+1} - t_n$, the change in time from level n to level $n + 1$. Also write $\lambda_{n+1,i}$ for the Arrow-Debreu price of node $(n + 1, i)$.

Then, we will see that

$$\lambda_{n+1,n+1} = e^{-r\Delta t} p_n \lambda_n \qquad (6.11.1)$$

$$\lambda_{n+1,n} = e^{-r\Delta t} \left(p_{n-1} \lambda_{n,n-1} + (1 - p_n) \lambda_{n,n} \right). \qquad (6.11.2)$$

Equation (6.11.1) follows because there is only one way to get to node $(n + 1, n + 1)$ from level n, and that is to come up from the previous time step. The probability of this is p_n. Remembering that the Arrow-Debreu price of a node is the present value of the probability of reaching that node, we obtain the first formula.

To understand the second formula, note that there are two ways of reaching node $(n + 1, n)$ from level n. We can come up from node $(n, n - 1)$ or come down from node (n, n). The probability of the former is p_{n-1}, while the probability of the latter is $1 - p_n$. Thus, we obtain the second formula.

To produce the Arrow-Debreu price of nodes at a given level, we have to know the Arrow-Debreu prices of all the nodes of the previous level that

D I S P L A Y   6.11.1

THE FORMULA FOR THE ARROW-DEBREU PRICE OF A NODE

We will compute the Arrow-Debreu price of all the nodes of a binomial tree at level $n + 1$, given that all the Arrow-Debreu prices at level n are known.

$\lambda_{n,i}$ = The Arrow-Debreu price of node (n, i)
$\lambda_{n+1,i}$ = The Arrow-Debreu price of node $(n + 1, i)$
p_i = The transition probability from node (n, i) to node $(n + 1, i + 1)$
r = Risk-free rate of interest
Δt = Length of time step

There are three formulas: the formula for $\lambda_{n+1,n+1}$, node $(n + 1, n + 1)$, the formula for $\lambda_{n+1,0}$, node $(n + 1, 0)$, and the formula for $\lambda_{n+1,i+1}$, $0 \le i \le n - 1$. We have

$$\lambda_{n+1,n+1} = e^{-r\Delta t} p_n \lambda_{n,n}$$
$$\lambda_{n+1,0} = e^{-r\Delta t} p_0 \lambda_{n,0}$$
$$\lambda_{n+1,i+1} = e^{-r\Delta t} (\lambda_{n,i} p_i + \lambda_{n,i+1}(1 - p_{i+1}))$$

---

can reach a given node and the transition probabilities from those nodes to the next level. In general, there will be two such nodes, unless you are at the top or bottom of the level. The general formula for the Arrow-Debreu price of a node is given in Display 6.11.1.

6.12   THE DISTRIBUTION OF RETURNS

In this section, we discuss how to compute the distribution of stock returns from a binomial tree. That one can easily compute the entire distribution of stock returns from the terminal nodes of the tree and their Arrow-Debreu prices is an important and useful feature of binomial trees.

The Procedure
Suppose we have a risk-neutral binomial tree. Then, we know or can compute the following data:

$$r = \text{risk-free rate of interest}$$
$$t_0 = \text{initial date of tree}$$

$$t_n = \text{ending date of tree}$$
$$\lambda_{n,i} = \text{Arrow-Debreu price of node } (n, i)$$

Where we recall that node (n, i) is the i-th node from the bottom at time t_n.

Now write $p_{n,i}$ for the probability of reaching node (n, i). From the definition of Arrow-Debreu prices, we know

$$p_{n,i} = e^{r(t_n - t_0)} \lambda_{n,i}.$$

With this information, we will compute the probability distribution of stock prices and returns from the binomial tree. The procedure is similar to creating histograms.

The probability distributions we make will be in the form of a bar graph. On the horizontal axis will be either returns or stock prices (depending on whether we want to look at the distribution of returns or prices). The vertical axis will represent the percent of returns falling in a particular range. Each bar in the resulting bar graph represents the fraction of stock price paths that yield a return (or price) that falls in the particular range. Thus, to produce these graphs, we must first decide on bin sizes we want in the bar graph.

Figure 6.12.1 displays an example of what we mean. The left-hand part of this figure (top part) is a portion of a 20-period Cox-Ross-Rubinstein binomial tree. The tree was constructed with the following data:

$$\sigma = 15\%$$
$$r = 10\%$$
$$T - t = 1 \text{ year}$$

That is, the tree represents a stock with 15 percent volatility and a risk-free rate of 10 percent over the period of one year. At the end of the tree, the figure displays both the stock prices of each terminal node (that is, the prices at the last period of the tree), as well as the annualized returns accrued at each node. We have listed the levels we wanted to bar graph for both prices and returns.

How to Make the Bar Graph

We can use a binomial tree to make two bar graphs: a distribution of stock prices, and a distribution of stock returns. To make bar graphs as in Figure 6.12.1, use the following procedure:

1. Decide on a set of "levels" for the bar graph. Equally spaced levels often work well; for example, in Figure 6.12.1, the returns

A 20-period binomial tree and the corresponding distribution of prices and distribution of returns

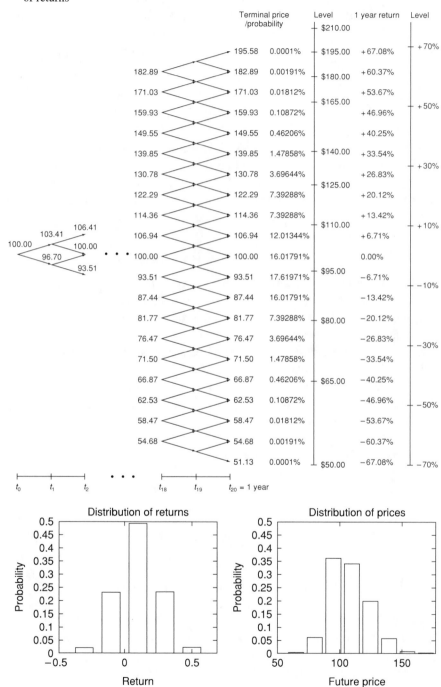

ranged from -70 percent to 70 percent spaced every 20 percent. Note we have also made levels for stock prices.

2. For each terminal node, compute the probability of reaching that terminal node.

3. For each level, compute the probability of being in that level by adding up all the probabilities of all terminal nodes within that level.

For example, consulting Figure 6.12.1, we see that there are four nodes in the $50 to $65 level, with probabilities of 0.0001, 0.00191, 0.01812, and 0.10872 percent respectively. Therefore, the probability of being in the range of $50 to $65 is the sum of these probabilities, which is 0.12885 percent (i.e. approximately 12/100 of one percent).

The Distribution of Returns of a Standard Tree

Until now we have only described how to measure the distribution of returns for a flexible binomial tree. This method, while perfectly general, does not exploit the regularity of a standard binomial tree. In the case of a standard tree, we have a lot more information and can produce precise formulas for the probability of reaching each terminal node, and therefore can significantly simplify the creation of distributions.

To begin, we collect several standard and important facts about standard trees relating to the distribution of stock returns. Before giving these formulas, we recall *factorial notation*.

Factorial Notation

Let n be some positive whole number, i.e., $0, 1, 2, \ldots$ Then, we have the standard notation:

$$n! = n(n-1)(n-2)\ldots 2 \cdot 1.$$

For example, $3! = 3 \cdot 2 \cdot 1$, which is equal to 6, and

$$8! = 8 \cdot 7 \cdot 6 \cdot 5 \cdot 4 \cdot 3 \cdot 2 \cdot 1.$$

Having dispensed with this, we give the main formulas.

Formulas

Here is the setup. We have an n-period standard binomial tree with the following data:

$$p = \text{up-transition probability at each node.}$$

Then, we have the following formulas:

$$\text{Number of paths reaching node } (k, i) = \frac{k!}{(k-i)!i!}$$

$$\text{Probability of reaching node } (k, i) = \frac{k!}{(k-i)!i!}p^i(1-p)^{k-i}.$$

Of course, the first formula holds for all binomial trees, not just standard trees. We illustrate this with a few examples.

Example
We'll start with a 10-period equal probability tree. Let's compute the probability of reaching each terminal node. Since each up-transition probability is 50 percent, we use the above formulas in a straightforward manner. The results are displayed in Figure 6.12.2.

F I G U R E   6.12.2

Terminal distribution of a 10-period equal probability tree

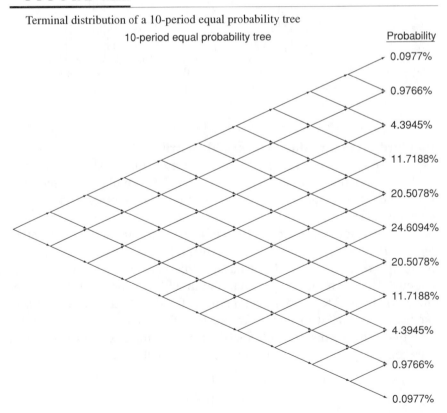

10-period equal probability tree   Probability

0.0977%

0.9766%

4.3945%

11.7188%

20.5078%

24.6094%

20.5078%

11.7188%

4.3945%

0.9766%

0.0977%

F I G U R E 6.12.3

Binomial trees approximate the log-normal distribution

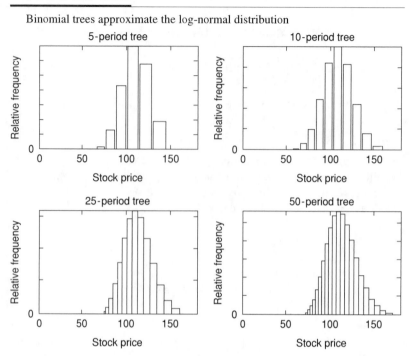

Standard Trees and the Log-Normal Distribution

As we have said before, standard trees are discrete time analogs of geometric Brownian motion. Now that we have a precise formula for the terminal distribution of a standard tree, it is possible to be more precise concerning what this means.

The distribution of stock prices of a standard binomial tree is called *approximately log-normal.* This statement has an exact mathematical meaning, however, we will not discuss this here. Rather, we will content ourselves with the concept that, intuitively, this means that the more time periods used to build a tree, the more the distribution looks and acts like the log-normal distribution. To illustrate this point, we use a picture.

Figure 6.12.3 displays terminal distributions for Cox-Ross-Rubinstein trees constructed with the following common input data:

$$\sigma = 15\%$$
$$r = 10\%$$
$$T - t = 1 \text{ year.}$$

That is, the tree models a stock with a 15 percent *per annum* volatility, assuming the risk-free rate of interest is 10 percent. The time from the initial date to the terminal date of the tree is one year.

We see from Figure 6.12.3 that as the number of periods increases, the terminal distribution looks more and more like a log-normal distribution.

This is what is meant by an approximate log-normal distribution. The basic shape of the distribution is log-normal, and as we increase the number of periods in a tree (with all other parameters fixed), the bar graphs become an increasingly accurate approximation of a log-normal distribution.

6.13   ARROW-DEBREU PRICES AND BUTTERFLY SPREADS

The concept of an Arrow-Debreu price may seem a little obscure, and perhaps of little practical importance, but nothing could be further from the truth. Arrow-Debreu prices have a natural manifestation in the world of trading, where they take the form of *butterfly spreads*. In this section, we discuss butterfly spreads and their relationship to Arrow-Debreu price.

Butterfly Spreads

A butterfly spread is formed from four options on the same underlying security: two short and two long. We fix three strike prices, K_1, K_2, and K_3,

FIGURE 6.13.1

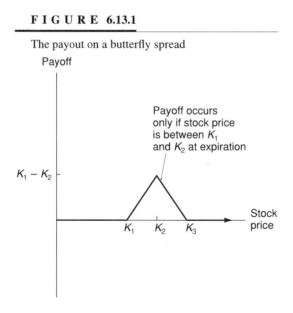

The payout on a butterfly spread

one greater than the next (e.g., $95, $100, and $105), and we assume that they are evenly spaced, so that the difference in price between K_2 and K_1 is the same as the difference in price between K_3 and K_2.

One way to form a butterfly spread is to create a portfolio consisting of one call option struck at K_1 long, two call options struck at K_2 short, and one call option struck at K_3 long, all expiring on the same date and all on the same underlying security.

The payout pattern of this portfolio is pictured in Figure 6.13.1. Except for the triangular region starting at a stock price of K_1, peaking at K_2, and returning to zero at K_3, the payout on this security is zero. The maximum payout is equal to $K_1 - K_2$, and this occurs at K_2.

Now, we can *normalize* the butterfly spread by dividing by $K_2 - K_1$. In this case, when K_1 and K_2 are close to one another, we have a security that pays $1 if the stock price is very close to K_2 at expiration and zero otherwise. Moreover, by moving K_1 and K_3 closer together, the region where the option payout is not zero or one shrinks.

One can see that the butterfly spread, regarded as a single financial instrument, is a very good approximation to a security that pays $1 at time T if and only if the spot price is K_2. If we were modeling this security on a binomial tree, and if there were a node at time T with value K_2, then the value of the butterfly spread would be exactly the Arrow-Debreu price of that node! Put another way, the butterfly spread is a trader's Arrow-Debreu price.

7

⑥ BASIC OPTION PRICING WITH BINOMIAL TREES

This chapter shows how to use the binomial tree model of stock price movements to price European call and put options. The method is quite general and will be extended in Chapter 11 to give pricing methods for barrier options. Almost any kind of option can be priced on a binomial tree. This explains why the binomial model is employed almost anywhere option pricing is taking place. In 1995, at the International Association of Financial Engineers awards dinner honoring Mark Rubinstein as financial engineer of the year, Stephen Ross, co-inventor (with Cox and Rubinstein) of the binomial model, remarked on the ubiquity of binomial trees, "The only thing I regret in developing the binomial model is that we didn't charge a penny a node."

Before beginning with the pricing methods, we emphasize the following fact. Binomial pricing is a two-step process: First we build a binomial tree, and then we price option. Therefore, the study of pricing on binomial trees is distinct from building binomial trees. In the previous chapter, we discussed the most basic binomial trees: standard trees. Later, we will study more advanced techniques for building flexible trees, and these trees will be powerful allies in option pricing. In either case, whether we build standard or flexible trees, the methods for pricing options on those trees remain the same. In this chapter, we study the most basic techniques for pricing on trees: pricing European options. Later, we will discuss pricing barrier options, as well as other options. In each case, when we study a pricing technique, we assume we *already have a binomial tree to price on.*

7.1 ONE-STEP MODELS

To get acquainted with the binomial method of option pricing, we begin our discussion with a very simple example: a one-step binomial model. Every binomial tree is composed of many one-step trees, and the pricing methods on multiple-step trees boil down to repeated applications of the single-step model. Therefore, understanding the single-step model in detail is crucial.

Binomial Pricing—The One-Step Model

Imagine we have a stock following a one-step model. The stock price can either rise or fall. Meanwhile, we also have an option on the stock that expires at the end of the time period. If the stock price rises, the option pays off a certain amount, C_u (the "up" payout), and if the stock price drops, the option pays off a certain amount, C_d (the "down" payout). Figure 7.1.1 displays this: The left-hand side is a one-step stock tree, and the right-hand side is the corresponding *option value tree*.

The option value tree, which we will encounter numerous times in option pricing, is a companion tree to the stock price tree; each node represents the value of the option when the stock price has the value of the same node in the stock price tree. Put another way, for each possible future stock price at each possible time, the option will have an associated value. The option value tree describes these values.

The Classic Arbitrage Argument

In the case of a plain vanilla, one-period European option struck at K, we can say explicitly what the up and down payments, C_u and C_d are:

$$C_u = \max(S_u - K, 0)$$
$$C_d = \max(S_d - K, 0).$$

F I G U R E 7.1.1

Stock and derivative option value tree for a one-step binomial model.

We are interested in knowing the value of the option C at time 0, which is denoted C_0 on the tree. Setting aside for a moment all we have learned in our study of Black-Scholes, let's ask the naive question

How do we know C has a value?

In other words, what makes us think we can assign a unique value to C? Maybe its value is something more like a work of art, which can only be valued based on some market's appraisal of its worth. Moreover, it is not even clear what we mean by "value." If we do come up with a value, what will its formula look like? What variables does it depend on?

Any attempt to come up with a value for C would have to involve the price of the underlying. But what else will this formula involve? What about p, the probability that the stock price will rise? What about economic data, like the short-term interest rates? More importantly, how do we determine which variables matter, and which can be ignored? We examine these questions next.

The Riskless Hedge

In the Black-Scholes analysis, we saw the arbitrage argument for the value of a European call involved forming a riskless hedge exactly replicating the payout of C no matter what price path the underlying takes. We would like to do this now in the (simpler) situation of the one-period binomial model.

Our hedging portfolio will have a certain number, Δ, of shares of stock at time t_0 and a riskless, zero-coupon bond maturing to a par value of B at time t_1. Thus, at time t_0, the value of the hedging portfolio is:

$$\Delta S_0 + e^{-r(t_1 - t_0)} B,$$

where r is the risk-free rate of interest.

The value of Δ and B will be determined in a moment. Right now, we will focus on what we want them to do for us. To get at this, consider Figure 7.1.2. In this figure, we see the value of the portfolio at time t_0 and the *possible* values of the portfolio at time t_1. Likewise, we see the option payout at time t_1, which consists of the two *possible* values of C at time t_1.

Now what we want Δ and B to do for us is clear:

We want to choose Δ and B so that the value of the portfolio is equal to C_u if the price of S rises and equal to C_d if the price of S drops.

In other words, we want the portfolio to *replicate* the payout of C. This means that the "up" node of the portfolio tree should equal the "up" node of the option value tree, and likewise for the down nodes. This translates into the following two equations:

F I G U R E 7.1.2

A comparison of the hedging portfolio tree and
the derivative value tree.

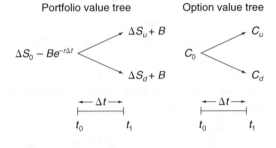

Portfolio value tree   Option value tree

$$\Delta S_u + B = C_u$$
$$\Delta S_d + B = C_d.$$

That is, the first equation represents the hedging portfolio's value at time t_1 if the stock price rises, and the second equation represents the value if the price falls. Solving these for Δ and B, we obtain:

$$\Delta = \frac{C_u - C_d}{S_u - S_d}$$

$$B = C_u - \frac{C_u - C_d}{S_u - S_d} S_u.$$

The readers who studied the Black-Scholes chapters of this book will quickly recognize the significance of the formula for Δ: The numerator is the "up" price minus the "down" price of C, while the denominator is the "up" stock price minus the "down" stock price. That is,

Δ *is the rate of change of the value of C at time t_1 with respect to S.*[1]

What about B—is there any significance there? Rewriting the formula a bit, we see:

$$B = \frac{S_u C_d - C_u S_d}{S_u - S_d}. \tag{7.1.1}$$

---

[1]Notice that this Δ is the rate of change at time t_1, *not* time t_0. Comparing this with the Black-Scholes model, we might wonder why Δ is not the rate of change at time t_0. The answer lies in the fact that the binomial model is a discrete time model. As the binomial model gets finer and finer, that is, as Δt gets closer and closer to zero, the value of t_1 gets closer to t_0 and the value Δ approaches the Black-Scholes delta.

At first glance, this does not seem to offer much, but we shall soon see differently. First, we answer the question, what is the value of C?

Valuing C

We still haven't produced a value for C. What we have done so far is produce a portfolio, consisting of Δ shares of stock and a bond maturing to B, which exactly replicates the payout of C at time t_1.

By a simple arbitrage argument, we then deduce that the value of C at time t_0 must be the value of the portfolio at time t_0. That is,

$$C_0 = \Delta S_0 + e^{-r\Delta t} B.$$

Writing this out with the formulas for Δ and B, we obtain:

$$C_0 = \frac{C_u - C_d}{S_u - S_d} S_0 + e^{-r\Delta t} \frac{S_u C_d - C_u S_d}{S_u - S_d}. \tag{7.1.2}$$

This is the value of the option at time t_0. Let's discuss a couple of points.

First, note that the formula has essentially four pieces of "input" data: the stock price, the option payout, and the risk-free rate of interest.[2] Conspicuously absent is the transition probability p. Thus, the question arises: Does the option value depend on the transition probability?

Option Value and Transition Probability

A first glance at equation (7.1.2) suggests that the transition probability plays no role in the option's value. On the other hand, we will see explicitly in Section 7.3 that the transition probability really is in there; in particular, we will see equation (7.1.2) is equivalent to

$$C_0 = e^{-r\Delta t} \left(p C_u + (1 - p) C_d \right),$$

where p is the risk-neutral transition probability. We'll explain this in detail later, but for now we make the following point. Since the one-period option value only depends on the up and down payouts, the risk-free rate, time to expiration and risk-neutral up transition probability, the option value contains no subjective assessment of the expected value of the stock. The only assessment at all is the *objective* one relating to the forward price of the stock. This refers to the fact that the risk-neutral up probability is the correct probability for pricing forward contracts (see page 243).

---

[2]There is also the time to expiration, but since we are speaking exclusively of a one-period model, we will ignore this for the moment.

Put another way, we do not have to state an opinion of what the probability of the stock rising is in order to value the option. We do have to know the risk-free rate of interest; this is related to making the "hedge work." The hedge is essential because it is what guarantees that we have really valued the option.

The Hedging Strategy

Our derivation of the formula for C_0 was derived from a hedging strategy. We know the price for C_0 is correct because we have essentially built our own "synthetic" version of C out of the underlying stock S and the bond B. In other words, if there really were in a "binomial" world in which the price of S precisely rises or falls to S_u or S_d respectively, then we could hold a hedging portfolio like the one above and obtain all the advantages of holding C. If C were available in the market for less, we could short the portfolio, use the proceeds to buy C, and be guaranteed a profit. Likewise, if C were priced above the value of the portfolio, we could short the option, use the proceeds to purchase the portfolio, and make a guaranteed profit.

In a moment, we will reinterpret equation (7.1.2) in terms of risk-neutral probabilities, but first let's look at how it gives us a "binomial" hedging strategy.

7.2 HEDGING THE OPTION

In the last section, we derived the price of C by constructing a hedging portfolio that replicates its payout. In this section, we study the hedging strategy obtained from this procedure.

Let's turn the formula in equation (7.1.2) around and see how we can derive our hedging strategy. Notice that the value of C_0 in equation (7.1.2) breaks up into the sum of two pieces:

$$\text{first piece:} \quad S_0 \frac{C_u - C_d}{S_u - S_d}$$

$$\text{second piece:} \quad e^{-r\Delta t} \frac{S_u C_d - C_u S_d}{S_u - S_d}.$$

These two pieces form the basis of the hedging strategy. The first piece is equal to the value of $\frac{C_u - C_d}{S_u - S_d}$ shares of S at its current price of S_0, while the second piece is equal to the value of a bond maturing to $\frac{S_u C_d - C_u S_d}{S_u - S_d}$ after Δt time expires. From this we obtain the following hedging strategy:

1. Buy $\frac{C_u - C_d}{S_u - S_d}$ shares of S at time t_0.

2. Sell a riskless, zero-coupon bond maturing to $-\frac{S_u C_d - C_u S_d}{S_u - S_d}$ at time t_1.

The second item requires a bit of explanation: $\frac{S_u C_d - C_u S_d}{S_u - S_d}$ is, in fact, always negative when the option is a European call.[3] For example, if $\frac{S_u C_u - C_u S_d}{S_u - S_d} = -\$28$, this means "sell a \$28 bond maturing in one time period."

We would like to verify two things: first, that the value of the hedging portfolio at time t_0 is the value of C_0; second, that the hedging portfolio replicates the payout of the call option at time t_1.

The first task is simple—the value of the hedging portfolio (at time t_0) is given by adding up the number of shares of stock purchased times the market price of S at time t_0, and the value of the bond at time t_0. We compute this value as:

$$S_0 \frac{C_u - C_d}{S_u - S_d} + e^{-r\Delta t} \frac{S_u C_d - C_u S_d}{S_u - S_d}.$$

The above equation is precisely the value of C_0 in equation (7.1.2).

The second point requires us to know what happens at time t_1. There are two possibilities—either the price of S goes up to S_u or it goes down to S_d. If it goes up, then the value of the hedging portfolio becomes

$$S_u \frac{C_u - C_d}{S_u - S_d} + \frac{S_u C_d - C_u S_d}{S_u - S_d} = C_u. \tag{7.2.1}$$

Notice that we have replaced S_0 by S_u and have eliminated the term "$e^{-r\Delta t}$." This reflects, respectively, the stock price rising and the bond maturing.

If the price of S moves down to S_d, the portfolio's value becomes:

$$S_d \frac{C_u - C_d}{S_u - S_d} + \frac{S_u C_d - C_u S_d}{S_u - S_d} = C_d. \tag{7.2.2}$$

Equations (7.2.1) and (7.2.2) mean the hedging portfolio's value becomes precisely the value of C (at time t_1), *no matter what*.

The "binomial hedging strategy" is summarized in Display 7.2.1.

Example
Suppose we have a one-year call option struck at \$100 on a stock, S, which has a spot price of \$100 per share. In one year, the price of S will either rise

---

[3]This is clear if $C_d = 0$, that is, if $S_d < K$. On the other hand, if both S_u and S_d are greater than K, we have $S_u C_d - C_u S_d = S_u(S_d - K) - (S_u - K)S_d = (S_d - S_u)K$, so $B = -1$. This scenario reflects a 100% probability that the option will expire in the money.

DISPLAY 7.2.1

THE BINOMIAL HEDGING STRATEGY

Suppose the spot price is at the indicated position:
Assuming that the risk-free rate of interest is r and the time between the periods indicated is Δt, then to hedge the position at the indicated node, a portfolio should be constructed consisting of the following:

1. $\frac{C_u - C_d}{S_u - S_d}$ shares of S.

2. A riskless, zero-coupon bond (short) maturing to $-\frac{S_u C_d - C_u S_d}{S_u - S_d}$ at the next period.

If the current value of S is S_0, then the current value of the portfolio is

$$\frac{C_u - C_d}{S_u - S_d} S_0 + e^{-r\Delta t} \frac{S_u C_d - C_u S_d}{S_u - S_d}.$$

to \$120 or fall to \$80 per share. The risk-free rate of interest is 5 percent. Figure 7.2.1 displays the stock tree and option payout value in this scenario.

We computed the risk-neutral probability by applying equation (6.8.2) as follows:

$$p = \frac{e^{r\Delta t} S_0 - S_d}{S_u - S_d} = \frac{e^{0.05} 100 - 80}{120 - 80} = 0.6282.$$

Next we compute the hedging portfolio using equation (7.1.2). We see the hedging portfolio should consist of the following:

1. $\frac{C_u - C_d}{S_u - S_d} = \frac{20}{40} = 0.5$ shares of S.

2. A riskless, zero-coupon bond maturing to $\frac{S_u C_d - C_u S_d}{S_u - S_d} = \frac{-20 \cdot 80}{40} = -\$40$ in one year. In other words, we short a riskless, zero-coupon bond maturing to \$40 in one year.

Now, what is the total cash flow in setting up this hedge? We have:

1. Long stock: total cost = \$50.00.

2. Short bond: total cost = −\$38.05.

Therefore, the total cost is \$11.95.

Let's check that this portfolio replicates the payout of the option. There are, of course, two scenarios:

F I G U R E 7.2.1

The stock and option value tree for a one-step binomial model.

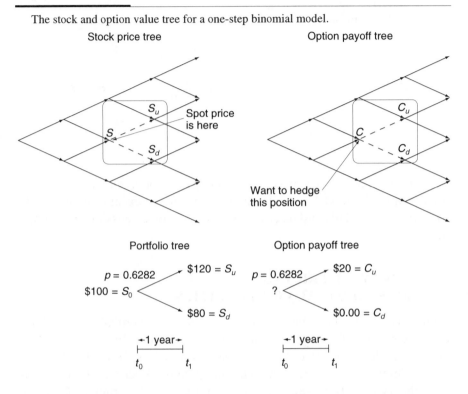

Stock price tree

Option payoff tree

Portfolio tree

Option payoff tree

1. The spot price of S rises to \$120 per share. The hedging portfolio will then be worth $\$0.5 \cdot 120 - \$40 = \$20$, the value of the option, C_u.

2. The spot price of S drops to \$80 per share. The hedging portfolio will then be worth $\$0.5 \cdot 80 - \$40 = \$0$.

We see that whether the price of the stock rises or falls, the portfolio replicates the payout of the option. Therefore, the value of the option at time t_0 is equal to the value of the hedging portfolio at time t_0: \$11.95.

Where Do We Go from Here?
Clearly, the one-step binomial model is only a stepping stone to our real goal of pricing options on a multi-period binomial tree. We studied the one-step model first because, as is depicted in Figure 7.2.2, multiple-step models are built up from one-step models. This will be studied in detail in Section 7.4.

F I G U R E 7.2.2

How a two-step binomial model is built up from one-step models.

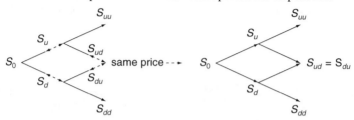

In fact, all the ideas necessary to hedge an option on a stock follow-ing the binomial model have already been discussed except for one: *back-ward induction.* This will be covered in our general discussion of binomial models.

7.3 BINOMIAL PRICING AND RISK-NEUTRAL PROBABILITIES

Equation (7.1.2) tells us the value of an option in a "binomial" world. More-over, we saw that the expected value of the stock in the binomial tree does not play a role in this price. Nevertheless, one wonders if probability theory is completely removed from the binomial picture. After all, in the contin-uous theory (i.e., Black-Scholes), probability played a crucial role in the form of the risk-neutral probability that the option expires in the money. Is there an analog of this in the binomial case? The answer is yes, and it's simple to understand.

We have to formally manipulate the terms of equation (7.1.2) into a slightly different form. To do this, we separate all of the terms involving C_u from all of the terms involving C_d and obtain:

$$C_0 = \frac{S_0 - e^{-r\Delta t}S_d}{S_u - S_d}C_u + \frac{e^{-r\Delta t}S_u - S_0}{S_u - S_d}C_d. \qquad (7.3.1)$$

The right-hand side of equation (7.3.1) has the form "something times C_u plus something times C_d." These "somethings" turn out to be very close to p and $1 - p$, the up- and down-transition probabilities.

Everything becomes much clearer if we compute the forward value of equation (7.3.1) by multiplying both sides by a factor of $e^{r\Delta t}$. Then, equa-tion (7.3.1) is transformed into:

$$e^{r\Delta t}C_0 = \frac{e^{r\Delta t}S_0 - S_d}{S_u - S_d}C_u + \frac{S_u - e^{r\Delta t}S_0}{S_u - S_d}C_d. \qquad (7.3.2)$$

Now, suppose we are in a risk-neutral world. Then, the left-hand side of the above equation is the expected value of C_0 after a time Δt: In a risk-neutral world, everything has an expected growth rate equal to the risk-free rate. What about the right-hand side?

Write $p = \frac{e^{r\Delta t}S_0 - S_d}{S_u - S_d}$. We see immediately that

$$1 - p = \frac{S_u - e^{r\Delta t}}{S_u - S_d},$$

and therefore equation (7.3.2) is transformed into:

$$e^{r\Delta t}C_0 = pC_u + (1 - p)C_d. \qquad (7.3.3)$$

On the other hand, the formula for p is exactly the formula for the risk-neutral transition probability of the binomial tree given in equation (6.8.2) of Chapter 6.

Thinking back to our discussion of probability theory (in Chapter 2), we see that the right-hand side of equation (7.3.3) is an expected value. Why? Think of the value of the option as a random event. There are two possible outcomes: C_u (the "up" payout) and C_d (the "down" payout). Then, the right-hand side of equation (7.3.3) reads "up probability" times "up payout" plus "down probability" times "down payout." That is, the equation is the sum of all possible outcomes times their respective probabilities—an expected value.

The conclusion is now obvious: The risk-neutral expected value of C computed one way—by taking the forward value under the risk-free rate—is the same as computing it another way—by computing the expected value of the "outcomes" C_u and C_d under the risk-neutral transition probabilities.

Finally, we conclude that the option's value is given by

$$C_0 = e^{-r\Delta t}(pC_u + (1 - p)C_d). \qquad (7.3.4)$$

In summary, we have shown:

> The value of an option is equal to its risk-neutral expected value, discounted to today's value at the risk-free rate of interest.

Here when we say risk-neutral expected value we mean the expected value computed with respect to the risk-neutral transition probabilities. Therefore, we have proved that the principle of risk-neutral valuation really works, at least for a binomial world.

7.4 PRICING EUROPEAN OPTIONS ON MULTIPLE-STEP TREES

In this section, we explain how to go from the one-step model to multiple-step models in order to value European options on any binomial tree. The principle is simple: We repeatedly apply the one-step model. We begin with an example.

General Binomial Trees

Suppose we have a European option settled at time t_0 and expiring at time T and a binomial tree modeling the stock price movement for the life of the option.

For example, in Figure 7.4.1 is a picture of a stock price tree and its corresponding option value tree for a call option with strike price $105. In this tree, we have

$$\Delta t = 1 \text{ month}$$
$$r = 5\% \text{ per annum.}$$

The tree is *not* a standard tree. The transition probabilities change at each node. We use this tree to emphasize that the type of tree we use is absolutely irrelevant to the valuation procedure we are going to employ.

F I G U R E 7.4.1

A multiple-step binomial tree and its accompanying option value tree for a $105 strike call.

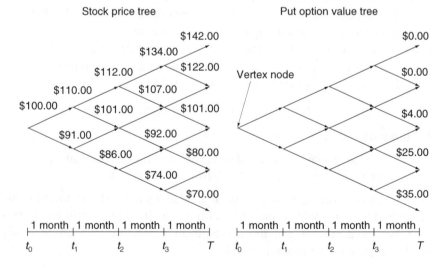

The risk-neutral, up-transition probability for the first node is pictured; it was computed using equation (6.8.2). We see the transition probability from node (0,0) to node (1,1) is

$$p = \frac{e^{0.05 \cdot 1/12} \cdot 100 - 91}{110 - 91} = 0.4957.$$

Once all the transition probabilities are computed, we will be able to compute the value of the option in Figure 7.4.1. To do this, we will apply the method of backward induction to "fill in" the empty nodes in the option value tree, ultimately working our way back to the "vertex node," which will represent the value of this $105 call.

Backward Induction

We are going to use the *boundary values* in the option value tree in Figure 7.4.1, along with the risk-neutral transition probabilities, to work backward from the terminal date to the settlement date using equation (7.1.2) to build the hedging strategy. The boundary values are the values of the option at the expiration date. We can compute these directly from the payout formula for the call option. These boundary values are displayed in Figure 7.4.1.

First, we compute all the transition probabilities from time t_3 to time T, using equation (6.8.2). What we are trying to do is shown in Figure 7.4.2.

F I G U R E 7.4.2

Backward induction from time T to time t_3.

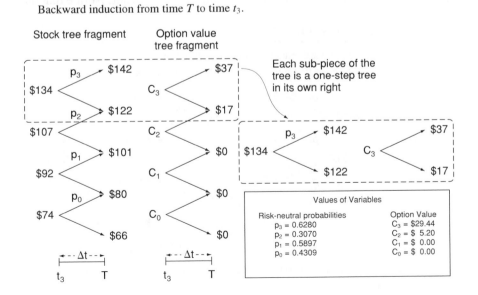

Risk-neutral probabilities	Option Value
$p_3 = 0.6280$	$C_3 = \$29.44$
$p_2 = 0.3070$	$C_2 = \$\ 5.20$
$p_1 = 0.5897$	$C_1 = \$\ 0.00$
$p_0 = 0.4309$	$C_0 = \$\ 0.00$

In the option value tree, the nodes labeled C_3, C_2, C_1, and C_0 should each be thought of as an option settled at that node and expiring at time T. For example, C_3 is an "option" settled at time t_3, when the stock is at \$134. The option has two possible payouts according to whether the stock price rises to \$142 or drops to \$122—its "up" payout is \$37 and its "down" payout is \$17. Therefore, using equation (7.3.4), we have

$$C_3 = e^{-r\Delta t}(p_3 \cdot 37 + (1 - p_3) \cdot 17) = \$29.44,$$

where $p_3 = 0.6280$ is the up-transition probability for the top node at time t_3.

Here is a complete list of equations used to compute C_3, C_2, C_1, and C_0:

$$C_3 = e^{-r\Delta t}(p_3 \cdot 37 + (1 - p_3) \cdot 17)$$
$$C_2 = e^{-r\Delta t}(p_2 \cdot 17 + (1 - p_2) \cdot 0)$$
$$C_1 = e^{-r\Delta t}(p_1 \cdot 0 + (1 - p_1) \cdot 0)$$
$$C_0 = e^{-r\Delta t}(p_0 \cdot 0 + (1 - p_0) \cdot 0).$$

We have computed all the values for $p_0, \ldots, p_3$ and $C_0, \ldots, C_3$; these values are displayed in Figure 7.4.2.

Backward Induction Continued—Time t_3 to Time t_2.

We continue with backward induction, now examining time t_2. Figure 7.4.3 displays a picture of what we have and what we want. Notice that the

F I G U R E 7.4.3

Backward induction from time t_3 to time t_2.

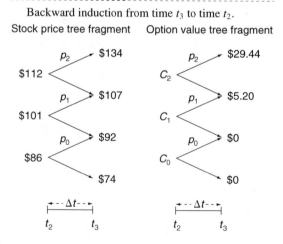

Stock price tree fragment   Option value tree fragment

right-hand side nodes on both the stock price tree fragment and the option value tree fragment are nothing but the left-hand nodes of the tree at time step t_3. For example, the right-hand nodes of the option value tree are, reading from top to bottom, $29.44, $5.20, $0.00, and $0.00.

We need to compute the transition probabilities p_2, p_1, and p_0, as well as the nodes labeled C_3, C_2, and C_1. We proceed exactly the same way as in the previous step. The equations for the transition probabilities are as follows:

$$p_2 = \frac{e^{r\Delta t}112 - 107}{134 - 107} = 0.2025$$

$$p_1 = \frac{e^{r\Delta t}101 - 92}{107 - 92} = 0.6281$$

$$p_0 = \frac{e^{r\Delta t}86 - 74}{92 - 74} = 0.6866.$$

Once we have the transition probabilities, we can immediately calculate C_2, C_1, and C_0. The equations are:

$$C_2 = e^{-r\Delta t}(p_2 \cdot 29.44 + (1 - p_2) \cdot 5.20) = \$10.07$$
$$C_1 = e^{-r\Delta t}(p_1 \cdot 5.20 + (1 - p_1) \cdot 0.00) = \$3.25$$
$$C_0 = e^{-r\Delta t}(p_0 \cdot 0 + (1 - p_0) \cdot 0) = \$0.00.$$

Backward Induction Continued—Time t_2 to Time t_1

We now compute the transition probabilities from time t_1 to t_2. This level is shown in Figure 7.4.4:

F I G U R E 7.4.4

Backward induction from time t_2 to time t_1.

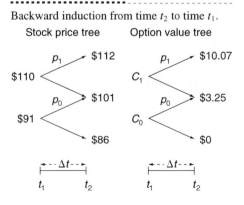

$$p_1 = \frac{e^{r\Delta t}110 - 101}{112 - 101} = 0.8599$$

$$p_0 = \frac{e^{r\Delta t}91 - 86}{101 - 86} = 0.3587.$$

With the values of p_1 and p_0 in hand, we can compute the values of C_1 and C_0. The equations are:

$$C_1 = e^{-r\Delta t}(p_1 \cdot 10.07 + (1 - p_1)3.25) = \$9.08$$

$$C_0 = e^{-r\Delta t}(p_0 \cdot 3.25 + (1 - p_0)0.00) = \$1.16.$$

Finishing the Backward Induction—Time t_0

We are now ready to finish backward induction by pricing time step t_0. Figure 7.4.5 displays the situation. We have to compute p_1 and C_1. We will make these computations and then discuss their meaning with regard to option pricing.

First, we compute the value of p_0. This is given by the equation

$$p_0 = \frac{e^{r\Delta t}100 - 91}{110 - 91} = 0.4957.$$

Next, we use this to compute C_0. We have

$$C_0 = e^{-r\Delta t}(p_0 \cdot 9.08 + (1 - p_0)1.16) = \$5.06.$$

In a moment, we will show that C_0 *is* actually the value of our call option, but first we discuss the meaning of the above numbers.

What the Numbers Mean

We have now computed everything we need—all the transition probabilities and all the nodes of the option value tree. But what do the numbers

FIGURE 7.4.5

Backward induction from time t_1 to time t_0.

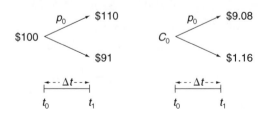

Stock price tree fragment   Option value tree fragment

FIGURE 7.4.6

Completed stock price and option value trees for the option described in Figure 7.4.1.

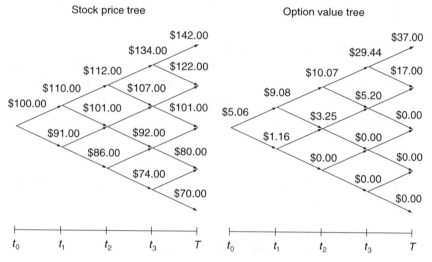

Stock price tree

Option value tree

really mean, and what good are they? To answer this, see the complete stock price tree and option value tree shown in Figure 7.4.6.

First of all, the extreme left node of the option value tree, priced at $5.06, *is* the option value in the binomial world described by the tree. What does this mean? Appealing to our notion of a self-financing, replicating hedging strategy, it means that there is a self-financing hedging strategy that replicates the call option described by the option value tree. Of course, this is subject to all of the earlier assumptions (e.g., on the economy) and to the restriction that the stock price stays *exactly* within the confines of the stock price tree.

The next question is, what does the *entire* option value tree represent? The answer is simple: We have not simply valued the option today; we have produced option values for *every possible* future stock price (subject to the restriction, of course, that the underlying stays within the binomial tree).

Let's see how to read off the hedging strategy from the diagrams in Figure 7.4.6. This is quite simple—we just use the hedging strategy described in Section 7.2. The only thing to make clear is what C_u, C_d, S_u, and S_d are in this context. The answer, of course, is that C_u and C_d are the "payouts" on the option for the next step, which are provided by the value tree. To understand what this means, let's work through an example based on one possible sample path through our tree.

Simulated Hedging Through a Single Sample Path

Figure 7.4.7 delineates a single sample path from the binomial tree in Figure 7.4.6. Let's compute and examine the hedging strategy we will follow to hedge the option as the stock follows the sample path.

The Hedging Portfolio at Time t_0

According to Figure 7.4.7, at time t_0, the stock price is $100 and can either increase to $110 or decrease to $91. The option value tree indicates that the corresponding payouts are $9.08 if the stock price goes up and $1.16 if the stock price goes down. Thus, we write

$$S_u = \$110 \qquad C_u = \$9.08$$
$$S_d = \$91 \qquad C_d = \$1.16.$$

Examining the hedging strategy in Section 7.2, we see we need to buy

$$\frac{C_u - C_d}{S_u - S_d} = \frac{9.08 - 1.16}{110 - 91} = 0.4168$$

shares of stock and short a one-month, zero-coupon bond in the next time period maturing to:

$$-\frac{S_u C_d - C_u S_d}{S_u - S_d} = -\frac{110 \cdot 1.16 - 91 \cdot 9.08}{110 - 91} = \$36.7726.$$

FIGURE 7.4.7

Sample path (dotted line) through stock price tree.

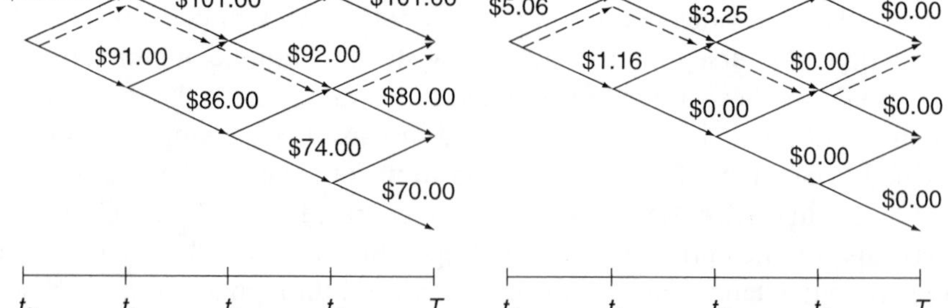

Let's compute the value of the hedging portfolio at this time. Since we buy 0.4168 shares of the stock and short a bond maturing to $36.7726, the portfolio's total value is

$$0.4168 \cdot 100 - e^{-r\Delta t} \cdot 36.7726 = \$5.06.$$

This value is to be expected: It is the value of the option at time t_0. Thus, the set-up cost of the hedge is equal to the value of the option. In other words, we have just purchased a hedging portfolio whose current value is equal to the value of the option as computed by our model.

What Happens at Time t_1

Let's move on to the next time period. In the sample path, the stock price moves up to $110.00. That is, if we examine Figure 7.4.7 we see that from time t_0 to time t_1 the stock price rises to $110.00. Let's see if our hedging strategy works by checking the value of the hedging portfolio at time t_1:

$$0.4168 \cdot 110 - 36.7726 = 9.08.$$

This was computed by observing that at time t_1, we still own 0.4168 shares of the stock, but the price went up to $110, and we are still short the bond, but it has matured to $36.7726. Note that the new value of the hedging portfolio, $9.08, is exactly equal to the value of the node we are at in the option value tree.

To continue, we have to rebalance the hedging portfolio at time t_1. To do this we have to do two things: 1) compute the new components of the hedge, and 2) compute how much stock and bond to buy or sell to bring the portfolio back in balance. First, we compute the components of the hedge. To start, notice we now have:

$$S_u = \$112 \qquad C_u = \$10.07$$
$$S_d = \$101 \qquad C_d = \$3.25.$$

Thus, the hedging strategy calls for owning

$$\frac{C_u - C_d}{S_u - S_d} = \frac{10.07 - 3.25}{112 - 101} = .6200$$

shares of the stock and having a one-month, riskless, zero-coupon bond maturing to

$$\frac{S_u C_d - C_u S_d}{S_u - S_d} = \frac{112 \cdot 3.25 - 101 \cdot 10.07}{112 - 101} = -\$59.37.$$

Since this is a negative dollar amount, we have to have short bond maturing to $59.37.

How much is this new hedging portfolio worth? We compute that the current value of this portfolio is

$$0.62 \cdot 110 - e^{-r\Delta t}59.37 = \$9.08.$$

This means the value of the new portfolio is *exactly* the same as the value of the old portfolio (i.e., the portfolio before rebalancing). All that has changed is its internal makeup. Therefore, the cost of rebalancing the portfolio is zero. (Note that it is exactly at this place where we use the "cost" of the no transaction costs assumption.) That is, in rebalancing, nothing has been added and nothing has been taken away (except transaction costs).

Let's turn our attention to what happens at time t_2. Examining Figure 7.4.7, we see that from time t_1 to time t_2, the stock price drops to \$101. Let's verify that the portfolio replicates the value of the option at the next time step. Its value at time t_2 is computed in the manner as above

$$0.62 \cdot 101 - 59.37 = 3.25.$$

This is precisely the desired value.

Rebalancing at Time t_2

At time t_2, we need to rebalance again. The portfolio should contain

$$\frac{5.20 - 0}{107 - 92} = 0.3467$$

shares of stock and a riskless, zero-coupon bond maturing to

$$\frac{0 - 92 \cdot 5.20}{107 - 92} = -\$31.89$$

in one month. The net value of this portfolio is

$$0.3467 \cdot 101 - e^{-r\Delta t} \cdot 31.89 = \$3.25.$$

Again, we see the strategy is self-financing.

Now, in the next time step (time t_3), the stock price drops to \$92, so the value of the portfolio becomes

$$0.3467 \cdot 92 - 31.89 = \$0.00.$$

At this stage (time t_3), the hedging is over. No matter what happens, the stock price cannot rise enough to make the option expire in the money. In any case, at each step, the cost of rebalancing was zero, so the total cost of hedging was equal to the initial cost of setting up the portfolio, which was \$5.06. Therefore, the hedging strategy accomplished exactly what we wanted it to:

1. **It** was self-financing. That is, at each step, the cost of rebalancing was zero, so that the total cost of hedging was equal to the setup cost.
2. **It** replicated the payout of the option.

European Put Options

The backward induction procedure for European call options works equally well for puts. The only difference is the first step of the backward induction procedure. With call options, we filled in the "terminal nodes" of the option value tree with the payouts of a European call and then proceeded backward to the initial node.

With put options, we do exactly the same thing, except using the payouts of a European put. Figure 7.4.8 displays a stock price tree and option value tree for a European put on the same stock as in the call pricing example (see Figure 7.4.1). The put is struck at $105, and we have filled in the terminal nodes.

We will not fill in the remaining unfilled nodes in Figure 7.4.8; the procedure for doing so is identical, *once the terminal nodes are determined.*

Summary of Pricing Procedure

To price a European option on a binomial tree, we use the following procedure:

FIGURE 7.4.8

A multiple-step binomial tree and its accompanying option value tree for a $105 strike European put.

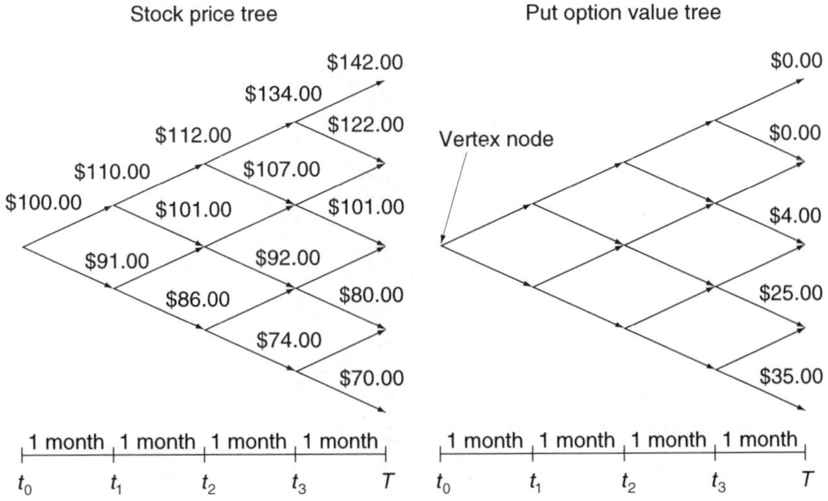

1. Build a binomial tree spanning the length of time from the option settlement date to the option expiration. The stock price tree can either be a standard tree or a more sophisticated tree. The choice depends on the nature of the application (more on this later).
2. Build an "empty" option value tree. This tree is the same size and shape as the stock price tree built in step 1; each node will represent the value of the option at the time and stock price represented by the "same" node in the stock price tree.
3. Fill in the terminal nodes of the option value tree. The terminal node values are determined by the *option payout structure*. For European calls and puts, we remind the reader:

$$\text{call option payout} = \max(S - K, 0)$$
$$\text{put option payout} = \max(K - S, 0).$$

4. Work back from the expiration date to the settlement date. At each "one-step piece" (see Figure 7.4.9) of the tree, use the formula:

$$C_0 = e^{-r\Delta t}\left(pC_u + (1 - p)C_d\right),$$

where p is the risk-neutral transition probability, r is the risk-free

F I G U R E 7.4.9

The one-step trees embedded in a multistep tree.

rate of interest, and C_u and C_d are the up and down values of the option.

Option Payout Structure and Path Independence

So far we have only discussed valuing European call and put options, but it is clear from the procedure we outlined that we can easily extend the basic techniques to many sorts of European options. The option payout structure can, in principle, be *anything* at all, as long as the option is European. As examples, we could define the following payout structures:

- Payout:

$$\begin{cases} 0 & \text{if } S < K \\ S & \text{if } S \geq K. \end{cases}$$

  This is a so-called cash-or-nothing payout, and the option is called a cash-or-nothing option. It pays the stock if the option is in the money and nothing otherwise.

- Payout:

$$\log S.$$

  That is, the payout is the natural logarithm of the value of the stock. This is called a log-payout, and the corresponding option is called a *log contract*.

- Payout:

$$\begin{cases} 0 & \text{if } S < K \\ 1 & \text{if } S \geq K. \end{cases}$$

  This is called a *digital,* or *binary,* payout, and the corresponding option is called a digital, or binary, option.

The above payouts all have one thing in common: They are *path independent payouts*. That is, the value of the payout is determined by only two things: 1) the terminal stock price value, and 2) the option payout structure. The backward induction procedure works perfectly for such payouts, but there are more complicated sorts of payouts for which backward induction does not work. The problem is, we can define even more complicated option payouts that depend not only on the final stock price and the payout structure but also on *how* the stock price arrived at the final price (e.g., the price might depend on the average value of the stock price throughout the life of the option). For now, we will avoid discussing such *path-independent* options; we will return to them later.

All of the above path-independent options are used (at least occasionally) by real investors and hedgers. Notice that there are myriad other *possible* payouts we could invent. In all cases, pricing European options with these payouts follows the procedure outlined above. The only step of the entire procedure particular to the specific contract is step 3, in which we fill in the terminal nodes at the option payout tree according to the payout.

7.5   OPTION VALUATION AND ARROW-DEBREU PRICES

In this section, we take another look at option pricing on a binomial tree, this time giving option pricing formulas in terms of Arrow-Debreu prices. That is, as opposed to building an option value tree via backward induction, we will show that the value of a European option of the type described in the last section (that is, with path-independent payouts) is determined by two types of information: 1) the option value at all nodes of a given time step, and 2) the Arrow-Debreu prices of all nodes of the same time step.

There are two reasons to study the methods in this section. First, they lead to insights regarding options pricing in general, and second, they are extremely useful in the method of implied volatility trees, which will be studied in Chapter 9.

Introduction
The main point of this section is to show that option values are intimately related to risk-neutral transition probabilities. To understand this, look back at the one-step model and equation (7.3.4). Recall that this equation means that the value of C today is the present value of the *expected value* of the option price one period later, where the expected value is calculated in terms of the risk-neutral transition probabilities.

The point of risk-neutral valuation is that this statement holds for *any* number of periods, not just one. To evaluate the value of an option on a binomial tree, we just need to compute its expected value in two different ways:

1. First, use the fact that in a risk-neutral world all securities have an expected value equal to growth at the risk-free rate.
2. Next, compute the expected value of the option by using the risk-neutral transition probabilities in the binomial tree and the payouts of the option.

Arrow-Debreu prices are precisely a way of combining the above two steps. We explain this with the example of a European call option.

European Call Options

Figure 7.5.1 shows the value tree for a European call option on some stock or index struck at K. We will write C for this option. We have only labeled the *terminal* nodes of this option, that is, the nodes at the expiration date.

By definition, the expected value of the call option is the sum over all nodes of the payout at each node times the probability of reaching that node. When we say "payout at a node," we mean the payout received on the option if the stock is at the price represented by that node (remember, we can use *any* payout structure we like). For example, in Figure 7.5.1, the payout at node (4,4) is $S_4 - K$.

In the case of Figure 7.5.1, the payout at a node is either zero, if the node is below the strike level, or $S_i - K$, if it is above the strike level. Thus, the expected value of the call is given by the formula

$$\pi_{4,3}(S_3 - K) + \pi_{4,4}(S_4 - K),$$

where $\pi_{4,3}$ is the probability of reaching node (4,3) and $\pi_{4,4}$ is the probability of reaching node (4,4).

Now we look at things from the point of view of risk-neutral valuation, which says that if the value of C at time t_0 is C_0, then its expected value at time t_4 is $e^{r(t_4 - t_0)}C_0$. We equate the two different ways of computing the

F I G U R E 7.5.1

The payout on terminal nodes in a European call option.

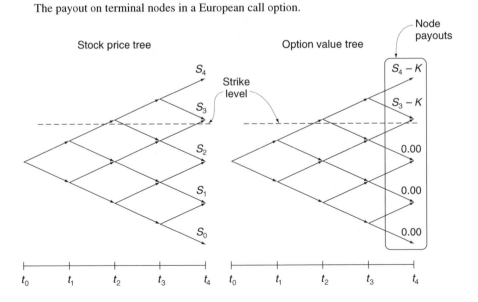

expected value and obtain $e^{r(t_4-t_0)}C_0 = (\pi_{4,3}(S_3 - K) + \pi_{4,4}(S_4 - K))$, or

$$C_0 = e^{-r(t_4-t_0)}(\pi_{4,3}(S_3 - K) + \pi_{4,4}(S_4 - K)). \qquad (7.5.1)$$

Now, recall the general fact that

$$e^{-r(t_4-t_0)}\pi_{4,3} = \lambda_{4,3}$$

$$e^{-r(t_4-t_0)}\pi_{4,4} = \lambda_{4,4},$$

where $\lambda_{4,3}$ and $\lambda_{4,4}$ represent, respectively, the Arrow-Debreu prices of nodes (4, 3) and (4, 4). With this noted, equation (7.5.1) becomes

$$C_0 = \lambda_{4,3}(S_3 - K) + \lambda_{4,4}(S_4 - K). \qquad (7.5.2)$$

In other words, the call value is equal to the sum over all the (non-zero) payouts, times the Arrow-Debreu prices.

The form of equation (7.5.2) is generally true. That is, the value of a path-independent European option is always equal to the sum over all the terminal nodes, times the Arrow-Debreu prices of those nodes.

F I G U R E 7.5.2

Formula for the value of a European call using Arrow-Debreu prices.

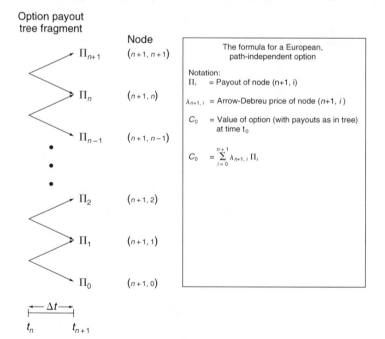

General Formula for a European Path-Independent Option
Given a European, path-independent option with any payout structure, we can value it using a binomial tree. To do this, all we need to know is the Arrow-Debreu price of each terminal node. This is summarized in Figure 7.5.2.

7.6   STOCK PRICE QUANTIZATION AND OPTION SPECIFICATION ERROR

The implicit assumption in the binomial model of option pricing is that there is a continuous model of stock price movements to which the discrete binomial model is *converging*. For example, consider a standard binomial model with expected return r and standard deviation σ. If we use the equations in Display 6.5.1 of Chapter 6, then increasing the number of time periods (or, equivalently, shrinking the size of Δt) will lead to option prices that get closer and closer to the corresponding Black-Scholes prices.[4]

We say that as the number of time periods increases, the standard binomial model *converges* to the Black-Scholes model of option pricing. Therefore, the idea of option pricing on a binomial tree is to obtain prices that are almost as good as the continuous theory, while retaining the power and flexibility of the discrete model.

Pricing options on a binomial tree is a powerful tool, but it is not without problems. There are two sources of errors directly associated with pricing options on a tree: *stock price quantization error* and *option specification error.*[5] We will discuss these now.

There are two components to pricing on a binomial tree: 1) the tree, which is a representation of stock price movements, and 2) the terms of the option, represented by a second binomial tree, the option value tree, derived from the stock price tree.

Stock quantization error is derived from the necessary coarseness of stock prices represented by a binomial tree. This means the "holes" between stock prices found in every binomial tree. For example, on a tree, two adjacent nodes at the same time step might represent stock prices of $87.50 and $90.00. This means that in this model and at this time, it is not possible for the stock to be $88.00, $89.00, or any other price between $87.50 and $90.00. Analogously, cption specification error is caused by the inability of the tree to accurately represent the terms of an option contract.

---

[4]This is by no means an obvious fact. It was discovered in 1979 by Cox, Ross, and Rubinstein.
[5]This terminology, and the associated ideas, are found in "Enhanced Numerical Methods for Options with Barriers," E. Derman, I. Kani, D. Ergener, I. Bardhan (1995).

We describe these sources of error in more detail below.

Stock Price Quantization Error

Stock price quantization error is the error on a binomial tree that arises because the binomial tree is not a continuous theory. In a continuous theory (e.g., Brownian motion), every possible spot price is represented by the theory. In a discrete theory, we necessarily "give up" many possible stock prices, and this "coarseness" can lead to discrepancies between the theoretical option price (that is, the price arrived at by a continuous time model) and the price arrived at by the tree.

The general remedy for quantization error is to increase the number of time periods in the binomial model. Doing this generally decreases the "space" between stock prices, therefore decreasing the stock price quantization error as well (see Figure 7.6.1). This remedy will always work provided we increase the number of periods enough; that is, all of these problems are resolved in the continuous limit. There are several problems associated with this solution, however, and it is important to discuss them.

Increasing the Number of Periods

To understand quantization error, we have to carefully sort out what we know and what we do not know. Imagine we are valuing an option that is

F I G U R E 7.6.1

Increasing the number of periods in a binomial tree decreases the space between spot prices

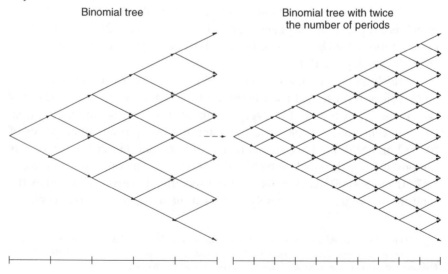

not at all familiar to us. We have a general payout structure of the option (e.g., a log contract), and we build a binomial tree to price the option. At the end of the day, we do end up with an option price, and this is where the trouble begins. The following questions immediately arise:

1. How do we know how "good" the option value we arrive at is?
2. If we suspect that the price is not "good" and we wish to build a tree with more periods, how do we know the new value we arrive at will be "better?"

For example, suppose we value a log contract and we obtain a value of $12 with a 100-period tree. Then we build a 200-period tree and obtain a value of $11. Which price is better?

The answer is, of course, we cannot say much about the two prices unless we know a little bit more about the option. In other words, it is impossible to use any option valuation model as a *black-box*. In general, we have to have some feel for what the correct price should be, either through actual trading and hedging experience or through seeing a great many values of options of the same type running through a variety of scenarios.

With this said, there is one general mathematical fact that can help us—convergence. We explain this now.

What Is Convergence?
In this subsection, we will stick to a single type of option (European and path independent for now), a plain vanilla European call struck at K and expiring in one year. We want to examine what happens if we price this option on the same underlying with trees of various numbers of periods.

Figure 7.6.2 shows six plots of European option values versus number of periods. All plots display option values obtained from a binomial tree in which all of the data about the option are fixed *except for* the number of periods in the binomial tree. The options have the following data:

$$T - t = 1 \text{ year}$$
$$\sigma = 15 \text{ percent}$$
$$r = 10 \text{ percent}$$
$$S_0 = \$100$$

That is, the time until expiration is one year, the underlying has 15 percent volatility, the risk-free rate is 10 percent, and the current spot price is $100.

The left-hand column of plots contains option values for three European call options: one out of the money (top graph), one at the money (middle graph), and one in the money (bottom graph). Similar graphs are displayed for put options.

F I G U R E 7.6.2

Value versus number of periods for puts and calls

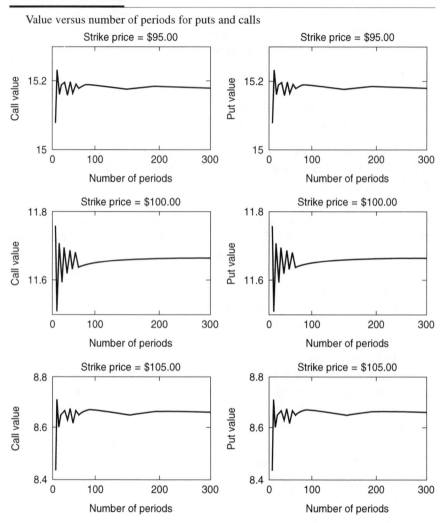

In each graph, the horizontal axis represents number of periods, and the vertical axis represents option value. In all cases we see that as the number of periods in the binomial tree is increased, for the first 50 periods or so, the option value at first moves up and down. After that the value settles in toward a fixed number (which turns out to be the Black-Scholes price of the option). This is a graphical picture of convergence.

We have made the plots to indicate two things. First, the "convergence pattern" of the prices is not simple (though it appears to be the same for puts and calls of the same strike. This is a consequence of put-call parity), and second, in all cases, when the number of periods becomes large enough, the option values *stabilize*. That is, the difference between values obtained by increasing the number of periods becomes very small.

This brings us back to the question of what is the correct number of periods to use when valuing an option on a binomial tree. The one way to get a feel for the "correct" number of periods to use is to know how large of a tree to use. The answer to this generally depends on the type of option (e.g., European versus American, path dependent versus path-independent), as well as the particulars of the option and underlying (e.g., the volatility of the underlying and the moneyness of the option).

Option Specification Error

Option specification error is the error in pricing on a binomial tree derived from the inability of the tree to accurately represent the terms of the option. Option specification error is not a major problem when pricing European options. We mention it because other types of options, particularly barrier options (which will be studied in more detail in Chapter 11), experience a great deal of option specification error, so much so that special numerical methods have to be implemented to handle them.

7.7 INTRODUCTION TO VALUING EXOTIC OPTIONS ON A BINOMIAL TREE

This section gives a brief introduction to the concepts behind valuing exotic options on a binomial tree. More complete information on both what exotic options are and how to price them may be found in Nelken (1995).

Exotic options are not a strictly defined class of options, but rather refer to options with more complicated properties than ordinary put and call options. For instance, barrier options are options that can become inactive, or conversely, only become active, if the stock price crosses a certain threshold price, called the "barrier price." (Chapter 11 will discuss barrier options in detail). The more complicated the nature of the payout scheme, the more difficulties we can expect in pricing.

The Difficulties of Pricing Exotic Options

Ideally, one would like to find closed form formulas for exotic option prices—that is, formulas like Black-Scholes. Unfortunately, this is highly unlikely because of the complicated nature of the payouts of these instruments. Moreover, most closed form solutions restrict the stock price model to geometric Brownian motion, something we do not want to do.

The principle behind pricing any option on a binomial tree is quite simple, and most aspects are captured in the one-step model. In that model, any option on a stock or index can be described by its payout at the two terminal nodes of the stock price tree. Once this option value tree is determined, it is quite straightforward to obtain a price.

When this technique is extended to multi-step trees, the same basic procedure works perfectly for European options. A general formula for the price of a European call or put option was derived merely by iterating the one-step model for several steps. One might think that this general picture is easily transferred to options other than plain vanilla European options. Unfortunately, *path dependency* makes this almost impossible.

In the case of European options, each terminal node of the stock price tree has a payout associated to it. For instance, if we are pricing a European call option struck at $100, and the terminal (i.e., expiration date) spot price is $110, then the payout of the option at this price is $10. If there is a node on the binomial tree representing the price $110, then the payout of the corresponding node on the option value tree is $10.

With many exotic options, a node's payout depends on how the stock price arrived at that node. For example, suppose an American put is written on ABC struck at $100. At expiration, the stock is at $80, but *this does not mean that the option pays $20 at that node*. What's missing is that the option might have been exercised at some earlier time, in which case the payout at the terminal node is equal the current value of the earlier payout. Thus, what the node pays off depends on the path that the stock price took to get there. This is an example of the general phenomena called *path dependency,* and options where payouts are path-dependent are called *path-dependent options*.

Path dependency means that the spot price of the underlying at expiration alone does not determine the payout of the option. In the case of American options, one needs additional information on whether the option was exercised early. An example of this is shown in Figure 7.7.1.

Degree of Path Dependency
There is no single, all-encompassing method for valuing path-dependent options on a binomial tree. (This is true with the possible exception of Monte Carlo methods; see below for more on this.) This is partly because path dependency is not a very precise term. Some options are more path dependent than others. Roughly speaking, degree of path dependency is a

FIGURE 7.7.1

Two different sample paths are displayed. An American put option has been written on this stock. If the stock follows the path indicated by the solid line, then the option is held until expiration. If the stock follows the dashed line, then it is exercised early. Both paths have identical prices at the expiration of the option, but the payout of the option is different depending on which path is followed.

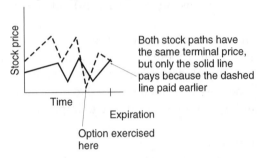

measure of how many different payouts a single terminal node can have. For instance, a European option is completely path independent because each terminal node has the same payout [$\max(S - K, 0)$], where S is the terminal value of the stock price (in the case of a call option) regardless of the path taken to reach the node. American options are path-dependent options, but of a very mild sort: The terminal node of an American call pays off either $\max(S - K, 0)$, if the option has not been exercised, or zero, if the option was exercised early.

Lookback Options

Of a more serious degree of path dependency are *lookback options*. Lookback options refer to a whole class of options whose payouts involve in some way the *maximum* or *minimum* value of the spot price of the underlying over the entire life of the option. These options come in two varieties. In the first, the strike price is determined by either the minimum (in the case of a call) or maximum (in the case of a put) of the spot of the underlying throughout the life of the option.

In the second variety, the payout is determined by the difference between the maximum or minimum of the spot price and a predetermined strike price. In either case, one can see that these options are highly path dependent. For example, in the case of a lookback call, two paths leading to the same node will have the same payout only when the two paths have the same maximum spot price along the path.

Asian Options

An even more extreme example of path dependency is found in *Asian options*. With Asian options, the payout of a node depends on the *average* value of the spot of the underlying over the life of the option. Thus, two paths leading to the same node have the same payout if, and only if, they have the same average value. Because of this, almost every price path has its own payout. Such options are extremely difficult to price, even on binomial trees.

As a general rule, the difficulty of pricing an option increases as the degree of path dependency increases. European options, at the bottom of the scale, are the least path dependent, so they are the easiest to value. As path dependency increases, the methods used to price these options become increasingly complex and time consuming to implement.

Monte Carlo Methods

One general method that can be used for pricing European options is called the Monte Carlo method. We describe the general idea here.

Suppose we have built a binomial tree and now we want to use it to price a particular European option. The option is path dependent, so we can't use the techniques derived in this chapter. Instead, we proceed in the following steps.

First, we devise a way to generate random sample paths through a binomial tree. We do this as follows. At each node of the tree, there are only two moves the spot price can make (up and down), and we know the probability of moving up or down.

Suppose that the up transition probability at node (i, j) is $p_{i,j}$. Then, starting at the vertex node, $(0, 0)$, we use a computer to generate a random number between zero and one. If the number is greater than $p_{0,0}$ (which has a $100p_{0,0}$ percent chance of happening), then we move to node $(1, 1)$ (i.e., we move up). Otherwise, we move down. Say we move up to node $(1, 1)$. Then we again generate a random number between zero and one and move up if the random number is greater than $p_{1,1}$. We continue in this way until we have created a path from node $(0, 0)$ to a terminal node of the tree.

Here is the key to the method: At each step of this process, we are creating a path for the stock price. As we generate the path, we can keep track of the option value *for that path*.

For example, say we are valuing a European lookback option whose payout at expiration is $\max(S_T - S_{min}, 0)$, where S_T is the spot price at expiration and S_{min} is the minimum spot price the underlying reached during the life of the option. We want to price it using the Monte Carlo method. We start by creating a sample path, and as we create it, we keep track of the minimum price of the stock along that path. When the expiration date is reached, we not only know the terminal price of the underlying but we also have a record of the minimum value of the spot price. In this way, we can assign an option payout to that path.

Let's understand where we are: We have just seen how to generate a stock price path in a binomial tree using random numbers. For each path we generate, we can say what the value of an option "on that path" is equal to. To proceed, we simply iterate this process. That is, we create not one but some large number of paths.[6]

After creating a sufficiently large number of paths, a rudimentary next step is to compute the average value of the option over all the different paths generated. This gives an estimate of the expected value of the option. Then, recalling that the option value (under risk-neutral valuation) is the present value of its expected value, we simply discount the expected value to the present time. This value is an estimate of the option value.

Of course, what we have described above only gives a feel for the Monte Carlo method. There are many subtle issues one must be aware of, such as:

1. How do we generate random numbers? What is a "good" method for generating random numbers? For example, are there random number generators that can potentially give inaccurate option values?

2. How do we estimate the accuracy of an option price obtained from the Monte Carlo method? For example, suppose we get a price from 50,000 sample paths. On average, how much better a price is this than a price obtained with 10,000 paths? Is the new answer "twice" as good as the old one?

3. Are there "tricks" for increasing accuracy? For example, in the above method for generating paths, we can also simultaneously generate the "mirror image path" (i.e., move down instead of up and vice versa at every step). If we compute two paths for the price of one each time, how much does this improve accuracy and efficiency?

---

[6]Remember, there are a lot of paths in a recombining binomial tree. We could never hope to cover them all. In an n-period tree there are 2^{n+1} paths. So, for example, in a 100-period tree there are approximately 1,267,650,600,230,000,000,000,000,000,000 paths.

See the end of this chapter for suggestions for further reading on the Monte Carlo method.

7.8 HEDGE PARAMETERS

Now that we have the basics of *pricing* options on a binomial tree, we turn to the calculation of hedge parameters. As we saw in Chapter 4, in order to hedge a European call or put option, we need to know its delta. We also studied other Greeks, such as Θ and Γ, which give important insights into the relative riskiness of the option with respect to changes in external parameters.

In this section, we show how to use the combination of a stock price tree and an option value tree to compute hedge parameters for options valued on that tree. With binomial trees, hedge parameters fall into two categories: 1) those that can be read directly off the tree; that is, those that can be computed by applying a formula directly to values at various nodes; and 2) those that can only be computed by a two-step procedure. In either case, the basic idea behind the computations is the same. All hedge parameters measure the rate of change of some variable with respect to another variable. Thus, these parameters can be estimated by physically seeing what happens (on the tree) when one variable is changed and measuring the change in the second variable. To show how this works, we begin with parameters whose values can be read directly off the tree.

Hedge Parameters from the Tree: Δ, Γ, Θ

Figure 7.8.1 shows a picture of the first two steps of a binomial stock price tree combined with an option value tree. There are two values at each node: the stock price and the option value. We have used the letter S for the stock price and C for the option value, combining the spot price tree and the option value tree into one.

To compute the delta of the option, we estimate the rate of change of the option value with respect to the stock price. We do this by looking at the two possible stock prices and option values at time t_1 and seeing how the option value changes when the stock price changes. Before doing this, let's discuss what this means.

The stock price at time t_1 has two possible values: S_u (the "up" price) and S_d (the "down" price). At these prices, the option is worth C_u and C_d, respectively. Thus, if the stock price changes from S_u to S_d, the option value experiences a corresponding change from C_u to C_d. Notice that in measuring this change, all other parameters—time, risk-free rate, and volatility—are held constant.

F I G U R E   7.8.1

How to compute the hedge parameters Δ, Γ, and Θ from a binomial tree
One needs to know the stock prices (denoted by S) and option prices (denoted by C).

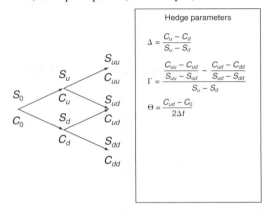

Hedge parameters

$$\Delta = \frac{C_u - C_d}{S_u - S_d}$$

$$\Gamma = \frac{\dfrac{C_{uu} - C_{ud}}{S_{uu} - S_{ud}} - \dfrac{C_{ud} - C_{dd}}{S_{ud} - S_{dd}}}{S_u - S_d}$$

$$\Theta = \frac{C_{ud} - C_0}{2\Delta t}$$

The rate of change of option price with respect to stock price, or Δ, is given by:

$$\Delta = \frac{C_u - C_d}{S_u - S_d}.$$

This is the ratio of option value change to stock price change. Now, the stock price never actually changes from S_u to S_d at time t_1, so one might wonder why we are examining this rate change.

We are isolating the effect of small stock price changes on the value of the option. In reality, of course, whenever the stock price changes, this happens along with a corresponding change in time. Therefore, when stock price changes, we are seeing the effect of at least two variables on option value: stock price and time. However, we want to ignore the effect of time to get an absolute measure of sensitivity of option value to stock price.

The Approximate Formula for the Delta Revisited
In Chapter 4, section 4.5, we gave an approximate formula for the delta of an option. We can now demonstrate that this is the "correct" approximate formula.

Continuing with the notation of the last section, let Δt be the length of time from time t_0 to time t_1, r be the risk-free rate, and p be the up-transition probability.

We know

$$C_0 = e^{-r\Delta t}(pC_u + (1 - p)C_d),$$

where p is given by the formula $p = \frac{e^{r\Delta t}S_0 - S_u}{S_u - S_d}$.

We have just seen the delta of our option is given by

$$\Delta = \frac{C_u - C_d}{S_u - S_d}.$$

Display 7.8.1 explains how to derive the following formulas:

$$\frac{C_u - C_d}{S_u - S_d} = \frac{C_0 - e^{-r\Delta t}C_u}{S_0 - e^{-r\Delta t}S_u}$$

and

$$\frac{C_u - C_d}{S_u - S_d} = \frac{C_0 - e^{-r\Delta t}C_d}{S_0 - e^{-r\Delta t}S_d}.$$

Notice that the right-hand side of each equation is exactly the approximate formula for the delta of the option given in equation (4.5.1) of Chapter 4.

Therefore, in the binomial world, the approximate formula for the delta is exactly equal to the binomial formula for the delta presented above.

DISPLAY 7.8.1

A DERIVATION OF THE APPROXIMATE FORMULA FOR THE DELTA

First we show $\frac{C_u - C_d}{S_u - S_d} = \frac{C_0 - e^{-r\Delta t}C_d}{S_0 - e^{-r\Delta t}S_d}$. To see this, note that since $C_0 = e^{-r\Delta t}(pC_u + (1 - p)C_d)$, we have

$$C_0 - e^{-r\Delta t}C_d = e^{-r\Delta t}p(C_u - C_d).$$

Substituting $p = \frac{e^{r\Delta t}S_0 - S_d}{S_u - S_d}$, we obtain

$$C_0 - e^{-r\Delta t}C_d = \frac{S_0 - e^{-r\Delta t}S_d}{S_u - S_d}(C_u - C_d).$$

Now, dividing both sides by $S_0 - e^{-r\Delta t}S_d$, we get our answer.

To see that $\frac{C_u - C_d}{S_u - S_d} = \frac{C_0 - e^{-r\Delta t}C_u}{S_0 - e^{-r\Delta t}S_u}$, we only have to observe that since $C_0 = e^{-r\Delta t}(pC_u + (1 - p)C_d)$, we have

$$C_0 - e^{-r\Delta t}C_u = e^{-r\Delta t}(1 - p)(C_d - C_u).$$

Now note that $1 - p = \frac{S_u - e^{r\Delta t}S_0}{S_u - S_d}$, and proceed as above.

But the binomial formula for the delta is an approximate formula for the Black-Scholes delta. Why? Because, as we have seen, the binomial world *converges* to the Black-Scholes world. Display 7.8.1 gives a derivation of the above equalities.

Two Ways to Compute Γ

Next, we compute the Γ of the option, that is, the rate of change of the Δ with respect to the stock price.

There are two different ways we can do this. When we compute the gamma, we have often already computed the Δ of the option for entire tree.

For example, in the adjoining figure, we see a tree frag- ment in which each of the nodes is labeled with a stock price (S_u or S_d) and a delta (Δ_u or Δ_d). The delta represents the delta of the option *if* the stock price is at that given node.

Then, since gamma is the rate of change of delta with respect to stock price, we have:

$$\Gamma = \frac{\Delta_u - \Delta_d}{S_u - S_d}.$$

If we do not want to compute the gamma using previously computed future deltas, we must go out to time t_2, where we can form two estimates of the delta. For the first estimate, we look at the upper two nodes, S_{uu} and S_{ud}, and write:

$$\Delta_1 = \frac{C_{uu} - C_{ud}}{S_{uu} - S_{ud}}.$$

This is the rate of change of the option as the stock price changes from S_{uu} to S_{ud}. To be consistent with our calculation at time t_0, we say that this is the delta of the option when the stock price is S_u.[7] Similarly, we write

$$\Delta_2 = \frac{C_{ud} - C_{dd}}{S_{ud} - S_{dd}}.$$

---

[7]Notice that S_u is a price that falls somewhere between S_{uu} and S_{ud}. In fact, we estimate the delta for *any* stock price between S_{uu} and S_{ud}. The error coming from this approximation is an example of stock price quantization error. The only way to improve accuracy is to increase the number of periods so that the difference between S_{uu} and S_{ud} decreases.

Now, Γ is the rate of change of the delta with respect to stock price, so we obtain

$$\Gamma = \frac{\Delta_1 - \Delta_2}{S_u - S_d}.$$

Option Theta

Lastly, we turn to Θ, the rate of change of the option price with respect to time. We give two methods in this section to compute theta. When discussing these formulas, we refer to Figure 7.8.1.

The first formula is

$$\Theta = \frac{C_{ud} - C_0}{2\Delta t}. \tag{7.8.1}$$

This equation compares the value of the option at time t_0 with the value of the option at time t_2 and the stock price equal to S_{ud}. This formula is perfectly adequate in the *special case* where $S_0 = S_{ud}$ because, in this situation, we are comparing the value of the option at time t_0 and time t_2 at the same spot price. Unfortunately, in flexible trees, and even trees centered at the forward, the condition $S_0 = S_{ud}$ will not always hold. In this case, equation (7.8.1) becomes an unreliable estimate of the actual theta.

A Second Method to Compute Θ

In order to deal with the possible inaccuracy of equation (7.8.1), M. Rubinstein has suggested using the Black-Scholes differential equation [equation (5.1.1)] to solve for theta based on the hedge parameters Δ and Γ. Recall the differential equation:

$$\Theta + rS_0\Delta + \frac{1}{2}\sigma^2 S_0^2 \Gamma = rC_0,$$

where σ is the *local volatility* at the given node of the binomial tree. If the binomial tree in question is a constant volatility tree, then σ represents the stock's overall volatility.

Observing this equation, we see that we can solve for theta, and obtain:

$$\Theta = rC_0 - \left(rS_0\Delta + \frac{1}{2}\sigma^2 S_0^2 \Gamma\right).$$

This formula for theta depends on knowing the risk-free rate of interest r, the option value C_0, the stock price S_0, the options delta, Δ and gamma, and the stock's local volatility. Given these parameters, the option's theta may be computed.

Note that the Black-Scholes differential equation is derived using the fact that the volatility of the underlying stock (of the option) is a constant. There exist extensions of this equation which hold when a constant volatility is replaced by local volatility, i.e., when volatility is a function of spot price and time. This is the equation we have used above for computing the value of theta.

Parameters That Cannot Be Read from the Tree: ρ and Vega

Recall that *rho* is the rate of change of option price with respect to the risk-free rate of interest, and *vega* is the rate of change of the option price with respect to volatility. Neither of these parameters can be read from a stock price and option payoff tree because, in both cases, the value of the parameters themselves—the risk-free rate in the case of ρ, and volatility in the case of vega—figure in the basic construction of the tree. Therefore, changing the risk-free rate or volatility (a basic input to the tree) necessarily changes the stock price tree itself. The only way to measure ρ and vega is to make two computations with two different trees.

We explain this in the case of ρ. Choose a value of the risk-free rate, say r, and construct a binomial tree and option value tree for the option in question based on the rate r. Write C_r for the value of the option based on this tree.

Next, change the interest rate by a small amount, Δr, to $r + \Delta r$, and recompute the price and option value trees. Write $C_{r+\Delta r}$ for the value of the option with respect to the new interest rate. Now, rho is approximated by the rate of change of the value of the option given the new interest rate. Thus,

$$\rho = \frac{C_{r+\Delta r} - C_r}{\Delta r}.$$

To compute vega, one proceeds similarly, starting by computing the option price based on a tree with volatility σ, C_σ, then computing the price, $C_{\sigma+\Delta\sigma}$, based on a tree with volatility $\sigma + \Delta\sigma$, where $\Delta\sigma$ is small. Then, vega is approximated by:

$$\text{vega} = \frac{C_{\sigma+\Delta\sigma} - C_\sigma}{\Delta\sigma}.$$

Examples

Let's use the formulas to calculate the delta, gamma, and theta of an option and then see how those parameters change over a period of time. In this example, we have a three-month vanilla European call option settled on January 1, 1996. We assume we have the following data:

$$S = \$100$$
$$K = \$100$$
$$r = 5\%$$
$$\sigma = 20\%$$
$$\text{Settlement date} = 1/1/96$$
$$\text{Expiration date} = 4/1/96$$

That is, the spot price of the underlying is $100, the strike price of the option is $100, the risk-free rate is 5 percent per annum, and the volatility of the stock is 20 percent per annum.

We are going to price this call option and compute its hedge parameters for January 1, 1996, on a three-month Cox-Ross-Rubinstein binomial tree with the time step equal to one day (to be precise, we use a 90-period tree).

We are going to see what happens one day later: We will price the same option on January 2, 1996, on the same tree with the time step equal to one day (now we use an 89-period tree), but assuming the price has risen to $100.50.

Figure 7.8.2 displays the first five days of both the January 1 stock price tree and option value tree and the January 2 stock price tree and option value tree. The values in these trees provide enough information to compute the parameters delta, gamma, and theta. These values are displayed to the right of the trees.

Figure 7.8.2 brings up an important point. Notice that on January 2, 1996, the stock price has risen to $100.50. But the January 1, 1996, tree does not have a node for $100.50 on January 2 (the two values on that date are $101.05 and $98.96). This is an example of stock price quantization error. The binomial tree did not accurately predict the possible stock prices for January 2, 1996. Consequently, it did not accurately predict the delta for those dates either. For example, had the stock price risen to $101.05, the delta and gamma would have been:

$$\Delta = 0.6085 \quad \text{and} \quad \Gamma = 0.0378.$$

In each case, notice how different these values are from the actual values on January 2.

The source of this error is stock price quantization. Since the stock price rose to the "wrong" value according to the January 1 model (the price rose to $100.50 instead of $101.50), the model did not accurately represent

F I G U R E 7.8.2

Cox-Ross-Rubinstein binomial trees and their hedge parameters.
Each tree is on a stock with 20 percent volatility and assumes a 5 percent risk-free rate.

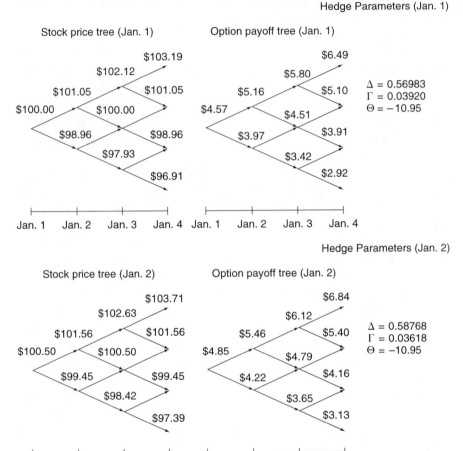

the stock price move. If we increase the number of periods, price quantization error is reduced, increasing the overall performance of the tree.

7.9 PRICING AMERICAN OPTIONS ON A FLEXIBLE TREE

This section is devoted to explaining how to value (plain vanilla) American options on a binomial tree. This is the first place where we see the real power of binomial trees over the Black-Scholes framework. The

Black-Scholes analytical formula is completely powerless in the face of American options, while binomial trees can value American options almost as easily as European options. The method we give here is a simple extension of the backward induction technique used for European options, and is due to Cox, Ross, and Rubinstein.

European options can only be exercised at their expiration dates. American options may be exercised at any time before expiration. In addition, options referred to as *Bermuda options*[8] may be exercised at any of a prespecified set of times before the expiration date. For instance, a Bermuda contract might specify that the option may be exercised on the third Friday of every month for the life of the option. Whatever the terms of the contract are, the exercise features of the option are specified *before* the option's life begins.

Any feature of an option contract that allows it to be exercised before the expiration date is called an *early exercise feature* of the option. American options have the most extreme early exercise features, while Bermuda options have very precise early exercise features. Another common early exercise feature is an option with a *first exercise date*. This date is the first date at which the option becomes American. In other words, the option may be exercised at any time between the first exercise date and the expiration date.

This section explains how to price any call or put option with an early exercise feature. The approach given here is standard and very general. To understand how it works, recall how we priced options on a binomial tree. Essentially, we worked backward from the expiration date and figured out what we needed at each node in order to replicate the next move forward. Because there are only two possible prices to which the spot price can move from each node, we are always able to replicate the option value at the next step. We used this observation to move backward from the terminal nodes of a binomial tree, to induce the correct "price" of each node in the option value tree.

The same concept applies in the case of American options. However, in order to replicate the option value at a given node, we must be prepared in case the option is exercised. In other words, the option is not truly hedged unless the possibility of early exercise is covered. This is summarized as:

> If we are hedging an option on a binomial tree, we must be able to cover
> the option at each time step, whether this means being able to cover the

---

[8] Again, this name is derived from the fact that Bermuda is somewhere between Europe and America.

next time step (from backward induction) or to cover immediate exercise. Thus, in hedging the American option, we must be able to cover the greater of the intrinsic value of the option and the value of holding the option through the next period.

To illustrate the above principle, we begin with examples using two-step trees.

Two-Step Examples

We consider a one-year plain vanilla American put option struck at $105 on a stock S whose spot price is $100, which we will value on a standard Cox-Ross-Rubinstein tree. We write σ for the volatility of S and assume it is 15 percent throughout the life of the option. We write r for the risk-free rate of interest and assume it is 5 percent. Since the total life of the option is one year and the number of time steps is two, each time step is one-half a year, and we write $\Delta t = 1/2$. Figure 7.9.1 displays the stock price and option value tree for this example.

In order to obtain this diagram we computed the following parameters using display 6.5.1 in Chapter 6.

$$\Delta t = 0.5$$
$$r = 5\%$$
$$u = e^{\sigma \sqrt{\Delta t}} = 1.1119 \quad \text{(up ratio)}$$
$$d = 1/u = 0.8994 \quad \text{(down ratio)}$$
$$p = \frac{e^{r\Delta t} - d}{u - d} = 0.5926 \quad \text{(up-transition probability)}$$
$$e^{-r\Delta t} = 0.9753$$

In this example, we use a standard binomial tree, so the transition probabilities are the same for every node.

To value the option in Figure 7.9.1, we must first deduce the values of the nodes labeled A and B. Write P_A for the value of node A in the option value tree. This is the value of the option when the stock price is at node A. Alternatively, this is the amount of money we need in a hedging portfolio at time t_1, with the spot price at node A (i.e., with the stock price at $111.19), in order to be perfectly hedged against the risk of holding the option.

To compute the value of P_A, we first compute the value of holding a European put (with the same strike and expiration as the American put) at node A. Writing P_A^{euro} for this value, we see

FIGURE 7.9.1

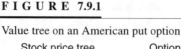

Value tree on an American put option

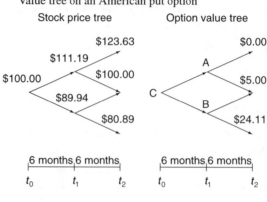

$$P_A^{euro} = e^{-r\Delta t}(p\$0 + (1-p)\$5)$$
$$= 0.9753(0.5926 \cdot 0 + 0.4074 \cdot 5)$$
$$= 1.9867,$$

where p is the risk-neutral up-transition probability at node A. The question is, is this the value of node A for the American option? The answer—due to the possibility of early exercise—depends on the intrinsic value of the option at node A.

The key point is that P_A is precisely the amount of money we need in the hedging portfolio at time t_1, with the stock price at node A, in order to hedge the value of the option at time t_2. Since the option is American, the holder has the right to exercise at node A. Consequently, the intrinsic value of the American option may be greater than that of the corresponding European option. Therefore, we have to ask:

Which is greater, the cost of hedging or the cost of paying for immediate exercise?

To answer this, we compute the *intrinsic value* of the option and compare it to the cost of hedging. In this case, the option is out of the money, so its intrinsic value is zero, and it is definitely more costly to hedge the option than to cover immediate exercise. Therefore, the value of node A remains equal to the value (at node A) of the European option, and is $1.9867.

We now apply the same analysis to node B. First, we compute the value of P_B without considering early exercise. We obtain the equation:

$$P_B^{euro} = e^{-r\Delta t}(p5 + (1-p)24.11)$$
$$= 0.9753(.5926 \cdot 5 + 0.4074 \cdot 24.11)$$

FIGURE 7.9.2

Value tree of the American put option from Figure
7.9.1

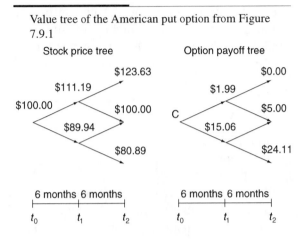

= 12.4694,

where now p is the risk-neutral up-transition probability at node B. Now, let's compare this to the intrinsic value of the option at node B. If immediately exercised, the option would pay out $105 - 89.94 = 15.0600$ (that is, the difference between the strike price, $105, and the stock price at node B). This is greater than P_B^{euro}, and the rational investor would exercise the option in the event the stock attains node B. Consequently, in hedging the option, we must prepare against paying out $15.0600 at node B instead of $12.4694. That is, to be fully hedged, we value node B at $15.0600, i.e.,

$$P_B = \$15.0600.$$

See Figure 7.9.2.

Lastly, we compute the value of P_C, which is the value at time t_0 of the option. Using the same analysis as above, we see that

$$
\begin{aligned}
P_C^{euro} &= e^{-r\Delta t}[p\$1.9867 + (1 - (1 - p)\$15.0600)] \\
&= 0.9753(0.5926 \cdot 1.9867 + 0.4074 \cdot 15.0600) \\
&= 7.1322.
\end{aligned}
$$

This is the value of the American option. Why? Because using the hedging strategy for an option on a binomial tree, we can be confident that no matter which way the stock price moves at each time, even if at any time the option is exercised (that is, if the intrinsic value of the option ever exceeds the value of holding the option), we can cover the short position.

Second Valuation Example

We now give a second example of pricing an American option on a binomial tree. This time, however, we use a flexible binomial tree.

Figure 7.9.3 displays a flexible stock price tree for a stock S whose spot price is initially $100; the figure also displays the corresponding option value tree for a one-year put option struck at $105. Since this tree is flexible, we have included the computations of risk-neutral transition probabilities. The notation is as follows:

u_A = up ratio from node A
u_B = up ratio from node B
u_C = up ratio from node C
p_A = up risk-neutral transition probability from node A
p_B = up risk-neutral transition probability from node B
p_C = up risk-neutral transition probability from node C

Let's compute the prices of nodes A and B. Using the values for p_A and p_B shown in Figure 7.9.3, we have

$$P_A = e^{-r\Delta t}(p_A \cdot 0 + (1 - p_A) \cdot 5) = \$1.76$$
$$P_B = e^{-r\Delta t}(p_B \cdot 5 + (1 - p_B) \cdot 33) = \$20.41.$$

Remember what these values mean: P_A is the value of the put option at node A; that is, it is the amount needed in a hedging portfolio that replicates the option payout at expiration, provided that the stock is at node A at time t_1. Likewise, P_B is the amount needed to replicate when the stock is

FIGURE 7.9.3

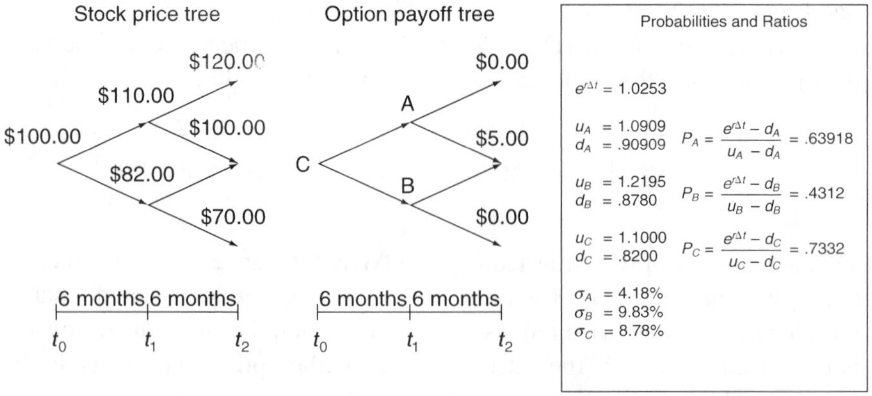

American put option on a stock following a flexible binomial tree

at $82 at time t_1. But to hedge the option, it is not enough just to replicate; one has to also hedge against the possibility of early exercise.

Referring again to Figure 7.9.2, if the stock is at $110 at time t_1 (i.e., at node A), then the option is out of the money and will not be exercised. On the other hand, if the stock is at $82 at time t_1, then the put's intrinsic value, that is, what it is worth if immediately exercised, is $105 - \$82 = \$23$. Now, imagine this from the point of view of hedging: If the hedging portfolio only contains $P_B = \$20.41$, the option position will not be fully hedged due to the possibility of early exercise. Thus, one has to replace P_B with the larger of the intrinsic value and the original value, which is $23. Therefore, node B is assigned a value of $23.

To perform the final step of backward induction, we have to compute the value of node C. We compute:

$$P_C = e^{-r\Delta t}(p_C \cdot 1.76 + (1 - p_C) \cdot 23).$$

Notice that we use $23 instead of the holding value of $20.41 as the value of the down node (node B, the bottom node at time t_1). This is because we want to hedge against having to pay out $23 if the stock price makes a down move. We have:

$$P_C = \$7.24.$$

Figure 7.9.4 shows the option value trees for both the American *and* European version of the put displayed in Figure 7.9.3.

Note that the American option's value is $7.24, while the corresponding European option's value is $6.57. The larger price exactly reflects the

F I G U R E   7.9.4

Comparison of hedging between American and European
put option of Figure 7.9.3

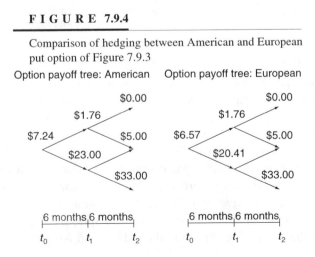

Option payoff tree: American   Option payoff tree: European

D I S P L A Y   7.9.1

PRICING AMERICAN OPTIONS ON A BINOMIAL TREE

To price an American option, proceed in the following steps.

1. Start with a binomial tree.

2. Create an option value tree for the binomial tree.

3. Assign the terminal payout of the option to the terminal nodes of the tree.

4. Work backward through the tree via backward induction.

5. To compute a node's value, proceed in two steps. First, compute the node's *holding value:* This is what it is worth to hold the option one more period; this value is computed by ordinary backward induction as with European options. Next, compute the option's *intrinsic value.* This is the value of immediately exercising the option. The value of the node is the greater of the holding value and the intrinsic value.

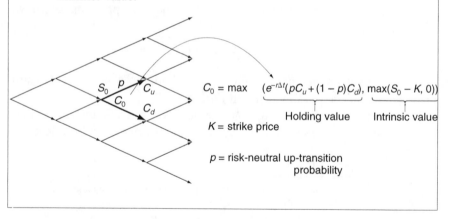

$$C_0 = \max \; \left(\underbrace{e^{-r\Delta t}(pC_u + (1-p)C_d)}_{\text{Holding value}}, \; \underbrace{\max(S_0 - K, 0)}_{\text{Intrinsic value}} \right)$$

K = strike price

p = risk-neutral up-transition probability

---

fact that anyone hedging the American option has to replicate a greater value at node *B* for the American than the European option (see Figure 7.9.3).

The Early Exercise Premium

The difference between the American option value and the European option value is known as the *early exercise premium*. The early exercise premium represents the extra value that the right to exercise an American option provides over an otherwise identical European option. Computing this premium is at the heart of determining the value of an American option.

FIGURE 7.10.1

10-period binomial tree for a stock with 15 percent volatility when the risk-free rate is 10 percent
The time from the start date to end date is one year.

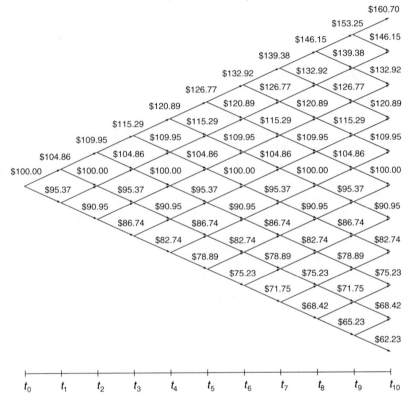

We summarize the procedure for pricing American options in Display 7.9.1.

7.10   THE EARLY EXERCISE BARRIER

Every American option has what is known as an early exercise barrier. The early exercise barrier defines for each time during the life of the option the interface between stock prices at which the option is optimally exercised early and stock prices at which it is more valuable to hold the option than to exercise it. Specifically, for put options, the early exercise barrier defines for each time the highest stock price for which the option is optimally exercised. For call options, the early exercise barrier defines at each time the lowest stock price for which the option is optimally exercised.

F I G U R E 7.10.2

The option value tree for an American put option on the stock in Figure 7.10.1
The dotted line represents the early exercise barrier. The circled prices represent the
first prices directly below the early exercise barrier.

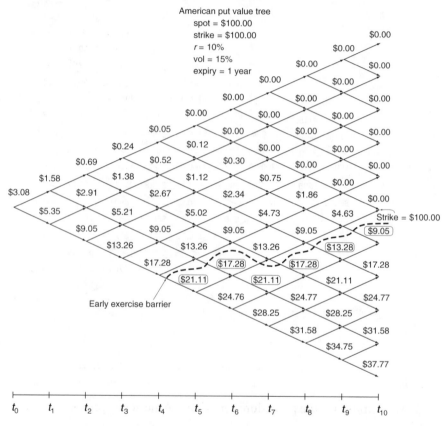

American put value tree
spot = $100.00
strike = $100.00
r = 10%
vol = 15%
expiry = 1 year

Early exercise barrier

Strike = $100.00

t_0 t_1 t_2 t_3 t_4 t_5 t_6 t_7 t_8 t_9 t_{10}

Figures 7.10.1 and 7.10.2 display a 10-period stock price tree and
option value tree for an American put option with the following parameters:

$$r = 10 \text{ percent}$$
$$\sigma = 15 \text{ percent}$$
$$T - t = 1 \text{ year}$$
$$S_0 = \$100$$
$$K = \$100$$

That is, the option is on a stock with 15 percent volatility *per annum* whose
spot price is $100. The American put is struck at $100 and has one year
until expiry. The risk-free rate of interest is 10 percent.

The option value tree displays the early exercise barrier.

COMMENTS AND
SUGGESTED READING

The binomial model of option pricing was introduced in 1979 by Cox, Ross, and Rubinstein. Its importance cannot be overstated. Many "extensions" of the basic methodology have been developed to tackle the various problems that arise in option pricing. An extension of the binomial method that models transaction costs is found in Boyle and Vorst (1992).

For a discussion of pricing and hedging log contracts, see Nelken (1995), chapter seven, and Neuberger (1994). For a discussion of pricing and hedging digital options, see Chriss and Ong (1995).

A basic explanation of the Monte Carlo method can be found in Kritzman (1993). A good introduction to option pricing using Monte Carlo methods is found in Nelken (1995), chapter 13. See the references therein for more information. See also the summaries in Press, Teukolsky, Vetterling, and Flannery (1992) for theoretical discussions, algorithms, and a wealth of computer code.

The discussion of the computation of theta in this chapter is taken from Rubinstein (1994).

For a nontechnical introduction to exotic options, see McVay (1992).

Our discussion of pricing American options focused solely on the mechanics of pricing options on binomial trees. To date, no one has come up with closed-form solutions for the value of an American option, but there has been a good deal of work on *analytic approximations* to the price of an American option. The advantage of analytic solutions, as with Black-Scholes itself, is speed. To get accurate values of American options on a binomial tree requires a lot of computing time, as compared to analytic solutions. Nevertheless, none of the analytic solutions provide nearly the flexibility or accuracy of pricing on a binomial tree. For information on these approaches, see Hull (1993), chapter 14, and Figlewski, Silber, and Subrahmanyam (1990), pp. 177–182, and the references therein. Also, see Carr and Faguet (1994).

8

⑥ THE VOLATILITY SMILE

This chapter discusses the volatility smile, the much talked about and very important real-world measure of the deviation of market option prices from Black-Scholes theory. The purpose of this chapter is to give a broad introduction to the volatility smile in simple language, and give emphasis to its importance in both stock price modeling and option pricing. To broaden our scope, along the way we talk about stochastic volatility and the structure of volatility, including mean-reversion.

8.1 IMPLIED VOLATILITY AND THE THEORY OF OPTION PRICING

Many options are traded on, and are therefore priced by, the market. The price of such an option is called its *market price*. Whenever the price of an option is known, we can compute its *Black-Scholes implied volatility*. This chapter explains what this is, and why it is one of the most important aspects of modern option pricing.

Here is an explanation of implied volatility for a European call. Suppose C is a European call option on a stock S struck at K. To use the Black-Scholes formula to produce a price for this option, we need to supply the values of all the input parameters; namely, we have to supply the spot price of the underlying, the strike price, the risk-free rate, time until expiration, and volatility of the underlying. One way to compute the stock's volatility is to look at historical data and employ the estimation procedure used in

Chapter 3. Then we may plug this, along with the other input parameters, into the Black-Scholes formula. What comes out is the Black-Scholes value of the option.

On the other hand, if the option has a market price, we can ask, What volatility would we have to plug into the Black-Scholes formula (along with the other parameters) to obtain the market price? Put another way, what volatility makes the Black-Scholes value agree with the market price?

The volatility that answers this question is called the *implied volatility* of the stock for the given option; an option on the same underlying with a different strike price or expiration might have a different implied volatility. This goes to say that a stock or index does not have one implied volatility, but rather has many—one for each option on the asset. Skeptics might protest that there could be more than one volatility that produces the same Black-Scholes value. This is not the case, however, for we recall that other things being equal, the greater the volatility of the underlying, the greater the value of the option.

Our first task in discussing implied volatility is to study the relationship between geometric Brownian motion and implied volatility.

Implied Volatility and Geometric Brownian Motion

Any option has an associated implied volatility. We can therefore ask, Are all the implied volatilities (for all listed options) on the same underlying stock the same?

According to the geometric Brownian motion model, the answer must be yes. This is because a fundamental assumption going into the model is that the volatility of a stock is exactly the same at all times. This means that if a stock follows a geometric Brownian motion with volatility σ and the market prices options according to the Black-Scholes picture (i.e., if the economic environment is exactly as the Black-Scholes theory describes it), then the Black-Scholes value of the option must be the market price of the option. On the other hand, the Black-Scholes price is computed using σ as an input; therefore, the implied volatility would also always be σ.

In reality, however, if we compute implied volatilities for a variety of options (on a given stock) with different strikes and times until expiration, we find, first of all, that implied volatilities change from strike to strike and expiration to expiration; we also find that there is a recognizable pattern to these changes (which we will explore in a moment).

If we assume that the market correctly values traded options and, moreover, that the basic economic assumptions of Black-Scholes are met—in particular, if we assume the market does not allow for arbitrage opportunities—then nonconstant implied volatilities is an indication that the underlying stock does not follow a geometric Brownian motion. Put another way, we have a large theory (the Black-Scholes point of view) that tells us what arbitrage-free option prices look like if a stock follows a geometric Brownian motion. In reality, option prices do not behave as the theory says they should. Namely, all implied volatilities of the same underlying are not the same. One possible explanation is that the underlying does not follow a geometric Brownian motion with constant volatility.

To account for this, at least *one* of the assumptions must be wrong. In reality, many are probably wrong to a greater or lesser extent. For example, there are probably some arbitrage opportunities, and stocks probably do not follow a geometric Brownian motion precisely. Our task is to analyze implied volatilities and see what they say about option values.

In this chapter, we will examine the implications of nonconstant implied volatilities for option pricing. We will focus on the exact nature of implied volatility in today's markets and what this says about the Brownian motion model and Black-Scholes values. Our first task is to describe how to compute implied volatility.

8.2   COMPUTING IMPLIED VOLATILITY

There is no general formula for implied volatility. That is, given an option price C on a stock S, there is no simple formula for producing the implied volatility of S with respect to C. To get a feel for why, look at the Black-Scholes formula:

$$C(S_t, K, T - t, \sigma, r) = N(d_1)S_t - N(d_2)Ke^{-r(T-t)}. \qquad (8.2.1)$$

As usual, S_t is the current stock price (at time t), K is the strike price, $T - t$ is the time until expiration, σ is the volatility of the stock, and d_1 and d_2 are defined in equations (4.8.1) and (4.8.2).

The formula relates the variables describing the option, $S_t, K, T - t$, σ, and r, to a single number, the Black-Scholes price of the option. If we already know the price of the option and want to compute which value of σ will produce that price, we need to *invert* the function $C(S_t, K, T - t, \sigma, r)$, which amounts to finding a formula that expresses the implied volatility as a function of the option price and the remaining Black-Scholes parameter; that is, we want a function

$$\sigma(C, S_t, K, (T - t), r)$$

that relates the price of the option, C, and the parameters $S_t, K, (T - t)$, and r to the implied volatility.

Unfortunately, the components of the Black-Scholes formula are fairly complicated, especially the cumulative normal distribution function $N(\cdot)$. Such complicated formulas are often not easily inverted, and other methods must be sought to get at the inverse. Fortunately, a variety of such methods exist, and we will explain two of them. Both are part of a broad class of techniques called iterative methods: We describe these first.

Iterative Methods

An iterative method is a technique that applies the same method to a problem repeatedly to get at an answer. The idea is that each time the method is repeated we are brought closer to the final answer. Iterative methods are often a useful alternative to formulas.

Generally, this sort of method when used for computing implied volatility works as follows. First, we make a rough guess at what the implied volatility should be and use this guess (along with the other input parameters) to compute the Black-Scholes value of the option with respect to the "guess" volatility. After comparing the "guess" Black-Scholes value to the market price of the option, we somehow modify the "guess" to produce a new "guess" volatility, and consequently a new Black-Scholes value that is closer to the market price than the first guess. We then "zero in" on the correct answer. How quickly we zero in is called the *rate of convergence*. Obviously, the key to such iterative methods lies in exactly how we modify each guess to move closer to the desired result.

We describe two iterative methods below. The first method, known as the method of bisections, is easy to implement and easy to understand. Its only drawback is speed. It converges rather slowly. For this reason, industry shops tend to use a faster method, known as the *Newton-Raphson method*. We will discuss the Newton-Raphson method after the method of bisections.

The Method of Bisections

Suppose C is a call option on a (non-dividend-paying) stock S struck at K, with time until expiration $T - t$ and a risk-free rate of interest r. We assume that we have produced all of these values at the start of this process.

Say the current market price of C is known to be C_t. The method of bisections for computing the implied volatility σ of C is carried out as follows.

First, we make a guess for the correct implied volatility and compute the Black-Scholes price using this volatility. Since we know the strike price, the stock price, the risk-free rate, and the time until expiration, we simply plug these parameters, along with the "guessed" volatility, into the Black-Scholes formula. For instance, if we have

$$\begin{aligned} K &= \$100 \\ S &= \$100 \\ T - t &= 1 \text{ year} \\ r &= 5\% \end{aligned}$$

and we guess the implied volatility is 20 percent, then we can compute $C(100, 100, 1, 20\%, 5\%)$, the Black-Scholes price of the option, using a volatility of 20 percent. See equation (8.2.1) for an explanation of this notation.

This "price" is just our first guess. We need to compare it to the market price. It is extremely unlikely that our first-guess volatility will yield a Black-Scholes price equal to the market price, so we have to make a second guess for the implied volatility—if the market price is higher than our "guessed" price, we need to raise the volatility guess, otherwise we need to lower it. Why? Because, as we know, all other things being equal, a higher volatility implies a higher option price.

So what do we require of our next guess? Simply put, we want to make sure we are moving in on the answer. If we can achieve this, then we can iterate our procedure producing more guesses, each guess moving us closer to the correct implied volatility. We can stop when our answers get "close enough" to what we want (we'll discuss how to know when to stop below).

The question remains: How do we produce a next guess that is closer to the actual implied volatility than our last guess? We explain this by giving a step-by-step procedure for the method of bisections.

The Method of Bisections: Step-By-Step
We now give a step-by-step procedure for carrying out the method of bisections.

STEP 1. Choose a first guess for the implied volatility. Write σ_0 for this guess. The first guess must be greater than the actual implied volatility. We may check that this condition is met by computing the Black-Scholes value of C, using σ_0, and then comparing it to the market price of C. If the Black-Scholes value is greater than the market price, then σ_0 is greater than the implied volatility.

STEP 2. This step produces the next implied volatility guess, which we will denote σ_1. To do this, compute $C(S, K, T - t, \sigma_0, r)$. We have already ensured that it is larger than the market price of the option (see step

1), so we need to make our next volatility guess lower. We set σ_1 to σ_0 *reduced* by 50 percent; that is,

$$\sigma_1 = \sigma_0 - \sigma_0/2 = 0.50\sigma_0.$$

This is our first "real" guess, so we call it σ_1.

STEP 3. Now we produce our next guess, σ_2. Compute $C(S, K, T - t, \sigma_1, r)$. If it is larger than the actual option price, then we make our next guess by reducing σ_1 by half as much as we did last time:

$$\sigma_2 = \sigma_1 - \sigma_0/4.$$

On the other hand, if $C(S, K, T - t, \sigma_1, r)$ is smaller than the actual option price, we increase σ_1 by $\sigma_0/4$, and set

$$\sigma_2 = \sigma_1 + \sigma_0/4.$$

STEP 4. Iterate the process. Compute σ_k from σ_{k-1} as follows. Compute the Black-Scholes value using σ_{k-1}, the volatility guess from the previous step. If it is larger than the market price, form the next guess by reducing σ_{k-1} by $\sigma_0/2^k$:

$$\sigma_k = \sigma_{k-1} - \sigma_0/2^k.$$

Otherwise, raise σ_{k-1} by $\sigma_0/2^k$:

$$\sigma_k = \sigma_{k-1} + \sigma_0/2^k.$$

As we continue, the computed value $C(S, K, T - t, \sigma_k, r)$ draws closer and closer to the actual options price, and the amount by which we adjust our guesses gets progressively smaller.

How Do We Know When to Stop?

When computing a number by successively approximating it by better and better guesses, we have to know when to stop, because the procedure itself never actually produces the correct answer. Rather, it just produces an answer that is "sufficiently close." For example, if we compute the implied volatility is 20.5234 percent, does it matter if the correct implied volatility is 20.5235 percent? This is a subjective question that must be answered within the context of the particular pricing scenario.

The most obvious place to stop is when we have a volatility that produces a Black-Scholes price exactly equal to the market price. We can also have a preset "error tolerance" that tells us how close we want to get to the actual answer. In some markets, for example, if we have many, many calculations to perform, we might be satisfied to get within, say, 0.1 of the actual answer. In other markets, which might be tighter, the tolerance could be as low as 0.01, or lower.

For example, if our tolerance is 0.1, then this means we will not stop until our implied volatility guess is within 0.1 of the actual implied volatility. How do we know when this is the case? Since each adjustment brings us closer to the correct answer, if an adjustment itself is less than 0.1, then we are certainly within 0.1 of the correct answer.

To compute σ_k, we adjust σ_{k-1} by $\sigma_0/2^k$. This adjustment is less than 0.1 when $\sigma_0/2^k < 0.1$, or, $\sigma_0/0.1 < 2^k$. This is the same as:

$$\log(\sigma_0/0.1)/\log 2 < k$$

where recall log means natural logarithm. Remember that in this situation K represents the step number in the procedure. If $\sigma_0 = 50$ percent volatility, then

$$\log(0.5/0.1)/\log 2 = 2.32,$$

so it takes three steps to get within 0.1 of the correct implied volatility.

In fact, an at-the-money option may require a tolerance of better than 0.01 to produce an implied volatility that exactly matches the market price. In this case, we have

$$\log(0.5/0.01)/\log 2 = 5.64.$$

That is, to get within 0.01 percent of the correct implied volatility requires more than five, and therefore six steps, three times as many as for a tolerance of 0.1 percent. This translates into a threefold time savings in computations if we are willing to go from a tolerance of 0.01 to a tolerance of 0.1.

A Formula for the Number of Steps
If we want to use the method of bisections to get within a tolerance of ϵ, then we must have:

$$k > \log(\sigma_0/\epsilon)/\log 2,$$

where k represents the number of steps. Here, σ_0 is the first guess (which had to be greater than the actual implied volatility). This formula says that the number of steps it takes to get within a tolerance of ϵ of the correct implied volatility is the first whole number greater than $\log(\sigma_0/\epsilon)/\log 2$.

Method of Bisections: Sample Computation
The algorithm described above is harder to visualize than to actually use. For this reason, we give a sample computation that illustrates the method

of bisections in action. The example can be followed along step-by-step or viewed as a whole in Table 8.2.1.

Suppose we have a call option C on a stock S struck at $100 expiring in two years. Suppose the risk-free rate of interest is 3 percent *per annum*. The current market price of S is $100 and C is trading at a price of $8.61. What is the implied volatility within a tolerance of 0.01 percent?

We compute this using the method of bisections, but first let's see how many steps it will take. For starters, we determine that the implied volatility is not greater than 20 percent, so we have:

$$\log(20/0.01)/\log 2 = 10.97.$$

Therefore, it will take eleven steps to get within 0.01 percent of the correct implied volatility.

The Procedure
We now carry out the procedure.

STEP 1. Since the option's actual implied volatility is not greater than 20 percent, set σ_0 to 20 percent. Therefore, σ_1 is given by:

$$\sigma_1 = \sigma_0 - \sigma_0/2^1 = 20\% - 20\%/2 = 10\%.$$

T A B L E 8.2.1

Computation of Implied Volatility Using the Method of Bisections
A call option struck at $100 with two years to expiration on a stock with current price $100 has a current listed price of $8.61.

Step	σ_i	Black-Scholes price
1	10%	$8.87
2	5%	$6.58
3	7.5%	$7.66
4	8.75%	$8.25
5	9.38%	$8.56
6	9.69%	$8.71
7	9.53%	$8.64
8	9.45%	$8.60
9	9.49%	$8.62
10	9.47%	$8.61

STEP 2. We compute the Black-Scholes price of C assuming the volatility of S is 10 percent. We obtain

$$C(100, 100, 2, 0.10, 0.03) = \$8.87.$$

This price is larger than the actual price of C, \$8.61, so we set:

$$\sigma_2 = \sigma_1 - \sigma_0/2^2 = 10\% - \frac{20\%}{4} = 5\%.$$

STEP 3. We compute the Black-Scholes price of S assuming the volatility of S is 5 percent. We obtain

$$C(100, 100, 2, 0.05, 0.03) = \$6.58.$$

This price is smaller than the market price of C, \$8.61, so we let

$$\sigma_3 = \sigma_2 + \sigma_0/2^3 = 5\% + 20\%/8 = 7.5\%.$$

STEP 4. We compute the Black-Scholes price of S assuming the volatility of S is 7.5 percent. We obtain

$$C(100, 100, 2, 0.075, 0.03) = \$7.66.$$

This price is smaller than the market price of C, \$8.61, so we let

$$\sigma_4 = \sigma_3 + \sigma_0/2^4 = 7.5\% + 20\%/16 = 8.75\%.$$

STEP 5. We compute the Black-Scholes price of S assuming the volatility of S is 8.75 percent. We obtain

$$C(100, 100, 2, 0.0875, 0.03) = \$8.25.$$

This price is smaller than the market price of C, \$8.61, so we let

$$\sigma_5 = \sigma_4 + \sigma_0/2^5 = 8.75\% + 20\%/32 = 9.38\%.$$

STEP 6. We compute the Black-Scholes price of S assuming the volatility of S is 9.38 percent. We obtain

$$C(100, 100, 2, 0.0938, 0.03) = \$8.56.$$

This price is smaller than the market price of C, \$8.61, so we let

$$\sigma_6 = \sigma_5 + \sigma_0/2^6 = 9.38\% + 20\%/64 = 9.69\%.$$

STEP 7. We compute the Black-Scholes price of S assuming the volatility of S is 9.69 percent. We obtain

$$C(100, 100, 2, 0.0969, 0.03) = \$8.71.$$

This price is larger than the market price of C, $8.61, so we let

$$\sigma_7 = \sigma_6 - \sigma_0/2^7 = 9.69\% - 20\%/128 = 9.53\%.$$

STEP 8. We compute the Black-Scholes price of S assuming the volatility of S is 9.53 percent. We obtain

$$C(100, 100, 2, 0.0953, 0.03) = \$8.64.$$

This price is larger than the market price of C, $8.61, so we let

$$\sigma_8 = \sigma_7 - \sigma_0/2^8 = 9.53\% - 20\%/256 = 9.45\%.$$

STEP 9. We compute the Black-Scholes price of S assuming the volatility of S is 9.45 percent. We obtain

$$C(100, 100, 2, 0.0945, 0.03) = \$8.60.$$

This price is smaller than the market price of C, $8.61, so we let

$$\sigma_9 = \sigma_8 + \sigma_0/2^9 = 9.45\% + 20\%/512 = 9.49\%.$$

STEP 10. We compute the Black-Scholes price of S under the assumption that the volatility of S is 9.49 percent. We obtain

$$C(100, 100, 2, 0.0949, 0.03) = \$8.62.$$

This price is larger than the market price of C, $8.61, so we let

$$\sigma_{10} = \sigma_9 - \sigma_0/2^{10} = 9.49\% - 20\%/1028 = 9.47\%.$$

This is the tenth step, and the last adjustment to our volatility was $20/1028 = 0.0019$, so we are within 0.01 percent of the actual implied volatility. Also,

$$C(100, 100, 2, 0.0947, 0.03) = \$8.61,$$

so we know our estimated implied volatility of 9.47 percent produces a Black-Scholes price equal to the market price of the option.

8.3   THE NEWTON-RAPHSON METHOD

The method of bisections is a reasonable and reliable way to compute implied volatilities, but it has one flaw: It is too slow. That is, it takes too many steps to converge to a reasonable answer. Therefore, most people serious about computing implied volatilities rely on a faster technique known as the *Newton-Raphson method.*

The technique is very general, and it arises in the study of calculus. The basic idea of Newton-Raphson is quite intuitive, and one *does not* need to know calculus to understand or use it. A graph of volatility versus the Black-Scholes option value is presented in the figure below. The x-axis represents volatility, and the y-axis represents the Black-Scholes value of a European call option of a fixed expiration and strike price. The graph examines the change of option value with respect to volatility.

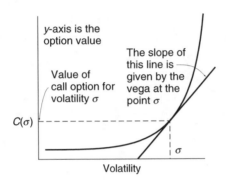

The straight line in the figure is called the *tangent* line to the graph at the point shown. Its *slope* (that is, its relative steepness) is equal to the instantaneous rate of change of the option price with respect to volatility. Therefore, by definition, the slope of this line is the vega of the option. A formula for the vega is given in Chapter 4, Display 4.10.1.

Graphical Example of Newton-Raphson Method
Examine Figure 8.3.1. In the upper left-hand inset (labeled 1), we have a graph of volatility versus the Black-Scholes value of a call, given a certain strike and certain expiration. The x-axis represents volatility, and the y-axis represents option value, so that a given point on the graph represents the Black-Scholes value of the call option assuming the underlying has the volatility represented by the x-axis. The horizontal dashed line represents the market price of the call option with given strike and expiration. We denote this as C. Our goal is to find the implied volatility of C—the volatility that makes the Black-Scholes value of the option equal to its market value. This is equivalent to finding the intersection point of the graph with the dashed line. We'll use the Newton-Raphson method.

To find this intersection point, we proceed in steps, following the four insets (numbered 1, 2, 3, and 4) in Figure 8.3.1.

The first step is to guess what the correct implied volatility is. Call this guess σ_1. Next, we compute the Black-Scholes value of our call option with volatility σ_1, denoted $C(\sigma_1)$, and the vega of this option, denoted $V(\sigma_1)$.

F I G U R E   8.3.1

The Newton-Raphson method for computing implied volatility

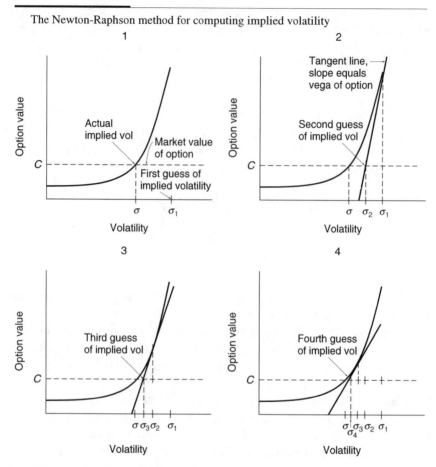

These can be computed using the formulas in Display 4.10.1, Chapter 4. Using these values, we compute the value of our next volatility "guess," depicted as σ_2 in inset 2, by equating the two different ways the slope of the tangent line to the graph can be written

$$V(\sigma_1) = \frac{C(\sigma_1) - C}{\sigma_1 - \sigma_2}.$$

Note that we do not yet know what σ_2 is. Rather, we will solve for it after computing the other terms in this equation.

The left-hand side is computed using the definition of vega: Vega is the slope of the line tangent to the graph of option price versus volatility.

The right-hand side comes from the definition of slope: Slope is the change in the y-axis—($C(\sigma_1) - C$)—divided by the change in the x-axis—($\sigma_1 - \sigma_2$). Here, σ_2 is the place on the graph where the tangent line meets the horizontal line $y = C$. We do not know the value of σ_2, so we have to solve for it:

$$\sigma_2 = \sigma_1 - \frac{C(\sigma_1) - C}{V(\sigma_1)}.$$

Notice in inset 2 that σ_2 is closer to the implied volatility than σ_1. In words, the equation means the second volatility guess is given by the difference of the Black-Scholes value, given a volatility of σ_1, minus the market price divided by the "current Black-Scholes" vega of the option, that is, the vega with respect to σ_1.

The next two insets—insets 3 and 4—show an iteration of this procedure. For example, in inset 3, we computed σ_3 by finding the tangent line to the graph at σ_2 and its intersection with the horizontal dashed line.

In general, the formula for σ_n, the nth volatility guess, is given by

$$\sigma_n = \sigma_{n-1} - \frac{C(\sigma_{n-1}) - C}{V(\sigma_{n-1})}. \tag{8.3.1}$$

Notice that the nth guess depends on the vega and the $n - 1$th guess.

We now give an example of using the Newton-Raphson method to compute implied volatility. We use the same option characteristics used in the demonstration of the method of bisections.

Newton-Raphson Method—Sample Computation

We now illustrate the Newton-Raphson method with a detailed example. The option is specified as follows:

type	vanilla European call
spot price (underlying)	$100
strike price	$100
expiration	2 years
risk-free rate	3%
market price	$8.61

We begin with a guess of $\sigma_1 = 20$ percent, as we did in the method of bisections. We will see how much faster Newton-Raphson converges than the method of bisections.

Iteration 1

We have to compute $C(\sigma_1)$, the Black-Scholes value of the option, assuming a volatility of 20 percent. The Black-Scholes value of the call with an input volatility of $\sigma_1 = 20$ percent is:

$$C(\sigma_1) = \$14.0721.$$

Next, we compute the $V(\sigma_1)$, the "Black-Scholes" vega of the option at a volatility of σ_1: $V(\sigma_1) = 53.0007$. To compute σ_2, we use equation (8.3.1) with $n = 2$:

$$\sigma_2 = 0.20 - \frac{14.0721 - 8.61}{53.0007} = 0.0969,$$

where the term 8.61 is the market price of the call.

Recalling that the actual implied volatility is equal to 9.47 percent (we computed this using the method of bisections), we see that in only one iteration, we have already moved quite close to the correct answer.

Iteration 2

Next, we compute the value of our call option with an input volatility of $\sigma_2 = 9.69$ percent and obtain:

$$C(\sigma_2) = 8.7144.$$

That is, the Black-Scholes price of the option given a volatility of 9.69 percent is $8.7144 (within 20 cents of the market price).

We now use Newton-Raphson to compute σ_3. To do this, we need to compute $V(\sigma_2)$. The answer is $V(\sigma_2) = 49.6346$. Newton-Raphson tells us:

$$\sigma_3 = \sigma_2 - \frac{C(\sigma_2) - C}{V(\sigma_2)} \qquad \sigma_3 = 0.0969 - \frac{8.7144 - 8.61}{49.6346}$$

Therefore, $\sigma_3 = 0.0948$.

Stopping

Next, we compute $C(\sigma_3) = 8.6103$, the Black-Scholes value of the call with an input volatility of σ_3.

We see that with an input volatility of 9.48 percent, we obtain a Black-Scholes price within 3/100 of a cent of the real price. In fact, this is a better estimate of the implied volatility than the method of bisections gave after nine steps! We see why the Newton-Raphson method is a better method for computing implied volatility than the method of bisections.

8.4 THE VOLATILITY SMILE

Most world equity markets have a particular *implied volatility* structure. The structure of implied volatility can be broken down into two components: the *volatility smile* and the *term structure of volatility*. The volatility smile is the way in which implied volatility (of a stock or index) varies with strike price for options of a fixed expiration. For example, suppose we have a stock S, and we look at all 6-month options (calls and puts) on S. Then, the graph of strike price versus implied volatility (for the six month option) is the volatility smile for 6-month options.

Term structure of volatility, on the other hand, describes the way at-the-money implied volatility varies with time until expiration (at-the-money implied volatility is the implied volatility of an at-the-money option). Thus, to look at the term structure of volatility of S, we graph time until expiration versus implied volatility for all of the at-the-money options on S. The name *term structure* derives from the *term structure of interest rates,* which looks at the relationship between interest rates and maturities.

Figure 8.4.1 depicts the volatility smile for European options on the S&P 500 index on January 24, 1996. Notice that implied volatility increases as strike price decreases for out-of-the-money options. This is called a negative skew.

The Volatility Smile and the 1987 Market Crash

By now, it is common knowledge that since the market crash of October 1987, the volatility smile for most world equity markets has become more pronounced. As of the writing of this book, nobody has produced a sound theoretical explanation for why this is the case. Rubinstein (1994) gives explicit examples of pre- and post-crash volatility smiles for the S&P 500. Moreover, he has a theory:

> One is tempted to hypothesize that the stock market crash of October 1987 changed the way market participants viewed index options. Out-of-the-money puts...became valued much more highly, eventually leading to the...situation where low striking price options had significantly higher implied volatilities than high striking price options. The market's pricing of options since the crash seems to indicate an increasing "crash-o-phobia"... [1]

---

[1] From Rubinstein, M. "Implied Binomial Trees" (1994), pp. 774–775.

F I G U R E 8.4.1

The volatility smile for the S&P 500 index for two different expiration dates
These graphs reflect the volatility smile on January 24, 1996.

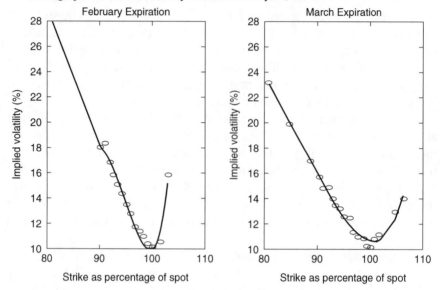

Volatility Skew and Option Prices

Examining Figure 8.4.1, one thing is clear: For out-of-the-money options as strike prices increase, implied volatility decreases. We want to examine the implications of this for option pricing.

First of all, we have already seen that all other things being equal, options trading at higher implied volatilities are more expensive. Put another way, Black-Scholes values increase as volatility of the underlying increases.

Let's consider what the volatility smile in Figure 8.4.1 says about S&P 500 options relative to the constant volatility hypothesis of Black-Scholes. We'll assume that the S&P 500 has a historical volatility of approximately 15 percent—somewhere in the middle of the smile.

As strike prices decrease, option prices increase relative to a flat smile. Therefore, out-of-the-money puts are more expensive than Black-Scholes theory predicts. Conversely, as strikes increase, option values drop (relative to a flat smile) due to the decreased volatility. Eventually, prices drop below the level given by historical volatility. Conclusion: In-the-money calls are less expensive than Black-Scholes theory predicts.

Another point of view comes from the trading floor. Traders view implied volatility as a measure of the market's "view" of volatility. For example, since a call option on the S&P 500 is a bet that the market will rise, a low implied volatility for an out-of-the-money call indicates that the market thinks volatility will drop if prices rise. Likewise, high volatilities for low strikes indicate that the market believes volatility will increase if prices drop.

What This Says About Local Volatility

We can formulate the relationship between market view and volatility in terms of local volatility. Recall that local volatility is the market's opinion today of what future volatility will look like for specific market conditions.

To be more precise, fix a certain time in the future and ask, What does the graph of spot price (at that future time) versus local volatility look like? More precisely yet, suppose we have a stock S and we fix some future time t. Graph x versus $\sigma(x, t)$, where x ranges over all future stock prices and $\sigma(x, t)$ is the local volatility of S for the price x and the time t.

The shape of this graph will be qualitatively quite similar to the volatility smile itself. For example, in the case of the S&P 500, a graph of stock price versus local volatility has the property that as stock price decreases, volatility increases. That is, the market says that if at some future date the stock price begins to drop, volatility will rise. (See Rubinstein (1994) for specific data.)

Theoretical Explanations

Given these facts, we can form three basic and opposite hypotheses regarding Black-Scholes: Either the market is wrong and Black-Scholes is right, the market is right and Black-Scholes is wrong, or they are both wrong. Let's say that the "market is right" *means* there are no arbitrage opportunities. If this is the case, then the existence of the volatility smile gives a strong indication that stock price volatility is not constant.

Now the question remains, What is the correct theoretical explanation for the volatility skew, and can we build a model that accounts for it? We discuss a popular class of models along these lines in the next section.

8.5 THE VOLATILITY OF VOLATILITY— STOCHASTIC VOLATILITY

We noted in the last section that if we believe the market prices options correctly, then the constant volatility assumption for stock prices is not correct. So we ask, If not constant, then what? Nobody knows the definitive answer. In this section, we discuss several popular theories.

The most obvious hypothesis to make regarding volatility is that volatility itself is random. Theories of stock price movements in which volatility is random are known as *stochastic volatility models*.[2] This means we hypothesize that as a stock price evolves, the volatility of the stock is randomly changing (random in the same sense that stocks following a geometric Brownian motion are random). The nature of this process and how it relates to the stock's own movements are among the issues we need to resolve in order to create a stochastic volatility model.

To understand how this relates to the geometric Brownian motion model, let's recall the basic assumptions underlying it. The model hypothesizes that the price of a stock is under continuous bombardment by "trades," which randomly jar the stock's price, and makes the following two assumptions:

1. The percentage return of each trade is random.
2. The distribution of returns (caused by trading) is independent of all previous trading and is normally distributed with mean value proportional to elapsed time and standard deviation proportional to the square root of elapsed time.

It is the second assumption that concerns us here. The volatility of the stock is directly linked to the probability distribution of the returns on each trade. For instance, if the probability distribution of returns is narrowly dispersed about its mean, then the volatility will be lower than if the dispersion is great. In the geometric Brownian motion model, each trade contributes to the overall volatility in the same way. This is the constant volatility assumption.

Viewing Brownian motion in this way, it is easy to see that one could replace the constant volatility assumption by something less restrictive. For instance, there is no reason to assume that the distribution of returns of a trade has to be the same at each trade and independent of previous trades. It may change over time. The probability distribution itself may be random in some way, or maybe it is random and also depends on time and stock price in a complicated way.

In this section, we want to briefly discuss models in which the distribution of returns' volatility component is randomly changing. One can

---

[2]The term *stochastic* is common in the vocabulary of stock price modelers and can be taken to mean *randomly changing volatility*.

derive such a model by positing that the probability distribution of the percentage returns on trades is a random variable. To make the model useful, however, we have to specify in a precise way how volatility changes. Before delving into these questions, we need to look at several broader questions.

Stochastic Volatility Models

Three important issues regarding stochastic volatility models are: 1) Is there any motivation for assuming volatility is random? 2) How do we determine how volatility "evolves" over time? and 3) If we derive a stochastic volatility model of price movements, can it be used to price options?

There are several ways to answer each of these questions, and we can only give partial answers here. First, deducing the exact nature of volatility is clearly a difficult question. We know that volatility is not constant[3] because we have a lot of data regarding historical volatility. The ideal model for volatility would predict future volatility. That is, given a set of inputs, the outputs of the model would tell us what future volatility would look like.

Digression: Predicting Volatility

There has been extensive research regarding the prediction of future volatility. In particular, researchers have examined what sources of information are the best predictors of volatility. Some obvious candidates are:

1. Historical volatility
2. Implied volatility
3. Some combination of the first two

Of course, the term *implied volatility* above is ambiguous, as there are many possible implied volatilities for a single stock.

The literature on this topic does not reach any firm conclusions. It seems that there are studies supporting just about any point of view one could choose to have. An excellent summary of the literature, however, is available in Mayhew (1994).

More on Stochastic Volatility

The first and most serious issue regarding stochastic volatility is, What kind of model do we use for the evolution of stock volatility? While there are

---

[3]There is strong theoretical evidence that the volatility smile implies nonconstant local volatility.

many possible theories we could put forward, there are solid theoretical reasons to assert that volatility itself follows a *mean reverting* process.[4] We explain this now.

Mean Reversion

It is a fact that in most world equity markets, historical volatility tends to move in cycles. There is a mean volatility around which historical volatility fluctuates. It can move away from the mean, but as it gets farther and farther away, it drifts back again. The farther away it is, the more quickly it drifts back. That is, unlike stock prices, which one expects will grow over time (i.e., the S&P 500 continues to reach "historical" highs), volatility tends to move away from a mean volatility and then come back again.

Figure 8.5.1 displays the historical annual and quarterly volatility of two major market indexes from two different countries: S&P 500 (United States) and TOPIX (Japan). In all four cases, one sees a pattern of mean reversion. We can easily model mean reversion mathematically; some stochastic volatility models make mean reversion a basic assumption. There are three parameters controlling mean-reverting processes: the mean to which volatility reverts, the strength of reversion; that is, how powerful the force pulling back to the mean is, and the volatility of volatility.

To get a feel for what the mean and strength of reversion are, Figure 8.5.2 displays nine computer-generated mean-reverting stochastic volatilities. The graphs depict time versus volatility. In each graph, the volatility of volatility is 15 percent and the volatility is set to revert to 15 percent. That is, over time, the value of volatility tends to drift back to 15 percent. The nine graphs depict mean-reverting volatility with increasing reversion strength. Notice that in general (but not always), the greater the reversion strength, the more sharply the volatility returns to the mean. For example, with a reversion strength of 15.00, the volatility moves irregularly, and returns to the mean only approximately 13 times, often moving beyond the upper limits of the graph before coming back down. Conversely, with a reversion strength of 200, whenever the volatility rises much above 15.02 it immediately and quickly bounces back to the mean.

A stochastic volatility model can incorporate mean reversion as a possible model for volatility. There are two main issues in such models. First, how do we measure the parameters of the model? This is called calibration.

---

[4]This is studied in many articles. See, for example, Merville and Pieptea (1989).

F I G U R E 8.5.1

Historical volatility of two major equity indexes

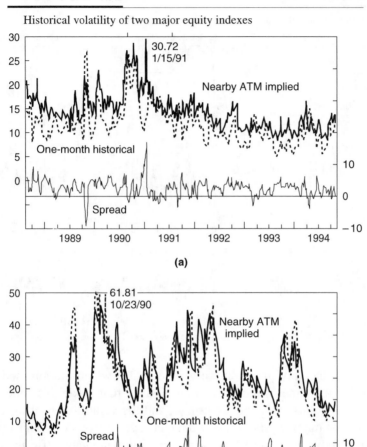

(a)

(b)

Source: Goldman Sachs Equity Derivatives Research publication, "Index Volatility in Global Option Markets," December 1994.

Next, how do we use the model to price options? We explain calibration first.

Calibration

After making a choice of a stock volatility process, the next step is to calibrate the model. That is, for every input parameter of the model, we have to find the appropriate values that fit what we are modeling.

FIGURE 8.5.2

Computer-generated mean-reverting volatility processes

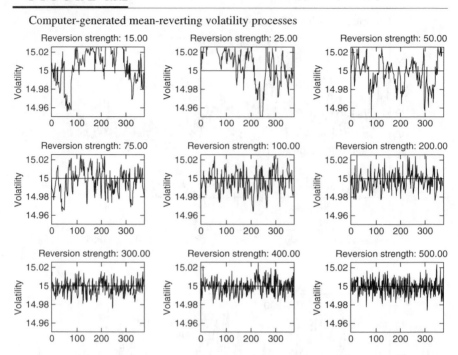

Recall the way in which the geometric Brownian motion model for stock price movements requires calibration. In that model it is necessary to compute the instantaneous return, μ, and the volatility, σ, of the stock. Assume now that volatility follows a mean-reverting process. This process itself must have a volatility, just as a stock following geometric Brownian motion has a volatility.

By analogy with calibrating volatility itself, what we need to model, then, are the percent changes in volatility over short periods of time. We can hypothesize that the relative size of the changes will be normally distributed (as we did in Brownian motion). We therefore need to determine the standard deviation of these changes—the *volatility of volatility*.

Compare this with the procedure for computing stock price volatility. The first step in this procedure is to obtain time series data for prices. For example, we might obtain the daily closing prices of the S&P 500 for the last six months. The analogous first step for computing the volatility of volatility is to create time-series data for volatility. This is problematic, however, because it is difficult to make so many measurements accurately—we are measuring how volatility changes over time. But we need to estimate volatility at many different times in order to measure this. To do this, we have to use price data.[5]

Suppose that we somehow make an estimate of the volatility of volatility. Then, there is another issue: the correlation between stock price and volatility. To understand this, recall the situation with the S&P 500 index. We already discussed that as the market level drops, the smile implies that volatility will increase. This is a correlation between price and volatility. In creating a model, we have to build into it what the correlation between price and volatility is. To understand this, we have to explain correlation in more detail.

Correlation

Mathematically, correlation is measured by a *correlation coefficient:* a number between minus one (completely negatively correlated) and one (completely correlated) in which a correlation of zero means completely uncorrelated. We denote the correlation coefficient by the Greek letter ρ.

Figure 8.5.3 gives examples of highly correlated (correlation = 0.8), moderately correlated (correlation = 0.3), uncorrelated (correlation = 0.0), moderately negatively correlated (correlation = -0.3), and highly negatively correlated (correlation = -0.8) stock price movements. In each picture there are two sample paths for stocks following geometric Brownian motion, with 15 percent volatility.

Notice that the highly correlated paths (correlation = 0.8) shadow each other closely with little deviation, while the moderately correlated paths (correlation = 0.3) have some of their movements correlated (for example, around the 250-day mark), but at other times they drift away from one another. Conversely, the highly negatively correlated paths (correlation = -0.8) mirror each others' movements: If one moves up, the other moves down. This is true, but to a lesser extent, for the moderately negatively correlated paths (correlation = -0.3).

Any mathematical model that contains two random processes (e.g., stock price movements with stochastic volatility) must address the issue of the correlation between processes, or the model is not complete. In the

---

[5]Alternatively, we could try to measure the volatility of volatility using implied volatilities, but then the question arises of how to incorporate the many *different* implied volatilities for a single underlying.

FIGURE 8.5.3

In each graph, there are two stock price paths. The top row of graphs shows correlated stock prices, the middle row shows uncorrelated stock prices, and the bottom row shows negatively correlated stock prices.

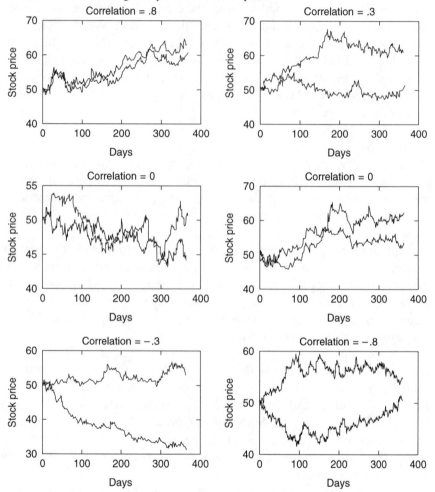

stochastic volatility situation, the question is, What is the correct model for the correlation between stock price and volatility?

The main problem with this is that it is difficult to estimate from historical data what the correlation between stock price and volatility should be. Contrast this with the situation with historical volatility. One of the strengths of Black-Scholes, we claimed, was that its key parameter, volatility, could be easily estimated from historical data.

F I G U R E   8.5.4

Sample paths for stocks with stochastic volatility
The volatility paths (right hand graphs) are mean reverting, and the changes in
volatility are positively correlated with changes in stock price.

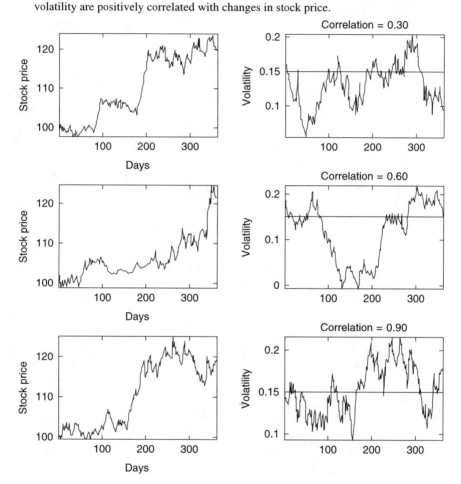

Sample Paths for Stochastic Volatility

Figures 8.5.4 and 8.5.5 display three sample paths each for stocks with
stochastic volatility. In both figures, volatility follows a mean-reverting
process with a mean volatility of 15 percent. In the first set of graphs, the
volatility is positively correlated with stock price movements. That is, when
stock price increases, to some extent so does volatility, and when stock price
decreases, volatility does as well. In Figure 8.5.5, stock price and volatility
are negatively correlated.

F I G U R E 8.5.5

Sample paths for stocks with stochastic volatility
The volatility paths are mean reverting, and the changes in volatility are negatively correlated with changes in stock price.

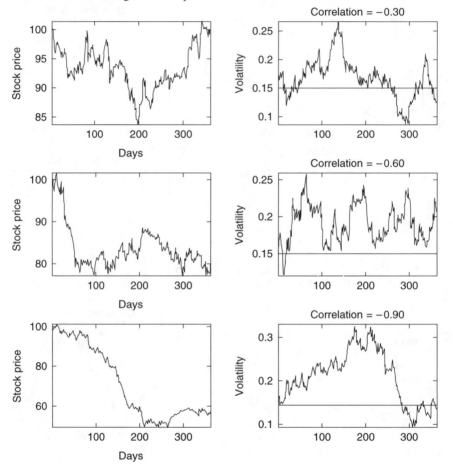

Hedging Volatility Risk

Before discussing how to hedge volatility risk, let's make clear what volatility risk is. Volatility risk is the risk associated with *unanticipated* changes in volatility. That is, any changes in volatility that are predictable can be hedged. For example, there are generalizations of Brownian motion in which volatility changes as some function of spot price and time. If this function is specified ahead of time so that for every possible spot price at every possible time we can say what the volatility of the underlying will be, then there is no volatility risk in the model. This is so because all the information regarding changes in volatility is reflected in changes in stock price. For instance, if the stock price rises, then we know the volatility will move to such-and-such value based on the function relating stock price and time to volatility. Therefore, in this case stock price risk already encodes all volatility risk.

More concretely, recall that in flexible binomial trees, volatility changes as a function of spot price and time: This is the notion of local volatility. See Figure 6.4.1 in Chapter 6. We saw in Chapter 7 that we can price any option with an underlying stock that follows a binomial process.[6]

On the other hand, if volatility changes randomly, then to some degree it moves independently from stock price. In this case, we cannot anticipate changes in volatility, and this type of volatility change gives rise to volatility risk that is independent of stock price risk. On the flip side, we also cannot build a simple binomial tree representing stochastic volatility.

A Volatility Instrument
One of the most vexing issues about stochastic volatility—and one which cannot be ignored—is the fact that in order to hedge volatility risk of an option, one must have available a *volatility instrument* for the underlying. A volatility instrument is a financial instrument whose price changes are 100 percent correlated with the changes in volatility. For example, suppose we are hedging options on the S&P 500 index. A volatility instrument in this context would be an instrument whose price rises or falls in proportion to respective increases or decreases in the volatility of the S&P 500. Using this instrument, we could hedge the risk from changes in volatility not anticipated by stock price changes.

Of course, one might suggest that if we have a stochastic volatility model, we might be able to do without a volatility instrument. The fact is, even with an accurate model of volatility fluctuations of an index, this would not improve our chances of hedging options on that index. We explain why in detail.

Why We Need a Volatility Instrument
In the "Black-Scholes" world, where volatility is constant, we are able to hedge options for a known cost. We observed that this was possible because

---

[6]This is related to the fact that stochastic volatility stock price models do not have simple discrete analogs such as binomial trees. Any discretization of a stochastic volatility model has to take into account the random nature of volatility.

the source of uncertainty in the option price (under the Black-Scholes set of assumptions) was limited to a single factor: stock price risk.

Imagine we are observing price changes in an option on a given stock, and over a period of time, the stock price does not change, but the volatility of the stock does. Then, the option price still changes, because as we have seen, the volatility of the underlying is a key determinant in the value of an option. The arguments we used to understand option pricing do not make sense now.

Recall that we approximated the delta of an option at some time t_0 as:

$$\frac{C_{t_0} - e^{-r(t_1-t_0)}C_{t_1}}{S_{t_0} - e^{-r(t_1-t_0)}S_{t_1}},$$

where t_1 is some time after t_0. But since volatility has changed (specifically, since its change was uncorrelated with stock price), this formula no longer reflects the rate of change of the option price with respect to the stock price—volatility has contributed to the change of the option price. Thus, we cannot use the above formula as a substitute for the theoretical formula for the delta of the option (given by $N(d_1)$). For this reason, all of our hedging arguments begin to break down.

The question is, can we produce new formulas that allow us to hedge the option even when volatility changes? The answer depends on *how* it changes. If volatility changes as a known function of spot price and time, that is, if it changes *deterministically,* then the answer is yes. We saw this above.

On the other hand, if volatility changes *randomly,* as in stochastic volatility models, then there is an essential difficulty in hedging. To understand this, think of how we hedge an option in the Black-Scholes model. If we are short the option, then we purchase delta shares of the underlying as a hedge against the uncertainty of the option price associated with stock price changes. This hedges us precisely because delta is the rate of change of the option price with respect to stock price. But stock price is now changing with respect to volatility as well. Thus, with this method, we can hedge away stock price risk and even all the volatility risk anticipated by stock price changes; that is, changes in the volatility (e.g., deterministic changes) that are correlated with changes in stock price. Despite this, we are still exposed to *volatility risk* uncorrelated with stock price.

To hedge away this risk, we need an instrument whose price is 100 percent correlated with stock price—a *volatility instrument.* This instrument could be used to hedge volatility risk, in much the same way as the underlying is used to hedge the risk associated with stock price changes. One could set up an instantaneously riskless portfolio consisting of the option, the underlying, and the volatility instrument and then proceed to derive an option pricing formula along the lines of Black-Scholes.

Unfortunately, such an instrument is not currently traded.[7] Without such an instrument, stochastic volatility risk cannot be hedged. Nevertheless, volatility instruments may be used to study option pricing formulas. The idea is to assume that there is a volatility instrument and then to create a model for how it behaves. Such an analysis has been carried out in Eisenberg and Jarrow (1994).

Stock Returns under Stochastic Volatility

We now look at stock returns under stochastic volatility. To understand the effect of stochastic volatility on stock returns, we use histograms to compare the probability distribution of returns under stochastic volatility to returns under a geometric Brownian motion.

Figure 8.5.6 displays six histograms. Each figure is a histogram of stock returns from stocks following a mean-reverting stochastic volatility stock process, with a mean volatility of 15 percent. What changes from histogram to histogram is the correlation between changes in stock price and changes in volatility. We generated the histograms by repeatedly generating one-year sample paths and binning the results for each of six different stock processes.

Recall that correlation is numerically determined by a number between -1 and 1, with -1 being completely negatively correlated, 1 being completely positively correlated, and 0 being uncorrelated. We display histograms with correlations equal to -0.8, -0.3, 0.0, 0.3, and 0.8. The sixth histogram is stock returns on a geometric Brownian motion. Let's discuss the results by referring to Figure 8.5.6.

We first examine the top two figures. In these, we see that relative to the "Normal returns," the left tail of the distribution is "fat." Likewise, the right tail of the distribution is "thin." That is, more sample paths have large negative returns compared with the returns in a Brownian motion path, and less sample paths have large positive returns compared with Brownian motion. What is the intuitive explanation for this?

Since volatility and stock price are negatively correlated, as stock price drops, volatility increases. This, in turn, has the effect of increasing

---

[7]There was an instrument traded on the CBOE called the Market Volatility Index (VIX). The VIX tracked the at-the-money implied volatility of options on the S&P 100 with 22 trading days to expiration. This is discussed in detail in Whaley (1993).

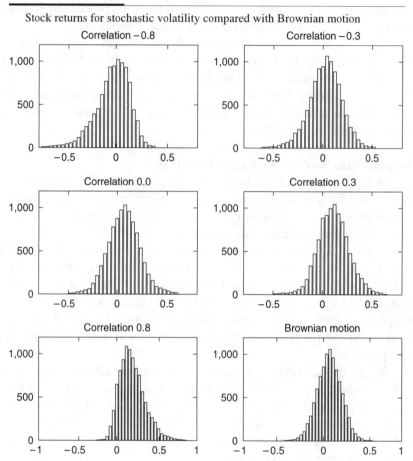

F I G U R E 8.5.6

Stock returns for stochastic volatility compared with Brownian motion

the probability of large changes relative to normal returns. When we consider many sample paths, as we do when we use histograms, the net result is that many more sample paths have large negative returns. Conversely, as stock prices increase, volatility decreases. Moreover, the greater the negative correlation between stock price and volatility, the greater the "skew" in the distribution; that is, the fatter the left tail of the distribution will be.

Similar reasoning shows that if stock price and volatility are *positively* correlated, then the distribution will have a fat right tail. Now, what if stock price and volatility are uncorrelated? In this case, both tails are fat and the distribution displays the classic fat-tailed *leptokurtosis*.

COMMENTS AND SUGGESTED READING

Murphy (1994) is a basic, nontechnical article describing stochastic volatility models, jump models, and the volatility smile. For a basic introduction to the volatility skew and some discussion regarding the S&P 500, see Clark (1994). Rubinstein (1994) has a great deal of information on the volatility smile of the S&P 500 and how it has changed since October 1987.

An interesting example of the use of volatility in practice is discussed in Star (1992). This article discusses Quantitative Financial Strategies, Inc. (QFS), founded by Wharton finance professor Sanford Grossman, and their practice of investing in volatility as an asset. As we have seen, options are "volatility class" assets; that is, their prices rise and fall in correlation with volatility swings.

In addition to the Newton-Raphson method and the method of bisections, several *approximate* formulas for computing the implied volatility of an option exist. See Chance (1993), Brenner and Subrahmanyam (1988), and Feinstein (1988).

A study of implied volatilities in stock index and interest rate options is given in Philippatos, Gressis, and Baird (1994). In particular, a framework is developed in this article for pricing options on the S&P 500 (spot and future) and Major Market Index options (spot). A study of options on the S&P 100 index and Black-Scholes prices is given in Cotner and Horrell (1989). This study compares historical and implied volatilities on options on the S&P 100 index and their effect on option prices.

There have been many attempts to study option pricing from the point of view of stochastic volatility. See Hull and White (1987), Ball and Roma (1994), Heston (1993), Stein and Stein (1991), and Wiggins (1987), as well as the other references. For an approach using a "volatility instrument," see Jarrow and Wiggins (1989). In Sheikh (1991) evidence is given that the S&P 100 exhibits stochastic volatility.

There are many more "alternative" approaches to option pricing than are discussed in this book. A classic example is Merton (1976), which introduces jumps into the stock price process. The stock process given in Merton (1976) is called a *jump diffusion process*. Such a process consists of two processes superimposed one onto the other. First, there is an ordinary Brownian motion, and then there is a "jump process," which allows for occasional jumps in the stock price. Merton derives an option pricing formula under the assumption that jumps are uncorrelated with moves in the market.

Option Pricing in the Presence of Jumps

A detailed study of option pricing in the presence of jumps is undertaken in Naik and Lee (1990). In this article, the authors show that if one applies the Black-Scholes hedging techniques in the case where stock prices jump, the strategy fails to be self-financing. Naik and Lee explain this as follows:

> Suppose that the underlying price process has jumps of random amplitudes occuring at random time intervals ... [in this setup] the Black-Scholes plan will neither be self-financing nor replicate the claim ....
>
> Consider first the case in which the agent attempts to replicate dynamically the payoff on a claim using the Black-Scholes trading strategy ..., the hedging plan fails to be self-financing at times when a jump occurs (and only at such times); at these jump times, either infusion of funds is needed to accomplish the intended replication or funds can be withdrawn.[8]

Given this example, one might ask if there are any situations in which jump risk can be at all managed. The answer is yes: If stock price jumps are uncorrelated with the market as a whole, then we can hedge it.[9] Jumps uncorrelated with the market do occur, as when some isolated or unexpected event related to a particular stock causes its price to jump. For instance, Kirk Kerkorian led a takeover bid of Chrysler Corporation on Wednesday, April 12, 1995, and this caused a one-day run-up in share prices of 34 percent. The stock price jumped because news of the takeover bid radically changed investors' opinion of the value of Chrysler stock. Thus, the jump had very little to do with changes in the market as a whole, and likely had a very small correlation with market moves that day.

A study of the pricing biases created by jumps in the market as a whole is given in Ball and Torous (1985). A discrete time version of a jump-diffusion model is given in Amin (1993). In this model, the author superimposes jumps on a binomial model and gives a pricing formula.

For more information on jumps in stock price modeling, see Jarrow and Rosenfeld (1984), Jorion (1988), and Press (1967).

Trading costs may possibly explain the volatility smile of the S&P 500. This is suggested in Jackwerth and Rubinstein (1995), but the authors warn:

---

[8]From "General Equilibrium Pricing of Options on the Market Portfolio with Discontinuous Returns," Naik and Lee (1990), pp. 506-507.

[9]This is studied in "Option Pricing When Underlying Stock Returns are Discontinuous," Merton (1976).

... those stalwarts who would place the blame on trading costs need to explain why—given the extreme shift in the option smile—these costs were apparently of much less importance before than after the crash.[10]

For a general survey of alternative option pricing models, see Cox and Ross (1976) and Hull (1993), Chapter 17 and the references therein.

---

[10]From Jackwerth, J. C. and Rubinstein M., "Recovering Probability Distributions from Contemporaneous Security Prices." *Journal of Finance,* 1995.

9

⑥ IMPLIED VOLATILITY TREES

This chapter deals with the *implied volatility tree* model of option pricing, introduced by E. Derman and I. Kani of the Quantitative Strategies Group of Goldman, Sachs & Co.

The motivation for implied volatility trees is the search for a stock price model that effectively deals with the volatility smile. We have seen the smile as a clear indication that something is wrong with Black-Scholes, and now we are introducing a way to deal with it.

Black-Scholes is based on the constant volatility geometric Brownian motion model of stock price movements. Stochastic volatility models, on the other hand, assume volatility changes randomly according to a process of its own—for example, a Brownian motion or a mean-reverting process. Implied volatility trees attack the problem from yet a different angle, turning option pricing on its head by accepting market prices of options as inputs to the model and building a stock price process (i.e., the *implied volatility tree*) based on those prices.

Consider the point of view of Fischer Black, codeveloper of the Black-Scholes model:

> It is rare that the [theoretical] value of an option comes out exactly equal to the price at which it trades on the exchange.
>
> ... there are three reasons for a difference between the value and price: we may have the correct value, and the option price may be out of line; we may have used the wrong inputs to the Black-Scholes formula; or the

Black-Scholes formula may be wrong. Normally, all three reasons play a part in explaining a difference between value and price.[1]

The implied volatility tree model takes a more extreme view than Black in this regard: The Black-Scholes formula is wrong, and the market is right. The justification for this extreme point of view is liquidity. We argue that if a particular option market is sufficiently liquid, then there will be no arbitrage opportunities available in these markets. In this sense, the market prices are correct, and it makes sense to build a model around the prices in these markets.

The Purpose of Implied Volatility Trees

First let's make clear what an implied volatility tree is.

> An implied volatility tree is a binomial tree that prices a given set of input options correctly.

For example, if we start with a certain underlying, an implied volatility tree for that security will price every option on it correctly. Contrast this with Black-Scholes or any other option pricing model: As Fischer Black points out, it is "rare" that the theoretical value (i.e., the value given by the model) agrees with the market value. The implied volatility tree model is the one exception to this rule. It is a model that, by design, agrees with the market.

There are two broadly defined reasons for using implied volatility trees. First, we use them to compute hedge parameters for standard options that we wish to hedge. The market itself only tells us the price of an option. If we want to hedge manage the risk of that option, we need to know hedge parameters. To infer hedge parameters, such as deltas or gammas, we need a model. The implied volatility tree model creates hedge parameters that make sense for the given option market.

Second, we use implied trees for pricing non-standard and exotic options. For example, we may want to price an OTC vanilla call that is not listed on the market. Essentially, we need to make a guess, based on the available set of option prices, as to what the price of the option might be. This alone does not require the implied tree model, but to produce this price, *along with* a hedge parameter, does require the implied tree model.

For more on this, we quote Emanuel Derman and Iraj Kani, who developed the implied trees model:

---

[1] From "The Holes in Black-Scholes," in *Black-Scholes to Black Holes*, RISK/FINEX (1992).

You can use this implied tree to value other derivatives whose prices are not readily available from the market—standard but illiquid European-style options, American-style options and exotic options that depend on the details of the index [or other] distribution—secure in the knowledge that the model is valuing all your hedging instruments consistently with the market.[2]

American Options and Implied Volatility Trees

The original work of Derman and Kani could only be used with an input set of options consisting entirely of European options. The method given here extends the Derman-Kani model to include input options of both the European *and* American variety.

Now let's take a closer look at the model.

A Detailed Look

Originally, binomial trees were introduced by Cox, Ross, and Rubinstein as an alternative way to get at the Black-Scholes formula. The idea was not to go beyond Black-Scholes but rather to come at it from a different angle. As mentioned earlier, the trees introduced by Cox, Ross, and Rubinstein are known as *standard binomial trees,* characterized by the fact that the up and down ratios are the same at each node of the tree (e.g., whenever the stock price rises, it rises by a fixed factor u, and whenever it falls, it falls by a fixed factor of d). Simply put, such a tree is a discrete time model that converges to Brownian motion. That is, as more time steps are introduced into the tree, it becomes a better and better representation of geometric Brownian motion.

From the perspective of stock price modeling, the standard binomial tree is subject to all the pitfalls and shortcomings of the geometric Brownian motion model. Accordingly, option pricing on these trees is subject to the same difficulties as the Black-Scholes model. This makes sense, because essentially all the assumptions of geometric Brownian motion are present in the standard binomial model. This was explained in detail in Chapter 6.

In the Black-Scholes model, one computes an historical volatility for a stock or index and then uses this value as an input to the model. Out of the model come both option prices and hedge ratios, crucial for managing the risk of the option. Alternatively, one could substitute implied volatilities as an input to the model in an attempt to predict correct hedge ratios. But which implied volatilities does one use? There are as many "input implied volatilities" as there are options on the index.

---

[2]From "The Volatility Smile and Its Implied Tree," Derman and Kani (1994b), from the introduction. This is also discussed in "Translatlantic Trees," Chriss (1996).

The implied volatility tree model uses *all of* the implied volatilities of options on the underlying—it deduces the *best* flexible binomial tree (see Chapter 6 for an explanation of "flexible") based on all the implied volatilities. This, in turn, gives prices and hedge ratios that feel the impact of the entire smile, not just a single volatility, implied or otherwise.

So, while the geometric Brownian motion model presumes that we understand volatility at the outset, the implied volatility tree model attempts to understand it by looking at current traded option prices. How? By demanding that the binomial tree price all listed options correctly. And what does this give us? It provides a tool to price a large number of options *other than traded options* and to calculate their hedge ratios, all reflecting the entire volatility skew, not just a single number, such as historical volatility or a particular combination of implied volatilities.

Terminology

This chapter assumes we have a fixed underlying and an *input set* of options on the underlying. These options are called the *input options*. Each input option is identified as European or American. We assume we know the *market price* of each input option. We say that the input set defines the current volatility smile, and we will often refer to the entire collection of input option prices as *the smile*.

The goal of this chapter is to produce, from a set of input options, a flexible binomial tree that values any option in the input set the same as its market price. A tree that performs in this way is called an *implied tree*.

9.1 PRELIMINARIES—INTERPOLATION AND EXTRAPOLATION

We shall soon see that in order to implement the implied volatility tree model, it is necessary to provide to the model prices of European options of strikes and expirations that may not appear in the market. These prices are supplied by means of *interpolation* and *extrapolation*.

What Is Interpolation?

Interpolation is the process of guessing unknown values from the patterns implicit in known values. A graphic example of this statement is given in Figure 9.1.1. The left-hand graph displays data points representing implied volatilities of call options on the same underlying index and with the same time until expiration, but with different strike prices. The horizontal axis represents different strike prices, and the vertical axis represents implied volatility.

FIGURE 9.1.1

Graphic example of interpolation.
The data points on the left represent implied volatilities of listed options for various
strike prices. On the right is an interpolated curve that allows one to find implied
volatilities for any strike price.

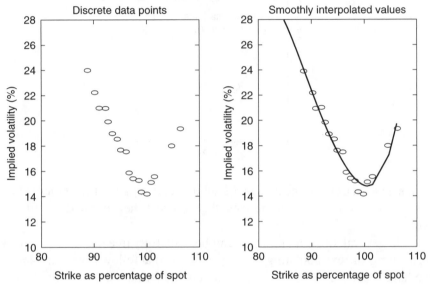

Suppose we want to know the implied volatilities of options with
strikes not in our data set. The right-hand figure plots a smooth curve that
is simultaneously "as close as possible" to all the different data points. This
can, in turn, be used to find an implied volatility for a strike price other than
the options listed by simply looking on the curve at the appropriate strike
price and observing the corresponding implied volatility. The values thus
obtained are called *interpolated values*.

Extrapolation

In the above picture of interpolation, we found values for implied volatilities for strikes between known values. Imagine a situation in which the
highest strike price for a traded option on an index is 575, but we need to
know values for strikes into the 600's. We can find these values by *extrapolating*.

When extrapolating, we make a best guess of the general trend of
the data and then continue this trend beyond the most extreme values of
the given data. For example, in the figure on page 366, we see real data
(solid line) and extrapolated data (dashed line). The dashed line was based

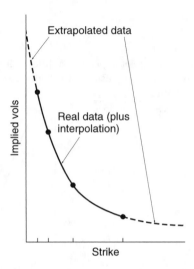

on the general trend of the data in the solid line. It suggests that if there were options with strikes in these ranges, this is where their implied volatilities would be.

In general, implementing the implied volatility tree model requires interpolating and extrapolating option prices. In what follows, we will assume we have a chosen method of interpolation and extrapolation available that allows one to produce option prices of arbitrary strikes and expirations.[3] That is:

> A preliminary step for implementing the implied volatility tree model is having a method for interpolating and extrapolating option prices.

How It Is Done in Practice

In practice, traders often quote option prices by means of their Black-Scholes implied volatilities. A two-by-two grid is built, with one dimension representing strike prices and another dimension representing expiry. The elements of the grid are the Black-Scholes implied volatilities of the options corresponding to the given strike and expiry.

Once the grid is in place, we use the option prices to build an implied tree by *forward induction*—building a binomial tree for stock or index prices node by node, starting at the spot price and moving forward in time.

---

[3] In Section 9.10 we describe the simplest method of interpolation: *bilinear interpolation*, which is suitable for building implied trees.

The value of each node (that is, the index price the node represents) is computed to ensure that the tree correctly prices all input options with strikes and expirations represented by the nodes of the tree. Since, in general, there are far more nodes of the tree than there are traded options, we can be sure that some (actually most) of the options for which we need market prices will not appear in the market. Therefore, part of any implementation of the implied volatility tree model is a "subroutine" that takes a data array consisting of all listed option prices and interpolates or extrapolates from this array the price of an option with a particular strike and expiration possibly not on the array.

Since option prices are quoted by means of their implied volatilities, one ends up interpolating and extrapolating implied volatilities, as opposed to option prices. These volatilities are then converted to option prices via the Black-Scholes formula or binomial model (in the case of European input options) or just the binomial model (in the case of American input options).

Example
Suppose we have a stock with a current price of $62 per share whose volatility is 15 percent *per annum* as estimated from historical data. Moreover, suppose the implied volatility for a 6-month European call struck at $65 is 15.3 percent *per annum,* as interpolated from the smile. Then, the Black-Scholes interpolated option price, assuming a risk-free rate of 3 percent, is $1.82. If one used historical volatility, the price of the option would only be $1.77.

9.2 BUILDING IMPLIED TREES—EUROPEAN OPTIONS

This section shows how to build implied volatility trees when the input set of options is European. After we demonstrate the method and give a few examples, we will show how to extend this method to American options. The presentation here is slightly different than the one found in Derman and Kani [(1994a) and (1994b)] and is taken from Chriss (1996). Finally, we will explain in detail how to implement the model into a computer system for building implied trees.

The Setup
In this section, we assume we have already computed a given time step and are moving on to computing the next time step (see Figure 9.2.1). In this way, we can start building the tree at the spot price and compute the values of all nodes one step at a time.

We will employ the following notation throughout this section, and in the entire section, we will use the numbering system of nodes in the binomial tree pictured in Figure 6.7.1. We have:

F I G U R E 9.2.1

Forward induction for building an implied binomial tree

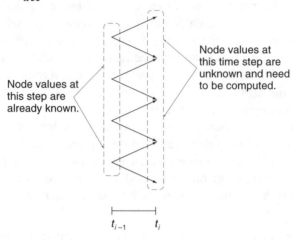

Node values at this time step are unknown and need to be computed.

Node values at this step are already known.

t_{i-1} t_i

$$t_{i-1} = \text{the date of time step } i - 1$$
$$\Delta t = \text{the amount of time between time step } i - 1 \text{ and } i$$
$$S_{i,j} = \text{the stock price value of node } (i, j)$$
$$r_i = \text{the risk-free rate applicable from time } i - 1 \text{ to } i$$

We assume that all of the stock price nodes at time t_{i-1} have been computed, and we are now going to compute the stock price nodes at time t_i.

We make the following general remarks about time steps and interest rates.

1. The values of Δt may vary from one time step to the next.

2. The interest rates may vary from time step to time step.

In other words, as we shall see, nothing about the formulas we derive below depends on fixing a certain risk-free rate throughout the tree, nor do we have to use one value of Δt throughout the tree. Thus one can vary the forward interest rates in the tree according to the yield curve.

Implied Volatility Trees and Dividends
The method of building implied volatility trees given here works perfectly well for stocks with dividends, and we explain how to incorporate dividends into the picture as we describe the method.

To incorporate dividends into this model, we have to produce a dividend schedule for the implied volatility tree. This is a list of ex-dividend dates and dividend payments for those dates. If there are no dividends, then we simply set all dividend payments to zero.

Derivation of the Formulas

Figure 9.2.2 displays a binomial tree fragment; we see times t_{i-1} and t_i. We make three assumptions:

- The values at all nodes of time t_{i-1} are known.
- The values of all Arrow-Debreu prices at time t_{i-1} are known.
- The value of S_u is known (see Figure 9.2.2).

Given these assumptions, our first step is to derive a value for S_d (see Figure 9.2.2) consistent with the value of a plain vanilla European put option struck at K and expiring at time t_i, denoted $P(t_i, K)$.

Suppose we know the value of $P(t_i, K)$ at node $(i - 1, j)$. In other words, suppose we know what the option will be worth if the stock price reaches node $(i - 1, j)$. Write $v^{\text{put}}_{i-1,j}$ for this value. Knowing this allows us to solve for the value of S_d. Display 9.2.1 derives the formula:

$$S_d = \frac{v^{\text{put}}_{i-1,j} S_u + (K - e^{-r\Delta t} S_u) K}{v^{\text{put}}_{i-1,j} + K - e^{-r\Delta t} S_u}. \tag{9.2.1}$$

Similarly, we can derive a formula for S_u if we know S_d and the value, $v^{\text{call}}_{i-1,j}$ of node $(i - 1, j)$ with respect to a European call option struck at K

F I G U R E 9.2.2

Fragment of a binomial stock price tree

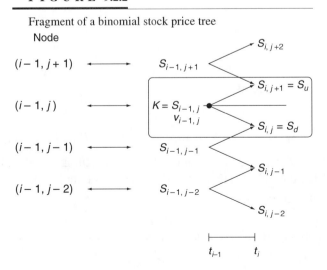

D I S P L A Y   9.2.1

DERIVATION OF EQUATION 9.2.1.

Write $v = v^{\text{put}}_{i-1,j}$. We have

$$v = e^{-r\Delta t}d(K - S_d),$$

where d is the risk-neutral down-transition probability from node $(i-1, j)$ to node (i, j) and $K = S_{i-1,j}$. But in this case,

$$d = \frac{S_u - e^{r\Delta t}K}{S_u - S_d},$$

and therefore we have

$$v(S_u - S_d) = (e^{-r\Delta t}S_u - K)(K - S_d).$$

Solving for S_d, we obtain:

$$S_d = \frac{vS_u + (K - e^{-r\Delta t}S_u)K}{v + K - e^{-r\Delta t}S_u}.$$

and expiring at time t_{i-1}. That equation is

$$S_u = \frac{v^{\text{call}}_{i-1,j}S_d + (e^{-r\Delta t}S_d - K)K}{v^{\text{call}}_{i-1,j} + e^{-r\Delta t}S_d - K}. \tag{9.2.2}$$

Moreover, we can derive the values of *both* S_u and S_d (when neither is known) just by knowing the value $v^{\text{put}}_{i-1,j}$. First, we compute the following auxiliary value:

$$u = \frac{v^{\text{put}}_{i-1,j} + K}{e^{-r\Delta t}K - v^{\text{put}}_{i-1,j}}. \tag{9.2.3}$$

Then, we set S_u and S_d according to the desired *centering condition*. Two possible examples are as follows.

- Center at the spot.[4] Set

$$S_u = Ku = S_{i-1,j}u \quad \text{and} \quad S_d = Kd = S_{i-1,j}d, \tag{9.2.4}$$

  where $d = 1/u$. This imitates Cox-Ross-Rubinstein trees, in which the up ratio times the down ratio is equal to one.
- Center at the forward. Set

---

[4]This was the original centering condition of Derman and Kani.

$$S_u = Ku = S_{i-1,j}u \quad \text{and} \quad S_d = (Ke^{r\Delta t})/u = (S_{i-1,j}e^{r\Delta t})/u.$$

$$(9.2.5)$$

This generalizes standard binomial trees centered at the forward.
There are many other possible centering conditions.

All of the above formulas are derived in the same spirit as equation (9.2.1).

Comments
So what have we accomplished? Referring to Figure 9.2.2, we see that there are three possibilities:

1. S_u is known, and we want to find the value of S_d.
2. S_d is known, and we want to find the value of S_u.
3. Neither S_u nor S_d is known, and we want to find both values.

Given these possibilities, we have to correspondingly do one of the following: 1) use equation (9.2.1) to compute the value of S_d, 2) use equation (9.2.2) to compute the value of S_u, or 3) use equation (9.2.3) to compute the value of u, and then use either equation (9.2.4) or equation (9.2.5) to compute the values of both S_u and S_d. To accomplish this, we next need to do, respectively, one of the following three things: 1) find the value of $v^{put}_{i-1,j}$, 2) find the value of $v^{call}_{i-1,j}$, or 3) find the value of $v^{put}_{i-1,j}$.

If we know the values of a European put or European call struck at K and expiring at time t_i, then we can give formulas for $v^{put}_{i-1,j}$ and $v^{call}_{i-1,j}$. We will explain this in a moment, but first we mention what happens when the input option is American.

Suppose we know the values respectively of an American put or an American call struck at K and expiring at time t_i. Then we can determine the necessary values of $v^{put}_{i-1,j}$ and $v^{call}_{i-1,j}$, but not by formulas. Instead, we determine the values by a simple iterative procedure. This will be discussed in the next section; right now, we discuss the case where the input options are European.

Finding the Values $v^{put}_{i-1,j}$ and $v^{call}_{i-1,j}$
We now give formulas for computing the values $v^{put}_{i-1,j}$ and $v^{call}_{i-1,j}$. To do this is simple, but we need some notation:

$$r = \text{the risk-free rate from time } t_i - 1 \text{ to time } t_i$$
$$D_i = \text{dividend payment with ex-dividend date } t_i$$

$$\lambda_{i-1,m} = \text{the Arrow-Debreu price of node } (i - 1, m)$$

$$P_{eu}(t_i, K) = \text{the market price of a European put option expiring}$$
$$\text{at time } t_i \text{ and struck at } K$$

$$C_{eu}(t_i, K) = \text{the market price of a European call option expiring}$$
$$\text{at time } t_i \text{ and struck at } K$$

First we compute the value of $v^{\text{put}}_{i-1,j}$ from the price of $P_{eu}(t_i, K)$. We start by writing the value of $P_{eu}(t_i, K)$ in terms of its payouts at time t_{i-1}. To do this, note that for any node above $(i - 1, j)$, that is, any node $(i - 1, k)$, $k > j$, the option cannot expire in the money, and therefore in this case, $v^{\text{put}}_{i-1,k} = 0$. On the other hand, for a node $(i - 1, k)$, $k < j$, we have from the put option payouts,

$$v^{\text{put}}_{i-1,k} = e^{-r\Delta t}\big(p(K - S_{i,k+1}) + (1 - p)(K - S_{i,k})\big), \qquad k < j, \quad (9.2.6)$$

where p is the risk-neutral up-transition probability from node $(i - 1, k)$ to $(i, k + 1)$. We use the one-period forward equation "with dividends,"

$$pS_{i-1,k+1} + (1 - p)S_{i-1,k} = e^{r\Delta t}S_{i-1,k} - D_i$$

to simplify equation (9.2.6) to

$$v^{\text{put}}_{i-1,k} = e^{-r\Delta t}K - S_{i-1,k} + e^{-r\Delta t}D_i, \qquad k < j. \quad (9.2.7)$$

Note that this new equation contains only known (that is, already computed) values.

The no-arbitrage value of any European option at any time is the sum over all nodes at that time of the payouts at each node times the Arrow-Debreu price of the node. Therefore, from equation (9.2.7) we may compute using equation (9.2.7)

$$P_{eu}(t_i, K) = \sum_{k=0}^{j} \lambda_{i-1,k}v^{\text{put}}_{i-1,k}$$

$$= \sum_{k=0}^{j-1} \lambda_{i-1,k}(e^{-r\Delta t}K - S_{i-1,k} + e^{-r\Delta t}D_i) + \lambda_{i-1,j}v^{\text{put}}_{i-1,j}.$$

Therefore, we have:

$$P_{eu}(t_i, K) = \Sigma + \lambda_{i-1,j}v^{\text{put}}_{i-1,j},$$

$$\Sigma = \sum_{k=0}^{j-1} \lambda_{i-1,k}(e^{-r\Delta t}K - S_{i-1,k} + e^{-r\Delta t}D_i).$$

Note that all of the values in the term Σ are known. Therefore, we may solve for $v^{\text{put}}_{i-1,j}$ and obtain:

$$v_{i-1,j}^{\text{put}} = \frac{P_{eu}(t_i, K) - \Sigma}{\lambda_{i-1,j}}. \tag{9.2.8}$$

In a similar manner, we derive

$$v_{i-1,j}^{\text{call}} = \frac{C_{eu}(t_i, K) - \Sigma}{\lambda_{i-1,j}},$$

$$\Sigma = \sum_{k=j+1}^{i} \lambda_{i-1,k}(S_{i-1,k} - e^{-r\Delta t}D_i - e^{-r\Delta t}K). \tag{9.2.9}$$

Keep in mind through all of this that $K = S_{i-1,j}$.

In summary, we have:

- To compute the value of S_d knowing the value of $P_{eu}(t_{i-1}, K)$ and S_u, we first compute the value of $v_{i-1,j}^{\text{put}}$ using equation (9.2.8), and then we compute the value of S_d using equation (9.2.1).
- To compute the value of S_u knowing the value of $C_{eu}(t_{i-1}, K)$ and S_d, we first compute the value of $v_{i-1,j}^{\text{call}}$ using equation (9.2.9), and then we compute the value of S_u using equation (9.2.2).
- To compute the value of S_u and S_d knowing only the value of $P_{eu}(t_{i-1}, K)$, we first compute the value of $v_{i-1,j}^{\text{put}}$ using equation (9.2.9). Next, we compute the value of u using equation (9.2.3). Finally, we compute S_u and S_d using either equation (9.2.4) or (9.2.5).

We have now shown how to derive the value of a given node (i.e., S_u, S_d, or both S_u and S_d) from the value of previously known nodes if the input options are European. But what if the input option values are American or Bermudan? We discuss what to do in this case next.

9.3 BUILDING IMPLIED TREES WITH AMERICAN INPUT OPTIONS

Let's begin by turning our attention back to Figure 9.2.2; assume again that S_u is known and S_d is unknown. This time, however, assume we know the value of an *American* put option, $P_{am}(t_i, K)$, struck at K and expiring at time t_i.

We want to find the value of S_d that makes the tree yield the "correct" price for $P_{am}(t_i, K)$. To do this, we need to make one crucial observation. Start with any option struck at K and expiring at time t_i (that is, the option can be American, European, Bermudan, or anything else). Then, the value of this option at every node at time t_{i-1}, except for node $(i - 1, j)$, is already determined by the tree's values at time t_{i-1}. That is, even though it seems that the value of the option depends on as yet uncomputed stock price nodes, we will be able to use risk-neutrality and information about options in general to compute the value of the option at time t_{i-1} without appealing to node values at time t_i. We will explain this in detail now.

Depending on the nature of the input option (i.e., put or call), the argument changes a little, but the basic idea is the same for all options. We illustrate how the computations work with American put options (on a stock possibly paying dividends) and next with American call options (on a stock possibly paying dividends).

American Puts

Suppose we have $P_{am}(t_i, K)$, an American put option expiring at time t_i and struck at K. Figure 9.3.1 displays the option value tree for this option (left-hand picture), along with the option value tree for the corresponding American call option $C_{am}(t_i, K)$ (right-hand picture), at time steps t_{i-1} and t_i. We claim that the value of every node below node $(i - 1, j)$ (which is the position of K; see Figure 9.3.1) is the intrinsic value of the option and that every node above $(i - 1, j)$ has value equal to zero.

The nodes at time t_{i-1} that are above the strike have value zero because the payout of the put option is zero in both the case when the stock price rises and in the case when it falls.

On the other hand, the option payout at time t_i for nodes below the strike are unknown (due to the fact that the node values are as yet uncomputed). However, it turns out that we do not need to know these values to compute the values at time t_{i-1}. We have already seen (see equation (9.2.7)) that the value of node $(i - 1, k)$ (for $k < j$) for a European put option is given by

$$v_{i-1,k}^{\text{put}} = e^{-r\Delta t}K - S_{i-1,k} + e^{-r\Delta t}D_i.$$

However, since the option is American, the above value is not necessarily the value of the option at node (i, k). The above value has to be compared to the intrinsic value of the option, which is $K - S_{i-1,k}$. We therefore have

$$v_{i-1,k}^{\text{put}} = \max(e^{-r\Delta t}K - S_{i-1,k} + e^{-r\Delta t}D_i, K - S_{i-1,k}). \quad (9.3.1)$$

Note that $v_{i-1,k}^{\text{put}}$ is completely determined by parameters known at time t_{i-1}. In particular, the dividend payments and ex-dividend dates are assumed to be known at the outset. In other words, $v_{i-1,k}^{\text{put}}$ can be computed when $k < j$.

In the special case where $D_i = 0$, that is, when t_i is not an ex-dividend date, the value of holding the option is $e^{-r\Delta t}K - S_{i-1,k}$, while the intrinsic value is $K - S_{i-1,k}$. Therefore, if interest rates are positive, we see the option will always be exercised at nodes below this strike.

F I G U R E 9.3.1

The option value tree for an American put option (left-hand side) and an American call
option (right-hand side) on a non-dividend-paying stock

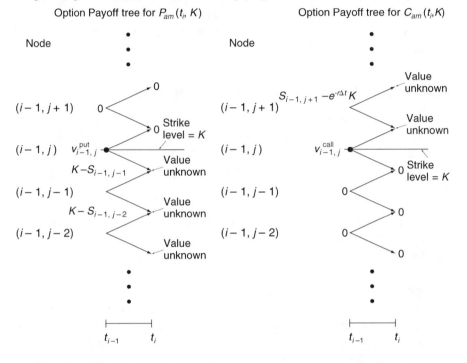

American Calls

The right-hand side of Figure 9.3.1 displays the option value tree for an
American call option struck at K and expiring at time t_i, denoted $C_{am}(t_i, K)$.
It is immediate that the value of each node at time t_{i-1} below the strike is
equal to zero, because the option cannot expire in the money once the spot
price has reached any of these nodes.

Now consider the node $(i - 1, k)$, where $k > j$. When the spot price
is at this node, the value of holding $C_{am}(t_i, K)$ is given by

$$S_{i-1,k} - e^{-r\Delta t} K - e^{-r\Delta t} D_i,$$

where $S_{i-1,k}$ is the value of the stock at node $(i-1, k)$ and D_i is the dividend
payment with ex-dividend date t_i.

The intrinsic value of the option, on the other hand, is $S_{i-1,k} - K$.
Therefore, the value of the option at node $(i - 1, k)$, $v^{call}_{i-1,k}$, is the greater of
the two values; that is,

$$v_{i-1,k}^{call} = \max(S_{i-1,k} - e^{-r\Delta t}K - e^{-r\Delta t}D_i, S_{i-1,k} - K). \quad (9.3.2)$$

Observe that this value is completely determined by values that are known at time t_{i-1}. This is true because, in particular, we assume that we know all of the dividend payments at the outset of building the tree.

In the special case where $D_i = 0$, we see that the intrinsic value is always less than the value of holding.

How to Build the Tree for American Options

We are now in a position to explain how we build up the entire tree when the input options are American. We illustrate the method for American put options, using Figure 9.3.1 as a reference point. Here is the setup:

1. We know the market price, P, of the American put $P_{am}(t_i, K)$.
2. All stock price nodes at time t_{i-1} have been computed.

With this information, we want to find the value of $v_{i-1,j}^{put}$ that makes the tree value $P_{am}(t_i, K)$ correctly. Specifically, this means that the tree, when used to price $P_{am}(t_i, K)$, should yield a value for $P_{am}(t_i, K)$ equal to P. Here is how we do it.

Recall that we showed that the only node in the option value tree for $P_{am}(t_i, K)$ at time t_{i-1} for which we do not know a value is node $(i-1, j)$, all other nodes can be computed. Therefore, if we assign any value to this one remaining node, then all of the nodes in the option value tree at time t_{i-1} have a value. Now we can use the tree, starting at time t_{i-1}, to perform backward induction for the option $P_{am}(t_{i-1}, K)$ to obtain a value for the option (a value based on the tree at hand). This value may or may not be equal to the "correct" value, P. However, it is enough information to go back and modify the original guess for the value of node $(i-1, j)$ and, in this way, iteratively solve for the correct node value.

In this, we may obtain an *iterative procedure* that allows us to zero in on the correct value for $v_{i-1,j}^{put}$, much as we use the Newton-Raphson method for finding Black-Scholes implied volatility.

Criteria for a Good Iterative Method

There may be more than one "good" iterative procedure for determining the value of $v_{i-1,j}^{put}$. In the next section, we will give a procedure that works well in applications. The procedure we use was chosen to have the following features:

1. It is fast; that is, it *converges* to the correct value in as few calculations as possible.

2. It is easy to implement.

3. It is foolproof; that is, it does not "blow up" or give wrong answers.

In Chapter 9, we gave two different iterative methods for finding implied volatility: the method of bisections and the Newton-Raphson method. The former method is too slow for our purposes (in practice it will take some 20 backward inductions to converge to a reasonable value). The latter method is not applicable in the situation, as the function relating the value of node $(i - 1, j - 1)$ to the value of $P_{am}(t_{i-1}, K)$ does not meet the criteria for the Newton-Raphson method.[5] Fortunately, there is an excellent method applicable in this situation, called the *false position method*. We discuss this now.

9.4 THE FALSE POSITION METHOD

The false position method is an iterative method to finding solutions to equations. The technique exploits the specific nature of the functional relationship between the node value $v_{i-1,j}^{\text{put}}$ and the value of $P_{am}(t_i, K)$ to obtain an iterative method that converges extremely quickly to the correct value of $v_{i-1,j}^{\text{put}}$. A reference for the false position method is Press, Teukolsky, Vetterling, and Flannery (1992).

Let's discuss the relationship between $v_{i-1,j}^{\text{put}}$ and the value of the option implied by the tree. First of all, we would like to be able to give a precise formula for $v_{i-1,j}^{\text{put}}$ in terms of the tree nodes. We cannot, however, because we do not know which nodes are early exercise nodes and which are not. Despite this, we can observe that the function relating $v_{i-1,j}^{\text{put}}$ to the value of an American put $P_{am}(t_i, K)$ is piecewise linear in $v_{i-1,j}^{\text{put}}$. In particular, the function is *not* differentiable at all points. On the other hand, its highly linear nature makes it an obvious candidate for the false position method. We describe it now.

The False Position Method

Let's get our bearings straight. We are in the situation of Figure 9.2.2. We have a market price, P, for the option $P_{am}(t_i, K)$, and we wish to determine the value, $v = v_{i-1,j}^{\text{put}}$, of node $(i - 1, j)$ that makes the "tree price" of $P_{am}(t_i, K)$ equal to the market price P. Moreover, given any value of v, we can perform backward induction to obtain the tree value of $P_{am}(t_i, K)$.

---

[5]In particular, the function is not differentiable; it is piecewise linear and therefore has a finite number of "corners."

Call this "tree value" $\pi(v)$. The problem of determining the correct value for v is now that of solving the equation:

$$\pi(v) - P = 0.$$

Let's write $P(v) = \pi(v) - P$, so that now we need to solve the equation $P(v) = 0$.

In order to implement the false position method, we need two initial guesses, v_0 and v_1, for the value of v. Moreover, we require that $P(v_0)$ is greater than P, and $P(v_1)$ is less than P; that is

$$P(v_1) < P < P(v_0).$$

Fortunately, these values are easy to supply. For v_0, we use equation (9.2.8) replacing $P_{eu}(t_i, K)$ with P; that is, we set

$$v_0 = \frac{P - \Sigma}{\lambda_{i-1, j}},$$

where Σ is described in equation (9.2.9). This is the correct value for v assuming $P_{am}(t_i, K)$ is European. As it is American, the tree will assign a premium to the option, and v_0 will be greater than the correct value of v. Conversely, we choose $v_1 = 0$. Since it is clear that $\pi(v)$ decreases when v decreases (that is, the greater the value of node $(i - 1, j)$ in the option value tree, the greater the option value), this is the obvious choice. We note that the method converges so quickly that it is not essential to make a very good guess for v_1.

Once the values v_0 and v_1 are computed, the next step is to compute a value v_2 as a "next guess" for the correct value of node $(i-1, j)$. Where does the value of v_2 come from? It is equal to the value where the line connecting $(v_1, P(v_1))$ and $(v_0, P(v_0))$ is zero, for which we will give a formula

$$v_2 = \frac{v_1 m + P(v_1)}{m}, \qquad m = \frac{P(v_1) - P(v_0)}{v_1 - v_0}.$$

Once we have determined v_2, we determine $P(v_2)$.

There are three possibilities for $P(v_2)$: It is either greater, less than, or equal to zero. If it is equal to zero, or rather, close enough to zero to satisfy us, we quit and set $v = v_2$. This is because all along our goal has been to compute the value of v such that $P(v) = 0$.

If $P(v)$ is not sufficiently close to zero, we seek a next trial, v_3, for the value of v.

To do this, we select from $P(v_0)$ and $P(v_1)$ the one that has the *opposite* sign as $P(v_2)$. Suppose this is $P(v_0)$. Then, we form the line connecting

$(v_0, P(v_0))$ and $(v_2, P(v_2))$. We write v_3 for the place where this is equal to zero, using the formula:

$$v_3 = \frac{v_2 m + P(v_2)}{m}, \qquad m = \frac{P(v_2) - P(v_0)}{v_2 - v_0}.$$

We then repeat the previous steps until we obtain a guess v_n such that $P(v_n)$ is sufficiently close to zero. Figure 9.4.1 gives a picture of this.

That concludes our discussion of the false position method. We now proceed to a discussion of the computation of Arrow-Debreu prices and some of the possible problems that occur when building implied trees.

9.5   ARROW-DEBREU PRICES AND BAD PROBABILITIES

Once we have computed all of the nodes at time t_i, we want to move on and compute the nodes at time t_{i+1}. To do this, we have to compute all of the Arrow-Debreu prices at time t_i. We do this using the techniques developed in Section 6.11 in Chapter 6.

In order to use those methods, we have to compute the transition probabilities from time t_{i-1} to time t_i. Let $p_{i-1,k}$ denote the up-transition probability from node $(i-1, k)$ to node $(i, k+1)$. Then, we have the formula

$$p_{i-1,k} = \frac{e^{r_i \Delta t} S_{i-1,k} - D_i - S_{i,k}}{S_{i,k+1} - S_{i,k}}, \qquad (9.5.1)$$

which follows immediately from the one-period forward equation "with dividends."

F I G U R E   9.4.1

The false position method

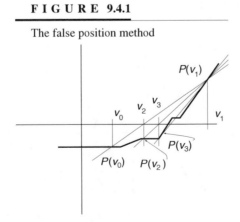

The Problem of Bad Probabilities

The above equation immediately suggests a potential problem. What if the transition probability computed from equation (9.5.1) is not between zero and one? After all, nothing guarantees that it will be. We see, for example, that if the forward price is less than $S_{i,k}$, the up-transition probability will be negative. We call a transition probability that is not between zero and one a *bad probability*. We now discuss where they come from and what to do about them.

What to Do about Bad Probabilities

When bad probabilities occur, something must be done to eliminate them. If we simply ignore them, then when we use the tree to value options, the corresponding values will be completely wrong. For example, a tree with negative probabilities will yield at least some negative option prices.

Suppose we compute the value of a node and the transition probability to that node is "bad;" that is, it is either greater than one or less than zero. We then have to replace the value of the node with a value that makes the corresponding transition probability "good." Naturally, there are many possible choices, so some additional criteria have to be introduced to help reduce the possible choices. A natural condition is to choose the node so that the local volatility structure of the tree remains as smooth as possible. We explain this in detail.

Figure 9.5.1 displays the situation we wish to resolve. There are two scenarios: either we are below the center of the tree and are computing the node below the last node we computed, or, conversely, we are above

F I G U R E   9.5.1

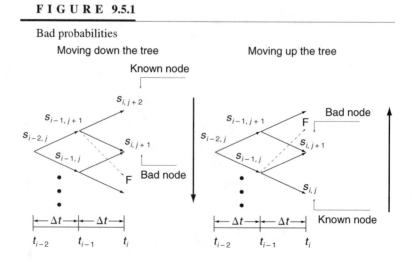

Bad probabilities

the center of the tree and are computing the node above the last node we computed.

In either case, node $(i, j + 1)$ is bad, and we want to change its value. For the left-hand figure, we know this because we have determined the forward price of node $(i - 1, j)$ lies above the price of node $(i, j + 1)$. In other words, the value of node $S_{i, j+1}$ that satisfies the implied tree equations is not high enough to make economic sense. In terms of an equation, we have:

$$e^{r\Delta t} S_{i-1, j} - D_i > S_{i, j+1},$$

where D_i is the dividend payment at time t_i. We say this is a *violation of the forward condition*. In the case of the right-hand figure, the forward condition is violated for the same reason. The value of node $S_{i, j+1}$ lies below the forward value of node $S_{i-1, j}$.

We have to change the value of node $(i, j + 1)$ so that the forward condition is not violated; that is, we want a new node value $S'_{i, j+1}$ such that

$$e^{r\Delta t} S_{i-1, j} - D_i < S'_{i, j+1}.$$

The problem is, there are many such choices, and we do not know *a priori* which one is the best. There are many possible strategies for dealing with this situation. We suggest one here that, roughly speaking, forces the new node to "smooth out" local volatility.

Replacing Bad Nodes with Good Nodes

The simplest way to correct for bad probabilities is to ensure that the spacing of the new node looks like the spacing of certain prior older nodes. Referring to Figure 9.5.1, we will choose $S'_{i, j+1}$ so that:

1. In the case of the left-hand figure, $S'_{i, j+1}$ and $S_{i, j+2}$ have the same "spacing" as $S_{i-1, j+1}$ and $S_{i-1, j}$.
2. In the case of the right-hand figure, $S'_{i, j+1}$ and $S_{i, j}$ have the same "spacing" as $S_{i-1, j+1}$ and $S_{i-1, j}$.

Why do we care about the spacing? Because of local volatility. Recall the formula for local volatility:

$$\sigma_{loc} = \frac{1}{\sqrt{\Delta t}} \sqrt{p \cdot (1 - p)} \cdot \log(S_u / S_d),$$

where S_u is an up node, S_d is a down node, Δt is the length of the time step, and p is the up-transition probability. The formula tells us that volatility is essentially controlled by the ratio of the up node to the down node. This is what we mean by the spacing between the nodes [this is called the "logarithmic spacing" by Derman and Kani (1994a)]. What we want to do is change the value of the bad node to something that preserves the logarithmic spacing of the tree.

A Formula for $S'_{i,j+1}$

Using the spacing criterion, we can now require that the logarithmic spacing between the nodes be the same as that of the closest node in the previous time step. We regard this as the most satisfactory solution; however, it does not always work.

Sometimes, we apply this procedure and we still get a bad node. In this case, we have to go to a (less desirable) second solution. We give this solution below, as an alternative to the solution involving spacing, to be used only after the first solution fails. We list the two solutions in detail here, referring to Figure 9.5.1.

1. In the case of moving down the tree (left-hand picture in Figure 9.5.1), set

$$S'_{i,j+1} = \frac{S_{i,j+2}S_{i-1,j}}{S_{i-1,j+1}}.$$

In the case of moving up the tree (right-hand picture in Figure 9.5.1), set

$$S'_{i,j+1} = \frac{S_{i,j}S_{i-1,j+1}}{S_{i-1,j}}.$$

2. If $S'_{i,j+1}$ is still bad after trying the above solution, that is, if it still lies on the wrong side of the forward, then we have to make a more extreme change. We choose essentially the smallest value for the $S'_{i,j+1}$ that still puts us above the forward. To do this, we choose some small number epsilon (to be determined exogenously by the needs of the situation):

$$S'_{i,j+1} = e^{r\Delta t}S_{i-1,j} - D_i + \epsilon,$$

where ϵ is some small number. This places the value of node $(i, j + 1)$ just a fraction above the forward price, making that node have (almost) as small a volatility as the forward condition will allow.

Example

We now give an example of how to replace a "bad" node with a good node. Figure 9.5.2 displays a situation in which bad probabilities occur. In this figure, the upper left-hand picture is for notational purposes only. We are interested in times t_{i-2}, t_{i-1}, and t_i of an implied volatility tree. In this example, the time step is one year and the risk-free rate is 10 percent.

F I G U R E 9.5.2

How to resolve bad probabilities.
In this figure, the risk-free rate is 10 percent.

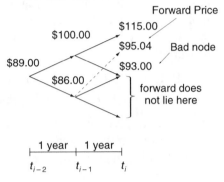

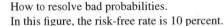

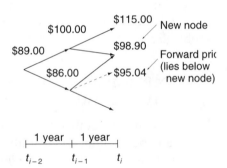

Solution

We choose node $S'_{i,j+1}$ to lie below
the forward price of node $S_{i-1,j}$
and so that node $S_{i-1,j+1}$ has
the same approximate spacing as
node $S_{i-2,j}$:

$$S'_{i,j+1} = \frac{115 \times 86}{100} = 98.90$$

What Happens When We Remove Bad Nodes?

If when building an implied tree we are forced to move nodes around to avoid bad probabilities, then these nodes do not reflect the best possible prices according to market data. Remember: The equation for the price of a given node involves the prices of other nodes, Arrow-Debreu prices, and option prices. If we ignore these equations and substitute "fake" node prices, then we are no longer building a tree directed by the market prices. So, what is the impact of these "fake" node prices?

The answer is that if the data we use as inputs, that is, if our smile, does not produce too many bad node prices, then the impact will not be too great. The reason this is true is that the "impact" of a node price on the total price of an option depends on the Arrow-Debreu price of that node and its payout.

In practice, nodes near the top and bottom of the tree (i.e., away from the forward price) have small Arrow-Debreu prices because few paths lead to them and the probability of traversing a particular path is small. Therefore, the probability of reaching such nodes is small. As a consequence these nodes do not contribute significantly to the total price of the option. In other words, a few bad probabilities do not spoil the tree.

In practice, when building an implied tree, one can do two things to measure the accuracy of an implied volatility tree:

1. Keep track of the number of bad probabilities.
2. Use the tree to price the input options.

The first item gives an idea of what occurred when building the tree. The more bad probabilities, the worse, in general, the tree will do. However, it is difficult to measure the extent of the impact of bad probabilities on the tree. Therefore, once the tree is completed, we use it to price all the input options that were used to create the tree. Comparing the "implied prices," the prices our final tree gives, to the "market prices" gives a feel for how well the tree does. The better the fit, the less the impact of bad probabilities.

9.6 IMPLEMENTING A SYSTEM FOR BUILDING IMPLIED TREES

In this section, we outline how to build a system that takes input options prices and builds implied volatility trees. This system will be able to handle both European and American input options. As this section is intended for those who wish to actually implement the system, we have arranged the notation accordingly. In the next section, we will give several sample computations demonstrating the technique.

We begin by explaining the necessary ingredients of the system.

The Setup

We will take as given the following input data:

1. An underlying stock or index, S, with a fixed spot price for today's date, denoted S_0.
2. A set of "input" options on S. Each option should be identified as a call or a put and as American or European, and its current market price should be recorded.

The system needs the following components:

1. A stock price tree (to be filled in).
2. An Arrow-Debreu price tree (to be filled in).
3. An interpolation method for producing option prices not available in the market. Namely, given the data "time," "strike," and "style," we should be able to produce a price for a "style" style option, expiring at time "time" and struck at "strike."
4. A "subroutine" for performing the false position method (American input options only).

The system will fill in the stock price tree and the Arrow-Debreu prices so that any option priced on this tree will price all input options correctly.

Notation
We will use the following notation in this section.

$$
\begin{aligned}
t_0, t_1, \ldots, t_n &= \text{dates of the tree nodes} \\
r_i &= \text{the forward interest rate applying from time } t_{i-1} \\
&\quad \text{to } t_i \\
D_i &= \text{dividend payment for ex-dividend date } t_i \\
S_{i,j} &= \text{stock price value of node } (i,j) \\
\lambda_{i,j} &= \text{Arrow-Debreu price of node } (i,j) \\
P_{eu}(t_i, K) &= \text{market price of a European put option on } S \\
&\quad \text{struck at } K \text{ and expiring at time } t_i \\
C_{eu}(t_i, K) &= \text{market price of a European call option on } S \\
&\quad \text{struck at } K \text{ and expiring at time } t_i \\
P_{am}(t_i, K) &= \text{market price of an American put option on } S \\
&\quad \text{struck at } K \text{ and expiring at time } t_i \\
C_{am}(t_i, K) &= \text{market price of an American call option on } S \\
&\quad \text{struck at } K \text{ and expiring at time } t_i \\
v^{put}_{i-1,j} &= \text{value of } P_*(t_i, S_{i-1,j}) \text{ at node } (i-1, j) \\
v^{call}_{i-1,j} &= \text{value of } C_*(t_i, S_{i-1,j}) \text{ at node } (i-1, j)
\end{aligned}
$$

Notice that we have not specified whether $v^{put}_{i-1,j}$ and $v^{call}_{i-1,j}$ refer to American or European options. The notation $P_*(t_i, K)$ (respectively, $C_*(t_i, K)$) means a put option (respectively, a call option) of American or European style, struck at K and with expiry t_i. Not specifying the style of the option is a matter of convenience only. It will always be clear from the context what we mean, so rather than cluttering the notation with additional decorations (e.g., $^{am}v^{call}_{i-1,j}$), we have stuck to the simpler way of viewing things.

Filling in the Tree

Filling in the stock price tree proceeds in several steps. This section explains these steps and, in the process, summarizes the results of the previous sections. We start by assuming that we have computed all time steps through time step t_{i-1}. This is possible, of course, because we know the value of the nodes at time t_0: There is only one, the spot price. Thus, we take as our starting point that we wish to compute the nodes at time t_i. We now proceed in the following steps.

Step 1—Starting the Time Step

We are at time step t_i and no nodes are known, so how do we start? We start in one of two ways, depending on whether the number of nodes in the time step is even or odd.

When the Number of Nodes in the Time Step Is Odd

If the number of nodes in the time step is odd, then there is a middle node in that time step, and we can simply declare the value of this node to be the spot price of the underlying. This builds a tree that looks like a Cox-Ross-Rubinstein tree, where all the middle nodes are equal to the spot price (see, for example, Figure 6.2.1). Note that if we are centering at the forward, we set the middle node to the forward value of the spot price at that time.

Let's examine this numerically, using the standard numbering system of the nodes in Figure 6.7.1. Notice that in this figure, time steps with an odd number of nodes are even-numbered time steps (e.g., time step 4 has 5 nodes), and if the time step is t_i, then the middle node is $(i, i/2)$. We have

- If we are centering at the spot set

$$S_{i,i/2} = S_0. \tag{9.6.1}$$

- If we are centering at the forward set

$$S_{i,i/2} = S_0 e^{ri\Delta t}. \tag{9.6.2}$$

When the Number of Nodes Is Even

If the number of nodes is even, the time step itself is odd, and we need to compute the values of nodes $(i,(i + 1)/2)$ and $(i,(i - 1)/2)$.

STEP (I). Compute the value of $v_{i-1,i/2}^{\text{put}}$. To do this, we find via interpolation the value of a put option struck at $S_{i-1,i/2}$ and expiring at time t_i. This is $P_{eu}(t_i, S_{i-1,i/2})$. There are obviously two cases: Case A, the input option is European, and Case B, the input option is American.

CASE A. The input option is European, so we use equation (9.2.8) to compute the value $v_{i-1,i}^{\text{put}}$. We reproduce it here for convenience:

$$v_{i-1,i/2}^{\text{put}} = \frac{P_{eu}(t_i,S_{i-1,i/2}) - \Sigma}{\lambda_{i-1,i/2}},$$

$$\Sigma = \sum_{k=0}^{i/2-1} \lambda_{i-1,k}(e^{-r_i \Delta t}S_{i-1,i/2} - S_{i-1,k} + e^{-r_i \Delta t}D_i).$$

(9.6.3)

CASE B. In this case, since the input option is American, we have to use the false position method. To start the false position method, we need two guesses, v_0 and v_1. Recall we set

$$v_0 = \frac{P_{am}(t_i, S_{i-1,i/2}) - \Sigma}{\lambda_{i-1,i/2}},$$

$$\Sigma = \sum_{k=0}^{i/2-1} \lambda_{i-1,k}(e^{-r_i \Delta t}S_{i-1,i/2} - S_{i-1,k} + e^{-r_i \Delta t}D_i).$$

and $v_1 = 0$. Once we have these values, we proceed with the false position method iteratively as described above. We continue until we obtain a value for $v_{i-1,i/2}^{\text{put}}$ that yields a tree-implied value of an American put struck at $S_{i-1,i/2}$ and expiring at time t_i that is within 0.005 of $P_{am}(t_i, S_{i-1,i/2})$.[6]

STEP (II). If we have completed STEP (I), then we have a value for $v_{i-1,i/2}^{\text{put}}$. Given this, proceed by applying equation (9.2.3), which in this case means we set

$$u = \frac{v_{i-1,i/2}^{\text{put}} + S_{i-1,i/2}}{e^{-r_i \Delta t}S_{i-1,i/2} - v_{i-1,i/2}^{\text{put}}}$$

(9.6.4)

and compute $S_{i,(i+1)/2}$ according to chosen centering condition. We have:

- For centering at the spot price, we set:

$$S_{i,(i+1)/2} = S_{i-1,i/2}u, \quad \text{and} \quad S_{i,(i-1)/2} = S_{i-1,i/2}/u. \quad (9.6.5)$$

- For centering at the forward, we set:

$$S_{i,(i+1)/2} = S_{i-1,i/2}u \quad \text{and} \quad S_{i,(i-1)/2} = (S_{i-1,i/2}e^{r_i \Delta t})/u. \quad (9.6.6)$$

STEP (III). Now, we compute the up-transition probability, $p_{i-1,i/2}$, from node $(i-1,i/2)$ to node $(i,(i+2)/2)$, using equation (9.5.1).

---

[6]Other values are valid as well. This is a reasonable suggestion, however.

In this case, we compute:

$$p_{i-1,i/2} = \frac{e^{r_i \Delta t} S_{i-1,i/2} - D_i - S_{i,(i-1)/2}}{S_{i,(i+1)/2} - S_{i,(i-1)/2}}. \tag{9.6.7}$$

Step 2—Moving Down the Tree

Continue to assume we are at time step t_i, and suppose we have just computed the value of node $S_{i,j+1}$, where $S_{i,j+1}$ is below the middle of the tree. We now want to compute the value of node $S_{i,j}$, the next node down. We proceed again in two steps.

STEP (I). First we determine the value of $v_{i-1,j}^{put}$. To do this, we first find (via interpolation) the value of a put option struck at $S_{i-1,j}$ and expiring at time t_i. This is $P_{eu}(t_i, S_{i-1,j})$. Again, there are two cases: Case A, the input option is European, and Case B, the input option is American.

CASE A. In this case, the input option is European, and we use our interpolation method to produce a value for $P_{eu}(t_i, S_{i-1,j})$. We apply equation (9.2.8), which in this case reads:

$$v_{i-1,j}^{put} = \frac{P_{eu}(t_i, S_{i-1,j}) - \Sigma}{\lambda_{i-1,j}},$$

$$\Sigma = \sum_{k=0}^{j-1} \lambda_{i-1,k}(e^{-r_i \Delta t} S_{i-1,j} - S_{i-1,k} + e^{-r_i \Delta t} D_i). \tag{9.6.8}$$

CASE B. In this case, the input option is American. First, we use our interpolation method to obtain a value for $P_{am}(t_i, S_{i-1,j})$. Next, we apply the false position method to determine a value for $v_{i-1,j}^{put}$. To do so, we need initial guesses v_0 and v_1. We have:

$$v_0 = \frac{P_{am}(t_i, S_{i-1,j}) - \Sigma}{\lambda_{i-1,j}},$$

$$\Sigma = \sum_{k=0}^{j-1} \lambda_{i-1,k}(e^{-r_i \Delta t} S_{i-1,j} - S_{i-1,k} + e^{-r_i \Delta t} D_i),$$

and $v_1 = 0$. We iterate the false position method until we have a value for $v_{i-1,j}^{put}$ within a tolerance of 0.005.

We now proceed to Step (II).

STEP (II). We now have a value for $v_{i-1,j}^{put}$, and we are ready to compute the value of $S_{i,j}$. For this we use equation (9.2.1), which in this case reads:

$$S_{i,j} = \frac{v_{i-1,j}^{put} S_{i,j+1} + (S_{i-1,j} - e^{-r_i \Delta t} S_{i,j+1}) S_{i-1,j}}{v_{i-1,j}^{put} + S_{i-1,j} - e^{-r_i \Delta t} S_{i,j+1}}. \tag{9.6.9}$$

Once this has been computed, we continue to move down the tree until all of the nodes below the middle node(s) have been filled in.

STEP (III). We now compute the transition probability, $p_{i-1,j}$, from node $(i-1, j)$ to node $(i, j+1)$. We have:

$$p_{i-1,j} = \frac{e^{r_i \Delta t} S_{i-1,j} - D_i - S_{i,j}}{S_{i,j+1} - S_{i,j}}.$$

Step 3—Moving Up the Tree

We continue at time step t_i. Suppose we have just computed the value of node $S_{i,j}$, where $S_{i,j}$ lies above the center of the tree. We now want to compute the value of node $S_{i,j+1}$. Once again we proceed in two steps.

STEP (I). First determine the value of $v_{i-1,j}^{call}$. To do this, we start by finding (via interpolation) the value of a call option struck at $S_{i-1,j}$ and expiring at time t_i. This is $C_{eu}(t_i, S_{i-1,j})$. As usual, there are two cases, Case A, the input option is European, and Case B, the input option is American.

CASE A. In this case, the input option is European, and we use our interpolation method to produce a value for $C_{eu}(t_i, S_{i-1,j})$. We apply equation (9.2.9), which in this case reads:

$$v_{i-1,j}^{call} = \frac{C_{eu}(t_i, S_{i-1,j}) - \Sigma}{\lambda_{i-1,j}},$$

$$\Sigma = \sum_{k=j+1}^{i} \lambda_{i-1,k}(S_{i-1,k} - e^{-r_i \Delta t} D_i - e^{-r_i \Delta t} S_{i-1,j}). \tag{9.6.10}$$

CASE B. In this case, the input option is American. We use our interpolation method to obtain a value for $C_{am}(t_i, S_{i-1,j})$, and we apply the false position method to determine a value for $v_{i-1,j}^{call}$. To do this, we need initial guesses v_0 and v_1. We have:

$$v_0 = \frac{C_{eu}(t_i, S_{i-1,j}) - \Sigma}{\lambda_{i-1,j}},$$

$$\Sigma = \sum_{k=j+1}^{i} \lambda_{i-1,k}(S_{i-1,k} - e^{-r_i \Delta t} S_{i-1,j} - e^{-r_i \Delta t} D_i),$$

and $v_1 = 0$. Now, we iterate the false position method until we obtain a value for $v_{i-1,j}^{call}$ within a tolerance of 0.005.

We now proceed to Step (II).

STEP (II). We now have a value for $v_{i-1,j}^{put}$, and we have to compute the value of $S_{i,j+1}$. For this, we use equation (9.2.2), which in this case reads:

$$S_{i,j+1} = \frac{v_{i-1,j}^{call} S_{i,j} + (e^{-r_i \Delta t} S_{i,j} - S_{i-1,j}) S_{i-1,j}}{v_{i-1,j}^{call} + e^{-r_i \Delta t} S_{i,j} - S_{i-1,j}}. \tag{9.6.11}$$

STEP (III). Compute the transition probability from node $(i - 1, j)$ to $(i, j + 1)$:

$$p_{i-1, j} = \frac{e^{r_i \Delta t} S_{i-1, j} - D_i - S_{i, j}}{S_{i, j+1} - S_{i, j}}.$$

Conclusion

That's all there is to it. After completing the above steps, every node of time t_i will be filled in, and we can proceed to compute Arrow-Debreu prices and move on to time t_{i+1}. Once the entire tree is built, it can be used to price a variety of options with the techniques described in this book.

General Theoretical Remark

We "start" time step t_i by providing one or two node values at the center of the time step. From there, we proceed in two steps. First, we move down the tree, filling in all nodes below the center using market put values. Next, we move up the tree, filling in all nodes above the known nodes using market call values. Why do we use puts below the center and calls above the center?

Nodes below the center will always have values below the spot price or forward price, depending on the centering condition (this is what "below the center" means). Therefore, the put values will correspond to puts struck below the spot price, that is, they will be out-of-the-money puts. Similarly, we will use call values struck above the spot price, out-of-the-money calls, for nodes above the center. Note that we could, in principle, use in-the-money puts above the middle and in-the-money calls below the middle. In fact, put-call parity (at least for European options) guarantees that these values are uniquely determined by the corresponding call and put values. There is, however, one important difference:

In-the-money options are not sensitive to changes in volatility.

Why should this matter? Recall that the whole purpose of building these trees is to capture the market's implied volatility. If we use volatility-insensitive in the money options, it is much harder to accurately do this with available market data.

9.7 SAMPLE IMPLIED VOLATILITY COMPUTATIONS

We now give several examples of how to implement the method for constructing implied trees given in Section 9.6. The two examples involve European input options only. In the first, we give a relatively simple smile, defined by a simple and easily computed formula relating implied volatility to strike price. In the second example, we give a more realistic example, in which the input options are options on the S&P 500. In this case, we define the smile in terms of a two-by-two table of implied volatilities arranged according to strike and expiration. We use bilinear interpolation to interpolate the option prices.

Example 1—Simple Smile

We begin with a simple example involving a simple formula for the smile. Here is the setup of our initial data:

$$r = 5\%$$
$$S_0 = 100$$
$$\Delta t = 1 \text{ year}$$
$$t_0 = \text{current time}$$

That is, we assume that the risk-free rate of interest is 5 percent (*per annum*), the current spot price of the underlying is $100, and the time step of the implied tree is one year. Therefore, t_1 represents one year from now, t_2, two years from now, etc. Moreover, we assume the underlying pays no income.

The Smile

We define the smile in terms of implied volatility by giving a formula relating strike price to implied volatility. We assume that the smile is *time independent*, that is, options of the same strike but different expirations have the same implied volatility.

$$\sigma_{imp} = -K/20 + 20 \quad \text{if } K \leq 110$$
$$\sigma_{imp} = -K/10 + 25.5 \quad \text{if } K \geq 110.$$

Here, K denotes strike price and σ_{imp} denotes Black-Scholes implied volatility. That is, the Black-Scholes implied volatility is given by the first formula for strikes less than $110, and by the second for strikes greater than $110. For instance, in this example, an option struck at $100 of *any* expiration has an implied volatility of 15 percent, while any option struck at $120 has a Black-Scholes implied volatility of 13.5 percent. A graph of this "smile" is given in Figure 9.7.1.

We now proceed step-by-step, following the procedure outlined in Section 9.6, computing the values of the nodes at each time step. We note here that in this example we center the tree at the spot.

F I G U R E 9.7.1

Graph of the volatility smile for
Example 1
Notice that the graph is kinked at
$K = \$110$.

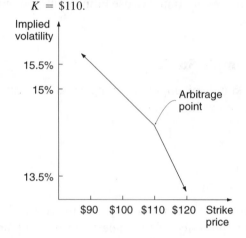

The Nodes at Time t_1

There are only two nodes at this time step: $S_{1,0}$ and $S_{1,1}$. In the notation of Section 9.6, $i = 1$. We have

$$S_{0,0} = 100.00,$$

and we will need to know

$$\lambda_{0,0} \quad \text{and} \quad P_{eu}(t_1, 100.00).$$

Of course, $\lambda_{0,0} = 1.00$ since the probability of being at node $(0, 0)$ is 100 percent. To compute $P_{eu}(t_1, 100)$, we first have to compute the corresponding implied volatility. Since the strike price is less than \$110, we use the first formula for σ_{imp}:

$$\sigma_{imp} = -100/20 + 20 = 15\%.$$

Next, we use a binomial tree to compute the value of $P_{eu}(t_1, 100)$. We obtain $P_{eu}(t_1, 100) = 4.8649$. The tree is a one-period tree, built with a volatility of 15 percent. Note that we have not included any of the computations for the input options. As an alternative method to this example, we could have used the Black-Scholes formula to compute the option value.

Now we use STEP I ("starting the time step") of the tree building process, using the case where the number of nodes is even. We start with STEP (I), CASE A, and compute $v_{0,0}^{\text{put}}$. We now compute, using equation (9.6.3), the value of $v_{0,0}^{put}$. Note the value of Σ in this case is zero. Therefore, we have

$$v_{0,0}^{put} = \frac{P_{eu}(t_1, 100)}{1.00} = 4.8649.$$

This makes sense: $v_{0,0}^{put}$ is the value of $P_{eu}(t_1, 100)$. Next, we set

$$u = \frac{4.8649 + 100}{e^{-0.05}100 - 4.8649} = 1.161834.$$

We center the tree at the spot, so we compute using equation (9.2.4)

$$S_{1,1} = 100 \cdot 1.161834 = 116.1834$$
$$S_{1,0} = 100/1.161834 = 86.0708$$

Having computed the stock prices, we now need to compute the Arrow-Debreu prices $\lambda_{1,1}$ and $\lambda_{1,0}$. We do this by first computing the up- and down-transition probabilities from node $(0, 0)$ to, respectively, nodes $(1, 1)$ and $(1, 0)$. We do this using equation (9.6.7). Writing p for the up-transition probability, we have

$$p = \frac{e^{0.05}100.00 - 86.0708}{116.1834 - 86.0708} = 0.6328.$$

Discounting this to time t_0, we obtain the Arrow-Debreu prices:

$$\lambda_{1,1} = 0.6020 \quad \text{and} \quad \lambda_{1,0} = 0.3493.$$

This completes the procedure for time t_1. We now move on to time step t_2.

The Nodes at Time Step t_2

We begin by starting the time step. There are three nodes at this time step $[(2, 0), (2, 1), \text{and} (2, 2)]$. Therefore, we set $S_{2,1}$, the middle node, equal to the spot price, and we have:

$$S_{2,1} = 100.$$

Next, we move "down" the tree and compute the value of $S_{2,0}$. First, we have to compute $v_{1,0}^{put}$, using equation (9.6.8). To do this, we have to determine values for $P_{eu}(t_2, S_{1,0}) = P_{eu}(t_2, 86.0708)$ and Σ. First of all, $\Sigma = 0$ because there are no nodes below node $(1, 0)$.

The implied volatility for $P_{eu}(t_2, 86.0708)$ is given by the formula

$$-86.0708/20 + 20 = 15.70.$$

Using this, we compute

$$P_{eu}(t_2, 86.0708) = 1.6693.$$

With this, we compute $v_{1,0}^{put}$ using equation (9.6.8):

$$v_{1,0}^{put} = \frac{P_{eu}(t_2, 86.0708)}{\lambda_{1,0}} = \frac{1.6693}{0.3493} = 4.7794.$$

With this in hand, we use equation (9.6.9) to compute the value of $S_{2,0}$. We have

$$S_{2,0} = \frac{4.7794 \cdot 100.00 + (86.0708 - e^{-0.05}100.00)86.0708}{4.7794 + 86.0708 - e^{-0.05}100.00} = 70.4897.$$

Next, we move "up" the tree and compute the value of $S_{2,2}$. First, we compute $v_{1,1}^{call}$, using equation (9.6.10). To compute this, we need to compute $C_{eu}(t_2, 116.1834)$. Its implied volatility is given by the formula:

$$\sigma_{imp} = -116.1834/10 + 25.5 = 13.88\%.$$

With this, we obtain

$$C_{eu}(t_2, 116.1834) = 6.0361.$$

To apply equation (9.6.10), we first note that $\Sigma = 0$ because there are no nodes above node (1, 1). Applying equation (9.6.10), we obtain:

$$v_{1,1}^{call} = \frac{C_{eu}(t_2, 116.1834)}{0.6020} = \frac{6.0361}{0.6020} = 10.0267.$$

With this value in hand, we apply equation (9.6.11) to obtain the value of $S_{2,2}$. We compute:

$$S_{2,2} = \frac{10.0267 \cdot 100 + (e^{-0.05}100 - 116.1834)116.1834}{10.0267 + e^{-0.05}100 - 116.1834} = 130.89.$$

Completing the Tree
We continue the above procedure until we have computed a five-period tree. Figure 9.7.2 displays the resulting stock price tree and Arrow-Debreu price tree.

Implied Distributions
We can use the data from the implied tree (Figure 9.7.2) to deduce the *implied distribution* of the underlying stock. What is this?

In our study of stock models and the Black-Scholes model, we saw that the distribution of stock prices and stock returns is at the heart of option pricing; moreover, we saw in Chapter 6 Section 6.12 that the distribution

F I G U R E 9.7.2

Completed stock price tree and Arrow-Debreu tree for the volatility smile in Figure 9.7.1

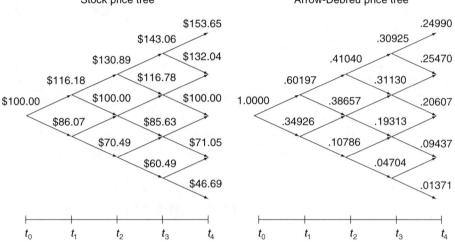

Stock price tree   Arrow-Debreu price tree

F I G U R E 9.7.3

Returns from an implied volatility tree versus returns from a standard binomial tree

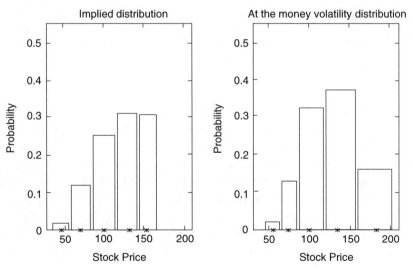

of prices or returns for a given future time (represented by the tree) can be read off of a binomial tree for the stock from the Arrow-Debreu prices and stock price nodes at the given time. When we arrive at a such a distribution from an implied volatility tree, we call the resulting distribution the *implied distribution* of the tree.

Figure 9.7.3 compares the implied distribution from example 1 to the log-normal distribution of prices. More precisely, we compare the implied distribution of a stock whose "smile" is defined by the implied volatility formula at the beginning of this section to a constant volatility stock, using the money implied volatility. In particular, if we use the at-the-money implied volatility of the stock in Figure 9.7.2 to produce a binomial tree of prices, the resulting distribution is displayed in the right-hand graph of Figure 9.7.3.

9.8   HYPOTHETICAL IMPLIED VOLATILITY TREE: THE S&P 500

In the previous sample computation, we used a formula for the volatility smile to obtain option prices. Each time we needed to compute an option price, we computed the implied volatility (of the underlying) via the formula and then computed its price from that volatility. In practice, there are actually a certain number of listed options, and all other option prices have to be interpolated or extrapolated from them. Ordinarily, the option prices are quoted by means of their Black-Scholes implied volatilities and implied volatilies are interpolated. This example demonstrates a procedure along those lines.

The Setup
Table 9.8.1 shows a list of hypothetical Black-Scholes implied volatilities for options on the S&P 500 for September 15, 1995. The displayed values are similar to the real values for that day. We have listed four expiration dates: October 20, 1995, December 15, 1995, March 15, 1996, and June 21, 1996. There are also five strike prices: 625, 595, 575, 540, and 500. Each entry of the table is an implied volatility for a given strike and expiration. We assume a market level (i.e., spot price) of $560.00, and that the risk-free rate of interest is a constant 5 percent. For convenience, we build our model assuming there is no dividend yield.[7] In reality, there are many more

---

[7] In reality we will always have to take into account the dividend payments of the constituent stocks of the S&P 500.

expiration dates and strike prices for options on the S&P 500, but we have restricted ourselves to this subset, again, for convenience only.

We will build a four-period implied volatility tree for the smile in Table 9.8.1, starting September 1, 1995, with each period representing three months, so that the entire tree covers one year.

How We Build the Tree

The procedure we use works as follows. Each time we compute a new node of the implied tree, we will need the price of a particular option; for example, at the first node, we need a December 1 call struck at $560 (this represents a call expiring at the end of the first time period). To obtain this price, we will use the table of implied volatilities (Table 9.8.1) and *bilinear interpolation* to compute the implied volatility of that option. We then compute the price of the option using that volatility.[8]

To compute option prices, we use a constant volatility binomial tree. What this means is, after determining the implied volatility of a particular option, we build a (separate) binomial tree with input volatility equal to the implied volatility of the input option and the number of periods specified by the node of the implied tree we are building. For example, suppose we need the price of a $545 strike call expiring at the end of the second time step. First, we use the table of implied volatilities and bilinear interpolation to obtain an implied volatility for this option. Say the implied volatility is 13.2 percent. We then build a two-step, risk-neutral binomial tree with a 13.2

T A B L E   9.8.1

Hypothetical Black-Scholes implied volatility
for the S&P 500 for September 1, 1995
The risk-free rate is assumed to be 5 percent.

Strike	Expiration			
	10/20/95	12/15/95	3/15/96	6/21/96
625	8.2	9.2	10.8	11.4
595	9.6	10.4	12.0	12.6
575	10.4	11.3	12.9	13.6
540	12.0	13.9	14.9	15.1
500	18.5	17.5	17.3	17.0

---

[8] See Section 9.10 for a quick tutorial on bilinear interpolation.

percent input volatility (and an input risk-free rate equal to 5 percent).[9] We then use this tree to price the $545 call.

It may seem strange that we use a constant volatility tree in this procedure, but remember: Implied volatilities are only a method for interpolating option prices. The implied volatilities themselves are computed from traded option prices.

Use Black-Scholes in Practice

In practice, when building trees with a large number of periods (e.g., 100), using binomial trees to compute option prices is much too slow, and instead we use the Black-Scholes formula for these computations.

We do not give a step-by-step account of the computation of the implied volatility tree for the hypothetical S&P 500, but rather only give the completed tree. If one is building a system to construct implied volatility trees, these completed trees, along with the data in Table 9.8.1 can be used as a control to check if the code is working properly.

Results

Figure 9.8.1 shows four "binomial trees." The first tree is the completed spot-price-implied binomial tree for the data in Table 9.8.1 computed using the methods described in the previous sections. The second is the completed Arrow-Debreu price tree for the implied tree.

The third tree describes the implied volatilities of the input options used in building the implied tree. Each node of the tree represents the implied volatility of a European put (or call) with strike price corresponding to that node. For example, node (1,0) (that is, the bottom node on December 1, 1995, which reads 12.37 percent) represents the implied volatility of an option struck at $526.69 and expiring on March 1, 1996.

The fourth tree describes the option prices derived from the implied volatilities in the third tree. Whether the option is a put or a call is determined by the position of the option on the tree (as specified by the implied volatility trees model). If it is below the spot, then it is a put; otherwise, it is a call.

Implied Distribution of the S&P 500

Figure 9.8.2 compares the implied distribution of the S&P 500 (from our example) to that of a stock following a four-period tree with constant 11.09

---

[9]In general, we can use any of the methods outlined in Chapter 6 for building risk-neutral trees. It is, however, a good idea to choose one method throughout the process.

F I G U R E 9.8.1

Implied volatility tree for S&P 500 example
The risk-free rate was set at 5 percent, and we assumed no dividend yield.

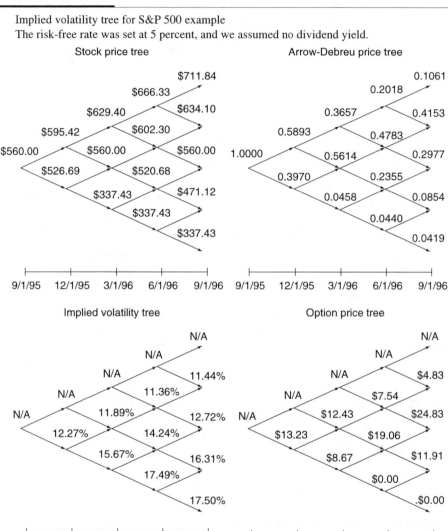

percent volatility (this is the interpolated at-the-money volatility of the hypothetical S&P 500).

Notice that the implied distribution of the S&P 500 is "fat tailed" on the left as compared to the at-the-money volatility distribution. That is, the probability of large price decreases is greater for the implied distribution than for the at-the-money volatility distribution.

F I G U R E 9.8.2

Implied distribution for S&P 500 example, compared with standard binomial tree with 11.09 percent volatility

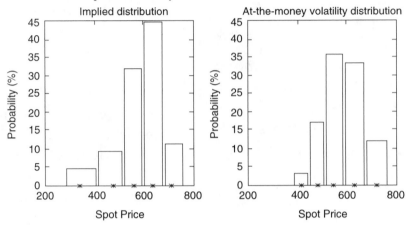

Examining Table 9.8.1, we hypothesize why. Options with low strike prices trade at a higher implied volatility than options with the same expiration at higher strikes. Intuitively, this means the market "thinks" that if market levels drop, options will gain value. This translates into a statement about local volatility: As spot price drops, volatility is expected to rise. Likewise, since options with large strikes trade at lower volatilities, if spot price increases, volatility is expected to drop. Assuming this is true, what does it say about the distribution of stock prices?

Consider what happens when the spot price drops. As it drops, volatility increases. This means that the likelihood of further large changes is greater, and in particular, the probability of lower stock prices increase — hence, a fat left tail.

An opposite logic applies to a rising spot price: the probability of large future price change decreases, and therefore the probability of large future prices decreases as well. This accounts for the skew toward the left in the implied probability distribution compared to the constant volatility distribution.

9.9 THE S&P 500 AND THE VOLATILITY SMILE

In this section, we briefly discuss the effect of the volatility smile on option prices on the S&P 500 index. The results in this section are reproduced from Derman, Kani, and Zou (1995b). The most notable observation is that

T A B L E 9.9.1

Pricing and Hedging in the Presence of the Smile
S&P 500 on 10/23/95, spot = 585, maturity =
9/20/96.

	Strike	BS implied (%)	BS delta	Skew delta
	625	12.44	0.40	0.29
	615	12.78	0.45	0.34
Calls	605	13.15	0.51	0.38
	595	13.57	0.56	0.43
	585	14.03	0.60	0.47
	575	14.52	−0.33	−0.46
	565	15.00	−0.29	−0.42
Puts	555	15.52	−0.26	−0.38
	545	16.02	−0.23	−0.34
	535	16.47	−0.20	−0.30
	525	16.87	−0.17	−0.27

Source: Goldman, Sachs & Co.

"skew deltas" and "skew prices" are much different than Black-Scholes deltas and prices.

Table 9.9.1 displays implied volatilities and delta values for European options on the S&P 500. The numbers were computed on October 23, 1995, when the S&P 500 spot price was 585. The options have an expiration date of September 20, 1996. In each case, the Black-Scholes implied volatility was computed. This volatility was then used to compute the Black-Scholes delta of the option. The delta was also computed in the "presence of the smile," using an implied volatility tree constructed from all available option prices on October 23, 1995.

American put values were also computed and were compared with skew values. "Black-Scholes" prices for American puts on a Cox-Ross-Rubinstein (constant volatility) binomial tree were computed and are compared with American put values computed on the same implied volatility tree used for the European options. Table 9.9.2 summarizes these results.

Here is a summary of the effect of the smile on options:

1. For European call options, the Black-Scholes delta is noticeably larger than the "skew delta," indicating that the Black-Scholes

T A B L E 9.9.2

Standard American (BS) Put Values versus Values "in the
Presence of the Smile"
S&P 500 spot 585, maturity 9/20/96.

Strike	BS price	BS vol (%)	Implied price	Implied vol (%)
625	44.65	12.44	43.49	11.72
605	32.78	13.14	31.78	12.65
585	24.14	14.03	23.36	13.66
565	17.85	15.00	17.37	14.76
545	13.27	16.02	12.99	15.84

Source: Goldman, Sachs & Co.

 formula is telling us to buy too much of the underlying when
hedging S&P 500 calls.

2. For European put options, the Black-Scholes delta is noticeably
   smaller in absolute value than the "skew delta," indicating that
   the Black-Scholes formula is telling us to short too little of the
   underlying in hedging S&P 500 puts.

3. American option "skew" values are significantly below Black-
   Scholes values.

Implied Distributions

Figure 9.9.1 displays the price distributions of the S&P 500 assuming a
Cox-Ross-Rubinstein tree using at-the-money volatility and the implied
probability distribution from market data.

 The implied distribution is noticeably "left fat tailed," indicating that
the market's "view" of the probability of large price decreases differs from
the constant volatility world's view.

What Implied Distributions Mean and Do Not Mean

The implied distribution should not be confused with an actual probability distribution for stock prices. First of all, it is a *risk-neutral* probability
distribution. To understand this, compare it with the distribution we obtain
from a standard binomial tree. Such a distribution is obtained from Arrow-
Debreu prices, which are in turn obtained from transition probabilities. But
these probabilities are themselves risk-neutral. That is, even in a one-step
binomial tree, the transition probabilities represent the probability in a risk-
neutral world of the stock price rising or falling.

F I G U R E 9.9.1

Implied distribution and constant volatility distribution
of S&P 500 stock prices on 10/23/95
Notice the implied distribution is left fat tailed.

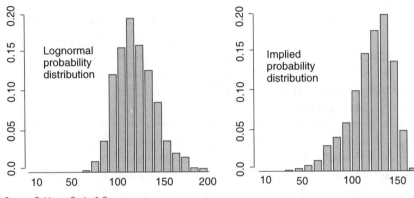

Source: Goldman, Sachs & Co.

Given this, we might ask what the point of implied distributions are. The answer is simple: The shape of the distribution is what matters.

For example, in a normal distribution, the shape is determined solely by the standard deviation (i.e., volatility). The mean of the normal distribution simply determines the position of its peak. Therefore, a risk-neutral normal distribution and another normal distribution with the same standard deviation have exactly the same shape, but they differ in the placement of their peaks. Likewise, we would think of an implied distribution as telling us the shape of the actual stock price distribution, but not the correct expected value.

Therefore, features such as "fat tails" and "leptokurtosis" have actual meaning. For example, the fat left tail in the implied distribution for the S&P 500 means that large price drops are more likely than the geometric Brownian motion model predicts (or at least the market's opinion, expressed through options trading, is such).

Other Empirical Work

The implied volatility trees model is new, and moreover, the idea of an implied theory, that is, a theory that "prices according to the market" is new as well. For this reason, as of the printing of this book, there has not been a lot of empirical work studying implied theories.

When studying implied theories, the main question we are interested in is, Do they improve our ability to hedge options? This is the most interesting sort of research from the practitioner's vantage point. In principle, the studies are easy to do. One simply needs to create simulated hedging using actual market data combined with hedge parameters computed from implied trees. These results should then be compared to hedging using other methods.

One such study was carried out by Dumas, Fleming, and Whaley (1996). In this study, the authors use the Black-Scholes differential equation to estimate a volatility function that prices options according to the market. That is, they find the local volatility function that, when plugged into the differential equation, produces option prices that are as close as possible to the market prices.[10]

The Dumas-Fleming-Whaley method is not precisely the same as the Derman-Kani method (nor is it the same as Rubinstein's method, which is reviewed in the next chapter) as a way to price options and obtain hedge parameters. In fact, the authors propose four models in their paper; they specify the form of the local volatility function in one of the four following ways:

$$\sigma(S, t) = a_0 \quad \text{(Model 0)}$$
$$\sigma(S, t) = a_0 + a_1 S + a_2 S^2 \quad \text{(Model 1)}$$
$$\sigma(S, t) = a_0 + a_1 S + a_2 S^2 + a_3 t + a_5 St \quad \text{(Model 2)}$$
$$\sigma(S, t) = a_0 + a_1 S + a_2 S^2 + a_3 t + a_4 t^2 + a_5 St \quad \text{(Model 3)}$$

Note that Model 0 is a constant volatility model, while Model 1 has volatility that only depends on spot price. One can posit any number of other models in this way as well.

Goodness of Fit
The first test the authors perform is on how well their models "fit" option prices. The authors computed the average root mean squared error between actual option prices and the ones computed from their model for a sample period from June 1988 through December 1993. They also compute the average error outside the bid-ask spread by computing the lesser of the absolute value of the difference between the theoretical price and the bid price of the option and the theoretical price and the ask price of the option.

The basic result is that the more terms in the model, the better the fits that could be achieved, with Model 3 performing slightly better over both types of error. The average error outside the bid-ask spread for all options

---

[10]Specifically, the authors study the generalization of the Black-Scholes differential equation involving a volatility function of time and spot price.

(both put and call) during the sample periods were $-0.034, 0.022, -0.009,$ $-0.011,$ and $-0.010,$ for Models 0, 1, 2, and 3, respectively.

The authors test hedging performance of the model on European options on the S&P 500 index in a sample period from June 1988 through December 1993. The hedging performance is tested by computing what the authors call the "hedging error" for an option position lasting one week. The error is defined as the difference between the one-week change in option price and the one-week change in the option's value as computed by the model. The surprising and contradictory result was that the hedging performance decreased from Model 0 to Model 3. The result is surprising because, intuitively, one would suspect that as the model produced prices closer to the market prices, hedging performance would automatically improve.

The authors offer no clear theoretical explanation for why hedging performance declines as the models grow more complicated. Moreover, they only do their tests on vanilla options and do not examine the hedging of more volatility-sensitive instruments such as barrier options. Clearly, it is important to study these matters further.

9.10 BILINEAR INTERPOLATION OF IMPLIED VOLATILITIES

In this section, we give a primer on bilinear interpolation for application in building implied volatility trees. The starting point for bilinear interpolation is producing a grid of known implied volatilities, called an *interpolation grid*.

The Interpolation Grid
We begin with a fixed underlying asset (e.g., the S&P 500) and a collection of options of various strikes and expirations. We put them into a two-by-two table much like Table 9.8.1.

We imagine this table as a two-by-two grid, which we display in Figure 9.10.1. We call this the *interpolation grid*. In this grid, we see "nodes" that represent strikes and expirations for which we know implied volatilities. The nodes are numbered according to their position in the grid, and we denote the values of the nodes as $v_{t,K}$, which means implied volatility of the node with time t and strike K.

The Unknown Node
Notice that we have displayed a lone node with coordinates (t, K). This is called the *unknown node*. We want to find the implied volatility $v_{t,K}$

FIGURE 9.10.1

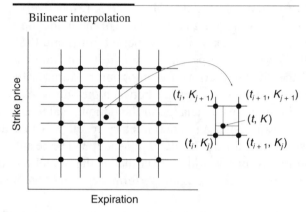

Bilinear interpolation

Strike price

(t_i, K_{j+1}) (t_{i+1}, K_{j+1})

(t, K)

(t_i, K_j) (t_{i+1}, K_j)

Expiration

corresponding to this node. The purpose of interpolation is to provide a value for $v_{t,K}$ based on the available information on the grid. The first step in bilinear interpolation is to find the *grid square* of the node, which is the four points immediately surrounding the unknown node.

The Grid Square
Figure 9.10.1 displays the grid square of the node (t, K) blown up. The grid square is the square of nodes that box in node (t, K). Notice that in the figure, nodes (t_i, K_j), (t_i, K_{j+1}), (t_{i+1}, K_j), and (t_{i+1}, K_{j+1}) form the grid square of node (t, K).

    Once the grid square of the unknown node is determined, we apply a simple formula to determine the value of the unknown node.

The Interpolation Formula
To find the value of $v_{t,K}$, we proceed in two steps. First, we compute

$$a = (t - t_i)/(t_{i+1} - t_i)$$
$$b = (K - K_j)/(K_{j+1} - K_j).$$

Then, the value of the unknown node is given by:

$$v_{t,K} = (1 - a)(1 - b)v_{i,j} + a(1 - b)v_{i+1,j}$$
$$+ abv_{i+1,j+1} + (1 - a)bv_{i,j+1} \qquad (9.10.1)$$

This value represents the bilinear interpolation of the unknown node in terms of the four nodes in its grid square. Figure 9.10.2 displays a graph of what bilinear interpolation looks like. The left-hand figure represents

F I G U R E 9.10.2

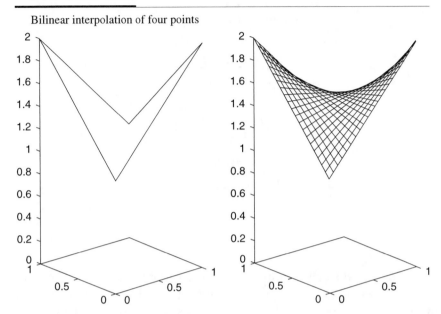

Bilinear interpolation of four points

a single grid square. At the bottom of the graph is the outline of the grid square, and the height of each vertex of the polygon above the grid square represents the value of implied volatility at the corresponding point of the grid square. In this context, the interpolation problem is to "fill in" the empty space above the grid square using the bilinear interpolation formula. The right-hand graph is a picture of just this.

Sample Computation

We now use Table 9.8.1 (page 397) to make a sample computation. That is, we will make a computation from our implied volatility tree's S&P 500 computation. We will compute the implied volatility of an option with expiration June 15, 1996, and a strike price of $560.00.

First, we compute the grid square. We see that Table 9.8.1 lists strikes for 540 and 575 and expirations for March 15, 1996 and June 21, 1996. Figure 9.10.3 displays the situation.

To compute the implied volatility of the 560 strike call, expiring June 15, 1996, we first compute a and b:

$$a = 90/96$$
$$b = 20/35$$

F I G U R E 9.10.3

The grid square for the sample computation

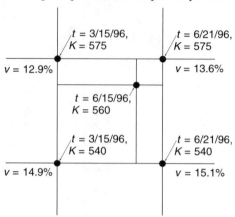

How did we make these computations? The variable a measures the difference between the unknown node's date (June 15, 1996) and the left node of the grid square (March 15, 1996)—90 days—divided by the length of the edge of the grid square (along the time dimension). This is the amount of time from June 21, 1996 and March 15, 1996—96 days.

The variable b is the difference between the unknown node's strike and the lower strike of the grid square, divided by the length of the edge of the grid square (along the "strike" dimension). This is 20/35.

Now, we compute

$$(1 - a)(1 - b)14.9 + a(1 - b)15.1 + ab14.6 + (1 - a)b12.9 = 14.213.$$

COMMENTS AND
SUGGESTED READING

The study of implied volatility trees covered in this chapter was developed by Derman and Kani [(1994a) and (1994b)]. The extension of implied volatility trees for use with American input options is due to N. Chriss, and may be found in Chriss (1996b).

At approximately the same time that Derman and Kani developed their work, similar work was published independently by Dupire (1994) and Rubinstein (1994). See Derman, Kani and Chriss (1996a), (1996b) for an in-depth look at implied volatility and trinomial trees. An alternative approach to the "bad probabilities" is discussed in Barle and Cakici (1995). An interesting non-technical account of these articles can be found in Hemmerick (1994).

For detailed information on interpolation techniques, see Press, Teukolsky, Vetterling, and Flannery (1992).

For a study of binomial processes as approximation to diffusion processes, see Nelson and Ramaswamy (1990).

10

ⓖ IMPLIED BINOMIAL TREES

This chapter discusses another innovation in derivatives pricing in the 1990s: implied binomial trees. These trees, introduced by M. Rubinstein (1994) of the Haas Business School of the University of California at Berkeley are similar in spirit to the implied volatility trees of Derman and Kani, but they are different in several important ways.

A Brief Introduction

We begin this chapter with a brief overview of the theory of implied binomial trees. The purpose of implied binomial trees is to start with a *given* stock price distribution for a particular future date and then build a binomial tree whose terminal distribution is equal to the given distribution. Thus, the key to implementing implied binomial trees is to have a particular (risk-neutral)[1] future stock price distribution in mind, build a binomial tree with this distribution, and then use this tree to value options. The question is, where does one find such a distribution? It turns out, there are two natural sources.

The first, and most important, source is option prices themselves. Going back to the work of Ross (1976), it was recognized that there is a close relationship between option prices and risk-neutral stock price distributions. Specifically, given a complete set of European option prices on a particular underlying for a particular expiration date (that is, given prices

---

[1] Due to the fact that we intend to use the distributions for option pricing, all the distributions we discuss have to be risk-neutral.

for options of every strike for that expiration) one can, in principle, deduce the risk-neutral probability distribution of the underlying for the given expiration date. Naturally, the key phrase is "in principle," and we must be able to translate this principle into an efficient computational tool. We'll return to this problem later. Right now, we discuss the second important source of stock price distributions: investor biases.

Investor Biases and Implied Binomial Trees

Some investors have strong opinions regarding the future distribution of prices. Where these opinions come from, and whether they are valid or not, is not important to us here. What concerns us is that they do exist, and therefore there should be a technique that allows us to incorporate such "biased distributions" into an option pricing model. The implied binomial tree provides such a technique.

The approach given here is to take a given distribution for stock prices and perturb some of its features to better represent a particular point of view. The idea is to use either a normal distribution of returns (e.g., generated via a Cox-Ross-Rubinstein binomial tree) or an "implied" distribution (e.g., obtained from market option prices as described in Section 10.1 of this chapter) and change certain of its qualities while preserving its mean and keeping its other features as close as possible to the original distribution. This method is described in Section 10.4.

Building the Tree

The starting point of the implied binomial tree model is a date and a risk-neutral stock price distribution for that date. Given this information, the model provides a simple, easy to implement method for producing a binomial tree with exactly the given distribution at the given date; the method does not, however, provide much flexibility regarding what happens at other dates. Specifically, the model builds a tree whose *terminal distribution* is the given distribution, but whose distribution on other dates is beyond the control of the model.

Once a binomial tree with the desired terminal distribution is built, it can be used, as we have emphasized from the start, to price a variety of options.

To summarize, the implied binomial tree model proceeds in three steps:

1. For a given underlying asset and future date, provide a risk-neutral probability distribution for the asset on the future date.

2. Build a binomial tree whose terminal date is the date given in step 1 and whose terminal distribution is the given distribution.

3. Use the tree to value options.

This chapter examines how to carry out steps 1 and 2 above. We've already discussed step 3. After this, we'll make some comments regarding the similarities and differences between the Derman and Kani implied volatility trees model and the Rubinstein implied binomial trees model.

10.1 INFERRING DISTRIBUTIONS DIRECTLY FROM OPTION PRICES

Recall that in the implied volatility trees model, we start with a set of input options and then build from these options an "implied volatility tree" with the property that it prices options consistent with the input set. Once this tree is built, we can compute the risk-neutral stock price distribution implied by the tree. We called this latter distribution the implied distribution of the tree. By contrast the implied binomial trees method takes the opposite approach by starting with a distribution and building a tree around that distribution.

The Setup

This section explains Rubinstein's method for inferring a risk-neutral probability distribution directly from a set of input option prices. We call this method Rubinstein's optimization method. Here is the specific framework.

We start with an underlying asset S with spot price S_0, and a collection of plain vanilla European options (all call or all put) on the asset, all of the same expiration date t_n. Specifically we write

$$C_1, \ldots, C_m$$

for the prices of m traded European call options with expiration t_n and strikes $K_1, \ldots, K_m$.

Note, if we have a set of input options, some puts and some calls, we have to convert all prices to either put or call prices using put-call parity.

Next, we supply a set of terminal nodes of a binomial tree for the underlying asset at the expiration date of the input options. Note that if the number of terminal nodes is $n + 1$, then this defines an n-period binomial tree. This defines a step size for each period of the tree.

Given this input data, we provide a method for determining the risk-neutral probability of reaching each terminal node.

F I G U R E 10.1.1

Sample setup for inferring implied distributions from option prices

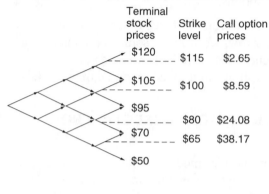

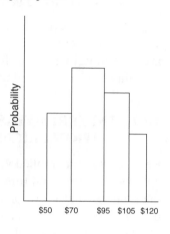

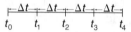

Sample Setup

Figure 10.1.1 graphically displays a possible set of input data for the implied binomial tree model. In this example, the current date is t_0, the terminal date is t_4, and the time step size is Δt.

There are five terminal stock price nodes with values $50, $70, $95, $105, and $120. We have four input options, all plain vanilla European calls and all expiring on the terminal date, with strikes $65, $80, $100, and $115. Their prices are, respectively, $38.17, $24.08, $8.59, and $2.65.

From this data, Rubinstein's method shows how to deduce the risk-neutral probability that the asset will reach each of the terminal stock price nodes. The figure displays a possible graph of the distribution, which is derived using *Rubinstein's optimization method,* which we describe now.

Rubinstein's Optimization Method

Rubinstein's method requires the user to have access to computer software capable of *quadratic optimization with constraints.* Before giving an outline of the approach, we need to establish some notation. In the above setup we have:

t_0 = today's date

t_n = end date

r = risk-free rate of interest *per annum*

$$\delta = \text{annual dividend yield on underlying}^2$$
$$S_{n,j} = \text{price of underlying at node } (n, j)$$
$$S_0 = \text{spot price of underlying}$$
$$C_j = \text{call option expiring time } t_n$$

STEP 1. Start with a given *prior distribution* for the terminal stock prices. This is nothing more than some risk-neutral distribution, and serves as a reference point for building the implied distribution.

A log-normal prior distribution for our setup may be generated as follows. Generate a standard Cox-Ross-Rubinstein tree whose terminal date is equal to the expiration date of our input options. Then the prior distribution of the tree is given by the risk-neutral terminal distribution of the tree. More specifically, the prior distribution is given by the set of terminal nodes of the tree, along with the probability of reaching each node.

Suppose the tree has n periods, so that the terminal nodes are labeled $S_{n,0}, S_{n,1}, \ldots$ etc., where $S_{n,i}$ represents the stock price of node (n, i).[3] Write P'_i for the probability of reaching node (n, i). The collection $P'_0, \ldots, P'_n$ is the prior distribution.

STEP 2. Minimize the following sum:

$$\min_{P_j} \sum_j (P_j - P'_j)^2. \tag{10.1.1}$$

Subject to the constraints:

$$\sum_j P_j = 1 \quad \text{and} \quad P_j \geq 0, \quad j = 0, \ldots n, \quad \text{and} \tag{10.1.2}$$

$$C_i = e^{-r(t_n - t_0)} \sum_j P_j \max(S_{n,j} - K_i, 0), \quad \text{for } i = 1, \ldots, m. \tag{10.1.3}$$

$$S_0 = e^{-(r-\delta)(t_n - t_0)} \sum_j P_j S_{n,j}. \tag{10.1.4}$$

Discussion

Minimizing the expression in equation (10.1.1) ensures that we find the set of probabilities $P_0, \ldots, P_n$ that is "closest" to the prior distribution. In fact, there is an infinite set of probability distributions that are close to the log-normal distribution. The constraint equations give a way of finding the ones that satisfy the various demands of the model, the most important

---

[2] We have specified this model for a continuous dividend yield. It can, in fact, be modified to accommodate lumpy dividends.

[3] See Figure 6.7.1 for a description of the numbering system of the nodes.

being: price options according to the input set (this is equation (10.1.3)). We discuss the constraints in more detail now.

The first constraint, $\sum_j P_j = 1$, is a natural one. It simply states that the sum of all the probabilities must be equal to one. In the language of random variables, this states that the terminal nodes describe all the possible outcomes of the stock price movement at time t_n *as a random variable*.

The second constraint, $C_i = e^{-(r-\delta)(t_n-t_0)} \sum_j P_j \max(S_{n,j} - K_i, 0)$ for $i = 1, \ldots, m$ is crucial. It states that the probabilities must "price" each input option correctly. Since the expression

$$e^{-r(t_n-t_0)} \sum_j P_j \max(S_{n,j} - K, 0)$$

is the expected value of a European call option that expires at time t_n and is struck at t_i (with respect to the stock price nodes $S_{n,0}, S_{n,1}, \ldots, S_{n,n}$), first, the equality

$$S_0 = e^{-(r-\delta)(t_n-t_0)} \sum_j P_j S_{n,j}$$

says that the risk-neutral expected value of the stock, adjusted for dividends and discounted to today's value, is equal to the spot price.

The minimization problem listed above can easily be solved by any non-linear optimization package.[4]

Loosening the Constraints

The constraint equations (10.1.3) and (10.1.4) can be relaxed a bit if we have bid and ask quotes for the call prices and stock prices. If we write C_i^a for the ask price of the option struck at K_i and C_i^b for the bid price, replace equation (10.1.3) with

$$C_i^b \le C_i \le C_i^a, \tag{10.1.5}$$

where

$$C_i = e^{-r(t_n-t_0)} \sum_j P_j \max(S_{n,j} - K_i, 0);$$

that is, we allow the theoretical value of the option to float somewhere between the bid and the ask price.

Similarly, suppose we have an ask price S^a and a bid price S^b for the stock. Then, we replace equation (10.1.4) with

---

[4]For example, all of the optimizations in this chapter were performed by the MATLAB™ Optimization toolbox.

$$S^b \leq S \leq S^a, \quad \text{where} \quad S = e^{-(r-\delta)(t_n-t_0)} \sum_j P_j S_{n,j}. \quad (10.1.6)$$

This equation is interpreted as follows. The left-hand side represents the forward price of the stock (at time t_n) discounted to time t_0. The right-hand side represents the present value of the expected value of the stock at time t_n. Therefore, the constraint equation says that the spot value of the asset *implied by the forward price* should fall between the bid and the ask.

10.2   BUILDING IMPLIED BINOMIAL TREES

The last section gave us a precise technique for determining a set of terminal nodes of a binomial tree and the corresponding probabilities of reaching each of them. If we discount each of these terminal probabilities to the current date, we obtain the Arrow-Debreu prices of each terminal node. Therefore, we are in the situation of knowing the *terminal data* of a binomial tree, and we now want to deduce from this data the entire tree.

Two questions arise at this point. First, can we use this data and some sort of backward induction procedure to deduce the tree? Second, if we can do this, to what extent is the tree we obtain unique? The answer to the first question is yes. The answer to the second is that there is an infinite number of possible trees with the same terminal data, and therefore we have to make some additional assumption in order to pin down the precise nature of the tree.

Binomial Path Independence

A very convenient assumption is the assumption of *binomial path independence* (BPI). The BPI assumption states that given a fixed node of a binomial tree, every path in the tree leading to that node has the same probability of being traversed. Put another way, if the probability of reaching node (n, i) is P, then if we delineate a single path leading to this node, the probability of traversing this path is equal to

$$\frac{1}{N} P, \quad N = \frac{n!}{i!(n-i)!},$$

where N is the total number of paths leading to node (n, i). This formula for N was given in Chapter 6.

Once we make the BPI assumption, it is incredibly simple to derive a backward induction method for building a binomial tree whose terminal data is equal to a given set of terminal data, the implied binomial tree. We illustrate this now.

Backward Induction for Building Implied Trees

Let's review the notation and add a little more:

$$
\begin{aligned}
t_0 &= \text{the start date of the tree} \\
t_n &= \text{the terminal date of the tree} \\
\Delta t &= \text{length of each time step} \\
S_{k,i} &= \text{the value of node } (k, i) \\
\lambda_{k,i} &= \text{the Arrow-Debreu price of node } (k, i) \\
P_i &= \text{the probability of reaching node } (n, i) \\
r &= \text{the risk-free rate of interest } per\ annum \\
\delta &= \text{annual dividend yield of the underlying}
\end{aligned}
$$

Note that we have the known relationship between probabilities and Arrow-Debreu prices:

$$\lambda_{n,i} = e^{-r(t_n - t_0)} P_i.$$

The idea of the backward induction method is to move backward through the tree, starting at the expiration date, computing all the stock price nodes and Arrow-Debreu prices at the "next earlier time." Here is a step-by-step procedure for the method.

1. Compute the terminal *path probabilities*. These are the probabilities of traversing a particular path to get to a particular end node. The path probability of the terminal node (n, i) is given by the formula:

$$\frac{i!(n - i)!P_i}{n!}, \qquad (10.2.1)$$

   where we recall $n! = n \cdot (n - 1) \cdot \ldots \cdot 2 \cdot 1$.

2. Perform backward induction. Consider the picture in Figure 10.2.1. Each letter P^* represents the *path probability* of the given node. For example, P^+ represents the path probability of the node labeled (P^+, S^+). Each letter S^* represents the stock price of the given node, and p represents the risk-neutral up-transition probability. We assume we already know $(P^+, S^+$ and $P^-, S^-)$, and we want to produce formulas for P, S. We have:

$$
\begin{aligned}
P &= P^- + P^+ & (10.2.2) \\
p &= P^+/P & (10.2.3) \\
S &= e^{-(r-\delta)\Delta t}\left(pS^+ + (1 - p)S^-\right). & (10.2.4)
\end{aligned}
$$

Once the Arrow-Debreu prices and transition probabilities have been computed, the Arrow-Debreu prices of the tree may also be computed.

F I G U R E   10.2.1

Backward
induction for
implied binomial
trees

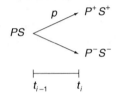

Explanation

The above two steps alone are enough to build an entire implied binomial tree. In the next section, we'll give an example of how to do this, but right now we discuss the derivation of the equations.

Equation (10.2.2) comes from the BPI assumption. Since P, P^+ and P^- represent path probabilities, the equation says the probability of reaching the node labeled P via a given path is equal to the sum of the probabilities of a path reaching the node labeled P^+ via a given path and reaching the node labeled P^- via a given path.

Equation (10.2.3) follows simply because if we choose any path leading to the node labeled P, the probability of traversing that path is P and the probability of traversing that path combined with a move up is pP. Equivalently, the latter is equal to the probability of traversing a given path to the node labeled P^+.

The third formula, equation (10.2.4), is simply the standard one-period risk-neutral forward equation. Recall that this says that a given node value is its expected value at the next period discounted to the given period.

Remarks

An obvious question is, what will the spot price of the binomial tree be when the procedure is completed? The answer, of course, is that the spot price will be exactly equal to the value of S_0. This is guaranteed in Rubinstein's approach by the constraint equation (10.1.4) combined with the equation (10.2.4). That is, in optimizing the end probabilities so that

$$S_0 = e^{-(r-\delta)(t_n-t_0)} \sum_{j} P_j S_{n,j}$$

and ensuring that at every time step the one-period forward equation (with dividends) is satisfied, we guarantee that the spot price of the tree (that is, the value of the vertex node of the tree) is equal to S_0.

10.3   SAMPLE IMPLIED BINOMIAL TREE

In this section, we compute a sample implied binomial tree in order to demonstrate the method. Here are the values for the model:

$$\Delta t = 0.20$$
$$r = 5.00\%$$
$$\delta = 0.00\%$$
$$t_0 = \text{today}$$
$$t_n = \text{one year from today}$$
$$n = 6$$

Thus, we are building a five-period tree starting today and extending one year into the future. Figure 10.3.1 displays the terminal nodes and distributions of our sample tree, along with the number of paths leading to each terminal node and the corresponding path probabilities. We tabulate the terminal stock prices and probabilities below for easy reference:

node	(5,0)	(5,1)	(5,2)	(5,3)	(5,4)	(5,5)
Stock price	$50.00	$70.00	$90.00	$110.00	$130.00	$150.00
Probability	15.00%	20.00%	35.00%	15.00%	10.00%	5.00%

The Spot Price

The spot price is nothing but the expected value of the future stock price discounted to today via the risk-free rate. Therefore, we have

$$S_0 = e^{-0.05}(0.15 \cdot 50 + 0.20 \cdot 70 + 0.35 \cdot 90 + 0.15 \cdot 110$$
$$+ 0.10 \cdot 130 + 0.05 \cdot 150) = 85.6106.$$

We will see this again after we have computed the entire implied tree.

Computing the Implied Binomial Tree

The procedure for computing the tree is so simple that we will only demonstrate the computations for the nodes at time t_4. We introduce some additional notation to make the computations more clear.

$$P_{i,j} = \text{the path probability of node } (i, j)$$
$$p_{i,j} = \text{the up-transition probability from node } (i, j) \text{ to node } (i + 1,$$
$$j + 1)$$

F I G U R E 10.3.1

Sample terminal data for an implied binomial tree

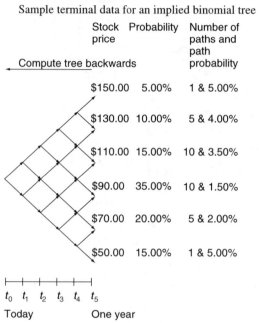

	Stock price	Probability	Number of paths and path probability
	$150.00	5.00%	1 & 5.00%
	$130.00	10.00%	5 & 4.00%
	$110.00	15.00%	10 & 3.50%
	$90.00	35.00%	10 & 1.50%
	$70.00	20.00%	5 & 2.00%
	$50.00	15.00%	1 & 5.00%

Compute tree backwards

t_0 t_1 t_2 t_3 t_4 t_5

Today   One year

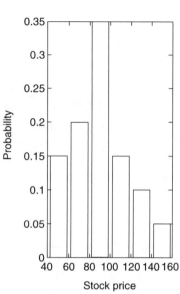

Thus, we have:

(5,0)	(5,1)	(5,2)	(5,3)	(5,4)	(5,5)
$P_{5,0} = 15\%$	$P_{5,1} = 4.00\%$	$P_{5,2} = 3.50\%$	$P_{5,3} = 1.50\%$	$P_{5,4} = 2.00\%$	$P_{5,5} = 5.00\%$

Remember: The path probabilities are the probabilities of reaching a given node by a single path. This is not the same as the total probability of reaching the node; rather, it is the probability of reaching that node divided by the number of paths leading to that node (due to the BPI assumption).

Now, we compute the path probabilities of the nodes at time t_4 via equation (10.2.2):

$$P_{4,4} = P_{5,5} + P_{5,4} = 7.00\%$$
$$P_{4,3} = P_{5,4} + P_{5,3} = 3.50\%$$
$$P_{4,2} = P_{5,3} + P_{5,2} = 5.00\%$$
$$P_{4,1} = P_{5,2} + P_{5,1} = 7.50\%$$
$$P_{4,0} = P_{5,1} + P_{5,0} = 19.00\%$$

F I G U R E 10.3.2

Completed implied binomial tree from Figure 10.3.1.

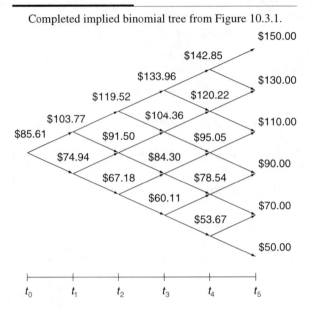

Next, we compute the transition probabilities from time t_4 to t_5 (via equation (10.2.3)):

$$p_{4,4} = P_{5,5}/P_{4,4} = 0.7143$$
$$p_{4,3} = P_{5,4}/P_{4,3} = 0.5714$$
$$p_{4,2} = P_{5,3}/P_{4,2} = 0.3000$$
$$p_{4,1} = P_{5,2}/P_{4,1} = 0.4667$$
$$p_{4,0} = P_{5,1}/P_{4,0} = 0.2105$$

Lastly, we compute the stock prices at time t_4 (via equation (10.2.4)):

$$S_{4,4} = e^{-r\Delta t}\left(p_{4,4}(S_{5,5} + (1 - p_{4,4})S_{5,4})\right) = \$142.85$$
$$S_{4,3} = e^{-r\Delta t}\left(p_{4,3}(S_{5,4} + (1 - p_{4,3})S_{5,3})\right) = \$120.2203$$
$$S_{4,2} = e^{-r\Delta t}\left(p_{4,2}(S_{5,3} + (1 - p_{4,2})S_{5,2})\right) = \$95.0448$$
$$S_{4,1} = e^{-r\Delta t}\left(p_{4,1}(S_{5,2} + (1 - p_{4,1})S_{5,1})\right) = \$78.5440$$
$$S_{4,0} = e^{-r\Delta t}\left(p_{4,0}(S_{5,1} + (1 - p_{4,0})S_{5,0})\right) = \$53.6711$$

We display the final implied binomial tree in Figure 10.3.2.

10.4   SKEWING A PROBABILITY DISTRIBUTION

This section discusses a methodology for taking a given risk-neutral probability distribution and "skewing" it to adhere to specific market views. This method is taken from Chriss (1996) "Skewing a distribution to a market view." We will illustrate the method by taking a normal distribution of returns (e.g., from a standard Cox-Ross-Rubinstein tree) and perturbing the probabilities of large negative returns so as to increase the possibility of a "crash." In so doing, we will create a whole array of returns that move smoothly from the normal returns to the skewed return. We will feed these returns into Rubinstein's method and build trees with these terminal returns. These trees will, in turn, be used to value a variety of options to show the effect that "skewing the distribution" has on option prices.

The Issues in Changing the Distribution

Suppose we are given a risk-neutral price distribution for a stock price one year from now. We look at the distribution and decide we want to increase the probability of large negative returns. How do we do this?

First of all, there are several issues we have to discuss. First, what features of the original distribution do we wish to preserve, and what features are we willing to sacrifice? For example, it is clear that we have to keep the mean of the distribution the same. Why? Because the mean is nothing but the expected value of the stock, and since we demand that the distribution be risk-neutral, this is the forward price of today's spot price computed with the risk-free rate.

What can we say about the standard deviation of the new distribution? Our position is as follows: Since we are using risk-neutral valuation with deterministic (i.e., non-stochastic) volatility, we are forced to allow volatility to change freely as we change the underlying distribution.

How to Change the Distribution

We now describe an optimization technique much like Rubinstein's optimization method for producing distributions implied by the market prices of European options. The setup is that we start with a given *prior* distribution (given, say, by Rubinstein's method arrived at from market option prices). We then try to find a new distribution that is as close as possible to the original distribution, subject to the following constraints:

1. The new distribution is risk-neutral; that is, its mean is equal to the forward price of the underlying computed at the risk-free rate.
2. The new distribution has the specific features we want to introduce.

We will make the second item precise in a moment. For now, we take this to mean that if we are not satisfied with a particular aspect of the prior distribution, we use a constraint equation to change it. We now describe the optimization problem mathematically.

The Optimization Equations

To describe the equations, we will need some notation. First, we assume we have a stock with spot price S and the risk-free rate of interest is r. Next, we assume we have a *prior* distribution of stock prices for specific time T. We present the distribution in the form of a list of prices and probabilities, which, naturally, we use as the terminal nodes in a binomial tree. We have

$$S_0, S_1, \ldots, S_n$$
$$P_0, P_1, \ldots, P_n$$

where $S_0 < S_1 < \cdots < S_n$ are the stock prices at some future time T, and P_i is the probability of the future price being S_i. Of course, we have to require

$$\sum P_i = 1.$$

Next, we propose changes to *some* of the probabilities in the list. That is, we prepare a list of probabilities

$$P'_{i_0}, P'_{i_1}, \ldots, P'_{i_m},$$

where the list represents proposed new values for the probabilities $P_{i_0}, \ldots,$ P_{i_m}. Here, $i_0, \ldots, i_m$ are integers between zero and n. Note that the above list proposes changes in only a subset of the probabilities.[5]

Our goal is to produce a new set of probabilities, $Q_0, \ldots, Q_n$, with the property that $Q_{i_0} = P'_{i_0}, \ldots Q_{i_m} = P'_{i_m}$. We do this by solving the following quadratic program. Minimize

$$\sum_{i=0}^{n} (P_i - Q_i)^2, \tag{10.4.1}$$

subject to the constraints:

$$S = e^{-(r-\delta)T} \sum_{i=0}^{n} Q_i S_i \tag{10.4.2}$$

---

[5]If this is confusing, see the example below.

$$\sum Q_i = 1.00 \tag{10.4.3}$$
$$Q_1 \geq 0.00, \text{ for } i = 0, \ldots, n \tag{10.4.4}$$
$$Q_{i_0} = P'_{i_0} \tag{10.4.5}$$

$$\vdots$$

$$Q_{i_m} = P'_{i_m}. \tag{10.4.6}$$

Equation (10.4.1) says that we want our new distribution $(Q_0, \ldots, Q_n)$ to be as close as possible to the old distribution $(P_0, \ldots, P_n)$.

Equation (10.4.2) says that the mean of the distribution discounted to today's value by the risk-free rate is equal to the spot price. This is the risk-neutrality assumption. Equation (10.4.3) states that the sum of all of the probabilities must be equal to one. This is the standard probability theory assumption. Lastly, equations (10.4.5)–(10.4.6) state that the given probabilities $Q_{i_0}, \ldots, Q_{i_m}$ should be equal to the specified probabilities $P'_{i_0}, \ldots, P'_{i_m}$.

Example

Since the above notation may be confusing, we give a simple example to explain what we mean. Suppose we have a five price distribution, presented in the form of a list:

$$S_0 = 70, S_1 = 90, S_2 = 110, S_3 = 130, S_4 = 150$$
$$P_0 = 0.1, P_1 = 0.20, P_2 = 0.4, P_3 = 0.20, P_4 = 0.10.$$

We assume the risk-free rate is zero percent, and the distribution represents stock prices one year from today. The mean of this distribution is given by:

$$0.1 \cdot 70 + 0.20 \cdot 90 + 0.4 \cdot 110 + 0.20 \cdot 130 + 0.10 \cdot 150 = 110.$$

Now, suppose we look at this distribution and believe the probability of the stock price being 70 or 150 is really 15 percent. Then, we set

$$P'_0 = 0.15, P'_4 = 0.15.$$

Our quadratic program is now as follows. We want a new distribution

$$Q_0, Q_1, Q_2, Q_3, Q_4$$

such that

$$(P_0 - Q_0)^2 + (P_1 - Q_1)^2 + (P_2 - Q_2)^2 + (P_3 - Q_3)^2 + (P_4 - Q_4)^2$$

is as small as possible, subject to the constraints:

$$Q_0 S_0 + Q_1 S_1 + Q_2 S_2 + Q_3 S_3 + Q_4 S_4 = 110$$
$$Q_0 + Q_1 + Q_2 + Q_3 + Q_4 = 1.00$$
$$Q_0 = 0.15$$
$$Q_4 = 0.15$$

F I G U R E 10.4.1

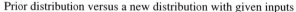

Prior distribution versus a new distribution with given inputs

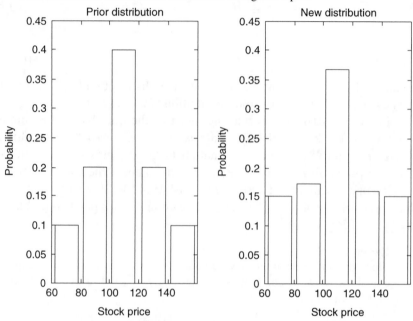

We solved this program using MATLAB's™ optimization package, and the results are displayed in Figure 10.4.1. The new distribution is:

$$Q_0 = 0.1500, Q_1 = 0.1733, Q_2 = 0.3674, Q_3 = 0.1615, Q_4 = 0.1500$$

That is, Q_i represents the new probability of reaching price S_i. Let's examine this new distribution. First, notice that we have:

$$0.15 \cdot 70 + 0.1733 \cdot 90 + 0.3674 \cdot 110$$
$$+ 0.1615 \cdot 130 + 0.15 \cdot 150 = 110,$$

so the mean of the distribution was not changed. Notice, however, that the symmetry of the distribution was broken. That is, the prior distribution was symmetric about the price 110, while this distribution is now skewed slightly to the left.

10.5   A COMPLETE EXAMPLE

We now give a much more detailed example of changing stock price distributions and then combining the new distributions with Rubinstein's methods to see the effect on option pricing. The basic idea is to take a 25-period standard Cox-Ross-Rubinstein tree and change the distribution by increasing the probability of large negative returns. We use these distributions, along with implied binomial trees, to price a variety of put and call options.

The Distributions

We start with a 25-period Cox-Ross-Rubinstein tree with the following data:

r = 5% (risk-free rate)
σ = 20% (volatility)
N = 25 (number of periods)
T = 1 year (time to expiration)
S = 100 (spot price today)

We created 20 distributions, starting with the normal distribution of returns given by the Cox-Ross-Rubinstein tree. The returns are numbered 1 through 20: Distribution 1 is the normal distribution of returns of the Cox-Ross-Rubinstein tree. As the number of the returns increases, the probabilities of the bottom five stock prices being achieved are increased 30 percent at a time. Figure 10.5.1 displays a three-dimensional graph of these distributions from two points of view.

Note how distribution 20 has an extra hump in the large negative returns region, indicating that the probability of these returns is much greater than a normal distribution would predict. Notice also how the returns near the peak of the normal curve dip downward to accommodate the fact that extra probability is concentrated in the negative returns region.

Option Prices

The distributions in Figure 10.5.1 were used to create implied binomial trees and to price options. We priced European calls and puts with strikes of 80, 100, and 110. The results are tabulated in Table 10.5.1. The rows of that table represent the prices for options valued using a particular distribution. The number of the distribution refers to the numbers on the x-axis (labeled 0 through 20) in Figure 10.5.1. In particular, distribution number 1 represents a normal distribution, and distribution number 20 represents the most skewed distribution.

Conclusions and Lessons Learned

What can we learn from the table of option prices, 10.5.1? First of all, let's compare distribution 1 (normal distribution) to distribution 20, the most-skewed distribution (see Figure 10.5.1), and ask ourselves the following

F I G U R E 10.5.1

Skewing a normal distribution to have greater than "normal" negative returns

Front view   Back view

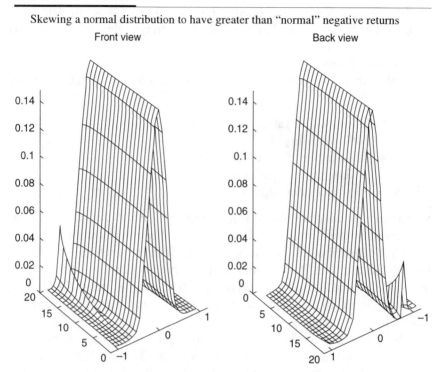

simple question:

What effect will the most-skewed distribution have on option prices?

At first blush, we might argue as follows: Since the probability of large downward moves of the stock has increased compared with a normal distribution of returns, the value of put options on the stock should increase, while the value of call options should decrease relative to the normal distribution.

The above logic, while tempting to the ear, is misleading. First of all, Table 10.5.1 does not corroborate this logic. More importantly, however, is that this logic violates one of our most basic principles of option pricing: put-call parity. Put-call parity says the difference between a call price and a put price (on the same underlying) of a given strike and expiration is independent of the future stock price distribution. Therefore, if we change the stock price distribution and the call value rises (falls), then the put value will also rise (fall).

T A B L E 10.5.1

Prices for European calls and puts valued with skewed
distributions

	Calls			Puts			σ
	80	100	110	80	100	110	
1	24.60	10.52	6.08	0.70	5.65	10.72	21.19
2	24.60	10.53	6.08	0.70	5.65	10.72	21.21
3	24.60	10.53	6.09	0.70	5.65	10.72	21.23
4	24.60	10.53	6.09	0.70	5.66	10.73	21.26
5	24.61	10.54	6.10	0.71	5.66	10.73	21.29
6	24.62	10.55	6.11	0.71	5.67	10.74	21.34
7	24.63	10.56	6.12	0.72	5.68	10.75	21.40
8	24.63	10.57	6.13	0.73	5.69	10.76	21.48
9	24.65	10.58	6.15	0.74	5.71	10.78	21.58
10	24.66	10.60	6.17	0.76	5.73	10.80	21.70
11	24.68	10.63	6.19	0.78	5.75	10.83	21.87
12	24.71	10.67	6.23	0.81	5.79	10.87	22.09
13	24.75	10.71	6.28	0.85	5.84	10.91	22.36
14	24.80	10.78	6.35	0.90	5.90	10.98	22.76
15	24.87	10.87	6.43	0.97	5.99	11.07	23.27
16	24.96	10.98	6.55	1.06	6.10	11.19	23.91
17	25.08	11.12	6.70	1.18	6.25	11.34	24.72
18	25.24	11.33	6.91	1.34	6.45	11.55	25.80
19	25.46	11.60	7.20	1.56	6.72	11.83	27.20
20	25.74	11.96	7.57	1.84	7.08	12.20	28.92

How then do we explain the option prices in Table 10.5.1? The answer is volatility. The final column of Table 10.5.1 indicates the volatility of each distribution. Notice the trend: As the distribution becomes more skewed away from normal, the volatility increases, and as volatility increases, option values increase as well.

The lesson is that adding the hump to the distribution creates more volatility. The "intuition" that tells us that an increased probability of a downward move in price raises the value of a put and lowers the value of a call ignores the basic premises of risk-neutral valuation and put-call parity. Remember the situation we encountered with binomial trees: The value of an option does not depend on the probability of the price rising or falling. Rather, it depends on the volatility.

10.6 IMPLIED BINOMIAL VERSUS IMPLIED VOLATILITY TREES

This section compares the implied binomial trees model with the implied volatility trees model. The purpose is to compare the fundamental concepts of each method. Figure 10.6.1 summarizes the conceptual framework of each.

The two models are in many senses complementary to one another. The chief difference of the two models is that Rubinstein's method only looks at option prices of a single expiration, while the Derman-Kani implied volatility trees look at all option prices with a given underlying.

The Derman-Kani model can be extended to work with input options that are American, while as yet there is no sound way to use Rubinstein's method in this way. The main advantage of the Derman-Kani method is that it makes the minimum number of assumptions on the underlying stock process. The only real assumption is that volatility itself is a function of

F I G U R E 10.6.1

Comparing implied volatility and implied binomial trees.

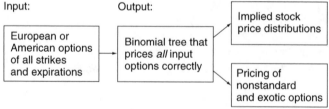

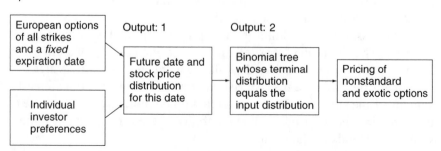

spot price and time (the local volatility function). This is not the case in Rubinstein's work, wherein the extraneous BPI assumption is employed.

The main disadvantage of the Derman-Kani method is that it is difficult to implement due to the problem of bad probabilities. No such problems ever occur in Rubinstein's method. With patience, however, it is possible to create a stable installation of the Derman-Kani method in which the effects of bad probabilities are minimized.

The main advantage of the Rubinstein method is that it is really a flexible method for building binomial trees with arbitrary terminal distributions. It is possible, with the aid of the optimization method given in Section 10.4, to take a given distribution and perturb it to meet a particular market view. Such a specialized distribution can be used in conjunction with the Rubinstein method to build a binomial tree to meet a particular point of view.

COMMENTS AND SUGGESTED READING

Rubinstein's implied binomial trees provide a novel approach to option pricing by providing a convenient way of starting with a given (arbitrary) risk-neutral probability distribution and building a binomial tree around that distribution. This, combined with a simple method for obtaining a distribution from market option prices or perturbing a given distribution to adhere to certain views, provides a different approach to option valuation than has been previously employed.

The idea of obtaining probability distributions from option prices has been variously attributed to Ross (1976) and Breedon and Litzenberger (1978). Other methods may be found in Shimko (1993) and Longstaff (1993). Both of these methods are summarized in Rubinstein (1994). Also, note that the Derman-Kani implied volatility trees method gives yet another way of inferring distributions from market option prices, and this method, with the extension in Chapter 9, can be used to infer distributions from American options.

The method of perturbing a known distribution into a new distribution that is discussed here may be found in Chriss (1996) "Skewing a distribution to a market view."

11

⑥ PRICING BARRIER OPTIONS IN THE PRESENCE OF THE SMILE

This chapter truly goes beyond Black-Scholes, combining the powerful techniques of implied volatility and implied binomial trees with the general methods of pricing options on these trees, which yields methods for pricing exotic options in the real world of volatility smiles.

Chapters 9 and 10 explained how to produce binomial trees that correctly price liquidly traded European or American (in the case of Chapter 9) options on a stock or an index. With these trees in hand, we can value options that are not liquidly traded in the market. This chapter uses the binomial model to price an important class of exotic options: barrier options.

Combining the techniques of this chapter with implied volatility and binomial trees is potentially very important. Barrier options are extremely sensitive to the shape of the volatility smile. Existing closed-form solutions for barrier option prices are based on the constant volatility assumption of Black-Scholes. It is more sound to price barriers on an implied volatility tree where the shape of the smile is explicitly taken into account. This chapter develops methods for pricing barrier options on *any* binomial tree—in particular, we combine implied volatility trees with the methods in the present chapter, and we present special techniques for guaranteeing that the tree produces the most accurate results possible.

11.1 WHAT ARE BARRIER OPTIONS?

We now study barrier options—a real example of an exotic option. We begin our study by explaining what barrier options are, and then we move on to discuss some of the features of barrier option values. Once we have completed this, we will give a method for pricing barrier options on a binomial tree; we conclude the chapter by giving a method due to Derman and Kani for "enhancing" the pricing of barrier options on binomial trees.

Barrier options are similar in some ways to ordinary options. There are put and call, as well as European and American varieties; but there are additional features to barrier option contracts that are not found in plain vanilla contracts. We illustrate these by explaining knock-out options.

Knock-out options start out as ordinary call or put options, but they become *null and void* if the spot price ever crosses a certain predetermined *knockout barrier.* For example, a European call option may be written on an underlying with spot price $100, and a knockout barrier of $120. This option behaves in every way like a vanilla European call, *except* if the spot price ever moves above $120, the option "knocks out" and the contract is null and void. Note that the option *does not* reactivate if the spot price falls below $120 again. Once it is out, it's out for good.

Next we have knock-in options. Knock-in options work in exactly the opposite manner. They start their lives inactive, in a sense null and void, and only become active in the event that the stock price crosses the *knock-in barrier.* For example, a European put option may be written on an underlying with spot price $100 and a knock-in barrier of $90. Then, this option contract is worthless to the owner unless the spot price falls below $90 at some time. Note that once the "knock-in" barrier is breached, the option is alive; crossing the $90 barrier again does not make the contract null and void.

In either case, if the option expires inactive, then there may be a *cash rebate* paid out. This could be nothing, in which case the option ends up worthless, or it could be some fraction of the premium.

We now examine barrier options in more detail. They fall into two broad categories: "in" options and "out" options. "In" options start their lives worthless and only become active in the event a predetermined knock-in barrier price is breached. "Out" options start their lives active and become null and void in the event a certain knock-out barrier price is breached.

Up-and-Out Options

Every up-and-out option starts active and is deactivated if the spot price of the underlying rises above a certain predetermined level, called the knock-out barrier. In this case a *cash rebate* may be paid out, as compensation for the knock-out. The predetermined level is called the barrier of the option.

Up-and-out options are so-named because spot price always starts below the barrier level, so that the spot has to move up in order for the option to be knocked out.

Up-and-out options, like all barrier options, come in both the put and call variety. In addition, the contract can also specify an early exercise feature; for example, there are American and Bermuda barrier options.

All up-and-out options have several features in common:

1. The specifications of the knock-out barrier are determined at settlement.
2. Once the option is knocked out, it remains knocked out, and there is no possibility of recovery.

Down-and-Out Options
Down-and-out options are exactly like up-and-out options—these options start as ordinary put or call options, but if the spot price ever goes below a certain barrier level, then the option contracts become null and void.

Up-and-In Options
An up-and-in option is almost the same as an up-and-out option, except the option begins its life inactive and only becomes active if the stock price rises above a certain predefined knock-out barrier. Thus, if the spot price never crosses the barrier, then the option is never activated and it expires worthless.

Down-and-In Options
Down-and-in options are exactly like up-and-in options except that the spot price starts above the strike price, so that the spot has to drop in order for the option to become activated.

Monitoring Barrier Options
In practice, one has to define precisely what it means for the barrier of an option to be crossed. The issue is how the spot price of the underlying is tracked. Does the option knock out (or in) at the moment the spot crosses the barrier, or does the spot price have to be beyond the barrier, for example, at the end of the trading day? This is the question of "barrier monitoring."

When Is the Barrier Crossed?
Barrier monitoring refers to determining when the barrier is deemed crossed. Barrier option contracts can specify that the barrier is only deemed crossed if it is crossed at the end of a trading day. This is called end-of-day monitoring.

For example, suppose we have a down-and-out put option on the S&P 500 with a barrier level of $540 and the barrier is monitored at the end of each trading day. If on a particular day the S&P 500 drops to $538 but closes at $541, then the barrier has not knocked out. The index must close below $540 for the option to knock out.

Conversely, if the barrier is monitored *intra-day,* then the barrier is deemed crossed whenever the spot price crosses the barrier. So in the last example, the barrier would be considered crossed and the option knocked out.

The method of barrier monitoring can affect option values. This makes a small difference in pricing, and it is discussed in detail in Heynen and Kat (1994).

Rebate Payment

If a knock-out option has a rebate, then when the rebate is to be paid has to be specified. The rebate can be paid at the moment the option knocks out or at some later date, such as the expiration date of the option. We shall see below that our pricing methods can accommodate any number of rebate payment possibilities.

Table 11.1.1 gives a complete list of barrier options and their properties.

11.2   IN-OUT PARITY AND BARRIER OPTIONS

In-out parity is the barrier option's answer to put-call parity. The principle is the same as in put-call parity: If we combine two different (barrier) options (one an "in" option and one an "out" option) with the same strikes and expirations, we get the price of a simpler instrument (in this case, a vanilla option). Here is how it works.

Start with a strike and expiration. Then, form two European options of the same type (i.e., both calls or both puts) on the same underlying, one a knock-in option and one a knock-out option, both with the same barrier. For example, we could have a one-year vanilla call option with strike price $100 on XYZ. Then, we decide on a barrier—in this case $120—and form a one-year knock-in call option with strike $100 and barrier $120, as well as a one-year knock-out call option with strike $100 and barrier $120.

In-out parity says that the "in" option value plus the "out" option value is equal to the value of the vanilla option. In symbols, we have

$$C = C_{in} + C_{out}.$$

T A B L E 11.1.1

Barrier options and their properties
All barrier options have the payouts of an ordinary call or put
option, provided they are active at expiration. This table describes
how these barrier options become active or inactive.

Barrier Options			
Knock-out Type		**Knock-in Type**	
Name	**Properties**	**Name**	**Properties**
down-and-out	Barrier lies below spot at settlement. The option starts active; it deactivates if the spot price drops below the barrier.	down-and-in	Barrier lies below spot at settlement. The option starts inactive; it only activates if the spot price falls below the barrier.
up-and-out	Barrier lies above the spot at settlement. The option starts active; it becomes inactive if the spot rises above the barrier.	up-and-in	Barrier lies above the spot at settlement. The option starts inactive; it activates only if the spot rises above the barrier.

One can verify that in-out parity holds with a simple arbitrage argument. The basic idea is that simultaneously holding the "in" and the "out" option guarantees that one and only one of the two will pay off. The argument only works for European options.

In the figure at the top of page 438, we see an example of how in-out parity works. In this picture, we see a barrier (denoted by the heavy horizontal line) and an expiration date (the vertical dashed line). In addition, there are two stock price paths—one that crosses the barrier and one that does not cross the barrier. The one that crosses the barrier simultaneously activates the knock-in option and deactivates the knock-out option.

Conversely, the path that does not cross the barrier behaves in the opposite manner: The knock-in option is never activated, while the knock-out option, which starts its life active, is never deactivated.

The expected payout of holding the "in and out" portfolio is therefore always the same: At expiration, the portfolio will always contain a single active option. Thus, holding the portfolio has exactly the same payout at

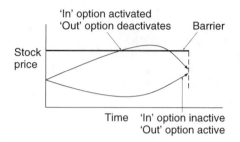

expiration as holding a simple option. Hence, by our standard arbitrage arguments, in-out parity holds. Of course, this argument relies on the fact that the options are European; we have to know that neither option was exercised prior to expiration in order for the argument to work.

Example of In-Out Parity

To get a feel for in-out parity, we will look at two options. Let XYZ be a stock or an index with a current spot price of $100. Consider an ordinary call option C with one year until expiration and a strike price of $110.

Now consider two European barrier options on XYZ:

type	knock-in	type	knock-out
strike	110	strike	110
barrier level	120	barrier level	120
expiration	one year	expiration	one year

The sum of the value of the "in" option and the value of the "out" option is equal to the value of C, the vanilla call.

11.3 HEDGE PARAMETERS OF BARRIER OPTIONS

Barrier options have much different price structures than their ordinary cousins. For example, suppose an investor is long an up-and-out call option struck at $100 with a knock-out barrier at $120, and the current spot price of the underlying is $101. Then, the maximum payout of the option is just under $20, because if the option is to expire active, then it must expire with the underlying under $120. For this reason, the investor is forfeiting some of the upside potential of an ordinary call, and therefore the up-and-out barrier option's value will be less than the value of the ordinary call. How much less depends on the amount of upside potential the investor is giving up.

This explains much of the appeal of barrier options: They can be tailored to fit an investor's view of the market. *Euromoney* magazine explains this as follows in the context of put options:

> Depending on the exact structure, these options either cap the potential insurance protection afforded by the put to the buyer, or leave open the possibility that if the barrier is reached, the put will extinguish worthless. Because of this, knock-out puts are cheaper than straight puts and so attractive to fund managers with defined market views and an aversion to large up-front premiums.[1]

Knock-in barrier options also have lower premiums than ordinary options. Suppose an investor purchases a call option on XYZ struck at $100 with a knock-in barrier of $105. This option only activates provided the stock price rises above $105 at some time during the option's life. If this fails to happen, then although the spot price may be greater than the strike, the option will expire worthless. Naturally, such an option cannot demand as high a premium as the corresponding call option with no barrier. If an investor believes there is a good chance that the price of the underlying will rise above $105, then he or she will not want to pay the part of the premium attached to payouts between $0 and $5.

Barrier Options and Their Hedge Parameters

The values and hedge parameters of barrier options differ from vanilla options due to the constant tug of war between the influence of the strike price, on the one hand, and the barrier on the other.

"In" options have no value until they knock in. Therefore at any given moment such an option's value is balanced between the possibility of *not* knocking in, and expiring out of the money. Similarly, an "out" option is constantly threatened by the possibility of knocking out, while at the same time fighting to expire in the money. All of this is exacerbated by the fact that barrier options are often set up so that the two forces are naturally working against one another, for example, when the spot moves toward the barrier in an up-and-in option, the intrinsic value of the option increases while simultaneously the probability of knocking out increases as well.

---

[1] From "Derivatives Sprout Bells and Whistles," *Euromoney,* August 1992, p. 29.

D I S P L A Y   11.3.1

THE VALUE OF VARIOUS BARRIER OPTIONS

All options are struck at $100 on an underlying with a spot price of $100. All options have one year until maturity. Note that the up-and-out call and up-and-in call can be used to verify in-out parity. The slight mismatches are due to rounding errors.

Down-and-in put		Down-and-out call	
Barrier	**Value**	**Barrier**	**Value**
90	$1.38	90	$6.525
92	$1.65	92	$6.36
94	$1.84	94	$5.93
96	$1.93	96	$4.98
98	$1.96	98	$3.15
100	$1.96	100	$0.00
Straight put	$1.96	Straight call	$6.60

Up-and-out call		Up-and-in call	
Barrier	**Value**	**Barrier**	**Value**
100	$0.00	100	$1.38
102	$0.06	102	$1.31
104	$0.50	104	$0.87
106	$1.02	106	$0.35
108	$1.29	108	$0.09
110	$1.36	110	$0.00
112	$1.38	112	$0.00
Straight call	$1.38	Straight call	$1.38

Worse yet, because of the all-or-nothing nature of option values at the barrier (in or out), option values "jump" when they cross the barrier. This fact, the radical changes that barrier options experience when they cross the barrier, has a fierce impact on hedge parameters that cannot be ignored. What follows is a discussion of hedge parameters and option values for the four basic kinds of barrier options: up-and-in, up-and-out, down-and-in and down-and-out. We illustrate the discussion with graphs of the values and (all of the) hedge parameters for European call and put options. Later when we discuss barrier option pricing on binomial trees, we'll show how to price American options as well.

Barrier Options and Delta

The delta of an option is the rate of change in its value with respect to changes in the price of the underlying. The most important thing to understand about the delta of *any* barrier option is that when the spot price (of the underlying) is near the barrier, the delta becomes very large. Just how large depends on some of the other parameters in the picture, such as stock price volatility. In general, however, a delta with absolute value of greater than two is not uncommon as the spot nears the barrier. In effect, this means that a barrier option becomes a highly leveraged instrument near the barrier, much more leveraged than a vanilla option.

To understand this better, let's consider an example. Take the up-and-out call in Figure 11.3.3. This call has a strike price of 100 and a barrier of 120. If the spot price exceeds the barrier, the option knocks out and is worthless. We want to study the effect this has on the delta, as the spot price approaches the barrier.

We consider spot prices very close to, but less than the barrier value of 120. For such spot prices, any move toward the barrier has the effect of increasing the probability of the option's knocking out, and therefore lowering the value of the option. On the other hand, moves away from the barrier decrease the probability of knocking out, and therefore increase the value of the option.

This effect is not limited to dollar-for-dollar changes with the stock value, as is the case with ordinary options. Rather, it is possible that a small change in stock price is magnified many times by the option. For example, the delta of the 120 barrier up-and-out call can be -5 for a close to expiration option (how great this delta is depends on the volatility of the underlying).

The Gamma of a Barrier Option

The dominant fact about the gamma of any barrier option is that it becomes infinite near the barrier. This means that as spot price moves toward the barrier, the gamma grows larger and larger, *without bound.*

To the consequences of "infinite gamma," let's remember what gamma is: a measure of how quickly delta changes as the underlying changes. In terms of delta hedging, gamma measures how quickly and how severely a delta hedge becomes out of balance. Thus, infinite gamma means extreme trouble when it comes to hedging near the barrier.

The root of the trouble with gamma at the barrier is the all or nothing nature of the option near the barrier. For a knock-out option near the barrier, all the value of the option will be lost if the barrier is crossed. Conversely, for a knock-in option, the option will expire worthless *unless* the barrier is crossed.

Intuitively, this possibility of extreme change has the effect of making hedging extremely difficult. The situation is exactly the same as being at the money very near to expiration while long a vanilla call or put. In this case, gamma can grow large without bound. The problem for hedging arises because of the large difference in amount of stock one has to hold to hedge, depending on whether the spot crossed or does not cross the barrier.

Consider, for example, the case of an up-and-in call with 100 strike and 120 barrier near to expiration (Figure 11.3.7). If we are short this option and the spot is near the barrier, but never crosses, then the option expires worthless, and we want to be holding no stock at expiration. Conversely, if the option knocks in, then we will be short a deep-in-the-money option with almost no time to expiration. In this case we wanted to be holding one share of the underlying in order to cover the call. Thus, our hedge has to maintain the balance between either holding no stock (if the option does not knock in) to holding one share (if the option knocks out).

The Other Parameters: Vega, Theta, and Rho

The hedge parameters vega, theta, and rho measure the sensitivity of an option to changes in volatility, time to expiration, and risk-free interest rate. In all three cases barrier options have a single feature that overpowers the rest. Near the barrier sensitivity to all three increases dramatically.

Barrier Options and the Smile

Let's examine the case of volatility in more detail because this relates to the issue of the volatility smile. Consider an up-and-out call option with strike 100 and barrier 120 (see Figure 11.3.3), and suppose the spot price is near the barrier and the option hasn't yet knocked out. In such a situation, the option's value is extremely sensitive to the volatility of the underlying, because the more volatile the stock is the greater the probability the option will knock out.

One might argue that this shouldn't be a big deal because while increased volatility does increase the probability of knocking out, it also increases the probability of the spot price slipping down. But the point is the barrier's influence dominates the other's. Put another way, the effect of knocking out on the option's value is extreme—knocking out wipes out the option. The effect of spot price dropping is graduated: each drop in stock price affects option value.

The upshot of all of this is twofold. First, the vega of our up-and-out option is very negative near the barrier. Increasing volatility hurts the option's value because the dominant effect of the knockout barrier looms larger. Second, the structure of local volatility (and hence the volatility smile) is crucial in the value of the barrier option.

Local volatility is the volatility the stock will have if the stock is a certain price at a certain time. Imagine local volatilities near the barrier. Tweak these, and the option value changes. Why? Because (look at the vega in Figure 11.3.3 one more time) the option value is extremely sensitive to volatility near the barrier.

A Note about Theta

Note, in this section, theta was calculated using the same convention set down in Chapter 4: A negative theta means as time passes, option value decreases.

Graphs of Barrier Option Values and Hedge Parameters

We now show you what we've been talking about with graphs displaying the relationship between spot price, time to expiration and value, delta, gamma, vega, theta, and rho. In what follows, each figure contains six graphs displaying values and hedge parameters for a single type of option. For example, Figure 11.3.3 represents an up-and-out call option with 100 strike and 120 barrier. Each graph within the figure represents a different feature of the option (e.g., value, delta, etc.) for *three different times to expiration:* three months (solid line), one month (wide dashed line), and two weeks (dotted line). Here is a complete table of the figures:

Figure	Option type	Strike	Barrier
11.3.1	down-and-out call	100	80
11.3.2	down-and-out put	100	80
11.3.3	up-and-out call	100	120
11.3.4	up-and-out put	100	120
11.3.5	down-and-in call	100	95
11.3.6	down-and-in put	100	80
11.3.7	up-and-in call	100	120
11.3.8	up-and-in put	100	105

In all the graphs, we used an underlying with 15 percent volatility and assumed the risk-free rate of interest was 5 percent.

F I G U R E 11.3.1

Down-and-Out Call: Strike 100, Barrier 80.
The out barrier of this option depresses out-of-the-money call values below what a
vanilla option's would be. As the spot price nears the barrier, the option moves deeper
out of the money, while at the same time the probability of knocking out increases.

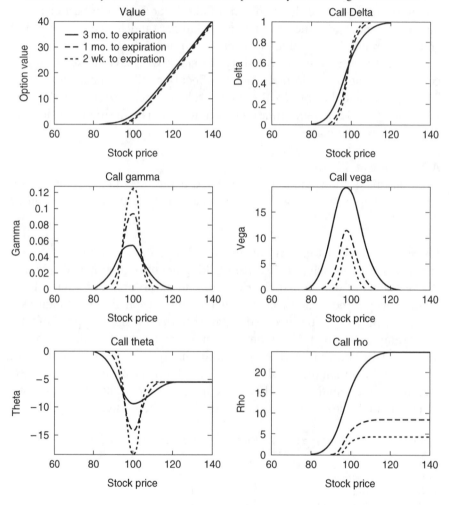

F I G U R E 11.3.2

Down-and-Out Put: Strike 100, Barrier 80.

This option clearly illustrates the "tug-of-war" between moving in the money and facing a possible knockout. As spot price drops toward 80, the option value increases for a while, but as the force of the knockout barrier begins to be felt, the option value precipitously drops until it reaches zero when the spot is at 80. Note in particular the vega of the option. As the spot nears the barrier, vega grows very negative. This indicates the severe negative effect volatility has near the barrier. Increasing volatility increases the probability of a knockout without the corresponding benefit to the option's non-knockout value.

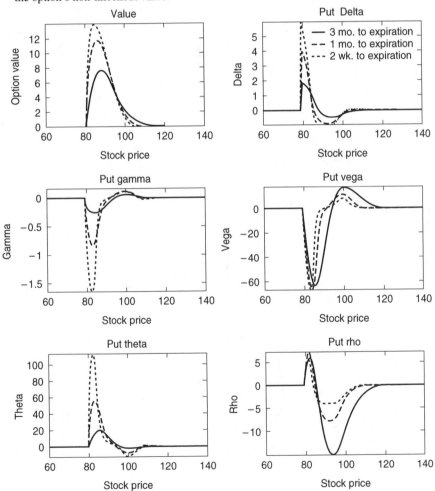

F I G U R E 11.3.3

Up-and-Out Call: Strike 100, Barrier 120.

This up-and-out call behaves quite similarly to a down-and-out put. As spot increases, the intrisic value of the option increases while the probability of knocking out increases as well. Near the barrier, the theta of the option is positive, and increases as time to expiration decreases. This is because the only threat to the option expiring deep in the money is the knockout barrier. As expiration nears, the probability of knocking out (at a given level of spot) decreases, and therefore the value of the option increases.

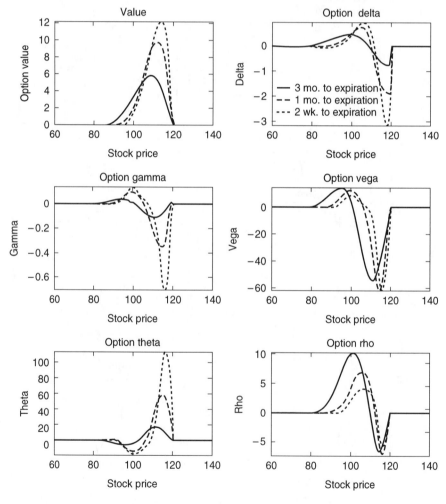

FIGURE 11.3.4

Up-and-Out Put: Strike 100, Barrier 120.

This option is straightforward to understand because as spot price increases, the force of the barrier diminishes the option's value, while at the same time the option moves out of the money.

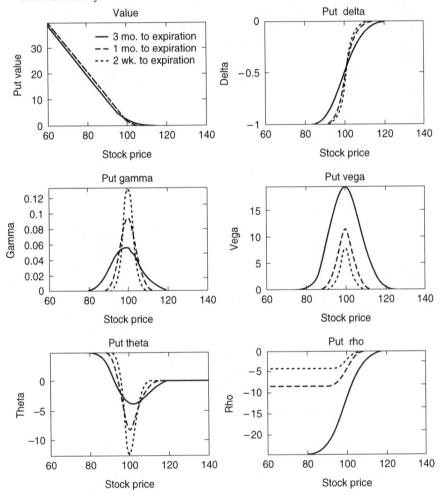

F I G U R E 11.3.5

Down-and-In Call: Strike 100, Barrier 95.

This down-and-in call moves out of the money as the spot price drops. Nevertheless, its value increases because it has not yet knocked in. When the option knocks in, the long position is left holding an out-of-the-money option. Further decreases in spot price rapidly diminish the value of the option. Note the extreme behavior of theta near the barrier. This indicates the danger of holding an inactive knocking option near the barrier. As time passes its value decays rapidly because the probability of knocking in decreases as time to expiration nears.

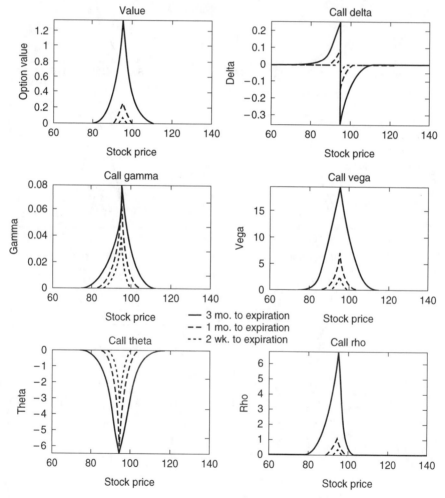

F I G U R E 11.3.6

Down-and-In Put: Strike 100, Barrier 80.
Of all the barrier options, this option's value behaves most like a vanilla option. Near the barrier, the option's value is depressed from the vanilla put's value due to the possibility of expiring worthless. This makes vega very large near the barrier, because increased volatility increases the probability of knocking in, while making theta very negative. Thus, while this option's *value* is similar to a vanilla option, near the barrier it is much more sensitive to volatility and time.

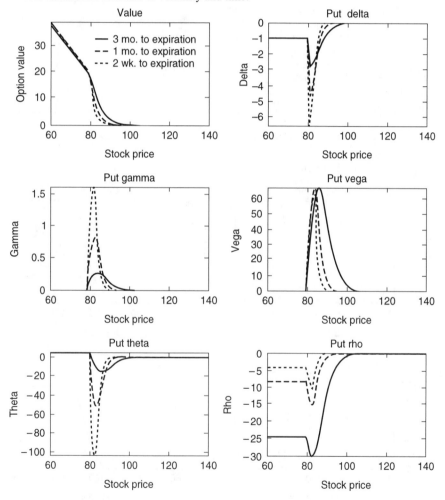

F I G U R E 11.3.7

Up-and-In Call: Strike 100, Barrier 120.
Let's focus on the delta of this call option. As the spot price nears the barrier, the delta grows to over four. This reflects the extreme nature of what happens if the option knocks in. The long position goes from having a probability of expiring worthless to being a deep-in-the-money call. Thus before the option knocks in, even fractional moves toward the barrier increase the option's value a great deal, thus accounting for the large delta. Once the option knocks in, the delta returns to almost one, appropriate for a deep-in-the-money call.

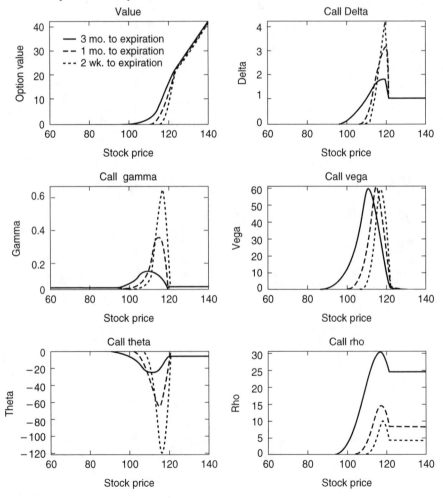

F I G U R E 11.3.8

Up-and-In Put: Strike 100, Barrier 105.

This option's value is complicated by the position of the barrier being exactly where the option is out of the money. This accounts for the very peaked appearance of the graphs near the barrier. As the spot price moves toward 105 (with spot less than 105), the option's intrinsic value remains zero, the probability of expiring in the money decreases, while the probability of knocking in increases. The net effect is that for a given level of spot, near the barrier the option's value is greatest furthest from expiration. Note how the delta jumps from very positive to very negative when the spot crosses the barrier. Once the option knocks in, it is a vanilla call, and its delta must be negative.

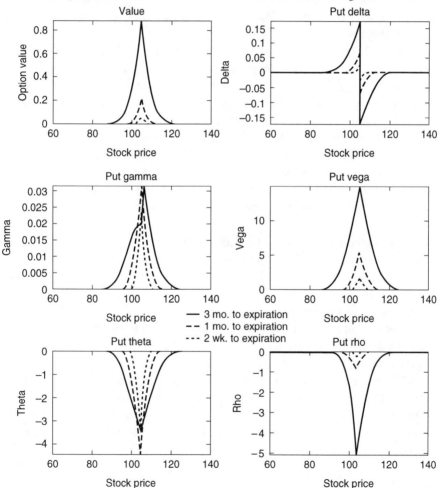

11.4 VALUING BARRIER OPTIONS ON A BINOMIAL TREE

We have seen some of the basic features of barrier option prices and hedge parameters. We now proceed to explain how to price barrier options on binomial trees.

Interestingly, the procedures for pricing knock-out and knock-in options work on exactly the same principle. The pricing method is a two-step procedure. In both cases, we first value the option at every point on the barrier. In the case of knock-out options, values along the barrier are equal to the value of the rebate. This reflects the fact that if the option knocks out, the short position has to "pay" the rebate to the long position. Thus, the amount of the rebate is the correct value for each node along the barrier. For example, if there is no rebate, the barrier values are all equal to zero.

In the case of knock-in options, barrier values are equal to the value of an ordinary put or call settled when the spot price breaches the barrier. We will explain this in complete detail below.

Once we determine the values along the barrier, the next step is to perform backward induction. This is similar to what is done in the case of ordinary puts and calls except we work backward from every point along the barrier, not just from the terminal nodes. All of these methods can be "Americanized" by testing at each node for early exercise.

Valuing Barrier Options—the Basic Idea

The fundamental idea in pricing barrier options is as follows: When the spot price crosses the barrier for the first time, a "target security" must be purchased by the short position and paid to the long position, according to the terms of the option contract.

For example, when a knock-in call option "knocks in," the contract instantly becomes an ordinary call option. This is the target option and is depicted in the figure at the top of page 453.

Thus, the short position must purchase the target option (or some equivalent security) at exactly the instant the barrier is breached; otherwise, it will not be fully hedged. Similarly, when a knock-out option "knocks out," a rebate is paid by the short position. In this case, the target security is cash in an amount equal to the rebate.

Some Terminology

The moment the spot price first breaches the barrier is called *first passage time*. The security that must be purchased at first passage time is called the *target security*. Table 11.4.1 displays a list of target securities.

Time

T A B L E   11.4.1

Target securities for barrier option

Knock-Out Type		Knock-In Type	
Name	**Target Security**	**Name**	**Target Security**
Down-and-out	Cash security whose value is equal to value of rebate	Down-and-in	Call (or put) option with terms equal to the terms of the "in" option
Up-and-out	Cash security whose value is equal to value of rebate	Up-and-in	Call (or put) option with terms equal to the terms of the "in" option

This terminology places knock-in and knock-out options on an equal footing, because it shows they are the same type of security, as they only differ in the nature of the target security. In fact, we can extend our "barrier" pricing methods to include any possible target security.

For example, consider a knock-out option with a "deferred rebate." This is a knock-out option in which the contract specifies that the rebate is paid on the expiration date instead of at the moment the barrier is crossed. This is exactly the same as an ordinary barrier with rebate, except now the target security is a bond maturing at expiration instead of cash.

The Target Security at Expiration

To complete our analysis, we have to say something about the expiration date of a barrier option. If an investor is holding a barrier option, then the option pays at expiration if the option expires "active." In this case, the in-the-money nodes at expiration that are in an active region (i.e., below an up-and-out knockout barrier) behave like barrier nodes, only the target security for these nodes is given by the standard payoff for the option. For example, a knockout call's in-the-money terminal nodes pay

$$S_T - K,$$

where S_T is the terminal spot of the underlying and K is the strike.

Hedging Barrier Options

The key difference between barrier options and the vanilla options we have studied so far is:

> To hedge the short position of a barrier option, at first passage time, we must be able to purchase the "target option," or an equivalent, and exit the contract.

Figure 11.4.1 shows a binomial tree with a barrier. The region above the barrier is the "out" region, and the region below the barrier is the "in" region. The darkened nodes are the first nodes reached after the spot price crosses the barrier—the barrier nodes. Notice that the terminal nodes below the barrier are darkened. We consider these barrier nodes because if the stock price reaches one of these nodes while the option is still active (that is, in the event that the option has not knocked out), then these nodes behave exactly like barrier nodes. The target security for these nodes is the standard payoff of the option.

American Options Are Barrier Options

In Chapter 7, Section 7.10, we discussed the early exercise barrier of an American option. Recall that this barrier is defined as the first possible node at each time at which an option will be optimally exercised.

From the point of view of barrier options, this is quite natural, and it says that an American option is nothing but a barrier option whose target security at each barrier node is the intrinsic value of the option. This is true since when the option is exercised, the payout is always $\max(S_t - K, 0)$, that is, the greater of the current value minus the strike and zero.

Unfortunately, this observation does not quite yield a new pricing method for American options; however, it does shed light on an important point: The true difficulty in pricing American options is determining exactly what the early exercise boundary looks like. If we could know this

F I G U R E   11.4.1

A binomial tree with a barrier.
The darkened nodes are the first-passage-time nodes.

Barrier

a priori for any option (e.g., by some sort of formula), we could produce pricing formulas for American options.

Backward Induction

Once we have determined the values of the target option at each of the first-passage nodes, we have to value the other nodes. This is done using the standard backward induction procedure (either European style or American style). The only difference is that when the barrier is crossed, the target security is purchased and the position is effectively closed out. We will illustrate how this works with a number of examples.

Figure 11.4.2 displays a four-period binomial tree for the spot price of a stock or index. This tree is a standard Cox-Ross-Rubinstein tree with the risk-free rate set at 5 percent, the volatility set at 20 percent, and with expiration equal to one year. In the next pages, we will value five different barrier options using this tree as the basic stock process. The options we value are specified as follows:

F I G U R E 11.4.2

Basic binomial tree. This is a
standard Cox-Ross-Rubinstein tree
with volatility equal to 20 percent,
risk-free rate equal to 5 percent,
and time until expiration of 1 year.

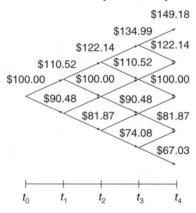

Example #	Type	Strike	Barrier	Rebate
1	knock-out call	$80	$120	$0
2	knock-out put	$110	$80	$1
3	knock-in call	$95	$120	$0
4	knock-in put	$110	$85	$0
5	double barrier call	$90	$120 (out)	$2
			$80 (out)	$5

The last option requires a bit of explanation. It is a double barrier
option; that is, it has two barriers. One is above the strike, and one is below
the strike. In the case of example 5, the option is a regular call option, but it
knocks out *if* the spot price drops below $80 or rises above $120. If the spot
price rises above $120, a $2 rebate is paid, and if it drops below $80, a $5
rebate is paid. We now proceed to value each example in complete detail.

Example 1: A Knock-Out Call with No Rebate
In this example, we value a knock-out call with the following specifications:

spot	$100
strike	$80
barrier	$120
rebate	0
expiration	1 year
risk-free rate	5%
volatility	20%

F I G U R E   11.4.3

Stock price tree and option value tree for example 1.
This knock-out call option has a barrier of $120, no rebate, and is struck at $80.

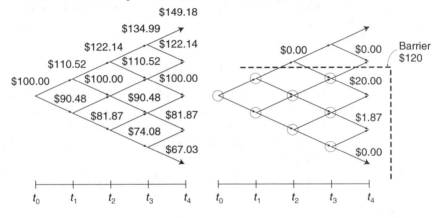

Figure 11.4.3 displays the stock price tree for this option accompanied by its option value tree. In the option value tree, we have only assigned values to *barrier nodes,* that is, those nodes that are the first nodes beyond the barrier.

The barrier nodes are valued in one of two ways. A barrier node before expiration has a value of zero, due to the fact that the option is a knockout with zero rebate. A barrier node at the expiration date of the option (time t_4) is valued according to the terms of the standard part of the option contract. Since the option is a vanilla call, the value of each barrier node at expiration is

$$\max(S_t - K, 0).$$

Completing the Tree in Example 1

To complete the tree in example 1, we proceed with backward induction "from the barrier." This means we value every node, inside the perimeter of the barrier, that has not already been assigned. These nodes have been circled in Figure 11.4.3.

We will value each of these nodes as if it were a one-step tree, using the formulas in equation (7.3.4) of Chapter 7. Given a node, we have to know the up and down values of the option, C_u and C_d, and the risk-neutral transition probability, p.

Since our tree is a standard binomial tree, the risk-neutral transition probability is the same at every node. It is given by:

$$p = 0.5378.$$

The computation of the value of nodes (3, 0) and (3, 1) proceeds exactly the same as in ordinary binomial trees, so we only explain the computation of node (3, 2), which is slightly different than with an ordinary call.

In computing node (3, 2), we will use standard backward induction based on the observed option payouts at time t_4. Looking at Figure 11.4.3, we see that these payouts are:

$$C_d = \$20.00 \quad \text{and} \quad C_u = \$0.00.$$

What's new here is that the "up" payoff from node (3, 2) is not the expected payout of a European call. Why? Because when the spot price moves up from node (3, 2) to node (4, 3), the spot price also crosses the \$120 barrier, and the option knocks out. Therefore, the correct amount to "hedge against" in this scenario is \$0.00.

The computations for the nodes at time t_3 are displayed below.

Node	Value
(3,2)	0.9876(.5378 · 0 + 0.4622 · 20) = 9.124
(3,1)	0.9876(.5378 · 20 + 0.4622 · 1.87) = 11.4762
(3,0)	0.9876(.5378 · 1.87 + 0.4622 · 0) = 0.9932

To compute the nodes at times t_2, t_1, and t_0, we proceed similarly as above, continuing backward first at time t_2, then at time t_1, and finally at time t_0. Figure 11.4.4 displays the completed option value tree for example 1.

Example 2: A Down-and-Out Put with Rebate
This example values a down-and-out put with the following data:

spot	\$100
strike	\$110
out barrier	\$80
rebate	\$1
expiration	1 year
risk-free rate	5%
volatility	20%

Figure 11.4.5 displays the stock price and option value trees for this down-and-out put. The rebate is paid if the spot price crosses the barrier and knocks the option out. The tree is constructed as in Figure 11.4.2.

Each barrier node prior to expiration is assigned the value \$1.00. Let's examine the meaning of this. Suppose the spot price at time t_2 is \$81.87; that is, suppose the spot price reaches node (2,0). The question is, If we

FIGURE 11.4.4

Stock price tree and option value tree for example 1.

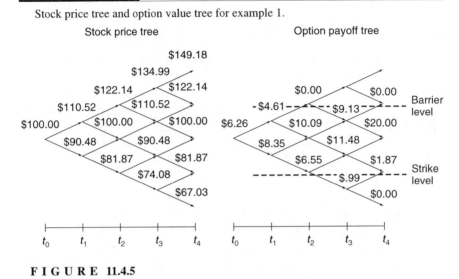

FIGURE 11.4.5

Stock price tree and option value tree for example 2.
This knock-out put option has a barrier of $80, is struck at $110,
and pays a rebate of $1.

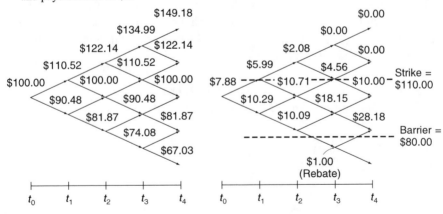

are hedging the short position of this option, what do we have to hedge against? If the spot price rises from time t_2 to time t_3, then our hedging portfolio has to have $18.15 in it at time t_3. On the other hand, if the spot drops, we only have to have $1 at time t_3—just enough to cover the rebate. These observations are reflected in the fact that nodes (3,1) and (3,0) are respectively labeled $18.15 and $1. Therefore, for node (2, 0) we have:

$$C_u = \$18.15 \quad \text{and} \quad C_d = \$1.00.$$

That is, the up payout is $18.15, the down payout is $1.00, and the value of node (2, 0) is

$$e^{-r\Delta t}(pC_u + (1 - p)C_d),$$

where r is the risk-free rate, Δt is the length of the time step, and p is the up-transition probability. This is the standard backward induction procedure.

One important note to make is that once the option enters the barrier region, the target option is purchased and no more hedging needs to take place. So, once the rebate is paid, there is no longer risk involved in the short position. Therefore, the nodes in the barrier region are not valued according to the "binomial formula." For this reason, we do not assign values to nodes "beyond" the barrier nodes.

Why Knock-Out Options Are Cheaper

Examining Figure 11.4.5 clearly demonstrates why knock-out options are cheaper than corresponding vanilla options. Examine node (4,0), the bottom node of time t_4. If this option were a vanilla put, then the value of this node would be $K - S = 110 - 67.03 = 42.97$. That is, since the node is a terminal node, the ordinary put's value would simply be $K - S$.

This, in turn, would cause the vanilla put's value at node (3,0) to be $34.56 rather than $1—a large difference. This increase would propagate backward through the tree, raising the value of all nodes that can possibly lead to node (4, 0). In particular, it would raise the value of node (0, 0), which is the value of the option.

Example 3: A Knock-In Call with No Rebate

This example studies a knock-in call with no rebate. The setup is as follows:

spot	$100
strike	$95
in barrier	$120
rebate	$0.00
expiration	1 year
risk-free rate	5%
volatility	20%

This is our first example of valuing a knock-in option. The procedure for valuing this option follows two steps.

1. First, we value the barrier nodes for the option. Because the "target option" is a call option with strike price $95, this means

that each barrier node represents a call option settled at the time of the node, struck at $95, and expiring the same time as the knock-in.

2. Next, perform backward induction "from the barrier." That is, ignore all nodes beyond the barrier and proceed with backward induction as in the case of knock-out options.

Hedging the Option

We discuss the above steps in more detail now. Figure 11.4.6 displays the stock price tree, and the beginnings of the option value tree for the knock-in call above. The most interesting node from our point of view is node (2, 2). This node is the first node in the tree (from the point of view of time) where the barrier could be crossed. What are the consequences of crossing the barrier when hedging the short position?

If the spot price reaches node (2, 2), then it is at $122.14, and the option knocks in. This means the short position must be prepared at this time to enter the long position (or its equivalent) in a $95–strike call expiring at time t_4. We have separately valued this option at $29.49, and this is the correct option value for node (2, 2).

With this completed, we move on to consider the terminal nodes in Figure 11.4.6. Note that all terminal nodes of the option value tree below the barrier are set to zero. At first, this may seem incorrect. What if the option knocks in and then dips below the barrier?

The point is, if the option ever knocks in, then all hedging stops because the target option is purchased. Therefore, at expiration, if we are still

F I G U R E 11.4.6

A knock-in call option with barrier $120 and strike $95.

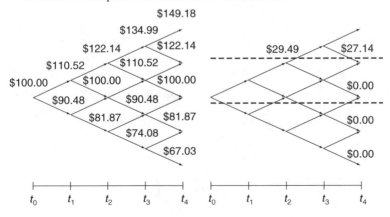

hedging the option, then we can assume that the option has not crossed the barrier. Since we are presently dealing with a *knock-in* option with no rebate, this means that should the spot price get to time t_4 inactive, then the option will be worthless. Figure 11.4.7 displays the completed option value tree for this example.

Example 4: Knock-In Put with $110 Strike and $82 Barrier
This example values a knock-in put with the following setup.

spot	$100
strike	$110
in barrier	$82
rebate	$0.00
expiration	1 year
risk-free rate	5%
volatility	20%

We do not go through the details of valuation in this example, but rather study the difference in value between the above option and a similar vanilla option. Figure 11.4.8 displays the regular "vanilla" option value tree (right-hand tree) and the "barrier" option value tree.

In the barrier option value tree, there are two nodes along the barrier, node (2,0) and node (4,1), valued at $25.41 and $28.13, respectively. Backward induction was performed from the barrier in the usual way.

F I G U R E 11.4.7

A knock-in call option with barrier $120, with all option value nodes filled in

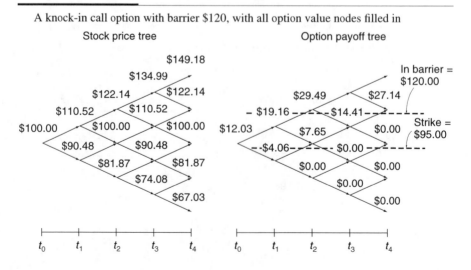

Stock price tree   Option payoff tree

F I G U R E 11.4.8

A knock-in put option with barrier $82 and strike $110 compared with a similar vanilla option.

See Figure 11.4.2 for the stock price tree of this option.

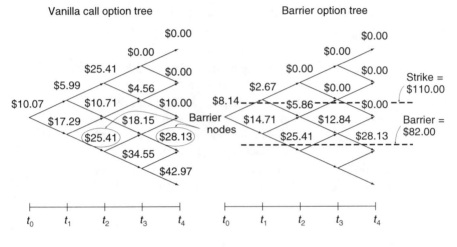

F I G U R E 11.4.9

The stock price tree and option value tree for a double barrier $90–strike call option. Option has a $120 out barrier with a $2 rebate, and an $80 out barrier with a $5 rebate.

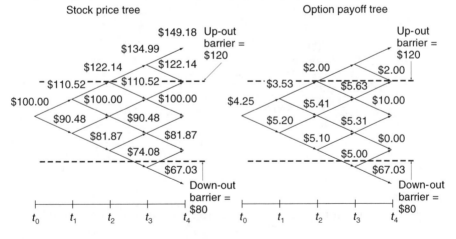

Example 5: Double Barrier Option

Figure 11.4.9 displays the stock price tree and option value tree for our example of a double barrier option. In this example, we price a double barrier. The underlying option is a call option struck at $90. There is a $120 out barrier with a $2 rebate and an $80 out barrier with a $5 rebate.

D I S P L A Y 11.4.1

HOW TO PRICE BARRIER OPTIONS

To price barrier options on a binomial tree, we proceed in several steps. The following steps are illustrated in the diagram below.

1. Build a binomial (stock) tree on which to price the option, and define where the barrier is on the tree.
2. Find all the "nodes along the barrier." These are the nodes that are touched immediately *after* first passage.
3. Value the nodes along the barrier according to the target security. If the option is a knockout option, the value of the target node is the cost of the rebate. If the option is a knock-in option, then an option must be valued at each node along the barrier.
4. Use backward induction "from the barrier." All nodes beyond the barrier (circled nodes in the figure) are to be ignored.

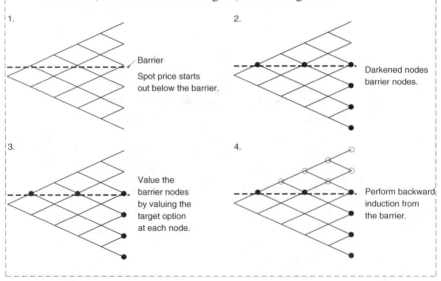

Summary

Display 11.4.1 summarizes the procedure for pricing barrier options.

11.5 ENHANCED NUMERICAL METHODS

While the above methods for computing barrier option prices are theoretically sound, there is one problem. Sometimes, in order to produce good option values, we have to use a tree with many more time steps than is computationally practical or convenient. In general, one wants to obtain reasonable option values with as few computations as possible.

The problem with valuing barrier options is that it can be difficult to know the "right" number of periods to use to calculate accurate option prices. Generally, we know that "binomial" prices converge to "analytical" prices as we increase the number of periods in our tree. That is, since all models for pricing options on a binomial tree can be built for any number of periods, if we price the same option with increasing numbers of periods, we expect to get better and better results. That is, results that are closer and closer to the analytical result.

In fact, the theory does imply something like this, but things are more complicated than they might appear at first. The theory actually says that if we want to get arbitrarily close to the analytical answer (i.e., to a given level of accuracy), there is always a tree large enough (i.e., with enough periods) to obtain prices that are accurate. However, the theory does not say how many periods we need to obtain this accuracy.

The heart of the problem is that as you increase the number of periods, the valuation of the barrier option can get worse instead of better.

This is at first counterintuitive, but the fact is that not every increase in periods is beneficial to the option price. The true nature of the convergence is, roughly speaking, that as you increase the number of periods, the approximation improves for a while and then suddenly gets worse. It proceeds to improve again, then worsens. This pattern repeats itself, and it is called a "saw-toothed" convergence pattern. Figure 11.5.1 depicts this. The root cause of this convergence problem is option specification error. We discuss this now.

Specification Error and Barrier Options

One can understand option specification error by noting that the nodes of a binomial tree do not necessarily lie near the barrier of an option. For example, in Figure 11.4.7, the option has a $120 barrier but none of the node prices are exactly $120. Therefore, according to the model, the option cannot knockout at exactly $120. Rather, when the stock price rises from $110.52, it rises to $122.14; therefore, the option must knock out essentially at this price.[2] The upshot of this is that the coarseness of the tree mis-specifies the option—option specification error.

---

[2] We could wax quite philosophical as to exactly where the option knocks out. One thing we do know for certain is that as long as the barrier lies between $110.52 and $122.14, we will obtain the same barrier option price.

F I G U R E 11.5.1

The convergence of binomial pricing of a barrier option.
As the number of periods is increased, the value converges slowly in an
irregular, saw-toothed manner.

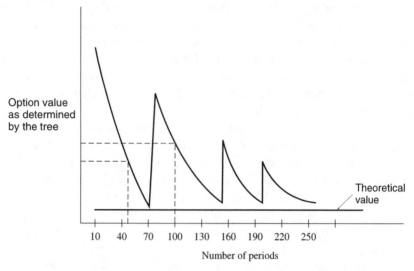

To overcome these mis-specifications, the most obvious solution is to
increase the number of periods. This will indeed solve the problem, but it
can require many more periods than one might think. Worse, the pattern
of *convergence* (that is, the general relationship between the number of
periods and the corresponding option prices) is not stable.

In general, increasing the number of periods will make matters worse
when adding a small number of periods.[3] This is illustrated in Figure
11.5.1. In this figure, the horizontal axis represents the number of periods
and the vertical axis represents the option value. The graph represents
the value of a single barrier option as valued on a binomial tree using a
varying number of periods. The theoretical value of the option is the solid
horizontal line below the saw-toothed pattern.

Imagine pricing this barrier option using a binomial tree with 50 time
periods. This tree would produce a certain price (see Figure 11.5.1). If we
increase the number of periods to 100, one can see from the picture that
rather than obtaining an option price closer to the theoretical value, we have
produced a price farther away.

---

[3]This was apparently first pointed out in "Binomial Pricing of Exploding Options," Margabre
(1989).

What makes this particularly difficult is that we do not know the exact nature of the convergence of the binomial price to the analytical price ahead of time. That is, we do not always know a "good" number of periods to choose for our binomial tree. The only way to find one is to start pricing options and make a graph. This is time consuming—exactly what we would like to avoid. We want a way to "speed up" the convergence.

Improving the Model

From our point of view, the problem is that the barrier may not be effectively represented by the tree. One way to correct this is to choose a tree in which the barrier is near the nodes of the tree.

In fact, this can be done if we are using a standard binomial tree with a simple barrier (i.e., the same barrier price for all times). This concept has been carried out by Boyle and Lau (1994). Their method (for standard trees only) gives a formula for choosing a "good" number of periods based on the barrier. In terms of Figure 11.5.1, their method tells you where the low points of the saw-toothed pattern are.

The Boyle and Lau method would be enough to successfully combat the saw-toothed convergence problem if we were only interested in standard binomial trees. Unfortunately, using a standard binomial tree is equivalent to assuming constant local volatility; and due to the implied volatility and binomial tree theories that we have available to us, we do not want to restrict ourselves to only standard trees. Therefore, we seek a better method.

The Enhanced Method

The methods discussed in this section provide computational enhancements to the techniques for valuing barrier options already discussed. In particular, these techniques largely suppress the saw-toothed pattern of convergence found in Figure 11.5.1. The methods can be found in Derman, Kani, Ergener, and Bardhan (1995), and we follow their work closely.

To start, we discuss the "effective" and "modified" barrier.

The Effective versus Modified Barrier

To illustrate these concepts, we will work with up-and-out options, though the methods are perfectly general and can be applied to any type of barrier option.

Consider the following barrier option on an underlying stock or index S with an annual volatility of 15 percent.

type	up-and-out
barrier	$120
strike	$80

Assume that the risk-free rate of interest is 5 percent. We have generated a stock price tree for this case; see Figure 11.5.2.

Due to the nature of the tree, the actual stock prices at which the option knocks out are given by the first prices (represented by the tree) above the barrier. These prices form the *effective barrier* of the tree (note that if this were a down-and-out option, we would look at the first prices *below* the barrier).

We want to create another barrier, the *modified barrier*, formed from the first stock prices directly before the barrier (in the case of down-and-out options, we would look at the first stock prices immediately *above* the barrier). To summarize, the effective barrier is the set of stock price nodes that are contacted immediately after first passage, and the modified barrier

F I G U R E   11.5.2

The effective (left diagram) and modified (right diagram) barrier for an up-and-out option with a $120 barrier

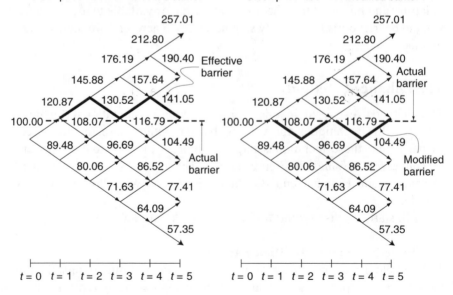

consists of the set of stock price nodes that are contacted directly before first passage.

The motivation for forming this second barrier is that neither barrier perfectly represents the actual barrier of the option—the effective barrier is a little "above" the real barrier and the modified barrier is a little "below" the real barrier. Therefore, the price of the barrier option is better calculated by taking some sort of average value of the two barrier options formed from the two barriers. The enhanced method we describe below makes this precise.

Description of the Enhanced Numerical Method

Roughly speaking, we are going to make two computations of the barrier option price. The first will be using the effective barrier (left diagram in Figure 11.5.2), and the second one will be using the modified barrier (right diagram in Figure 11.5.2). We will combine these estimates at each node according to how close the actual node is to the two barriers.

In the adjoining diagram, we see a piece of a binomial tree with a barrier. We are assuming that the barrier lies above the initial spot price (i.e., the option is an up-and-out or an up-and-in type), so that the effective barrier lies above the pictured node and the modified barrier lies below it.

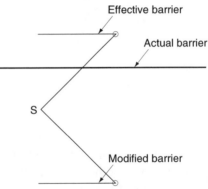

How the Method Works

Recall that the key to pricing barrier options is to evaluate all the nodes along the barrier (according to the target option) and then perform backward induction "from the barrier." With the enhanced barrier method, we do almost exactly the same thing, except we evaluate each barrier node in two ways—first assuming that the barrier is the effective barrier and then assuming that the barrier is the modified barrier—and then average the two values, placing the resulting value on the modified barrier. We now describe the steps in detail, referring to Figure 11.5.3.

F I G U R E 11.5.3

Steps in performing the enhanced method

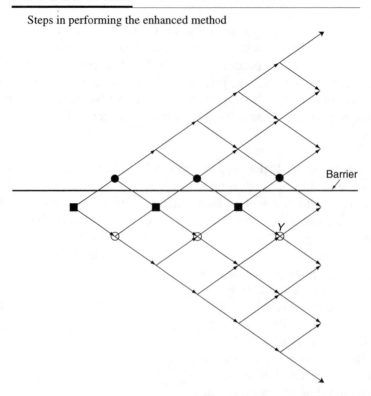

To perform the enhanced numerical methods, we use the following steps. The goal of the enhanced method is to assign values to all of the nodes directly before the nodes along the barrier. In Figure 11.5.3, the nodes along the barrier are displayed as darkened circles. The nodes directly below the barrier are displayed as open circles. The values of nodes that are displayed as darkened rectangles can be deduced from the circled nodes *once the values of the circled nodes have been established.* We point this out, because it is easy to think that since these nodes are near the barrier, they should be enhanced as well.

We will explain how to compute the "enhanced value" of the node directly below the barrier, labeled Y.

1. Value node Y as if the barrier is the effective barrier (as in ordinary pricing of barrier options). Call this value V_e, for effective value.

2. Now value node Y again, this time assuming that the barrier is the modified barrier. When we move the barrier to the modified barrier, node Y becomes a node along the barrier and therefore takes the value of the target option at that node. We call this value V_m, for modified value.

3. Finally, we compute the value of node Y by averaging the values V_e and V_m according to how far the effective and modified barriers are from the actual barrier. The formula is as follows. Write B_a for the actual barrier value, B_e for the enhanced barrier value, and B_m for the modified barrier value. Then, V is defined by the following formula:

$$V = \frac{B_a - B_m}{B_e - B_m} V_e + \frac{B_e - B_a}{B_e - B_m} V_m. \qquad (11.5.1)$$

To help understand equation (11.5.1), it is helpful to substitute the "extreme" values for B_a, the actual barrier, into it. First, assume $B_a = B_e$, that is, the actual barrier is equal to the effective barrier. Then, we have:

$$V = \frac{B_e - B_m}{B_e - B_m} V_e + \frac{B_e - B_e}{B_e - B_m} V_m = V_e.$$

In other words, when the actual barrier is equal to the effective barrier, the value of node Y is equal to V_e. Likewise, when $B_a = B_m$, we have

$$V = \frac{B_m - B_m}{B_e - B_m} V_e + \frac{B_e - B_m}{B_e - B_m} V_m = V_m$$

and the value of V is V_m. When the actual barrier lies somewhere between the effective and modified barrier, the value of node Y lies somewhere "between" V_e and V_m. Let's give an example of using the method.

Sample Computation
We now give a sample computation of the enhanced numerical methods at work. In this example, we apply the method to a knockout call option. Here are the relevant data for the option:

spot price	$100
strike price	$90
expiration	1 year
option style	European
option type	knockout call
barrier	$115.00
risk-free rate	5%
volatility	15%

FIGURE 11.5.4

Stock tree used in the enhanced numerical method example.
The tree is a Cox-Ross-Rubinstein constant volatility tree. The risk-free rate of interest is 5 percent and the volatility is 15 percent. The tree is used to price a knockout call option with a $115 barrier.

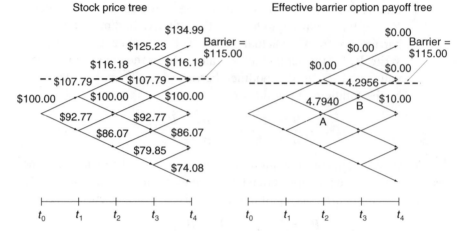

The left-hand side of Figure 11.5.4 displays a Cox-Ross-Rubinstein tree constructed with a 5 percent risk-free rate and a 15 percent volatility. Each time step is three months. At time t_2 the effective barrier is $116.18, and the modified barrier is $100.00. At time t_3 the effective barrier is $125.23 and the modified barrier is $107.79.

The right-hand side of Figure 11.5.4 displays a partially filled in "effective barrier tree." That is, this is the option value tree for our barrier option if we use the effective barrier. The nodes labeled A and B are what interests us. The values of these nodes reflect the use of the effective barrier. If we use the modified barrier, then these nodes both have a value of $0.00 (because in the modified barrier, nodes A and B both lie on the knockout barrier).

We want to find values of nodes A and B that reflect the effective values (derived from the effective barrier) and the modified values (derived from the modified barrier) and their relative distance to the actual barrier ($115).

We do this for node A first. We have:

Barrier	Value	Node value
effective	$116.1834	$4.7940
actual	$115.00	to be computed
modified	$100.00	$0.00

We have to find the node value at the actual barrier. To do this, we apply the interpolation formula:

$$\text{Value of node A} = \frac{115.00 - 100}{116.1834 - 100} \cdot 4.7940$$
$$+ \frac{116.1834 - 115.00}{116.1834 - 100} \cdot 0.00 = 4.444.$$

Now, we repeat the computation for node B. We have:

Barrier	Value	Node value
effective	$125.2323	$4.7940
actual	$115.00	to be computed
modified	$107.7884	$0.00

We have to find the node value at the actual barrier. To do this, we apply the interpolation formula:

$$\text{Value of node B} = \frac{115.00 - 107.7884}{125.2323 - 107.7884} \cdot 4.2956$$
$$+ \frac{125.2323 - 115.00}{125.2323 - 107.7884} \cdot 0.00 = 1.7759$$

With the values of nodes A and B in hand, we can finish valuing the option.

Valuing the Option

Figure 11.5.5 displays our barrier option priced using the enhanced nodes. Notice that once the values for nodes A and B are computed, the rest of the procedure for pricing the option is no different than the unenhanced methods.

11.6   FINAL WORDS . . . WHAT'S IT ALL GOOD FOR?

This concludes *Black-Scholes and Beyond*. If you have read this entire book carefully, you have received an introduction to the theory of options pricing as it is understood today.

In this book we have presented a theory of option pricing revolving around the single idea of a self-financing, replicating hedging strategy. This concept stayed with us through the original Black-Scholes formula, through binomial trees, and finally to implied volatility and binomial trees. All of these models have a single purpose: to help traders (or, more generally,

F I G U R E 11.5.5

The final option pricing tree for the enhanced method.

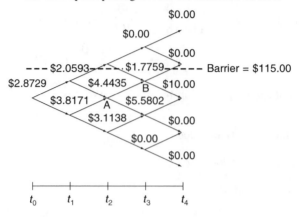

$0.00

$0.00

$0.00

--- $2.0593 --- $1.7759 --- Barrier = $115.00

$2.8729 $4.4435 B $10.00

$3.8171 A $5.5802

$3.1138

$0.00

$0.00

t_0 t_1 t_2 t_3 t_4

anyone handling option positions) better manage the risk of hedging: If there were a magical formula that could see the future and tell us which way stock prices (or even volatilities) were going to move, then sophisticated theories would not be necessary.

Unfortunately, in the absence of such information, we need *good* theories. Now the question is: What is a good theory? This is a question this book has not addressed enough. A simple definition of a good theory is one that performs well. Let's agree that good performance is reflected in low "model error." For more on this, we quote from Eric Jacquier and Robert Jarrow:

> Textbook treatments of option pricing theory ignore model error when discussing risk management... yet model error is of immense importance in the application of options pricing and related risk management techniques.[4]

Jacquier and Jarrow (1995) address what is possibly the most important issue facing the next generation of option pricing models. Do the models work? The above article gives a methodology for computing the risk inherent in a model based on what really happens in the markets, or as *RISK* magazine puts it, they "present a new framework for evaluating error in option pricing models."

With this said, an appropriate final word might be *skepticism*. It would be wise to approach all the models in this book, and all the new models yet

---

[4]From "Vital Statistics", Jacquier and Jarrow (1995).

to come with an appropriate dose of skepticism. This is not to say that the models are not valuable tools. The models in this book are intuitively appealing, make sense, and are logically self-consistent. But, do they work? This is a question that needs to be evaluated today and continually reevaluated as markets evolve.

Where Do We Go from Here?

The good practioner knows that no model, no matter how well it represents reality, is worth anything if the trades required by the model cannot be executed in the prevailing markets. In this situation, costs not predicted by the model can arise. Thus, the next generation of research is starting to focus not strictly on valuation models (though it is true there is much work still to be done there), but also on *hedging;* that is, the practical side of hedging must be blended with the theory of options pricing to produce models that perform in the real world. This book has layed out the basic framework of the theory of options pricing. Yet another book is necessary to discuss hedging.

COMMENTS AND
SUGGESTED READING

The material barrier options in this chapter were derived from a number of sources. Interesting general articles on barrier options include Benson and Daniel (1991), Derman and Kani (1993), Heynen and Kat (1994), Hudson (1991), Kat and Verdonk (1995), Kunitomo and Ikeda (1992), Margrabe (1989), and Reiner and Rubinstein (1991). The work on "enhanced numerical methods" was taken from Derman, Kani, Ergener, and Bardhan (1995).

Analytic formulas for pricing barrier options may be found in Derman and Kani (1993) and Reiner and Rubinstein (1991). We caution the reader, however, that these formulas are based on the Black-Scholes assumptions for stock price movements. Since barrier option prices are especially sensitive to volatility, these models may not be very accurate.

A completely different approach to pricing and hedging barrier options is found in *static hedging*. Static hedging is based on the idea of hedging exotic options by creating a hedge consisting of vanilla calls and puts in special combinations that guarantee replicating the payoff of the option. The term *static* is used because the hedge is set up once and not modified throughout its life, in contrast to dynamic hedging, which is continuously modified. Naturally, static and dynamic hedging are linked by the fact that vanilla calls and puts may be themselves replicated through a dynamic hedging strategy, thus supplying a method for transforming any static hedge into a dynamic hedge. For more on the subject of static hedging see Bowie and Carr (1994), Carr, Ellis and Gupta (1996) and Derman, Ergener and Kani (1994, 1995), and the references therein.

Bibliography

Alexander, S. "Price Movements in Speculative Markets: Trends or Random Walks?" *Industrial Management Review* 2, no. 2 (May 1961), pp. 7–26.

———. "Price Movements in Speculative Markets: Trends or Random Walks, No. 2." *Industrial Management Review* 5, no. 2 (Spring 1964).

Amin, K. "Jump Diffusion Option Valuation in Discrete Time." *Journal of Finance* 48, no. 5 (Dec. 1993), pp. 1833–1863.

Bachelier, L. "Theory of speculation." In *The Random Character of Stock Market Prices.* Cambridge, MA: MIT Press, 1964.

Ball, C., and A. Roma. "Stochastic Volatility Option Pricing." *Journal of Financial and Quantitative Analysis* 29, no. 4 (Dec 1994), pp. 589–607.

Ball, C., and W. Torous. "On Jumps in Common Stock Prices and Their Impact on Call Option Pricing." *Journal of Finance* 40, no. 1 (Mar 1985), pp. 155–173.

Barclay, M. "Dividends, Taxes and Common Stock Prices: The Ex-dividend Behavior of Common Stock Prices Before the Income Tax." *Journal of Finance* 19, (1987), pp. 31–44.

Barle, S., and N. Cakici. "Growing a Smiling Tree." *RISK* 8, no. 10 (Oct 1995), pp. 76–81.

Barone-Adesi, G., and R. Whaley. "Efficient Analytic Approximation of American Put Values." *Journal of Finance* 42, no. 2 (June 1987), pp. 301–320.

Benson, R., and N. Daniel. "Up, Over and Out." *RISK* (June 1991).

Bernstein, P. L. *Capital Ideas.* Canada: The Free Press, 1992.

Black, F. "The Pricing of Commodities Contracts." *Journal of Financial Economics* 3, Jan–March 1976, pp. 167–179.

———. "How We Came Up with the Option Formula." *Journal of Portfolio Management* 15, Winter 1989, pp. 4–8.

Black, F., and M. Scholes. "The Valuation of Option Pricing Contracts and a Test of Market Efficiency." *Journal of Finance* 27, no. 2 (May 1972), pp. 399–418.

———. "The Pricing of Options and Corporate Liabilities." *Journal of Political Economy* 81, May/June 1973, pp. 637–657.

Bookstaber, R. M. *Option Pricing and Investment Strategies.* Chicago: Probus, 1987.

Bowie, J., and P. Carr. "Static Simplicity." *RISK* 7, no. 8 (Aug. 1994), pp. 45–49.

Boyle, P., and A. Ananthanarayanan. "The Impact of Variance Estimation in Option Valuation Models." *Journal of Financial Economics* 5, 1977, pp. 375–388.

Boyle, P., and S. H. Lau. "Bumping Up Against the Barrier with the Binomial Method." *Journal of Derivatives* 1, Summer 1994, pp. 6–14.

Boyle, P., and T. Vorst. "Option Replication in Discrete Time with Transaction Costs." *Journal of Finance* 47, no. 1 (Mar 1992), pp. 271–293.

Brealey, R. A. *An Introduction to Risk and Return from Common Stock.* 2nd ed. Cambridge: MIT Press, 1983.

Breeden, D., and R. Litzenberger. "State Contingent Claims Implicit in Option Prices." *Journal of Business* 51, (Oct. 1978), pp. 621–651.

Brenner, M., ed. *Option Pricing: Theory and Applications.* Lexington, MA: DC Heath and Co., 1983.

Brenner, M., and M. Subrahmanyam. "A Simple Solution to Compute Implied Standard Deviation." *Financial Analysts Journal* 44, no. 5 (Sept–Oct 1988), pp. 80–83.

Campbell, C., and R. Whaley. "Dividends and S&P 500 Index Options." *Journal of Futures Markets* 12, no. 2 (Sept. 1992), pp. 123–137.

Canina, L., and S. Figlewski. "The Information Content of Implied Volatility." *Review of Financial Studies* 6, no. 3 (1993), pp. 659–681.

Carr, P., K. Ellis, and V. Gupta, "Static Hedging of Exotic Options," forthcoming, *Journal of Finance.*

Carr, P., and D. Faguet. (1996) "Fast Accurate Valuation of American Options." Forthcoming.

Chance, D. M. "Leap into the Unknown." *RISK* 6, no. 5 (May 1993), pp. 60–66.

——. "The ABCs of Geometric Brownian Motion." *Derivatives Quarterly* (Winter 1994).

——. "Empirical Tests of the Pricing of Index Call Options." *Advances in Futures and Options Research* 1, pt. A, 1986, pp. 141–166.

——. *An Introduction to Options and Futures.* Chicago: Probus, 1987.

Chen, N. F.; B. Grundy; and R. Stambaugh. "Changing Risk, Changing Risk Premiums, and Dividend Yield Effects." *Journal of Financial Economics* 19, 1987, pp. 31–44.

Chriss, N. "Skewing a Distribution to a Market View." Working paper, 1996a.

——. "Transatlantic Trees." *RISK* 9, no. 7 (July 1996b).

Chriss, N., and M. Ong. "Digitals Defused." *RISK* 8, no. 12 (Dec 1995), pp. 56–59.

Christie, A. "The Stochastic Behavior of Common Stock Variances." *Journal of Financial Economics* 10, Dec 1982, pp. 407–432.

Clark, R. "Estimating and Using Volatility: Part 2." *Derivatives Quarterly* (1994), pp. 35–40.

Constantinides, G., and J. Ingersoll. "Optimal Bond Trading with Personal Taxes." *Journal of Financial Economics* 13, Sept 1984, pp. 299–335.

Constantinides, G., and M. Scholes. "Optimal Liquidation of Assets in the Presences of Personal Taxes: Implications for Assets Pricing." *Journal of Finance* 35, no. 2 (May 1980), pp. 439–443.

Cookson, R. "Moving in the Right Direction." *RISK* 6, no. 10 (Oct 1993), pp. 22–26.

Cootner, P. H., ed. *The Random Character of Stock Market Prices.* Cambridge: MIT Press, 1964.

Copeland, T.; T. Koller; and J. Murrin. *Valuation: Measuring and Managing the Value of Companies.* New York: John Wiley & Sons, 1990.

Cotner, J., and J. Horrell. "An Analysis of Index Option Pricing." *Journal of Futures Markets* 9, no. 5 (Nov. 1989), pp. 449–459.

Cox, J., and S. Ross. "The Valuation of Options for Alternative Stochastic Processes." *Journal of Financial Economics* 3, Jan–Mar 1976, pp. 144–66.

Cox, J.; S. Ross; and M. Rubinstein. "Option Pricing: A Simplified Approach." *Journal of Financial Economics* 7, Sep. 1979, pp. 229–263.

Cox, J., and M. Rubinstein. *Option Markets.* Englewood Cliffs: Prentice Hall, 1985.

Cox, J. C.; J. E. Ingersoll; and S. Ross. "The Relationship between Forward Prices and Futures Prices." *Journal of Financial Economics* 9, Dec 1985, pp. 321–346.

Dehrad, K., M. Janel, C. MeVay. "Mundane Problems, Exotic Solutions." *Euromoney* (Aug 1992), pp. 42–46.

Derman, E.; D. Ergener; and I. Kani. "Static Options Replication." Goldman Sachs Quantitative Strategies Research Notes, 1994a.

——. "The Ins and Outs of Barrier Options." Goldman Sachs Quantitative Strategies Research Notes, 1993.

——. "Riding on a Smile." *RISK* 7, no. 1 (Feb 1994b), pp. 32–39.

——. "Static Options Replication," *Journal of Derivatives* 2, no. 4 (Summer 1995), pp. 78–95.

——. "The Volatility Smile and its Implied Tree." Goldman Sachs Quantitative Strategies Research Notes, 1994.

Derman, E.; I. Kani; and N. Chriss. "Implied Trinomial Trees of the Volatility Smile." To Appear, *Journal of Derivatives.*

Derman, E., I. Kani, D. Ergener, and I. Bardhan. Enhanced Numerical Methods for Options with Barriers, *Financial Analysts Journal* 5, (Nov–Dec 1995), pp. 65–74.

Derman, E., I. Kani, and J. Zou. The Local Volatility Surface, *Financial Analysts Journal* 52, (Jul–Aug 1996).

Dixit, A., and R. Pindyck. *Investment Under Uncertainty.* Princeton: Princeton University Press, 1994.

Duffie, D. *Futures Markets.* Englewood Cliffs: Prentice Hall, 1989.

——. *Dynamic Asset Pricing Theory.* Princeton: Princeton University Press, 1992.

Dumas, B.; J. Fleming; and R. Whaley. "Implied Volatility Functions: Empirical Tests." Working paper, 1996.

Dupire, B. "Pricing with a Smile." *RISK* 7, no. 1 (Jan 1994), pp. 18–20.

Duque, J., and D. Paxson. "Implied Volatility and Dynamic Hedging." *Review of Futures Markets* 13, 1993, pp. 381–421.

Eisenberg, L., and R. Jarrow. "Option Pricing with Random Volatilities in Complete Markets." *Review of Quantitative Finance and Accounting* 4, 1994, pp. 5–17.

Engle, R. "Statistical Models for Financial Volatility." *Financial Analysts Journal* 49, no. 1 (Jan/Feb 1993), pp. 72–78.

Fabozzi, F. J., and G. M. Kipnis, eds. *Stock Index Futures.* Homewood, IL: Dow Jones-Irwin, 1984.

———. *Handbook of Stock Index Futures and Options.* Homewood, IL: Dow Jones-Irwin, 1989.

Fabozzi, F. J., and E. E. Peters. "Hedging with Stock Index Futures." In *Handbook of Stock Index Futures and Options,* ed. F. J. Fabozzi and G. M. Kipnis. Homewood, IL: Dow Jones-Irwin, 1989.

Fama, E. "The Behavior of Stock Market Prices." *Journal of Business* 38, no. 1 (Jan 1965), pp. 34–105.

———. "Random Walks in Stock Prices." *Financial Analysts Journal* (Sept–Oct 1965), pp. 55–59.

Farlow, S. *Partial Differential Equations for Scientists and Engineers.* New York: Dover Publications, Inc., 1993.

Feinstein, S. "A Source of Unbiased Implied Volatility." Working Paper 88–9, Federal Reserve Bank of Atlanta, 1988.

Figlewski, S.; W. Silber; and M. Subrahmanyam, eds. *Financial Options: From Theory to Practice.* Homewood, IL: Business One Irwin, 1990.

Fink, R. E., and R. B. Feduniak. *Futures Trading: Concepts and Strategies.* New York: New York Institute of Finance, 1988.

Fisher, L., and J. Lorie. "Rates of Return on Investments in Common Stocks." *Journal of Business* 37, no. 1 (Jan 1964) pp. 1–24.

Fortune, P. "An Assessment of Financial Market Volatility: Bills, Bonds and Stocks." *New England Economic Review* (1989), pp. 14–28.

French, K. "A Comparison of Futures and Forward Prices." *Journal of Financial Economics* 12, Nov. 1983, pp. 311–342.

Friedman, B. M., and D. I. Laibson. "Economic Implications of Extraordinary Movements in Stock Prices." *Brookings Papers on Economic Activity* 2, no. 2 (1989), pp. 137–189.

Galai, D. "Tests of Market Efficiency and the Chicago Board Options Exchange." *Journal of Business* 50, (Apr 1977), pp. 167–197.

Garman, M. "Charm School." *RISK* 5, no. 7 (Jul 1992), pp. 53–54.

Garman, M., and M. Klass. "On the Estimation of Security Price Volatilities from Historical Data." *Journal of Business* 53, no. 1 (Jan 1980), pp. 76–78.

Gould, J., and D. Galai. "Transaction Costs and the Relationship Between Put and Call Prices." *Journal of Financial Economics* 6, (1978), pp. 187–211.

Hammer, J. "On Biases Reported in Studies of the Black-Scholes Option Pricing Model." *Journal of Business* 41, no. 2 (1989), pp. 153–169.

Harris, L. "S&P 500 Cash Stock Price Volatilities." *Journal of Finance* 44, no. 5 (1989), pp. 1155–1175.

Heath, D., and R. Jarrow. "Ex-dividend Day Stock Price Behavior and Arbitrage Opportunities." *Journal of Business* 61, no. 1 (Jan 1988), pp. 91–108.

Hemmerick, S. "New Options Pricing Models Gain Ground." *Pension & Investments* 22, no. 10 (May 16, 1994), p. 3.

Heston, S. "A Closed-Form Solution for Options with Stochastic Volatility with Applications to Bond and Currency Options." *Review of Financial Studies* x, no. 6 (1993), pp. 326–343.

Heynen, R. "An Empirical Investigation of Observed Smile Patterns." *Review of Futures Markets* 13, (1994), pp. 317–353.

Heynen, R., and H. Kat. "Crossing Barriers." *RISK* 7, no. 6 (June 1994), pp. 46–51.

Hodges, S., and A. Neuberger. "Optimal Replication of Contingent Claims Under Transaction Costs." In *Options: Recent Advances in Theory and Practice,* volume 2: Manchester University Press (1989).

Hudson, M. "The Value of Going Out." *RISK* 4, no. 3 (Mar. 1991).

Hull, J. *Options, Futures and Other Derivative Securities.* 2nd ed. Englewood Cliffs: Prentice Hall, 1993.

Hull, J., and A. White. "The Pricing of Options on Assets with Stochastic Volatilities." *Journal of Finance* 42, no. 2 (June 1987), pp. 281–300.

———. "The Analysis of the Bias in Options Pricing Caused by a Stochastic Volatility." *Advances in Futures and Options Research* 3, (1988), pp. 29–61.

Ingersoll, J. *Theory of Financial Decision Making.* Ottawa: Rowman and Littlefield, 1987.

Itô, K. "On Stochastic Differential Equations." *Memoirs of the American Mathematical Society*, 1951, pp. 1–51.

Jackwerth, J. C., and M. Rubinstein. "Recovering Probability Distributions from Contemporaneous Security Prices." *Journal of Finance, 1995.*

Jacquier, E., and R. Jarrow. "Vital Statistics." *RISK* 8, no. 4 (Apr 1995), pp. 62–64.

Jarrow, R., and E. Rosenfeld. "Jump Risks and the Intertemporal Capital Asset Pricing Model." *Journal of Business* 57, (1984), pp. 337–351.

Jarrow, R., and A. Rudd. *Option Pricing.* Homewood, IL: Richard Irwin, Inc., 1983.

Jarrow, R., and J. Wiggins. "Options Pricing and Implicit Volatilities: A Review and a New Perspective." *Journal of Economic Surveys* 3, 1989, pp. 59–81.

Jarrow, R. A., and G. S. Oldfield. "Forward Contracts and Futures Contracts." *Journal of Financial Economics* 9, no. 4 (Dec 1981), pp. 373–382.

Johnson, H., and D. Shanno. "Option Pricing When Variance is Changing." *Journal of Financial and Quantitative Analysis* 22, (1987), pp. 143–151.

Jones, C., and J. Wilson. "Is Stock Price Volatility Increasing?" *Financial Analysts Journal* (1989), pp. 20–26.

Jorion. "On Jump Risk in the Foreign Exchange and Stock Markets." *Review of Financial Studies* 1, (1988), pp. 427–445.

Karatzas, I., and S. Shreve. *Brownian Motion and Stochastic Calculus.* New York: Springer-Verlag, 1988.

Kat, H., and L. Verdonk. "Tree Surgery." *RISK* 8, no. 2 (Feb 1995).

Kawai, M. "Spot and Futures Prices of Nonstandard Commodities Under Rational Expectations." *Quarterly Journal of Economics* 98, 1983, pp. 235–254.

Kawaller, I. G. *Financial Futures and Options.* Chicago: Probus, 1992.

Kawaller, I. G.; P. D. Koch; and T. W. Koch. "The Relationship Between the S&P 500 Index and S&P 500 Index Future Prices." *Federal Reserve Bank of Atlanta Economic Review* 73, (May-June 1988), pp. 2–10. Reprinted by the Chicago Mercantile Exchange as a CME Financial Strategy Paper, 1988.

Klemkosky, R., and G. B. Resnick. "Put-Call Parity and Market Efficiency." *Journal of Finance* 34, no. 5 (Dec 1979), pp. 1141–1155.

———. "An Ex-ante Analysis of Put-Call Parity." *Journal of Financial Economics* 8, 1980, pp. 363–378.

Kritzman, M. " . . . About Monte Carlo Simulation." *Financial Analysts Journal* 49, no. 6 (Nov. 1993), pp. 17–20.

Kunitomo, N., and M. Ikeda. "Pricing Options with Curved Boundaries." *Mathematical Finance* 2, no. 4 (1992), pp. 275–298.

Latane, H., and R. Rendleman. "Standard Deviation of Stock Price Ratios Implied in Option Prices." *Journal of Finance* 31, no. 2 (May 1976), pp. 369–381.

Leland, H. E. "Option Pricing and Replication with Transaction Costs." *Journal of Finance* 40, no. 5 (Dec 1985), pp. 1282–1301.

Leong, K. "Estimates, Guesstimates and Rules of Thumb." In *From Black-Scholes to Black Holes,* 1993 RISK Magazine, London.

Litzenberger, R., and K. Ramaswamy. "The Effect of Personal Taxes and Dividends on Capital Asset Prices: Theory and Empirical Evidence." *Journal of Financial Economics* 61, 1988, pp. 95–108.

Longstaff, F. "Martingale Restriction Tests of Option Pricing Models." Working paper, University of California, Los Angeles, 1993.

MacBeth, J. D., and L. J. Merville. "An Empirical Examination of the Black-Scholes Call Option Pricing Model." *Journal of Finance* 34, no. 5 (Dec 1979), pp. 1173–1186.

Malkiel, B. *A Random Walk Down Wall Street.* 4th ed. New York-London: Norton & Company, 1985.

Margrabe, W. "Binomial Pricing of Exploding Options." *Topics in Money and Securities Markets* 149. Bankers Trust Company, 1989.

Mayhew, S. "Implied Volatility." *Financial Analysts Journal* (July-August 1994), pp. 8–20.

McDonald, J. B., and R. M. Bookstaber. "Option Pricing for Generalized Distributions." Working paper, Brigham Young University, 1988.

McMillan, L. G. *Options as a Strategic Investment.* 2nd ed. New York: New York Institute of Finance, 1986.

Merton, R. (1973a) "The Relationship Between Put and Call Prices." *Journal of Finance* 28, no. 1 (Mar 1973), pp. 183–184.

———. (1973b) "Theory of Rational Option Pricing." *Bell Journal of Economics and Management Science* 4, Spring 1973, pp. 141–183.

———. (1976) "Option Pricing When Underlying Stock Returns Are Discontinuous." *Journal of Financial Economics* 3, (Jan-Mar. 1976), pp. 125–144.

———. (1990) *Continuous Time Finance.* Cambridge: Blackwell Inc., 1990.

———. (1995) Chap. 1 in *The Influence of Mathematical Models in Finance on Practice: Past, Present and Future.* London: Chapman & Hall, 1995.

Merville, L., and D. Pieptea. "Stock-Price Volatility, Mean Reverting Diffusion, and Noise." *Journal of Financial Economics* 24, (Sep 1989), pp. 193–214.

Michaely, R. "Ex-dividend Day Stock Price Behavior: The Case of the 1986 Tax Reform Act." *Journal of Finance* 46, no. 3 (Jul 1991), pp. 845–860.

Michaely, R., and J. L. Vila. "Investors' Heterogeneity, Prices and Volume Around the Ex-dividend Day." *Journal of Financial and Quantitative Analysis* 30, no. 2 (Jun 1995), pp. 171–198.

Modigliani, F., and G. Pogue. "An Introduction to Risk and Return: Concepts and Evidence." *Financial Analysts Journal* (Mar-Apr 1974), pp. 18–30.

Murphy, G. "When Options Price Theory Meets the Volatility Smile." *Euromoney* no. 299 (Mar 1994), pp. 66–74.

Naik, V., and M. Lee, "General Equilibrium Pricing of Options on the Market Portfolio with Discontinuous Returns." *Review of Financial Studies* 3, no. 4 (1990) pp. 493–521.

Natenberg, S. *Option Volatility and Pricing: Advanced Trading Strategies and Techniques.* Burr Ridge, IL: Richard D. Irwin, 1994.

Nelken, I., ed. *The Handbook of Exotic Options.* Burr Ridge, IL: Richard D. Irwin, 1995.

Nelson, D., and K. Ramaswamy. "Simple Binomial Processes as Diffusion Approximations in Financial Models." *The Review of Financial Studies* 3, (1990), pp. 393–430.

Neuberger, A. J. "The Log Contract." *Journal of Portfolio Management* (Winter 1994), pp. 74–80.

Norman, A., and C. Annandale. "Index Futures on Stocks." *FT-SE 100 Index Futures Review (LIFFE),* Fourth Quarter 1991, pp. 3–4.

Officer, R. "The Variability of the Market Factor of the New York Stock Exchange." *Journal of Business* 46, (1973), pp. 434–453.

———. "The Distribution of Stock Returns." *Journal of the American Statistical Association* 67, (1972), pp. 807–812.

Osborne, M. "Brownian Motion in the Stock Market." *Operations Research* 7, (Mar-Apr 1964), pp. 145–173.

Park, H. Y., and A. H. Chen. "The Difference Between Futures and Forward Prices: A Further Investigation of Marking to Market Effects." *Journal of Futures Markets* 5, no. 1 (Feb 1979), pp. 77–88.

Parkinson, M. "The Extreme Value Method for Estimating the Variances of Rates of Returns." *Journal of Business* 53, no. 1 (Jan 1980), pp. 61–65.

Perrakis, S., and P. Ryan. "Options on Thinly Traded Stocks." *Canadian Journal of Administrative Sciences* 11, no. 1 (Mar 1994), pp. 24–42.

Peters, E. E. *Chaos and Order in the Capital Markets.* New York: John Wiley & Sons, 1991.

Philippatos, G.; N. Gressis; and P. Baird. "Implicit Volatility and the Pricing of Stock Index and Interest Rate Options in U.S. markets." *Mathematical Finance* 20, no. 5 (1994), pp. 79–89.

Praetz, P. "The Distribution of Share Prices." *Journal of Business,* 45, pp. 49–55.

Press, S. "A Compound Events Model for Security Prices." *Journal of Business* 40, (1967), pp. 317–335.

Press, W.; S. Teukolsky; W. Vetterling; and B. Flannery. *Numerical Recipes in C.* Cambridge: Cambridge University Press, 1992.

Putnam, B. "Staying Out of the Holes in Black-Scholes." *Global Investor* 65, (Sep 1993), pp. 19–21.

Reiner, E., and M. Rubinstein. "Breaking Down the Barriers." *RISK* 4, no. 9 (Sep 1991), pp. 28–35.

Rich, D. "The Mathematical Foundations of Barrier Option Pricing Theory." *Advances in Futures and Options Research.* (1996).

———. "The Valuation and Behavior of Black-Scholes Options Subject to Intertemporal Default Risk." *Review of Derivatives Research* 1. Forthcoming.

Robertson, M. "FT-SE 100 Futures and Options." *LIFFE/LTOM,* 1990.

Ross, S. "Options and Efficiency." *Quarterly Review of Economics* 90, (Feb 1976), pp. 75–89.

Rubinstein, M. "Exotic Options." Paper presented at FORC Conference, Warwick.

———. "Non-parametric Tests of Alternative Option Pricing Models Using All Reported Trades and Quotes on the 30 Most Active CBOE Option Classes from August 23, 1976 through August 31, 1978." *Journal of Finance* 40, no. 2 (Jun 1985), pp. 455–480.

———. "Derivative Asset Analysis." *Economic Perspectives* 1, no. 2 (Fall 1987), pp. 73–93.

———. "Implied Binomial Trees." *Journal of Finance* 69, no. 3 (July 1994), pp. 771–818.

———. "As Simple as One, Two, Three." *RISK* 8, no. 1 (Jan 1995), pp. 44–47.

Scholes, M. "Taxes and the Pricing of Options." *Journal of Finance* 31, no. 2 (May 1976), pp. 319–332.

Schwert, G. W. "Why Does Stock Market Volatility Change Over Time?" *Journal of Finance* 44, no. 5 (Dec 1989), pp. 1115–1153.

Scott, L. "Option Pricing When the Variance Changes Randomly: Theory, Estimation and Application." *Journal of Financial and Quantitative Analysis* 22, no. 4 (Dec 1987), pp. 419–438.

Sheikh, A. "Transaction Data Tests on S&P 100 Call Option Pricing." *Journal of Financial and Quantitative Analysis* 26, no. 4 (Dec 1991), pp. 459–475.

Shiller, R. *Market Volatility.* Cambridge, MA: MIT Press, 1989.

Shimko, D. *Finance in Continuous Time.* Miami: Kolb Publishing, 1992.

———. "Bounds of Probability." *RISK* 6, no. 4 (April 1993), pp. 33–37.

Star, M. "Betting on Market Moves—Quantitative Financial Sees Volatility as Distinct Asset." *Pension & Investments* 20, no. 21 (Sep. 18, 1992) pp. 6, 46.

Stein, E., and C. Stein. "Stock Price Distributions for Estimating Stochastic Volatility: An Analytic Approach." *Review of Financial Studies* 4, (1991), pp. 727–752.

Stein, J. "Over-reactions in the Options Market." *Journal of Finance* 44, no. 4 (Sep 1989), pp. 1011–1023.

Stoll, H. "The Relationship Between Put and Call Option Prices." *Journal of Finance* 31, no. 5 (Dec 1969), pp. 319–332.

Sullivan, E. J., and T. M. Weithers. "The History and Development of the Option Pricing Formula." *Research in the History of Economic Thought and Methodology,* volume 12. JAI Press, Inc., 1994.

Sutcliffe, C. M. S. *Stock Index Futures.* London: Chapman & Hall, 1993.

Taylor, S., and X. Xu. "The Magnitude of Implied Volatility Smiles: Theory and Empirical Evidence." *Review of Futures Markets* 13, (1993), pp. 355–380.

Thorp, E. O. and S. T. Kassouf. *Beat the Market.* New York: Random House, 1967.

Tompkins, R. *Options Analysis.* Chicago: Probus, 1994.

Turner, A. L., and E. J. K. Weigel. "An Analysis of Stock Market Volatility." Technical report, Frank Russell, Co., Tacoma, WA, 1990.

———. "Daily Stock Market Volatility: 1928–1989." *Management Science* 38, Nov 1992, pp. 1586–1609.

Varian, H. R. "The Arbitrage Principle in Financial Economics." *Economic Perspectives* 1, no. 2 (Fall 1987), pp. 55–72.

Whaley, R. E. "On the Valuation of American Call Options on Stocks with Known Dividends." *Journal of Financial Economics* 9, no. 2 (June 1981), pp. 207–211.

———. "Derivatives on Market Volatility: Hedging Tools Long Overdue." *Chicago Board Options Exchange Risk Management Series* 9 no. 2 (June 1981).

Wiggins, J. "Option Values Under Stochastic Volatility." *Journal of Financial Economics* 19, no. 2 (Dec. 1987), pp. 351–372.

Wilmott, P.; J. Dewynne; and S. Howison. *Option Pricing: Mathematical Models and Computation.* Oxford: Oxford Financial Press, 1993.

Working, H. "A Random Difference Series for Use in the Analysis of Time Series." *Journal of the American Statistical Association* 29, (Mar 1934), pp. 11–24.

Young, C. "What's the Right Black-Scholes Value?" *Financial Executive* 9, no. 5 (Sep/Oct. 1993), pp. 57–59.

AUTHOR INDEX

Annandale, C., 33
Bachelier, L., 99, 117
Baird, P. 357
Ball, C., 357, 358
Bardhan, I., 299, 467, 476
Barle, S., 409
Barone-Adesi, G., 207
Benson, R., 474
Bernstein, P. L., 57, 117
Black, F., 119, 182, 188, 190,
    207, 361, 362
Bookstaler, R.M., 182
Bowie, J., 476
Boyle, P., 325, 467
Brealey, R. A., 117
Breedon, D., 432
Brenner, M., 182, 357
Cakici, N., 409
Carr, P., 325, 476
Chance, D. M., 117, 182, 357
Chriss, N. 3, 325, 363, 367,
    409, 423, 423
Clark, R., 117, 357
Constantinides, G., 182
Cookson, R., 182, 202, 204
Cootner, P. H., 117
Copeland, T., 54–55
Cotner, J., 357
Cox, J., 2, 54, 182, 190, 207,
    219, 220, 233, 273, 299, 325,
    359, 363
Daniel, N., 476
Derman, E., 3, 6, 226, 227,
    299, 361, 362–363, 367, 370,
    381, 400, 409, 411, 467, 476
Dewynne, J., 182, 207
Dixit, A., 55
Duffie, D., 54, 182, 207
Dumas, B., 404
Dupire, B., 3, 409
Ellis, K., 476

Engle, R., 117
Ergener, D., 299, 467, 476
Fabozzi, F. J., 54
Faguet, D., 325
Fama, E., 116
Feduniak, R. B., 54
Feinstein, S., 357
Figlewski, S., 117, 325
Fink, R. E., 54
Flannery, B., 325, 377
Fleming, J., 404
French, K., 54
Friedman, B. M., 116
Galai, D., 44
Garman, M., 182
Gould, J. 44
Gressis, N. 357
Gupta, V., 476
Hammer, J., 182
Harrell, J., 357
Harris, L., 117
Hemmerick, S., 3–4, 409
Heston, S., 357
Heynen, R., 436, 476
Hodges, S., 182
Howison, S., 182, 207
Hudson, M., 476
Hull, J., 54, 117, 182, 207,
    239, 325, 357, 359
Ikeda, M., 476
Ingersoll, J., 182
Ito, K., 102
Jackwerth, J. C., 116, 358
Jacquier, E., 474
Jarrow,R., 182, 357, 358, 474
Jorion, ., 358
Jones, C., 117
Kani, I., 3, 6, 226, 227, 299,
    361, 362–363, 367, 370, 381,
    400, 409, 411, 467, 476
Kassouf, S. T., 188,

Kat, H., 436, 476
Kawaller, I. G., 54
Keller, T., 54–55
Kipnis, G. M., 54
Klemkosky, R., 44
Koch, P. D, 54
Koch, T. W., 54
Kritzman, M., 325
Kunitomo, N., 476
Laibson, D. I., 116
Lau, S. H., 467
Lee, M., 358
Leland, H. E., 182
Leong, K., 117
Litzenberger, R., 432
Longstaff, F., 432
MacBeth, J. D., 182
McMillan, L. G., 54
McVay, J., 325
Malkiel, B. G., 93–94, 117
Margrabe, W., 466, 476
Mayhew, S., 345
Merton, R., 57, 117, 161, 182,
    207, 357, 358
Merville, L., 117, 182, 346
Murphy, G., 357
Murrin, J., 54–55
Naik, V., 358
Natenberg, S., 182, 207
Nelken, I., 54, 303, 325
Nelson, D., 409
Neuberger, A., 182, 325
Norman, A., 33
Ong, M., 325
Osborne, M., 97, 117
Perrakis, S., 182
Peters, E. E., 54, 115, 116, 117
Philippatos, G., 357
Pieptea, D., 117, 346
Pindyck, R., 55
Press, W., 325, 377, 409

Press, S., 358
Putnam, B., 183
Ramaswamy, K., 409
Reiner, E., 476
Resnick, G.B., 44
Rich, D., 182
Robertson, M., 54
Roma, A., 357
Rosenfeld, E., 358
Ross, S., 2, 190, 207, 219, 220, 233, 273, 299, 325, 359, 363, 411, 432
Rubinstein, M. 2, 3, 7, 54, 116, 182, 219, 220, 233, 273, 299, 312, 325, 341, 357, 358, 363, 409, 411, 432, 476

Rudd, A., 182
Ryan, P., 182
Scholes, M., 182, 188, 190, 207
Sheikh, A., 182, 357
Silber, W., 117, 325
Star, M. 357
Stein, C., 357
Stein, E., 357
Subrahmanyam, M., 117, 325, 357
Sullivan, E. J., 117, 182
Sutcliffe, C.M.S., 33, 44, 54
Tenkolsky, S., 325, 377
Teukolsky, S., 409
Thorp, E. O., 188

Tompkins, R., 182
Touros, W., 358
Turner, A. L., 115, 116
Vedon, K. L., 476
Vetterling, W., 325, 377, 409
Vorst, T., 325
Weigel, E. J. K., 115, 116
Weithers, T. M., 117, 182
Whaley, R. E., 3, 54, 207, 355, 404
White, A., 357
Wiggins, J., 357
Wilmott, P., 182, 207
Wilson, J., 117
Young, C., 183
Zou, J., 400

INDEX

above the center, 390
American options
    arbitrage argument, 45–46
    as barrier options, 454–455
    call option on non-dividend
      paying stock, 45–46
    call options, 375–376
    early exercise, 45–46
    early exercise barrier,
      323–324
    early exercise boundary,
      186
    early exercise feature, 316
    early exercise premium,
      322
    example, 317-323
    first exercise date, 316
    holding value, 322
    implied volatility trees,
      363, 373–377
    optimal exercise date,
      47–48
    paying dividends, 46–47
    pricing on flexible tree,
      315–323
    put options, 374–375
    put-call parity, 42–43
    two-step examples,
      317–318
    valuing
      on a binomial tree, 316
      summary of valuation,
      322
annualized continuously
    compounded return, 64–65
approximate formula for delta,
    135–136
    comments on, 137–138
    in derivation of
      Black-Scholes, 150
approximately log-normal, 270

arbitrage, 38–45
    forward contracts, 48–51
    forward price, 51–53
    no-arbitrage hypothesis, 39
    put-call parity, 40–45
arbitrage argument, 39–40,
    200, 274–275
    American options, 45–46
    valuing options, 156–157
arbitrage assumptions, 38–39
arithmetic change, 97
Arrow-Debreu prices, 260–265
    bad probabilities, 379–384
    and binomial trees,
      265–271, 296–299
    butterfly spreads, 271–272
    and distribution of returns,
      265–271
    formula, 265
    general definition, 263
    implied binomial trees, 418
    iterative procedure,
      263–265
    sample computation,
      261–263
Asian options, 25–26, 306
asset pricing
    monotonic relationships to
      risk, 192
    and volatility, 191–192
at-the-money options, 30, 341
average squared dispersion
    from the mean, 76

backward induction, 282
    barrier options, 455–463
    binomial trees, 285–288
    European options, 293
    implied binomial trees, 418
bad probabilities, 379–384, 431

balancing a portfolio, 143
barrier nodes, 457
barrier options, 433–473
    American options,
      454–455
    backward induction,
      455–463
    barrier nodes, 454-455
    cash rebate, 434
    definition and types,
      434–436
    and delta, 441
    double, 463
    down-and-in options, 435
    down-and-out options, 435
    effective versus modified
      barrier, 467–469
    end-of-day monitoring,
      435–436
    enhanced numerical
      methods, 464–473
    first passage time, 452
    gamma and, 441–442
    graphs of values and hedge
      parameters, 443–451
    hedge parameters,
      438–451
    hedging, 454, 461–464
    in-out parity, 436–438
    infinite gamma, 441–442
    intra-day monitoring, 436
    knock-in, 434
    knock-out, 434
    monitoring, 435
    option specification error,
      465–467
    price behavior, 439–440
    pricing on binomial tree,
      452–464
    properties of, 437
    rebate payment, 436

barrier options, cont.
  rho barrier, 442
  target securities, 452–454
  theta barrier, 442
  up-and-in, 435
  up-and-out, 434–435
  vega barrier, 442
  and volatility smile,
    442–443
barrier price, 303
below the center, 390
Bermuda options, 24, 316
biased distributions, 412
biased estimator, 105
bilinear interpolation, 397,
  405–408
binary option, 198, 295
binning, 82
binomial hedging strategy, 280
binomial models, discrete time
  model, 221
binomial option pricing
  components of model, 299
binomial path independence,
  417, 430
binomial pricing
  arbitrage argument,
    274–275
  one-step model, 274–278
  process, 273
binomial stock price model,
  69–70
  expected value, 71–76
binomial trees, 219–272,
  273–324
  American options pricing,
    315–323
  and Arrow-Debreu prices,
    260–265, 296–299
  and forward interest rates,
    243–250
  approaches to building,
    233–239
  background, 220–221
  backward induction,
    285–288
  centering condition, 226
  convergence, 299,
    301–303
  defining equations,
    240–241
  definition, 221–223
  with dividends, 250–260

binomial trees, cont.
  European options on
    multiple trees, 284–296
  exotic options, 303–308
  flexible, 225, 227,
    320–322
  general standard, 239–241
  generic, 284–285
  geometric, 226–227
  hedge parameters,
    308–315
  hedging portfolio,
    278–282, 290–296
  hedging strategy, 278–282
  implementation, 412–413
  implied, 411–431
  inferring distributions from
    prices, 413–417
  with known dollar
    dividends, 253–260
  with lumpy dividends,
    255–256
  Monte Carlo methods,
    306–308
  negative probabilities,
    238–239
  node numbering system,
    241
  one-period expected value,
    228
  one-period forward
    equation, 242–243
  one-step models, 274–278
  one-step tree, 274
  option pricing, 273–324
    American options,
      315–324
    early exercise barrier,
      323–324
    European puts, 293
    hedge parameters,
      308–315
  option specification error,
    299–303
  parameters, 240
  path-dependent options,
    304–306
  principles behind, 304
  returns
    distribution of,
      265–271
    multiple-period model,
      229–230

returns, cont.
  one-period model, 228–229
  risk-neutral probabilities,
    282–283
  risk-neutral worlds,
    241–243
  riskless hedge, 275–277
  simulated hedging,
    290–296
  standard, 225–226
    Cox-Ross-Rubinstein
      tree, 233–235, 238,
      249–250, 256–258,
      317–319
    equal probability
      approach, 236–237
    most general, 239–241
    negative probabilities
      and, 238–239
  stock price quantization
    error, 299–303
  terminal distribution,
    412
  time periods, 221
  transition probabilities,
    224, 277–278
  up and down ratios,
    223
  valuing barrier options,
    452–464
  varying forward rates,
    248–250
  and volatility,
    230–232
black box, 301
Black-Scholes formula,
  119–183
  arbitrage argument,
    200
  at expiration, 149–150
  binary option, 198
  binomial model, 2
  Black on, 361–362
  boundary conditions,
    186–187
  cash-or-nothing option,
    198–199
  charts, 179–181
  components, 120
  constant interest rate
    assumption, 202, 245
  continuous dividend yield,
    154, 159–162

Black-Scholes formula, cont.
continuous trading
assumption, 202–203
delta, 132–139
delta hedging, 195–197
differential equation,
187–190, 313
dividend assumption, 16
with dividends, 154–162
dynamic hedging,
129–132
economic assumptions,
200–204
equations, 140–141
expected rate of return,
127–128
function, 5
geometric Brownian
motion assumption,
203–204
hedge parameters, 162–181
charts, 180–181
delta, 137
gamma, 162, 176–178
rho, 162, 178–179
theta, 137, 162,
169–176
vega, 162, 164–169
hedging, 128–129
hedging argument,
199–200
hedging costs, 208–217
hedging strategy, 119–124,
140–145
how it works, 145–152
implied volatility, 204,
327–341, 345
liquid markets assumption,
201–202
lumpy dividends, 154,
155–159
method of bisections,
330–336
misconceptions, 197–200
and Newton-Raphson
method, 336–340
no transaction costs,
143
no-arbitrage assumption,
203
no-transaction-costs
assumption, 203
payoff replication, 129

Black-Scholes formula, cont.
preliminary version,
140–141
put-call parity, 141–142
questions about, 185–186
rebalancing portfolio,
145–146
risk-neutral valuation,
190–195
riskless hedge, 188–190
self-financing dynamic
hedging, 130–132
self-financing hedging
strategy, 144–145
self-financing, replicating
hedging strategy, 120–126
short selling, 201
simulated hedging, 204–206
value of an option, 140
and volatility smile,
342–343
what it is, 152–154
bonds, 23–24
borrowing, 43
boundary conditions, 186–187
boundary values, 285–286
BPI; *see* binomial path
independence
Brownian motion particles, 97
Brownian motion; *see*
geometric Brownian motion
butterfly spreads, 271–272

calendar days, 15
calibration, 347–349
call options, 12, 24–25
and Arrow-Debreu prices,
298-299
binomial tree valuation
formula, 298–299
expected rate of return,
127–128
implied probability trees,
375–376
optimal early exercise,
47-48
probability in the money,
114
value, 274
valuation with lumpy
dividends, 160
cash rebate, 434

cash-or-nothing option,
198–199
centering, 226
centering condition, 226, 240,
370–371, 387
Chrysler Kerkorian takeover
bid, 358
clearinghouse, 32–33
closed-form solutions, 188
coin-tossing game, 121–126
assumptions, 125–126
compound interest, 58–63
exponential, 61
general rule, 59–60
rules for, 65
computing volatility,
106–108
constant interest rate
assumption, 23, 202, 245
constant interest rates
versus yield curve, 245
constant volatility assumption,
104, 232, 344
constant volatility binomial
tree, 397–398
continuous dividend yield
model, 154, 159–162
continuous random variables,
79–81
modeling, 81–84
continuous trading assumption,
202–203
continuous-time geometric
Brownian motion, 220–221
continuously compounded rate
of return, 16
continuously compounded
return, 65
convergence, 299, 301–303,
311, 376
rate of, 330
saw-toothed pattern,
465–467
correlation, 349–350
sample paths, 351–352
correlation coefficient, 349
Cox-Ross-Rubinstein tree,
233–235, 238, 240–241,
249–250, 256–258, 317–319,
427
crash of 1987
and geometric Brownian
motion, 115–116

crash of 1987, cont.
and volatility smile, 341
cumulative distribution
function, 86–87
cumulative normal
distribution, 85–91
standard, 86–89
cumulative normal distribution
function, 87, 330
properties, 90–91
currencies; *see* foreign
currency

deep-in-the money option, 442,
450
default risk
and clearinghouse, 32
deferred rebate, 453
delivery date, 30
delivery price, 30
delta, 132–139, 162
approximate formula,
135–136, 309–311
comments on, 137–139
and barrier options, 441
deriving formula for,
194–195
equation, 147
European options, 138–139
geometric Brownian
motion, 203–204
hedge parameter, 137
put and call relationship,
143–144
put-call parity, 138–139
using binomial model,
309–312
delta hedging, 195–197
dependent random events, 77
derivative securities
binomial trees, 411–431
definition, 24
exotic options, 25–26
options, 24–25
deterministic dividend models,
16–17
deterministic price movement
component, 99–101
deterministic volatility, 354
differential equation, 187–190
Black-Scholes, 313
digital option, 295

discrete time model, 221
distribution
binning, 82
skewing, 423–426
of variables, 66
distribution of return
hypothesis, 115–116
distribution of returns
and binomial trees,
265–271
log-normal, 270–271
distributions
inferring from prices,
413–417
dividend models, 16–17
dividend reinvestment,
19–21
dividend schedule, 154, 155
dividend yield model, 20
dividends, 16; *see also* lumpy
dividends
binomial trees with,
250–260
in Black-Scholes, 154–162
forward contracts, 49–51
and implied volatility trees,
368–369
known-dollar, 253–260
option-paying, 46–47
and options, 19
as percentage of spot price,
251–252
and short position, 36–37
and stock indexes, 18–19
double barrier option, 463
down ratio, 223
down transition probability, 70
down-and-in option, 435, 437
graph, 448
down-and-out options, 435
graphs, 448
with rebate, 458–460
down-transition probability,
224
dynamic hedging, 129–132,
143
self-financing, 130–132
dynamic portfolio, 130

early exercise barrier, 323–324
early exercise boundary, 186
early exercise feature, 316

early exercise premium, 322
economic assumptions of
Black-Scholes, 201–204
effective barrier, 468
end-of-day monitoring,
435–436
enhanced numerical methods,
464–473
equal probability
implementation, 236–238,
250
equity options, 11, 13
error tolerance, 332–333
European call options
and Arrow-Debreu prices,
297–299
European options, 124, 127
and binomial trees,
273–274
Black-Scholes formula,
140–142
delta, 138–139
delta hedging, 195–197
implied volatility, 327–328
implied volatility trees,
367–373
Monte Carlo pricing,
306–308
on multiple trees,
284–296
put-call parity, 40–45
European put options
backward induction,
293
ex-dividend behavior, 16n
ex-dividend date, 16, 158
exercise, 12, 316–317
of American options,
45–48
optimal date, 47–48
exotic options, 25–26
barrier option, 303
Bermuda options, 24
in binomial trees,
303–308
implied volatility trees,
362–363
path dependency, 304–305
expected rate of return, 228
call options, 127–128
expected value, 71–76, 296
of continuous random
variable, 81

expected value, cont.
definition, 73
one-period, 228–229
of a stock return, 127–128
expiration
target security at, 453–454
three different times to,
443
expiration date, 187
expiry, 25
exponential, 57–66
and compound interest, 61
inverse function, 64
rules for, 64–65
extrapolation, 365–366

factorial notation, 268
fair value, 27–28
fake node prices, 383
false position method,
377–379
fat-tailed distribution, 399,
402, 403
first exercise date, 316
first passage time, 452
flexible tree, 220–221, 225,
227, 320–322
foreign currency, 21–22
continuous dividend yield,
22
economic assumptions,
22–23
forward contract, 51
forward price, 53
forward contracts
assets with continuous
dividend yield, 49–50
assets with lumpy
dividends, 50–51
delivery price, 30
expected return, 127
foreign currency, 51
payoff on, 30–31
settling in cash, 31
valuation, 48–51, 52
forward equation, 236, 242
forward induction, 366
forward interest rates
and binomial trees,
243–250
general, 247–248
yield curve, 245–248

forward price, 51–53
in binomial tree, 239
foreign currency, 53
stock index, 53
forward rates
varying, 248–250
fractional numbers, 14
fractional power, 62
futures contracts, 31–33
clearinghouse, 31–33
margin account, 32–33
margin requirements,
31–33
marking to market, 31–33
options pricing, 33

gamma, 162, 176–178
and barrier options,
441–442
computing, 311–312
and hedging, 176–177
infinite, 441–442
put versus call, 177–178
using binomial model,
308–312
general forward rates, 247–248
geometric Brownian motion,
93–116, 157–159
assumption in
Black-Scholes, 203–204
basic assumptions, 97–98
and binomial trees, 219,
221
and crash of 1987, 116
calibration of model,
103–109
conclusions of model,
98–99
constant volatility
assumption, 104, 232
continuous-time model,
221
description of model,
96–103
distribution of stock prices,
109–111
distribution of return
hypothesis, 115–116
fact or fiction, 115–116
heuristic argument, 102
and implied volatility,
328–329

geometric Brownian motion,
cont.
Itô's lemma, 102–103,
157
log-normal process, 111
numerical example,
108-109
returns less than expected,
99–100
scaling, 103, 116
and stochastic volatility,
344
volatility and risk in,
94–96
geometric change, 97
geometric trees, 226–227
goodness-of-fit test,
404–405
grid square, 406
guess volatility, 330–332

hedge
instantaneously riskless,
188–190
riskless, 188–190,
275–276
hedge parameters, 29, 162–181
barrier options, 438–451
in binomial trees, 308–315
Black-Scholes, 162–181
charts, 180–181
delta, 133, 137, 308–312
gamma, 162, 176–178,
308–312
general features, 162–163
implied volatility trees,
362
rho, 162, 178–179,
313–315
theta, 137, 162, 169–176,
308–313
vega, 162, 164–169,
313–315
hedging, 14, 128–129
barrier options, 454,
461–464
costs associated with,
130–131
delta, 195–197
dynamic, 129–130
economic assumptions of
Black-Scholes, 201–204

hedging, cont.
  gamma and, 176–177
  no transaction costs, 143
  self-financing, 144–145
  simulated, 204–206
  volatility risk, 352–353
hedging costs, 208–217
hedging error, 405
hedging portfolio
  in binomial model,
    290–296
  in Black-Scholes,
    129–130, 142–143
  one-step binomial model,
    278–282
  rebalancing, 132, 143,
    292–293
  weighted, 130
hedging strategy
  Black-Scholes, 119–124,
    140–145
  for European options,
    278–282
  properties, 123–124
histograms, 82–84
  binning, 82
  of stochastic volatility,
    355–356
historical volatility, 346–347
holding value, 322
hypothetical implied volatility
  tree, 396–400

implied binomial trees,
  411–431
  Arrow-Debreu prices,
    418
  backward induction, 418
  binomial path
    independence, 417, 430
  construction, 417–420
  example, 426–429
  investor biases, 412
  optimization equations,
    424–426
  path probabilities, 418
  Rubinstein's optimization
    method, 413–415
  sample computations,
    420–422
  skewing probability
    distribution, 423–426

implied binomial trees, cont.
  terminal data, 417
  theory of, 411–412
  versus volatility trees,
    430–431
implied distribution, 394–396,
  412
  fat-tailed, 402–403
  S&P 500, 398–400
  S&P 500 options, 402–403
implied tree, 364
implied volatility, 327–343
  and Black-Scholes, 327–330
  at-the-money, 341
  computing, 329–336
  cumulative normal
    distribution, 330
  formula for number of
    steps, 333
  and geometric Brownian
    motion, 328–329
  iterative methods, 330
  method of bisections,
    330–332
  Newton-Raphson method,
    336–340
  non-constant, 329
  out-of-the money options,
    342
  stochastic volatility,
    343–356
  tangent line, 337–339
  term structure, 341
  tolerance, 332
  volatility smile, 341–343
implied volatility trees, 28n,
  361–409
  and American options,
    363, 373–377
  and Arrow-Debreu prices,
    379–384
  bad and good nodes,
    381–382
  bad probabilities, 379–384
  bilinear interpolation, 397,
    405–408
  and Black-Scholes,
    361–362
  and dividends, 368–369
  and European options,
    367–373
  centering condition,
    370–371, 387

implied volatility trees, cont.
  definition, 362
  derivation of formulas,
    369–371
  detailed look at, 363–364
  empirical evidence, 403–404
  extrapolation, 365–366
  fake node prices, 383
  false position method,
    377–379
  filling in, 386–390
  first example, 391
  goodness-of-fit test,
    404–405
  hedging values, 371–373
  implementation, 384–390
  versus implied binomial
    trees, 430–431
  implied distribution,
    394–396, 398–400,
    402–403
  in practice, 366–367
  input options, 364
  interpolation formula,
    406–407
  interpolation, 364–365
  iterative procedure,
    376–377
  logarithmic spacing,
    381–382
  notation, 385
  one-period forward
    equation, 372
  purpose, 362–363
  S&P 500, 396–400
  S&P 500 options, 400–405
  sample computations,
    390–396
  setup, 384–385
  system for building,
    384–390
  terminology, 364
  unknown node, 405–406
  violation of forward
    condition, 381
in-out parity, 436–438
in-the-money options, 29–30,
  390
independent random events,
  76–78
infinite gamma, 441–442
infusion of funds cost, 130,
  144

initial date, 221
initial margin, 32
initial time, 221
input options, 364
input to the model, 228
instantaneous expected return, 98
instantaneous rate of return, 190
instantaneous standard deviation, 98
instantaneously riskless hedge, 189–190
interest
    simple, 58
        time periods other than one year, 58
interest rate conversion, 62–63
interest rate risk, 23
interest rate sensitivity, 178–179
interest rates; *see also* compound interest *and* rate of return
    term structure, 341
interpolation, 364–365
    bilinear, 397, 405–408
interpolation formula, 406–407
interpolation grid, 405
intra-day monitoring, 436
intrinsic value, 29, 318, 322
inverse function, 64
investor biases, 412
iterative procedure, 330, 376–377
Itô's lemma, 102–103, 157

jump diffusion process, 357
jump risk, 134, 203–204

kappa; *see* vega
knock-in options, 434
    no rebate, 460–461
    premium, 439
    target securities, 453
knock-out options, 434
    cheapness, 460
    graph, 445
    no rebate, 456–457
    target securities, 453
knockout barrier, 434

leptokurtosis, 115, 356, 403
limit, 61
liquid markets assumption, 201–202
liquidity, 34
liquidity issues, 14
liquidity of markets, 43
local volatility, 220, 231, 312, 381, 400
    binomial tree implementation, 236
    formula, 230
    and volatility smile, 343
local volatility equation, 236
log contract, 295
log-normal hypothesis, 111, 115–116
log-normal process, 111
log-normal variable, 111
logarithmic spacing, 381–382
long position, 32, 34–35, 37–38
lookback options, 305–306
lumpy dividends, 50–51, 154, 155–159, 160, 255–256

maintenance costs, 49, 130
margin account, 32
margin requirements, 31–33
market impact, 14, 34
market impact assumption, 126
market liquidity assumption, 201–202
market price, 327, 364
market priced options, 28–29
marking to market, 31–33
mathematics, 57–91
    exponential, 57–64
    fractional numbers, 14
    fractional power, 62
    multiplier, 58
    natural logarithm, 64
    probability, 66–91
    return on investments, 64–66
    rules for compound interest, 65
    rules for exponentials, 64–65
    rules for logarithms, 65

mean deviation, 84–85
    formulas, 79
mean formula, 91
mean reversion, 346–347
method of bisections, 330–333
    error tolerance, 332–333
    formula for number of steps, 333
    procedure, 334–336
    sample computation, 333–334
    step-by-step, 331–332
modified barrier, 468
moneyness, 29–30
monitoring
    barrier options, 435–436
    end-of-day, 435–436
    intra-day, 436
monotonic relationships, 192
Monte Carlo methods, 306–308
multiple binomial trees, 284–296
multiplier, 58
mutually exclusive events, 68

natural logarithm, 64
near-the-money options, 30
negative probabilities, 238–239
negative skew, 341
Newton-Raphson method, 336–340, 376–377
    graphical example, 337–339
    iterations, 340
    sample computation, 339
    stopping, 340
no-arbitrage assumption, 203
no-arbitrage band, 44n
no-arbitrage hypothesis, 39
no-transaction-costs assumption, 203
nodes, 222
    above or below the center, 390
    Arrow-Debreu prices, 260–265
    bad and good, 381–382

nodes, cont.
  implied volatility
    computations, 392–393
  implied volatility trees,
    386–390
  numbering system, 241
  removing bad, 383–384
nonconstant implied volatility,
  329
normal density curve, 82–84
  mean and standard
    deviation, 84–85
normal distribution, 78–85
  bell curve, 82
  cumulative, 85–91
    formula, 88
  limiting behavior, 90
  standard, 85–86
  standard cumulative, 86–88
  symmetry formula, 90–91
normal distribution function
  formula, 88
normalized vega, 169
notation, 76, 414–415, 418
  for stocks, 14–15
  implied volatility trees,
    385
numerical methods, 464–473
numerical solution, 188

obligation to cover, 38
one-period expected value,
  228–229
one-period forward equation,
  236, 242–243, 372
one-step binomial model,
  274–278
optimal exercise, 26
optimization equations,
  424–426
optimization method, 413–415
  prior distribution, 415
option payout structure,
  295–296
option positions, 38
option premium, 27–28
  early exercise premium,
    322
  intrinsic value, 29, 318
  time value, 29
option pricing, 13
  binomial, 273

option pricing, cont.
  binomial tree model,
    452–464
  contract specifications,
    24–25
  exotic options, 303–304
  fair value, 27–28, 132–133
  from implied binomial tree,
    427–429
  futures contracts, 33
  implied volatility, 327–329
  implied volatility trees,
    361–409
  inferring distributions
    from, 413–417
  long position, 34–35
  market price, 28–29, 327
  normalized vega, 169
  principles behind, 304
  risk-neutral valuation,
    190–195
  short position, 35–37
  trading days, 15
  versus valuation, 1n
option specification error, 303
  and barrier options,
    465–467
option theta, 312
option value, 26–33
  Black-Scholes, 140
  gamma, 176–178
  jump in, 440
  rho, 178–179
  time decay, 169–176
  and volatility, 164–166
option value tree, 274, 299
  American options, 329
  boundary values, 285–286
  hedge parameters,
    308–315
  meaning of numbers,
    288–289
option valuation
  moneyness, 29–30
options, 11–17; see also
  American options and
  European options
  arbitrage and, 38–45
  at-the-money, 30
  basics of, 4
  binary, 198
  boundary conditions,
    186–187

options, cont.
  cash-or-nothing, 198–199
  delta, 132–139
  and dividends, 19
  early exercise feature, 316
  exercise, 316–317
  exotic, 25–26
  first exercise date, 316
  in-the-money, 29–30
  on interest rates, 19
  near-the-money, 30
  out-of-the-money, 30
  over-the-counter, 24
  plain vanilla, 25
  preliminary definition, 11–13
  puts and calls, 24–25
  and stock price uncertainty,
    134
  underlying asset, 12–13
options pricing
  volatility skew, 342–343
options valuation
  forward contracts, 30–31
  futures contracts, 31–33
out-of-balance portfolio, 130
out-of-the money options, 341
  graph, 444
  implied volatility, 342
out-of-the-money option, 26, 30
over-the-counter deals, 24

path-dependent options,
  295-296, 304–305
  Asian options, 306
  lookback options,
    305–306
path independent options,
  295–296
  formula, 298–299
path probabilities, 418
payoff graphs, 26–27
payoff replication, 129
perfect hedge, 128–129
plain vanilla options, 25; see
  also European options
  binomial model pricing,
    315–323
portfolios, 129–130
predictive models, 94
premium; see option
  premium
price versus value, 1n

prior distribution, 415, 423
probabilistic models, 94
probability, 66–91
 biased estimation, 105
 cumulative normal
  distribution function,
  85–91
 distribution, 68
 expected value, 71–76
 independent random
  events, 76–78
 mean deviation, 84–85
 normal density curve,
  82–84
 normal distribution, 78–85
 notation, 76
 random events, 67–71
 random variables, 67
 range, 68
 of simple occurrence,
  70–71
 standard deviation, 74–76,
  84–85
 unbiased estimation, 105
 up and down transitions,
  69–70
 variance, 74–76
probability distribution
 skewing, 423–426
put options, 12, 24–25
 formula, 153–154
 implied volatility trees,
  374–375
put-call parity, 303
 American options, 42–43
 and in-out parity, 436
 Black-Scholes, 141–142
 delta and, 138–139
 economics of, 43–45
 European options, 40–45
 gamma and, 177–178

quadratic optimization with
 constraints, 414

random component of price
 movement, 99–101
random events, 67–71
 concept, 69
 expected value, 71–76
 independent, 76–78

random events, cont.
 variance of, 74–76
random variables, 67, 416
 continuous, 79–81
 log-normal, 111
random volatility, 344, 354
random walk assumption, 204
*Random Walk Down Wall
 Street,* 93
randomly changing volatility,
 344n
range, 68
rate of convergence, 330
rate of return
 expected, 228
 instantaneous, 190
 risk-neutral, 242
rebalancing costs, 292–293
rebalancing portfolio
 with Black-Scholes, 130,
  145–146
rebate payment, 436
recombining tree, 222
replication, 123–124
 payoff, 129
returns
 and binomial trees,
  265–271
 less than expected, 99–101
 mathematics of, 64–66
 multiple-period model,
  229–230
 on stocks, 16
 one-period model, 228–229
 standard deviation of daily,
  108
 standard trees, 268–269
rho, 162
 and barrier options, 442
 in binomial tree, 313–315
 interest rate sensitivity,
  178–179
risk; *see also* hedging
 monotonic relationship
  with, 192
 stock price, 94–96
risk-neutral binomial tree,
 243
risk-neutral probabilities,
 282–283
risk-neutral probability
 distribution, 402
risk-neutral rate of return, 242

risk-neutral transition
 probabilities, 241
risk-neutral valuation,
 190–195, 296
risk-neutral world, 191–192
 and binomial trees,
  241–243
riskless hedge, 188–190,
 275–276
riskless zero-coupon bonds,
 23–24
Rubinstein's optimization
 method, 413–415

S&P 500; *see* Standard and
 Poor 500
sample path, 95
 Monte Carlo method,
  307
 simulated hedging through,
  290–296
 for stochastic volatility,
  351–352
saw-toothed convergence
 pattern, 465–467
scaling, 103, 116
securities
 derivatives, 24–26
 forward contracts, 48–51
 indexes, 17–23
 long position, 34–35
 short position, 35–37
 stocks, 13–17
 zero-coupon bonds, 23–24
self-financing, 123
self-financing dynamic
 hedging, 130–132
self-financing hedging
 in Black-Scholes,
  144–145
self-financing replicating
 hedging strategy, 120–126
set-up costs, 130, 144
settling in cash, 31
short position, 35–37, 38
 and dividends, 36–37
 profit from, 36
short selling
 with full use of proceeds,
  44, 201
short squeezed, 36
simple interest, 58

simple smile, 391
simulated hedging,
    204–206, 290–296
skew delta, 401–402
skewing probability
    distribution, 423–426
slope, 337
smile, 364
    simple, 391
spot price, 420
    dividends as percentage of,
        251–252
    first passage time, 452
    and local volatility,
        400
    of stocks, 13–14
    and theta, 171–172
Standard and Poor 500
    historical volatility,
        346–347
    implied distribution,
        398–400, 402-403
    implied volatility, 396-405
    volatility instrument,
        353–355
    volatility smile, 341–342,
        400–405
standard cumulative normal
    distribution, 86–88
    formula, 88–89
standard deviation, 84–85; *see
    also* volatility
    computation, 77
    computing, 105
    continuous random
        variables, 81
    of daily returns, 108
    definition, 74–76
    formulas, 79
    in geometric Brownian
        model, 98
standard normal distribution,
    85–86
standard trees, 225–226, 363
    building, 233–239
    Cox-Ross-Rubinstein tree,
        249–250
    equal probabilities
        implementation, 250
    and log-normal
        distribution, 270–271
    multiple-period, 229–230
    returns, 268–269

stochastic dividend models,
    17
stochastic volatility, 101,
    343–356
    calibration, 346–349
    correlation, 349–350
    hedging, 352–353
    mean reversion, 346–347
    models, 345
    predicting volatility, 345
    sample paths, 351–352
    stock returns, 355–356
    volatility instrument,
        353–355
    volatility of volatility,
        348–349
    and volatility risk,
        352–353
stock indexes, 17–23
    assumptions, 17–18
    dividend reinvestment,
        19–21
    and dividends, 18–19
    foreign currency, 21–23
    forward price, 53
    Standard and Poor's 500,
        17
stock price models
    binomial trees, 219–324
    geometric Brownian
        motion, 93–116
    notation, 14–15
    predictive, 94
    probabilistic, 94
    stochastic volatility, 344
stock price quantization error,
    300, 314–315
stock price uncertainty
    implied volatility, 328
    jump risk, 134
    options and, 134
    volatility risk, 134
stock prices
    binomial model, 69–70
    binomial trees, 219–272
    deterministic component,
        99–101
    distribution of,
        109–111
    effective versus modified
        barrier, 467–469
    ex-dividend behavior, 16n
    local volatility, 220

stock prices, cont.
    random component,
        99–100
    scaling property, 103, 116
    stochastic component, 101
    volatility and risk, 94–96
stock returns, 16, 110
    expected rate of, 127–128
    Itô's lemma, 102–103, 157
    under stochastic volatility,
        355–356
stock sample paths, 95
stocks, 13–17
    and stock indexes, 18
strike price, 12
symmetry formula, 90–91

tangent line, 337–338
target option, 454
target security, 452–454
term structure of interest rates,
    341
term structure of volatility, 341
terminal data, 417
terminal date, 221
terminal distribution, 412
terminal time, 221
theoretical value, 27
theory, 474
theta, 137, 162
    and barrier options, 442
    computing, 311–313
    and spot price, 171–172
    time decay, 169–176
    and time to expiration,
        172–173
    using binomial model,
        308–313
    what it measures, 169–171
time decay, 169–176
time independent smile, 391
time value, 29
trading days, 15
transaction costs, 33, 130, 143
transition probabilities, 224,
    241, 277–278
    computing, 285–286

unbiased estimator, 105
underlying asset, 12–13
unknown node, 405–406

up ratio, 223
up transition probability, 69, 224
up-and-in options, 435
up-and-out option, 434–435
    graph, 446

valuation, risk-neutral, 190–195
value versus price, 1n
values
    interpolated, 365
    jump in, 440
variance, 74–76
    definition, 75
varying forward rates, 250
vega
    and barrier options, 442
    in binomial tree, 313–315
    of options, 162, 164–169
violation of the forward condition, 381
volatility, 2; *see also* implied volatility *and* local volatility
    and binomial trees, 230–232
    asset pricing, 191–192

volatility, cont.
    Black-Scholes-implied, 204
    constant volatility assumption, 104
    guess, 330–332
    historical cycles, 346
    and in-the-money options, 390
    market view, 343
    of options, 164–166
    steps in computing, 104–105
    stochastic, 343–356
    stock price, 94–96
    term structure, 341
volatility instrument, 353–355
volatility of volatility, 348–349
volatility risk, 352–353,-354
    hedging, 352-353
    unanticipated volatility changes, 352
volatility skew, 342–343
volatility smile, 2–4, 327–359

volatility smile, cont.
    and barrier options, 442–443
    and crash of 1987, 341
    impact of S&P 500 options, 400–405
    local volatility, 343
    simple, 391
    time independent, 391

weighted portfolio, 129–130
without bound, 441
writing a call option, 128
writing the option, 38

yield curve, 245
    versus constant interest rates, 245
    and forward rates, 245–248

zero-coupon bonds, 23–24